Missile
Envy

MISSILE ENVY
A Bantam Book / published by arrangement with
William Morrow and Company

PRINTING HISTORY
William Morrow edition published June 1984
Bantam edition published May 1985
Bantam special revised edition / June 1986

Grateful acknowledgment is made for permission to reprint the following:
Pictures of burn victims courtesy of Dr. John Constabel. Cover of Aviation Week &
Space Technology *courtesy of McGraw-Hill, Inc., Vol. 117, No. 26, December 27,*
1982. Action and Reaction Chart reprinted from Stop Nuclear War! A Handbook *by*
David P. Barash, Ph.D., and Judith Eve Lipton, M.D. (Grove Press, Inc.: 1982,
p. 127). Contracts Chart copyright © 1980 by NARMIC (National Action/Research on
the Military Industrial Complex). Foreign Military Sales Chart reprinted from Council
on Economic Priorities newsletter, December/January 1981–1982. Installations Chart
courtesy of Superintendent of Documents, U.S. Government Printing Office, Washing-
ton D.C.

ISBN 0-553-19384-8

60,680

Contents

Introduction

I write this book with a tremendous sense of urgency—as a mother, as a pediatrician, and as a woman—aware that we live on a planet that is terminally ill, infected with lethal macrobes (nuclear weapons) that are metastasizing rapidly, the way a cancer spreads in the body. I have been concerned about nuclear war since I was a young teenager, when I read Nevil Shute's book *On the Beach*. I lived then in Melbourne, Australia, the scene of the story, and the image of the people of Melbourne giving cyanide to their babies as the radioactive fallout was about to strike has stayed with me all my life. The empty streets of my beloved city, bereft of life, with newspapers blowing vacantly in the wind, signaled the end of human existence.

Since that time, I have never felt protected by the adults around me and have never understood why the governments of the world build more nuclear weapons. When I started my first year of medical studies in 1956, at the age of seventeen, I was prompted to speak out about the carcinogenic and mutagenic effects of radioactive fallout from the atmospheric explosions detonated by the Soviet Union, the United States, and Great Britain. Unfortunately, I spoke in the refectory at lunchtime, and my male medical colleagues gazed absentmindedly at me, obviously wondering who this crazy lady was, as they ignored my comments and continued their poker game. During the remaining years of medical school, I managed to suppress my fear and practice a degree of denial—psychic numbing. It wasn't until 1963, when I was three months

1

pregnant with my first baby, that my fears began to re-emerge. I was worried about bringing a child into a world where he or she might not have the opportunity to enjoy a full life-span without the specter of nuclear war. Because the wonder and creativity of birth so enchanted me, my husband and I proceeded to have three babies in as many years. But always the danger of nuclear war lurked in the background. I could never really enjoy anything totally without a little voice asking, "How much longer will life continue?"

Being intensely curious, I read every article about nuclear weapons that I could find. I was pleased and relieved when the partial test-ban treaty was signed by President John F. Kennedy and Soviet Premier Nikita Khrushchev in August 1963. President Kennedy had already started making some unilateral moves toward the Soviet Union. In June 1963, he made his famous "Strategy of Peace" speech at American University. For the first time since Franklin Roosevelt, an American president praised the Soviets for their sacrifices and bravery during World War II, and announced a unilateral act—the United States would stop all atmospheric tests and would not resume them unless the USSR did so first. The Soviets were apparently so thrilled by this praise that for months afterward they carried in their wallets clippings of the *Pravda* and *Izvestia* articles reporting the speech. On June 15, Khrushchev responded by welcoming the initiative and announcing a halt to Soviet plans for the production of strategic bombers. Further agreements followed, and a "hot-line" agreement was reached on June 20. The Soviets were so pleased with this process that they called it the "Policy of Mutual Example." On October 9, Kennedy announced a $250 million wheat sale, and tensions between the Soviet Union and the United States were at an all-time low. On November 22, President Kennedy was assassinated.

I was in my sitting room in Canberra, Australia, on a lovely sunny morning when my brother, who works in foreign affairs, came to tell me of the murder. My first thought as I emerged from the shock was, "Will we survive?" Kennedy had sparked a light of hope in the hearts of millions of people around the world, and when he died, the light faded. Men on the golf courses in Australia took off their caps and openly wept when they heard the news. Years later, when my husband and I visited Iran in 1974, we discovered to our amazement that pictures of Jack Kennedy adorned almost every shop window. This was not atypical of the respect people felt for him throughout the world. A young president whose soul had been scarified by the Cuban missile crisis had reached out to America's nuclear adversary to foster a climate of hope and peace in the world.

For the next ten years, the Vietnam War became the dominant theme in world affairs. Nuclear war and weapons were forgotten, much to everyone's subconscious relief, for to contemplate nuclear war is to entertain the concept of the end of immortality. We need to feel that we leave a part of ourselves behind when we die—our children, a great work, books, buildings, paintings—or that we live on in the spiritual or organic life cycle. Nuclear war obliterates these possibilities.

At the same time, the test-ban treaty had moved nuclear testing underground. Since out of sight is out of mind, we all heaved a sigh of relief and proceeded with normal everyday life. Meanwhile, the Kremlin and the Pentagon unobtrusively continued to enlarge and refine their nuclear arsenals.

In 1979, I was asked to join a delegation of Americans visiting the Soviet Union as guests of the Soviet Peace Committee. The group included journalist Arthur Macy Cox, formerly of the CIA and an adviser to Paul Warnke during the SALT II negotiations; Everett Mendelsohn, professor of the history of science at Harvard University; Bill Coffin, formerly of the CIA and fluent in Russian; and Marta Daniels, a Connecticut activist who was highly versed in and articulate on nuclear-weapon strategies. We started off at the lower bureaucratic levels, where we received our daily doses of propaganda *ad nauseam*. We argued vociferously with our Soviet hosts when we visited the State Committee on Atomic Energy and the Ministry for Health, on topics ranging from health and safety measures at nuclear reactors to the storage of radioactive waste and the alleged huge nuclear accident at Kyshtym in 1958—an event that nobody could either "remember" or "explain."

Because our arguments obviously demonstrated a sophisticated level of knowledge, we were invited to move up the bureaucratic ladder. We had lunch with Anatoly Petrovich Alekandrov, the prestigious president of the Soviet Academy of Sciences. At the end of ten days, the red carpet was unrolled, and we met with the two ambassadors who had spent the previous seven years negotiating the SALT II treaty. At just that time, we learned that Senator Frank

Church had discovered the "Soviet Brigade" in Cuba and that all hell was breaking loose in the Congress of the United States. It was obvious to us and our hosts that SALT II did not stand a chance of being ratified. Nevertheless, Arthur Cox presented to the ambassadors the concept of a bilateral freeze in testing, development, production, and deployment of any new nuclear weapons and delivery systems. They argued for hours about it, made phone calls, ran in and out speaking and consulting with their colleagues, and, finally, at the end of two hours, said with a sigh, "Well, we'd vote for that with both hands!"

The freeze concept was new to me, as was the extreme state of emergency that the arms race was to present to the world. But with knowledge comes responsibility. When I learned that a launch-on-warning policy would be commonplace by late 1983 or 1984 and that the advent of cruise missiles would signal the practical end of arms-control treaties, I knew I would have to leave medicine. This decision was made more obvious by two experiences in the Soviet Union. First, I was impressed by the depth of hardship and suffering undergone by the Soviets in World War II—experiences they recounted to us again and again. They lost approximately 20 million people; almost every family was bereft. Seventy-two thousand towns and cities were razed, and Leningrad (perhaps the most beautiful, majestic city on earth) was under siege by the Germans for three years. Hundreds of thousands of people starved in Leningrad; we visited a cemetery on the outskirts of the city where 500,000 people are buried in mass graves. The cemetery is large, and a long path leads down its center to a distant figure of Mother Russia holding an olive branch. As we walked silently in the bitterly cold, rainy weather, the sounds of Bach's Double Violin Concerto just audible, we saw parents bringing their children to pay homage to aunts, uncles, and grandparents who had died during the war. As we walked back through the rain, I said to Arthur Cox, "Arthur, if there is another war and anyone survives, if they come back here they will say, 'They didn't learn.'"

My other moving experience occurred in Moscow. Red Square seemed to be full of brides. I asked our guide, "What are all these brides doing?" (I love brides), and he said, "Whenever a girl marries, she takes her flowers and puts them on a peace memorial, so that her children will never know war." He also told me, as he recounted the deprivations during World War II, "My grandmother has seen people eat people twice in her lifetime."

Toward the end of our stay, we visited the U.S. embassy in Moscow. Because the ambassador was unavailable that day, we were met by two young men who sat down and proceeded to assail us with figures about nuclear weapons and war-fighting strategy. Their diatribe went on for about thirty minutes, and it was obvious that theirs were two brilliant, computerlike minds; but as they talked, a question occurred to me: Did they actually function like human beings, make love, have feelings, or were they robots? As we left, I turned to one of them and said, "Do you think we will survive?" and he said, "What?" Somewhat taken aback, I repeated my question. Without batting an eyelash, he replied, "Of course."

The whole delegation staggered out into the streets of Moscow almost in a state of acute clinical shock. Here we were in the Soviet Union, having had long, heated discussions with high-ranking Soviet officials on the topics of nuclear weapons and strategies, always with an overwhelming sense of the tragedy of war. Yet these two young, totally oblivious Americans had just presented to us a cold, immoral analysis of a nuclear war-fighting strategy that could be contemplated as the arms race proceeded. As we wandered down the street in a state of disarray, I realized that Washington was full of young men like these, who have never suffered any real pain, deprivation, starvation, or tragedy, and who have never allowed their emotional or moral reasoning to impinge upon their rational and objective analyses.

The Reverend William Sloane Coffin spoke and sang fluent Russian, and we often left our group and guides and wandered through the city streets and subways, speaking freely with the Soviet people. After admiring our jeans and telling us how much they liked America and its music, they universally spoke of their fear of nuclear war.

After I returned from the Soviet Union, I often wandered into the labs at Harvard Medical School, where brilliant young doctors conducted experiments on rare and diverse diseases. I thought, "What are they doing that for? We have three years before the world is out of human control. Don't they know that?" The fact is that most of them did not. And as I speak around the country, I find that less than 1 percent of American audiences even know what a strategic weapon is. The level of ignorance about the arms race is frightening.

It took me one year to decide finally that I had to leave the day-to-day practice of clinical medicine. Although I loved my forty patients with cystic fibrosis (the most common genetic disease of childhood), I realized that I had a conflict of interest. What was the use of keeping these children alive for another five, ten, or twenty years with meticulous and loving medical care when during this time they could all be vaporized in a nuclear war? Further, as a pediatrician, I felt a sense of responsibility for all children—present and future—on the planet.

I went to the door of my chief three times, and three times I walked away. I thought, "Will I lose my credibility if I leave Harvard? I will cut my ties with Harvard forever, and I love this place." Finally I opened the door. I was relieved to discover that he had understood my conflict for some time. Afterward I wandered down the corridor and into the street, feeling naked. I had lost the image of myself as a clever doctor working at Harvard, and I felt like a nobody. I was very depressed for several weeks until the work for our survival absorbed my energy and time.

About a month later, I received a letter from the chief of medicine at Children's Hospital Medical Center, Harvard Medical School. She was sorry I had left, but she wrote that if I ever wished to return, she would reappoint me to my positions at both the hospital and the medical school. Then senior physicians on the faculty at Harvard started to approach me, saying, "It's because of what you did that I have decided to get involved in Physicians for Social Responsibility." I realized the empathy that doctors have for one another as they recognize the scarifying experience involved in the acquisition of the art and science of medicine. Finally, the dean of a prestigious medical school in New York told me, "You've left medicine to save lives," and I felt vindicated. I learned from that experience that in the future I must do what is right, not because it *feels* right but because it *is* right.

The Terminal Event

The logical consequence of the preparation for nuclear war is nuclear war. The behavior that perpetuates this race to oblivion can be changed only when people actually allow themselves to contemplate the true medical and ecological implications of such an event. Only then will they make a conscious decision to devote their lives, their fortunes, and their sacred honor to save the creation.

As you read this chapter, think of everything you hold most dear in your life—your children; parents; spouse; friends; home; the beauties of nature in spring as she unfolds the lilacs, dogwood, wisteria, roses, magnolias, and daffodils. Then transpose the following facts into your own life. After you have read this chapter, you will realize the intellectual and moral imperatives of understanding the dynamics of the arms race in all its manifestations. Then you can take the law into your own hands and use your democracy to save your world.

After the button is pressed (either by accident or by design), the bombs will begin to hit coastal cities about fifteen minutes after launch from nearby Soviet submarines and thirty minutes after launch from ICBM silos in the Soviet Union. However, because satellites and radar take some time to detect the attack and for warning then to be relayed via your radios and TV sets, advance warning to the general populace will be fifteen minutes or less. Of course, you may not have the radio or TV on when the attack occurs. You may be at work, or you may be sound asleep, in which

7

case (if you live in a city) you will be instantly annihilated. In its plans for civil defense, the Reagan Administration has said that it may provide a special monitor that could be attached to your radio or TV set, which would turn on automatically to give you warning of the impending attack. I'm not sure why you would need this few minutes' warning—perhaps just to say good-bye.

To understand the magnitude of a nuclear war, we must compare the number of available targets to the number of available weapons. America has 11,469 nuclear weapons it can drop on the Soviet Union; 7,855 in thirty minutes or less, and 3,614 over several hours. The Soviet Union has 8,794 strategic bombs it can land on America or other countries, 8,094 in thirty minutes or less. Approximately 60 percent of Americans live in an area of 18,000 square miles and could be annihilated with only 300 1-megaton bombs. This enormous redundancy of nuclear weapons is called, appropriately enough, overkill. For instance, the United States has a policy of not specifically targeting population areas—only military and industrial facilities. Yet because most of these targets are near population areas, current U.S. war plans target all 200 major Soviet cities and 80 percent of the 886 cities with populations above 25,000. Most of these cities would be bombed by more than 10 weapons; approximately 60 warheads would land on Moscow alone. Not a single tree or building would be left standing. The Soviet Union has similar targeting plans for the United States.

The Royal Swedish Academy of Sciences, in *Ambio* magazine, devised a scenario for nuclear war and examined the medical and ecological consequences of such an event. Because there is such a huge number of bombs, the academy could find appropriate targets for fewer than half the strategic and tactical nuclear weapons expected to be in the arsenals of the superpowers by 1985. Nevertheless, the horrific targeting plan goes like this:

All cities with populations over 100,000 people in the United States, Canada, Western Europe, Eastern Europe, the USSR, Japan, North and South Korea, Vietnam, Australia, South Africa, and Cuba would be targeted. According to the *Ambio* study, the bombs landing on these cities would be ground-burst weapons, which produce enormous quantities of fallout. The bombs and yields allocated to each city would be as follows:

1. Cities with 100,000 to 1 million people: 1 megaton (three 300-kiloton and one 100-kiloton bomb)
2. Cities with populations of 1 million to 3 million people: 3 megatons (three 1-megaton bombs)
3. Cities with 3 million people or more: 10 megatons (ten 500-kiloton and five 1-megaton bombs)

Cities with populations greater than 500,000 people would be targeted in China, Southeast Asia (except Vietnam and North and South Korea), India, and Pakistan:

1. Cities with 500,000 to 1 million people: 1 megaton (three 300-kiloton and one 100-kiloton bomb)
2. Cities with populations of 1 million to 3 million people: 3 megatons (three 1-megaton bombs)
3. Cities with 3 million people or more: 10 megatons (ten 500-kiloton and five 1-megaton bombs)

The important industries in these cities that are not directly destroyed are targeted with air bursts, as are all the energy supplies and the mineral resources of these countries and other areas in both the Northern and Southern hemispheres.

Military targets not close to cities are also targeted with ground bursts. These include the airfields and ports in both the Northern and Southern hemispheres.

In the event of a nuclear war, it is highly likely that the arsenals of the two superpowers, as well as those of Great Britain, France, and China, would be depleted—probably within several days. These reserves represent a total of some 50,000 bombs.

To give you an idea of the magnitude of destruction suggested by these statistics, let me drop a 20-megaton bomb on a major city. Twenty megatons is equivalent in explosive power to 20 million tons of TNT—more than the collective explosive power of all the bombs used to date in the history of the human race. Of course, it could be 10 or 60 smaller hydrogen bombs, or a MIRVed "footprint," but it is easier to describe the physical effects of a single large bomb. The Soviets have between 100 and 200 weapons of this size. They will almost certainly be used on large cities, where the leadership resides and where the major command, control, and communications centers are located.

The bomb will come in on a missile traveling at about 20 times the speed of sound, moving on a ballistic trajectory that loops some 750 miles into space. If it explodes at ground level on a clear day, it will release heat equivalent to that of the sun—several million degrees Celsius—in a fraction of a millionth of a second. It will dig a hole three quarters of a mile wide and 800 feet deep, converting all the people, buildings, and earth and rocks below to radioactive fallout particles, which will be shot up into the atmosphere in the mushroom cloud.

Six miles from the epicenter, every building will be flattened and every person killed. Because the human body is composed mostly of water, when it is exposed to thousands of degrees Celsius, it turns into gas and disappears. There are photographs of shadows of people on pavements in Hiroshima—that is all they left behind them.

Twenty miles from the epicenter, all people will be killed or lethally injured, and most buildings will be destroyed. People just beyond the 6-mile, 100-percent lethal range who happen to glance at the flash could have their eyes melted. John Hersey's book *Hiroshima* gives a clinical description of this event:

> There were about thirty men . . . all in exactly the same nightmarish state: Their faces were wholly burned; their eye sockets were hollow; the fluid from their melted eyes had run down their cheeks. . . . Their mouths were mere swollen, pus-covered wounds which they could not bear to stretch enough to admit the spout of a teapot. . . .

Other people will be charcoalized from the heat. In a book called *Unforgettable Fire,* Hiroshima survivors drew pictures of scenes they remembered. One depicted a mother holding her baby, standing on one foot, running; she and the infant had been turned into a charcoal statue.

Enormous overpressures will create winds of up to 500 miles per hour, causing hundreds of thousands of injuries. (A normal hurricane wind has a velocity of approximately 120 miles per hour.) These winds will literally pick people up off the pavement and suck them out of reinforced-concrete buildings, together with the furniture, converting them into missiles traveling at 100 miles per hour. When they hit the nearest wall or solid object, they will be killed instantly from fractured skulls, brain trauma, fractured long bones, and internal-organ injuries. The overpressures also will convert bricks, mortar, and other solid objects into missiles traveling at high speeds until they might hit the nearest human being. These overpressures will enter the respiratory tract and lungs through the nose and mouth and produce acute pneumothorax with rupture of the lungs, with accompanying sudden death. They will also rupture the tympanic membranes, or eardrums, causing deafness.

Glass is also very vulnerable to overpressures. Windows will be "popcorned"—extruded outward or inward—by these forces before they shatter into millions of sharp pieces of flying glass. Traveling at 100 miles an hour, the shards could penetrate human flesh and produce shocking lacerations and hemorrhage. The Pentagon has published a large book called *The Effects of Nuclear Weapons* in which complex equations and formulas calculate how far a piece of glass traveling at 100 miles an hour will penetrate human flesh.

In a major city, the huge buildings will collapse into the streets, taking their occupants with them. People will be crushed, mangled, and trapped under falling debris.

Thirty-five percent of the energy of the bomb is released as heat. This radiant heat will produce hundreds of thousands of severe burns. A patient with extensive burns is one of the most difficult challenges in medicine. Burn victims require intensive medical care day and night for at least six months, elaborate isolation techniques, operations and skin grafts every couple of days, hundreds of units of blood and blood products, antibiotics, analgesics, and sedation. Even after this intensive treatment, they often die or end up grotesquely deformed. Because of the cost and intensive medical care involved, there are only about 1,000 beds for acute-burn victims in the whole of the United States (a country with the most sophisticated medical technology in the world).

Twenty-six miles from the epicenter, the heat from the explosion will still be so intense that dry objects such as clothes, curtains, upholstery, and dry wood will spontaneously ignite. People could become walking, flaming torches. Wooden houses will also burn spontaneously.

Forty miles from the flash, people who glance reflexively at the incredible light will be instantly blinded by burns to the retina or back of the eyes. (Animals 345 miles from the Bikini explosions in the Marshall Islands were found to have focal retinal burns to their eyes.)

Huge fires will begin to burn over the entire area. A typical American city contains 5 to 25 potential ignition points per acre. As the bomb explodes, a huge pressure wave is created, which travels at a speed greater than that of sound. It spreads out from the center of the explosion, followed by winds that transiently exceed 1,000 miles per hour. This wind creates a low-pressure area as it moves upward, and surrounding oxygen-rich air rushes in and feeds the many fires that have been ignited in houses, gasoline tanks, liquid natural-gas facilities, oil tanks, and other flammable objects. This fire storm could cover an area with a radius of 16 to 21 miles. Such a fire storm occurred in Hamburg after a fire bombing in 1943 and produced temperatures up to 1,472 degrees Fahrenheit. So intense was this heat that days later, as bomb shelters were opened, the fresh air rushing in caused them to burst into flames.

A massive conflagration could also occur in which flammable objects ignited. The resultant fires, fanned by prevailing winds, could spread to cover an area of up to 3,000 square miles. Such a conflagration increases the lethal area of bomb damage by a factor of five. Within this area, of course, fallout shelters would be useless because the fires would suck all the oxygen out of them. They would fill with noxious gases, carbon dioxide, and carbon monoxide, asphyxiating the occupants. The intense blast and heat would convert most shelters into crematoria.

The *Ambio* study determined that in a global nuclear war, of the 1.3 billion urbanized population in the Northern Hemisphere, 750 million people will be killed instantly from blast alone, and a further 340 million will be seriously injured. Within minutes, the urban population will be reduced to less than one third; more than half of the survivors will be injured. These figures do not include all the other effects of fire, radiation, and thermal burns I have described, let alone the long-term effects on the survivors.

The World Health Organization produced a report in 1983 titled *Effects of Nuclear War on Health and Health Services.* They

Acute phase

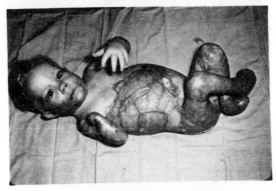

After months of medical treatment and many operations

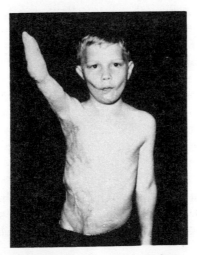

Child growing up minus a hand, and very scarred

predicted that nuclear war using the stockpile of the *Ambio* scenario would result in 1 billion dead and 1 billion injured. All the nations of the world endorsed this report save the U.S. administration and some of its close allies.

Fallout

Much of the targeted city and its people would now be radioactive dust, which would be shot up into the atmosphere in the mushroom cloud. It is difficult to calculate the size of the area that would be covered by lethal fallout because there has never really been a proper ground-burst nuclear test, but one 15-megaton bomb exploded 7 feet above the coral reef at Bikini atoll caused substantial contamination of an area of 7,000 square miles. A 20-megaton ground-burst explosion over New York, for instance, probably would produce a similar amount of fallout, and if the prevailing went blew this fallout onto populated areas, it could kill about 20 million people—almost 10 percent of the U.S. population.

People die in various ways after exposure to fallout, depending upon the doses of radiation they have received. Radiation is measured in units called rads. The national background level of radiation we all receive every year is 170 millirads (1 millirad equals 1/1000th of a rad). A huge exposure of 5,000 rads or more, received by people closest to the explosion, will produce the *central nervous system syndrome*, whereby the brain cells are severely damaged, and the brain swells inside its fixed box or skull. Because there is no room to accommodate such swelling, symptoms of acute raised intracranial pressure occur—immediate excitability, severe nausea, vomiting, and diarrhea, followed by drowsiness. Prostration and respiratory failure precede death, which occurs within twenty-four to forty-eight hours.

Doses greater than 1,000 rads and less than 5,000 rads will induce death from *gastrointestinal symptoms*. Such high doses of radiation produce death of the cells lining the gut, all the way from the mouth to the anus. The bone marrow, which produces white blood cells to fight infection and platelets to induce clotting, also is severely damaged by this dose of radiation. Consequently, mouth ulcers, colicky abdominal pain, loss of appetite, nausea and vomiting, and bloody diarrhea all occur within seven to fourteen days. Death is produced by fluid and electrolyte loss, infection, hemorrhage, and starvation.

Doses less than 500 rads are followed immediately by symptoms common to all the other syndromes: nausea, loss of appetite, fatigue, and possibly diarrhea. Fifty percent of patients experience these effects, which subside after several days' duration.

Doses of 200 to 1,000 rads cause bone-marrow death. Fifty percent of patients who receive 450 rads will die from this exposure; the incidence of death decreases below this dose and increases above it. Typical symptoms are immediate vomiting and diarrhea, which subside after six or seven days, followed within three or four weeks by severe illness. People will start to feel tired and weak, notice that their hair is falling out, and become bald. They will develop bloody diarrhea and bleeding under the skin and from the gums, and die from extensive internal hemorrhage and often generalized septicemia or infection.

These radiation syndromes are exacerbated by mechanical injuries and burns. Severe burns occur at 100 rads, the dose at which 50 percent of the population dies. Infants, children, and old people are also more sensitive to these lethal effects of radiation than are healthy adults, and 50 percent may die at doses of 200 rads.

Doctors will be killed in higher proportions than the average population because they work and reside in heavily targeted areas. A study done by Physicians for Social Responsibility and published in *The New England Journal of Medicine* in 1962 estimated that after a 20-megaton attack on Boston, there would be one physician for 17,000 injured patients. If that doctor then worked twenty hours a day for fourteen days, he or she could see each patient only once for a ten-minute period (assuming they could be identified among the debris of the flattened city). Such cursory care virtually assures that all the patients would die. Of course, the doctor would also be exposed to lethal levels of radiation during that initial period. This, in turn, would decrease the number of physicians available to treat people in coming months.

Within the bombed areas, fatalities will occur from a combination of trauma, burns, radiation illness, and starvation. Many will be trapped under girders, rafters, and beams in the most intense agony, with no relatives and no help from doctors or health workers even to give them pain-relieving drugs. The federal government has, indeed, stock-piled 70,000 pounds of morphine in case there is a nuclear war. Some officials would like to increase this amount to 130,000 pounds, but the Reagan Administration, early in 1983, decided to defer the purchase of more morphine to avoid frightening people. This drug is stored in central depots, is certainly not distributed to the few people who know how to use it following a nuclear attack, and obviously will be useless.

After I describe this scenario in lectures, I am accused of making people feel uncomfortable. I believe it is therapeutic to induce the feeling of severe discomfort in people *before* a nuclear war so they will be motivated to prevent such an event—the final epidemic of the human race.

You have just read the description of one bomb landing on one city, but there are enough bombs to target all towns and cities with populations down to 10,000 people in both the United States and the USSR. The Soviet Union and the United States also target each other's energy facilities, which include nuclear power plants. Steven Fetter and Kosta Tsipis wrote an article in *Scientific American* describing the consequences of a 1-megaton bomb exploding on a 1,000-megawatt nuclear reactor (standard size). If the radiation in the reactor and in the cooling pools containing spent fuel rods were released into the atmosphere, it could contaminate an area the size of West Germany. In fact, the *Ambio* scenario states that an attack just on the numerous nuclear reactors in Western Europe and North America would render these and neighboring countries uninhabitable, by ordinary radiation standards, for years or even decades. If the plants that reprocess spent reactor fuel were also hit, to say nothing of the storage tanks containing vast quantities of radioactive waste, the radiation levels I've discussed here would be greatly increased.

In a full-scale nuclear war, the United States probably would be covered by lethal fallout for the first forty-eight hours. Subsequent consequences would be so devastating that up to 90 percent of Americans could be dead within thirty days. A similar magnitude of devastation would also be visited upon the Soviet Union, continental Europe, Great Britain, and much of the other territory described in the *Ambio* scenario.

Nikita Khrushchev once said that after a nuclear war, "the living will envy the dead." For survivors in targeted and nontargeted countries alike, life would not be worth living.

Disease

The immediate aftereffects will depend very much on the season. It has been postulated by the U.S. Forest Service that if the holocaust occurs in the summer months, up to 80 percent of the United States could be consumed in fire. Millions upon millions of decaying human and animal bodies will fill the air with the most unbelievable stench as bacteria and viruses multiply in the dead flesh. The high levels of background radiation will cause mutations in these organisms, so even bacteria that normally live in harmony with the human body could become more dangerous and virulent. Because birds are very sensitive to radiation, it is possible that most of them in heavily targeted countries will die. Meanwhile, insects— which are extremely resistant to high levels of radiation—will multiply prolifically in the absence of their natural predators. Trillions of flies, fleas, lice, and cockroaches will crawl and fly unimpeded over corpses, transmitting disease from the dead to the living. Rodents will also multiply in these unhygienic conditions. All sewage-disposal and sanitation systems will be destroyed, and the cities of the world will become perfect culture media for pathogens (bacteria, viruses, rodents, and insects).

In 1944, during World War II, the U.S. Army entered Manila and faced the problem of burying 39,000 bodies of Japanese and Filipinos killed during the preceding weeks. It was soon found that American troops were unable to withstand the psychological aspects of this work. "With a few exceptions, nausea, vomiting, and loss of appetite occurred within a few days." Local laborers were recruited at double pay to place the dead in large pits; nevertheless, the burial of these 39,000 dead, unhampered by such complications as radioactivity and lack of equipment, required eight weeks.

The unfortunate survivors of nuclear war will be extremely susceptible to contracting disease. A radiation dose as low as 50 rads can diminish the normal functioning of white blood cells, which fight infection. Such a dose will be rapidly accumulated by people in rural areas or on the periphery of lethal areas of fallout. Radioactive elements in fallout decay rapidly; even so, low background levels of radiation emitted from fallout, accumulated on the ground, will quickly add up to a significant dose if people stay outside for many hours.

Adequate supplies of antibiotics and vaccines will most likely have been destroyed, and there will be few if any medical personnel available to treat survivors. Susceptibility to infectious disease will be further enhanced by a lack of first-class protein, by malnutrition or starvation, and by unsanitary conditions.

Epidemics of diseases now controlled by mass-immunization programs—polio, tetanus, whooping cough, measles, influenza, typhus, smallpox, and diptheria—probably will spread among the nonimmunized population. Diseases that are relatively rare in a pre-attack world will become common, and other diseases common in Third World countries will spread rapidly in the postattack developed nations. This is because excellent sanitation and a high standard of living, including immediate therapy with antibiotics, have deprived most people of routine exposure to these diseases and an opportunity to develop appropriate immunities to them. These diseases include cholera, malaria, plague, rabies, shigella, typhoid fever, yellow fever, amoebic dysentery, botulism, food poisoning, hepatitis A, meningococcal meningitis, pneumonia, and tuberculosis.

Because of the intensely unhygienic conditions in bombed cities, a growth rate of up to 11 percent per week is expected in the rat population. Rat-transmitted plague, or bubonic plague, is characterized by infection and swelling of the lymph glands. Under stressful conditions, this form of the disease can change to a virulent pneumonia called pneumonic plague, which is then highly contagious among humans. It can spread rapidly under conditions of crowding, which will be inevitable in postwar fallout shelters. Some people believe that plague represents "the major national threat among the set of vectorborne diseases."

Many of these disease epidemics could be transferred to nontargeted countries by insects, where a highly susceptible population will guarantee widespread contagion.

In Europe, American plans call for the integrated battlefield, which refers to simultaneous use of conventional, nuclear, and chemical weapons. Therefore, any survivors from a nuclear war on the European battlefield will most likely die from the dreadful effects of these chemical weapons.

Evacuation

The Federal Emergency Management Agency (FEMA) plans to evacuate people from "risk areas" to "host areas"—that is, from targeted cities to small country towns and villages. It claims to need three to five days' advance notice and plans eventually to be able to evacuate 250 cities with populations of more than 50,000 people. That is two thirds of the U.S. population—a total of 145 million people.

Apparently, this will be done at a time of heightened international tension, such as during a conflict in the Persian Gulf, Central America, or Eastern Europe, or when the Soviet Union appears to be evacuating her cities. These evacuation plans require eight to ten years to complete at current funding levels, and the sheltering components will require another eight to ten years' planning. Therefore they will not be complete until the turn of the century, at which point American demographic patterns will have altered sufficiently to render the plans obsolete. If we have been unsuccessful in arms control and disarmament, the Soviet Union will have enough bombs by then to blanket America with blast as well as radiation effects, making the plans totally irrelevant.

They are ludicrous anyway because Soviet satellites could observe all significant population-movement activities in America, and U.S. satellites could observe similar activities in the Soviet Union. If Soviet leaders see that the United States is evacuating its cities, especially with all the new first-strike weapons sitting on the shelf, they will naturally conclude that America is preparing for a first-strike nuclear war. At that point they could initiate their own first strike against the military targets, the evacuating populations, and the evacuated cities themselves. In this context, evacuation is an open invitation to nuclear war.

Apparently the Soviet Union has similar plans, but conditions there make potential evacuation even more difficult. Very few people have cars. The roads are mostly dirt tracks, which are extremely uncomfortable to travel on, and people would be reduced to walking. If either the United States or the USSR had to evacuate during the winter, people would find it impossible to dig holes or shelters in the frozen ground, and they would literally freeze to death out in the tundra or U.S. countryside.

FEMA has decided that during this three- to five-day preemptive period before a nuclear war, the evacuating population will remain calm, orderly, and well behaved. Pets are to stay at home with an adequate supply of food and water. We must not forget to take our bankbooks, credit cards, insurance policies, and wills; we must submit change-of-address cards to the post office; we must not take with us drugs or alcohol (although, as Dr. Herbert Abrams, professor of radiology at Harvard Medical School, has said, that is exactly what he might like to have when trapped in a massive traffic jam on the highway, waiting to be vaporized).

There are actually plans for car breakdowns on the highway. You are to move your car to the side of the road, get out your shovel—which you should remember to take—dig a large hole, and drive the car over the top of the hole. Cover the car and hole with a tarpaulin and hide underneath until the bombs have stopped falling. After some days or weeks, get out your Geiger counter and measure the ambient radiation levels. If they are safe, you may leave your shelter!

In most cases, people in the designated host areas will not have been adequately informed of their roles in the event of nuclear war. They are hospitably to receive thousands, perhaps hundreds of thousands of people in their small villages and offer them shelter in their basements. Plans are available to teach people how to make their basements radiationproof: One merely piles tons of dirt onto the roof of the basement or the first floor of the house. Unfortunately, many floors will collapse under such an enormous weight.

T. K. Jones, deputy undersecretary of defense for strategic theater nuclear forces, has determined that all people really need to do is dig a hole, cover it with two doors (presumably detached from the nearest available house), and pile three feet of dirt on top. T. K. says, "It is the dirt that does it." One might ask: "Who will put the dirt on top once you have safely entered your hole?"

Fallout Shelters

Let us talk about fallout shelters after a nuclear war. Within targeted areas, most people will have been asphyxiated in their shelters. But perhaps you live in a rural, nontargeted area and happen to be awake and listening to your radio or TV. When you hear the emergency signal to tell you a nuclear war is about to occur, you will have, at the very most, fifteen minutes to reach the nearest fallout shelter (if there is one) before the bombs start to explode and release their fallout. Once in the shelter, you will not be able to re-emerge for a period ranging from three weeks to three months— even longer near cities or other highly radioactive areas. In most places where people live and work, typical one-week doses will reach tens of thousands of rads. There, even shelters with high protection factors will not protect people from lethal doses of radiation. (Doses will be lower in some rural areas.)

Conditions in these shelters will be horrendous. They probably will be crowded with adults and children. Since some will doubtless have entered after the nuclear war and thus may have already received a lethal dose of radiation, they will develop vomiting with liquid and bloody diarrhea and die there. Of course, there will be no adequate sanitation, no toilets or sewage system. At best, there may be a small chemical unit. People will have to live with decomposing bodies and revolting sanitary conditions. They cannot go outside without risking exposure to lethal levels of radiation.

The shelters will have various protection factors (PF). Their effectiveness at radiation shielding will depend upon the thickness of dirt and concrete above them. Even with adequate PFs, they will need to be equipped with air-ventilation facilities to filter out the alpha-, beta-, and gamma-emitting isotopes from the fallout. Otherwise, people inside the shelter will become contaminated by inhalation or ingestion of these radioactive materials—which, incidentally, have no taste or smell and may be invisible or look like dust. Furthermore, the blowers and fans could be rendered inoperable by overpressures of one pound per square inch (which is minimal overpressure created on the very periphery of the area of deleterious effects from a nuclear explosion). The systems would also be blocked by electric power failure (apart from the fact that the power stations are likely targeted, the electromagnetic pulse, or EMP, emitted from the explosions will have rendered all power stations, cables, and electric lines inoperable).

If the war occurs during the winter, people in shelters could develop severe hypothermia at temperatures of 40 degrees Fahrenheit or less and would freeze to death. In the summer, the absence of a continuous flow of fresh air would make for unbearable heat and humidity. Stagnant, foul-smelling air; crowding; dead bodies; and poor sanitation will encourage the spread of microorganisms. Almost certainly the water supply will become sparse or almost nil. Because the average person needs one gallon of water per day to maintain basic health, people will be especially susceptible to disease. Insects will proliferate both inside and outside the shelters. Diseases that thrive in such shelter conditions include meningococcal meningitis and septicemia, influenza and viral respiratory diseases and pneumonia, gastrointestinal disease with vomiting and diarrhea, and hepatitis.

The supply of food almost certainly will be inadequate. Many people probably will die without ever emerging from their shelters. A study published in *The Journal of Health Physics* recommended that old people be sent outside as food gatherers, because they would not live long enough to die of leukemia and cancer resulting from their high radiation exposure. Such a scheme would allegedly spare the children and young adults who are also very susceptible to the carcinogenic effects of radiation.

Afterward

A colleague of mine had a nightmare recently. An emergency room physician, she dreamed there had been a nuclear war and Boston had been demolished. She had reached the fallout shelter and remained inside until the radiation levels had become relatively safe. As she prepared to leave the shelter to search for her parents, and clothed in a radiation-resistant suit and with an oxygen and food supply strapped to her back, she realized there would be no landmarks in Boston, making it impossible to navigate. Then she thought of the millions of decaying corpses and realized that as a physician she could not face the devastation. It became apparent then that what she lacked was an adequate supply of sleeping tablets.

What, indeed, will the world be like as the few survivors emerge from the underground graves? There will be millions of decaying human and animal bodies. More than 90 percent of the urban housing will have been destroyed. There will be no available food—no roads or railways to transport it, no one to coordinate distribution or even determine the areas of greatest need where the survivors have gathered. Since all oil refineries and storage facilities are targeted, 90 percent of the American fuel supply will have been destroyed. If the survivors do obtain any food, it probably will be raw grain, which needs to be processed or cooked before it is edible—but there will be no processing facilities and very few places to cook. Much of this food will already have been contaminated by the fallout.

Estimates suggest that after such a massive disaster, from 12 to 25 percent of the survivors will develop acute psychoses. (It is well known that all people exposed to significant psychological stress will develop symptoms. The intensity of the stress is more important in determining the nature of these symptoms than is the pre-existing personality.) Seventy-five percent would be dazed and stunned; 12 to 25 percent of these individuals might remain effective. In settings of massive destruction, people become so isolated that they may develop psychoses derived from sensory deprivation, and their symptoms will be exacerbated by fatigue and physical trauma. Survivors of the Japanese atomic bombings experienced pervasive images of the horror and continual fears of the radiation effects, with primal anxieties about cancer and leukemia, and profound guilt that they had survived and their relatives had not.

Severe grief and mental disturbance will persist as victims of nuclear war attempt to grow their own food on radioactive land without machinery, fertilizers, or insecticides. Given the almost troglodytic conditions under which people will have to live, will any of them be able to overcome their grief sufficiently to initiate sexual relations to reproduce the species? Fertility will be low; spontaneous abortion and infant mortality will be high. People are also bound to realize that their pervasive exposure to radiation, both immediately after the war and chronically thereafter, will almost certainly increase their chances of developing leukemia five to ten years later or solid cancers fifteen to fifty years after initial exposure.

The incidence of genetic diseases will rise over all future generations of humans, animals, and plants. The *Ambio* scenario, which for the sake of simplicity used only the accumulated seven-day fallout dose, estimated that such a war would induce 5.4 million to 12.8 million fatal cancers eight to twenty years after the war in the Northern Hemisphere. Within one hundred years, it estimated that 6.4 million to 16.3 million people in the Northern Hemisphere would suffer genetic defects attributable to their ancestors' exposure in 1985. Of those people who do not die from massive radiation exposure, between 3 million and 5 million North Americans are likely to be permanently sterilized by fallout—if, indeed, these people survive the other horrors visited upon them in the aftermath of nuclear war. If these scientists had chosen a more realistic 25-year accumulated dose, the incidence of cancer and genetic defects would be hugely increased.

The long-term ecological consequences of nuclear war probably are more important than the acute effects because the state of life on the planet may be permanently altered by such an event. Let us consider the known consequences.

There is only a thirty-day supply of food in the world at any one time, supplied to many Third World nations by Canada, the United States, Argentina, and Australia. Because most of these countries are targeted; because distribution of food depends upon ships, fuel, and people; and because most of the grain will be destroyed during the war anyway, hundreds of millions of people in the Third World will die from starvation in the first couple of months. International trade and exchange networks will suffer total collapse. Seven hundred fifty million immediate deaths in the Northern Hemisphere would escalate to between 1 billion and 3 billion deaths in tropical regions and in the Southern Hemisphere. That is three quarters of the earth's population.

People in targeted countries will also die from famine because most of the crops will likely have been burned in continental fires. It is not easy to estimate how much grain will be left to plant after the war, or where it will be, or who in fact will plant it. Only 6 percent of the U.S. population is currently involved in agriculture, so the majority of the surviving population will have had no experience in farming. They will have to hand-till the radioactive land, since 99 percent of the U.S. oil-refining capacities will be destroyed, and there won't be fuel to run farm machinery. Neither fertilizers nor pesticides will be available. Since the insects will have proliferated in the trillions and mutated to become more virile, the crops will almost certainly fail. If the attack occurs in the spring, tender new shoots will be killed. Seventy percent of the U.S. crop could be destroyed, as well as Soviet and European crops and those of other vulnerable nations. An attack prior to harvest may not induce so much damage—unless the country is covered with fire—but the crops may well be too radioactive to harvest.

Crops grown in following years will present other problems—if, indeed, all the seed has not been eaten by the starving survivors. Plants concentrate the radioactive elements that have landed on the soil as fallout. These elements then concentrate even more in a nonuniform fashion in various organs of the human body, exposing people to the threat of cancer years later.

More than 50 percent of the grazing livestock will be killed, and more than one quarter of the large farm animals fed on stored food will die immediately. These estimates are based only on blast and fallout effects.

Other long-term ecological effects will ravage the planet.

Ozone

The function of our planet's ozone is to protect multicellular organisms from the damaging effects of ultraviolet (UV) light emitted from the sun. Before multicellular organisms were formed, there was no ozone. Then tiny unicellular organisms learned how to create oxygen by metabolizing carbon dioxide through photosynthesis. As the oxygen formed, it rose up into the stratosphere to form the ozone layer. As the lethal levels of UV light at ground level began to diminish, multicellular organisms began to evolve.

Normal quantities of UV light induce sunburn at the beach and snowblindness during the winter. However, if the UV light increased dramatically in the Northern Hemisphere, fair-skinned people could develop incapacitating sunburn within 10 minutes, and blistering or even lethal third-degree sunburn with 30 to 60 minutes' exposure.

In 1975, the National Academy of Sciences published a study called *Long-Term Worldwide Effects of Multiple Nuclear Weapons Detonations*. They estimated that in a 10,000-megaton nuclear war in the Northern Hemisphere, if many of the weapons exploded were of 1 megaton or bigger, 30 to 70 percent of the stratospheric ozone layer could be destroyed in the Northern Hemisphere and 20 to 40 percent in the Southern Hemisphere. They based their estimates on such large bombs because according to past atmospheric data, nuclear clouds from detonations with yields greater than 1 megaton penetrate into the upper atmosphere or stratosphere. There are at least several thousand bombs in the nuclear arsenals of the world today with yields of this size. Both superpowers are moving toward smaller, more accurate bombs, but the old ones probably will still be used in an all-out nuclear war.

These large explosions oxidize vast quantities of nitrogen in the air to form nitrous oxide. Depending on size, altitude, and conditions of the explosion, each megaton would release about 5,000 tons of nitrous oxide. These nitrous oxides would be injected with the fireball and mushroom cloud into the stratosphere high above the earth, where there is a layer of ozone molecules (each molecule composed of 3 atoms of oxygen). At ground level this layer would be only 3 millimeters thick at normal temperature and pressure. The nitrous oxide molecules combine chemically with the ozone molecules and destroy them. The lowest levels of ozone after such destruction would occur six months after the war; it would not be totally replenished for ten years.

Because of the damage to the ozone layer, UV radiation could be increased tenfold in the Northern Hemisphere three months after a nuclear war, and doubled in the Southern Hemisphere for a period of up to two years after the war.

In addition to severe sunburn, increased UV light will induce a variety of pathological effects. It is very damaging to the eyes of humans, animals, birds, and insects and contributes to several kinds of eye lesion. *Photophthalmia,* or snowblindness, results in a partial, albeit temporary, loss of sight. *Conjunctivitis* is the painful red inflammation of the membranes surrounding the cornea. *Photokeratitis* is debilitating damage to the cornea—the clear, curved plaque that overlies the pupil and iris. Repeated UV injury eventually causes scarring of the cornea, which results in blindness. UV light can also damage the lens and the iris and can produce *cataracts,* or opaque areas, in the lens, causing blindness. Among Australian aborigines, who live in intense sunlight for years, significant correlations have been found between cataract prevalence and sunshine, or UV intensity.

Birds, animals, and insects will all be susceptible to these eye injuries. For humans privy to the same kind of damage, the use of sunglasses may be counterproductive. Many sunglasses absorb more visible light than UV light, causing pupil dilation which increases the eyes' vulnerability.

If birds, animals, and insects are blinded over time, much of the ecosystem will collapse. The bees will not be able to fertilize the crops, for example.

The National Academy of Sciences study also reported that a 50 percent loss in the ozone shield, lasting three years, would increase the incidence of skin cancer and malignant melanoma from 3 percent to 30 percent at midlatitude, the effect of which would persist for 40 years. Of course, fair-skinned people will be more susceptible to these effects than dark-skinned people.

UV light also induces the production of vitamin D in the skin. Although this is normally a healthy process, too much UV light would raise the levels of production of vitamin D in man, animals, and birds, inducing vitamin D toxicity. This can cause kidney and bone damage and even renal failure. The NAS report states, "We do not know whether man and other vertebrate animals could tolerate an increased vitamin D synthesis that might result from a large and rapid increase in UV exposure." They urgently recommended further study of this problem.

The ecological balance can also be adversely affected by an increase in UV light. According to Carl Sagan, recent scientific evidence suggests that the single-celled organisms, or bacteria, that live in the soil and upon which all other life depends are extremely sensitive to the effects of UV light. Because this radiation is so toxic to bacteria, it is used frequently for sterilization of equipment. These microorganisms form the base of the pyramid of life, with man at the apex. Should they be destroyed after a nuclear war, the pyramid of life will collapse.

The oceanic web of life depends upon its smallest organisms, which live at the surface of the sea. Recent data indicate that these single-celled or small multicellular organisms are extremely sensitive to UV light. Some wait until evening hours to divide because their replicating DNA is very much exposed to the lethal effects of UV light during cell division. Some have enzymes by which damage done during the day is repaired at night, and some dive below the surface of the water if the sun appears from behind a cloud.

Evidence suggests that if the ozone were decreased by 60 percent, this diving organism would be killed in middive. Although information about this subject is patchy, it could pose a most serious threat to much of life in the sea and on land. These life forms produce much of the oxygen that normally replenishes the ozone layer. If they were destroyed by the increase of UV light, the ozone probably would never reaccumulate. Crops and plants have also been found to be damaged by UV light. The sensitivity varies according to the species.

Climatic Change

Although reduction of the stratospheric ozone layer would allow more heat from the sun to enter the atmosphere, decreased ozone levels would also prevent much of the heat radiated up from the earth from being reflected back to the atmosphere. The combination of these two dynamics could result in a cooling of the earth by 1 degree Fahrenheit, which would have serious ecological implications. Further, the effect of the subsequent cooling of the upper troposphere and lower stratosphere is likely to be more severe than the cooling at the surface of the earth. It could cause alterations in the cloud cover, which could also influence the climate. These two events, as well as cooling induced by the injection of vast quantities of dust and smoke into the atmosphere, could lower the temperature of the earth by 2 degrees Fahrenheit.

Another scenario envisioned by *Ambio* is an all-out nuclear war using hydrogen bombs of a smaller yield than those of 1 megaton or more projected by the National Academy of Sciences. In this event it is unlikely that significant quantities of nitrogen oxide would initially be injected into the stratosphere to cause the ozone depletion previously described. The most significant atmospheric effect will result from the enormous number of huge fires—in forests, oil wells, military installations, urban and industrial centers, and gas-production facilities. Such fires would create sufficient quantities of toxic airborne particulate matter in the lower atmosphere, or troposphere, to screen out the sun for weeks or months. The subsequent reduction or even elimination of agricultural crops over large areas of the Northern Hemisphere would ensure that no food could be grown by the survivors. Dark aerosol deposits probably would kill any plants that did manage to grow.

The vast quantities of nitrogen oxide created from the smaller nuclear explosions and from the fires would make the rain extremely acidic, with a pH of less than 4. As is well known, acid rain kills trees, plants, and aquatic life. Nitrogen oxide in the low-lying troposphere would also induce ozone production. This new tropospheric ozone would cause severe photochemical pollution like that in Los Angeles and could also severely damage crops. Thus the troposphere would become heavily polluted by a toxic dark smog consisting of particulate matter from the fires and aerosolized dirt from the ground-burst nuclear explosions, the nitrogen oxides, and ozone produced by the nitrogen oxides, dioxins, furans, and cyanide.

If this smog induced a reduction of solar penetration to the earth by a factor of one hundred, it is quite possible that most of the plants in more than half of the Northern Hemisphere's oceans would die. Similar darkening of the planet is thought to have occurred 65 million years ago during the Cretaceous-Tertiary boundary era, when a large extraterrestrial body is said to have hit the earth, possibly causing the widespread and massive extinctions evident in geological history.

But if the ground fires were extremely powerful, the flames could reach reach up into the stratosphere, carrying nitrogen oxide with them, and cause further reduction of stratospheric ozone. Nitrogen oxide might also be transported upward when the heavy, dark, aerosol, low-lying layer was heated by the sun, thus setting up convection currents and wind systems that could transport a large amount of the fire effluents into the stratosphere.

The Nuclear Winter

Since this chapter was written, Carl Sagan, Paul Ehrlich, and their colleagues have published two papers in *Science* that examine the concept of nuclear winter. The dense cloud of smoke produced by urban fires, forest fires, and burning oil wells could blanket the Northern Hemisphere for many months, causing a drop in temperature of 13 degrees Fahrenheit, in midsummer. This severe change would occur within three or four weeks after a major nuclear exchange. Light from the sun would be reduced to 17 percent of normal. At least a year would be required for light and temperature values to return to normal conditions. The subfreezing dark conditions in the Northern Hemisphere could destroy the biological support systems of civilization, resulting in massive starvation and death from hypothermia and thirst (most fresh water could be frozen to a depth of three feet).

Sagan found that radiation levels would be much higher than previously calculated, as most radioactive nuclear debris remained in the troposphere and fell to the ground as intermediate-term fallout. Thirty percent of the Northern Hemisphere would receive a dose greater than 250 rems (rem—Roentgen equivalent man—is a unit of radiation dosage) and 50 percent of northern midlatitudes would receive a dose greater than 100 rems.

Because of the large temperature gradients at the equator, it is predicted that the smoky cloud would move rapidly down to the Southern Hemisphere, inducing marked cooling and subsequent global disruption of the biosphere.

According to these new data, the population of man could conceivably be reduced to prehistoric levels; indeed, the extinction of Homo sapiens cannot be dismissed. Certainly extinction of a large fraction of the earth's animals, plants, and microorganisms seems inevitable.

These biological effects were calculated from the Ambio nuclear-war scenario of a 5,000-megaton exchange, but the threshold for such global cooling was found to be an exchange of only 100 megatons (100 kilotons apiece on 1,000 cities).

If the world were to fall prey to such a nuclear disaster, we will have destroyed most of the germ cells that would have produced all future generations of humans, animals, and plants. We will take with us not only all present earthly life but also all past generations and the magnificent heritage they bequeathed: Beethoven, Mozart, Bach, Rembrandt, Picasso, Dickens, Shakespeare, Gothic cathedrals, beautiful ancient monuments of Europe and Asia. We hold in our hands the ability to destroy most of creation. It could happen any day.

The Iron Triangle

The late General of the Army Omar Bradley once said, "We have grasped the mystery of the atom and rejected the Sermon on the Mount. Ours is a world of nuclear giants and ethical infants. We know more about war than we do about peace. We know more about killing than we do about living."

Somewhere in the past thirty-eight years, the United States of America has lost its direction and its soul. In 1984, it appropriated approximately $264 billion for the military—7.24 percent of the total Gross National Product. For 1985, the administration requested authority for $313 billion and received $293 billion.

In Australia, where I come from, tax dollars are used for the benefit and not the death of society. We have nationalized medicine (medical insurance is either national or private, according to the patient's preference), and all medical care is subsidized. University education is free. All citizens are provided with adequate old-age pensions so they can maintain their dignity, and poor people are provided with aid. Australia is a capitalist country, but she cares for her people. What has happened to the great United States of America?

In 1983, a total of $30 billion was withdrawn from programs to help people: Medicare; legal services; food stamps; school lunches; assistance to low-income families for heating costs; welfare; aid to cities; student loans; Social Security; job opportunities and training; elementary, secondary, and higher education; child-nutrition programs; housing-assistance programs; Aid to Families with Dependent Children programs; and compensatory education for disadvan-taged children. By August 1983, a total of 34.4 million people in the United States were below the poverty line—defined as $9,900 annual income for a family of four.

Instead, in the five years from 1985 to 1989, the Reagan Administration plans to spend $1.8 trillion (if hidden costs are included, $2.5 trillion) on "defense." It has earmarked $21.6 billion for MX missiles, $28.2 billion for B-1 long-range bombers (which will be obsolete by the time they are ready at the end of the 1980s), $69.8 billion for Trident submarines and missiles, $42.9 billion for production of FA-18 attack bombers, $12.7 billion for procurement of Patriot missiles, $2.6 billion for Pershing II missiles, and $2.3 billion for nerve gas. In the past thirty-eight years, America has spent a relatively paltry $1.5 trillion on defense.

If one subtracts from the federal budget the government's self-funding trust accounts (such as Social Security and Medicare, which are funded separately from income taxes), the Defense Department is by far the biggest single spender. The Council on Economic Priorities recently reported that the "total military budget" in 1981 used 48 percent of all federal general funds. In 1984 the figure was 55 percent. Projecting to 1986, the "total military budget" would use up 59 cents of every federal dollar. When Reagan was elected, his administration and the Pentagon, military corpora-tions, and scientists behaved like little boys let loose in a candy shop. They ordered every weapon on the shelves—whatever struck their fancy.

This sort of wild spending, using people's hard-earned tax dollars, will destroy the American economy. Such a downfall will doubtless be bad for America but probably worse for the rest of the world, which depends on the value of the U.S. dollar for economic survival, and on U.S. exports of food, U.S. technology, and the U.S. market.

The dynamics of the pathology of the U.S. arms race has several different sources. It involves the activities of scientists in specialized "think tanks" and at American universities. But the whole government policy on weapons development and procure-ment, with its implications for U.S. foreign policy, is dominated and controlled by what some political scientists call the Iron Triangle. The three sides of this triangle are:

- the Pentagon and other agencies related to defense in the executive branch of the government—the National Aeronautics and Space Administration, and the Nuclear Weapons Branch of the Department of Energy
- the key committees of Congress—House and Senate Armed Services committees and Defense Appropriation subcommittees—and the members of Congress from districts and states where the defense industry is concentrated
- private industry—the corporations, research institutes, laboratories, trade associations, banks, and defense-related trade unions

All three sides of the Iron Triangle engage in frequent socializing and an almost constant exchange of personnel. Many politicians become handmaidens to this powerful corporate monopoly instead of representing their constituents or their children. And millions of Americans feel trapped in jobs orchestrated by large military corporations. In order to feed their children, they make weapons and delivery systems of hideously destructive power.

In his classic eighteenth-century treatise *The Wealth of Nations*, Adam Smith wrote, "The whole Army and Navy are unproductive laborers. They are the servants of the people, and are maintained by a part of the annual product of the industry of other people." Thirty percent or more of America's best engineers work on military projects because they pay better and are technologically more interesting. It is evident that the military-industrial complex neither stimulates the economy nor provides many jobs for the amount of money it spends. For every $1 billion spent by the Pentagon in the private sector, 28,000 direct and indirect jobs are created. But the same amount of money would create 32,000 jobs if spent for new public transportation, 57,000 jobs if used for personal consumption, or 71,000 jobs if spent for education. Those professions that military spending benefits with increased employment are primarily specific and highly skilled—such as aircraft production, electronics, and engineering (there are also opportunities in skilled and semiskilled metal work). More than 30 percent of the country's mathematicians work somewhere in the military-industrial complex, as do 25 percent of the nation's physicists, 40 percent of its aeroastronautic engineers, and 11 percent of its computer programmers. On the other hand, domestic spending creates jobs in areas of high public interest—medicine, social work, civil engineering, construction, and education. And as the defense sector becomes more capital-intensive, fewer and fewer new jobs are created through new defense expenditures.

The military industry also creates dead-end products in economic terms. Huge amounts of money are spent on the most deadly weapons of mass genocide, which, if they function as intended, will never be used. Because they sit on the shelf, so to speak, the money used to create them is never injected back into the economy, where it might contribute to further economic production. People can't eat bombs, wear them on their heads, or use them for pleasure.

America's military expenditures are partly responsible for her declining economy. Japan, which spends a mere 1 percent of its Gross National Product on military expenditures; and West Germany, which spends 3.5 percent on them, are way ahead of us in terms of relative economic growth. Their scientists develop wonderful things that people can buy and sell, instead of contributing to a weapons stockpile of deadly proportions. At present, defense accounts for a full 10 percent of U.S. manufacturing output and 38 percent of its export sales, while Japan is edging America out of the marketing of advanced computer technology, and the European consortium Airbus Industries is challenging Boeing in the world market for the new generation of fuel-efficient jumbo jets.

During World War I, business leaders were used by the federal government as wartime production planners for all sections of U.S. industry. During and after World War II, businesspeople were recruited into government as policymakers. Regulatory commissions have been staffed for years by personnel from the industries they regulated. The administration of military spending has also been staffed, especially in wartime, by executives and officials from the defense industry. During the 1960s and 1970s, major corporations became adept at influencing government and executive branch policymakers to affect legislation, administrative decision-making, and the regulatory process. Most of the *Fortune* 500 companies now have Washington offices. The staffs from these offices make connections between the companies' needs and government requirements. They gather information and exert political pressure;

campaign for company spending; organize political grass-roots support; and influence members of Congress and government officials, even in the administration itself. These firms work to achieve a high degree of intimacy between the Pentagon and its contractors, which tends to inhibit cost control, and most Department of Defense contracts eventually become cost-plus. In addition, federal procurement policies give many defense contractors much rent-free production space and equipment and interest-free loans for "progress" on work completed by contractors.

Military-related jobs account for a large percentage of the U.S. work force. Over 8 million people in America are supported by jobs in defense. Of the more than 3.3 million who work directly for the defense industry, 1.1 million are civilians employed in support and clerical positions with the Department of Defense. Uniformed personnel account for 2.2 million workers; and 1.4 million are with the National Guard and Reserve.

Business interests work in tandem with scientists and the armed forces. In 1983, about 2.9 million American jobs depended on the manufacture of weapons (this figure doesn't include those on active military duty). Of every four dollars the government spends on procurement, the Pentagon spends three. In other words, the jobs of one of every ten American workers depend directly or indirectly on defense spending. The Pentagon is the largest single purchaser of goods and services in the nation. Defense industries account for 10 percent of all U.S. manufacturing. In certain states, defense-related employment is the largest single source of personal income (California, for example, boasts twice as many defense workers as farmers).

Business is very cynical about how it obtains government contracts. The defense industries have no moral scruples in their quest to achieve those contracts. In fact, in the area of defense, America does not have a working democracy. It has become instead a system of socialism for the rich and capitalism for the poor. Many big defense corporate chiefs sit on advisory boards to the Department of Defense, the Department of Energy, and NASA. They lobby extensively throughout the federal bureaucracy; support politicians financially through their political action committees (PACs); work hand-in-hand with the armed forces at the Pentagon; entertain and befriend relevant representatives and senators; use the large banks that fund them and the investment firms that support their activities in deals; and work with huge trade associations that represent their special interests in Washington. They also practice fraud, allowing cost overruns that cost the American people billions of dollars.

There is a story to be told about the corruption and intrigue in the defense industry that is bigger than Watergate ever was. If we are to expose the dynamics of the pathology of our planet, we must be prepared to examine the Iron Triangle and the military-industrial complex in minute detail.

Let me first enumerate the activities of the scientists, many of whom have spearheaded the arms race since 1945. At that time, the Air Force, having used the two atomic bombs in Japan, maintained a proprietary right over nuclear weapons. For many years, it was the strongest force in the Pentagon with respect to nuclear arms. The Air Force generals were enthusiastic about the first use of nuclear weapons at a time when the Soviet Union possessed very few, if any. Their policy was to bomb the Soviet Union flat if it misbehaved on the international scene.

The Air Force, which appreciated the great consultative value of scientists during World War II, also established the RAND Corporation in 1946 to advise and formulate policies for a rational use of nuclear weapons. As described by Fred Kaplan in *The Wizards of Armageddon,* its faculty represented a broad range of scientific expertise, including biologists, engineers, physicists, mathematicians, chemists, and astronomers, as well as social and political scientists. RAND was instrumental in leading military thinking into the nuclear area and has had enormous impact on U.S. policy about nuclear weapons and nuclear war. Herman Kahn, Albert Wohlstetter, Charles Hitch, Alain Enthoven, Daniel Ellsberg, James Schlesinger, Thomas Schelling, William Kaufmann, Harold Brown, Bernard Brodie, and others became godlike figures to the Air Force and to the federal politicians at large. RAND has largely planned and devised the strategy and doctrine that has been adhered to for the past thirty-eight years. Most of the language associated with nuclear war was coined in its corridors—terms such as superpowers, balance of terror, nuclear exchange, first strike, counterforce, nuclear deterrence, and nuclear-war fighting.

RAND attracted some of the most brilliant minds of the time.

Most of them, unfortunately, became almost completely divorced from reality as they daily tried to devise scenarios to make nuclear war practical and winnable. They created strategies for massive civil defense programs, working with complex mathematical formulas about how many people would survive with adequate protection factors. They talked endlessly about imagined Soviet motives and attack scenarios, so much so that their projected fantasies became reality in their minds. They had tremendous influence over Air Force decisions and over official U.S. government policy. Although the RAND approach is now under heavy attack by some main-stream experts, for many years it was considered something of a sacred cow—rarely if ever questioned by officials in the Pentagon, the administration, or Congress. Certainly the public has had very little input over the past thirty-eight years into these esoteric plans because the language devised by RAND made use of thousands of complex acronyms. The situation is only now beginning to change as some scientists have started to translate the esoterica into ordinary English and explain to people the true meaning of their nation's nuclear strategies.

Many prominent businessmen were also involved in helping to establish the RAND Corporation—Donald Douglas of McDonnell Douglas, Henry Ford II, Rowan Gaither (a prominent lawyer), Arthur Raymond of TRW, and others. Many of these men have remained in the defense industry and are producing weapons to this day.

The first plan for counterforce nuclear war was formulated in 1951 by a RAND strategist named Bernard Brodie. Brodie's plan called for first use of nuclear weapons by the United States on the Soviet Union, but because he was so appalled by the Air Force's Sunday Punch plan (which called for massive bombing of cities), he excluded the bombing of Soviet cities. A small number of nuclear weapons were designated for nonurban targets, such as airports. Meanwhile, in order to have some leverage at the bargaining table, the United States maintained a strenuously guarded reserve force of atomic weapons. These represented a threat to the Soviet Union that unless it stopped fighting, America would begin to bomb its cities one by one. In 1951 the Soviet Union possessed hardly any nuclear weapons and could not possibly have delivered nuclear bombs on America. At this stage, however, the Air Force and RAND planned to use nuclear weapons on the Soviet Union to discipline it for conventional acts of aggression.

In 1960, RAND faculty member Herman Kahn wrote a 652-page book called *On Thermonuclear War*. In it he noted that while nuclear war would boost the number of children born with genetic defects, 4 percent are born that way anyway. He wrote, "War is a terrible thing, but so is peace. The difference seems, in some respect, to be a quantitative one of degree and standards." He predicted that while human tragedy would increase after nuclear war, "the increase would not preclude normal and happy lives for the majority of survivors and their dependents."

A huge fallout shelter program costing $200 billion over a twenty-year period would save tens of millions of American lives. Kahn thought such a massive civil defense program was necessary to "enable the U.S. to take a much firmer position" in the Cold War with the Soviet Union. He believed that Soviet-American relations would become so tense that it was "perfectly conceivable . . . that the U.S. might have to evacuate two or three times every decade." He also said that after a nuclear war, "we can imagine a renewed vigor among the population with a zealous, almost religious, dedication to reconstruction, exemplified by a 50–60-hour work week."

In one of Kahn's lectures, he talked about the postnuclear war environment in almost surrealistic terms:

> Now, just imagine yourself in a postwar situation. Everybody will have been subjected to extremes of anxiety, unfamiliar environment, strange foods, minimum toilet facilities, inadequate shelters and the like. Under these conditions, some high percentage of the population is going to become nauseated and nausea is very contagious. If one man vomits, everybody vomits. It would not be surprising if almost everybody vomits. Morale may be so affected that many survivors may refuse to participate in constructive activities, but would content themselves with sitting down and waiting to die. Some may even become violent and destructive.
>
> However, the situation will be quite different if radiation meters were distributed. Assume now that a man gets sick from a cause other than radiation. Not believing this, his morale begins to drop. You look at his meter and say, "You have received only 10 roentgens; why are you vomiting? Pull yourself together and get to work."

The mathematician James R. Newman wrote in *Scientific American* that Kahn's book was "a moral tract on mass murder; how to plan it, how to commit it, how to get away with it, how to justify it." This prompted Kahn to write a second book, *Thinking About the Unthinkable*, to justify his rational approach to so ghastly a topic. He fashioned himself as the ultimate defense intellectual: cool, calm, rational, and fearless.

In fact, most of the scientists at RAND exhibited no moral scruples in their writings or discussions about their systematic plan to murder hundreds of millions of Soviets. They spent all their time fascinated with the plans they had devised, drawing graphs, calculating models based on economic principles, and playing never-ending war games. They had an enormous influence on government thinking, and their strategies and terminologies became so sacred that they still are set in stone.

Kahn was most influential in his discussions on nuclear targeting strategy. He argued in the fifties that simply threatening to destroy Soviet cities in response to a nuclear attack was not enough to maintain peace. He contended that the Soviets could impose "nuclear blackmail" by first destroying the U.S. nuclear arsenal and then threatening to destroy its cities with a protective "reserve force" of missiles if the United States dared to retaliate. (The Soviets had four nuclear missiles by 1962.) To prevent being checkmated in this nuclear chess game, Kahn urged the United States to develop a "credible first-strike capacity" to allow the United States to respond to Soviet conventional aggression (an invasion of Western Europe) by knocking out the Soviet strategic forces, and also a "tit-for-tat" capability to enable the United States to use first very small nuclear salvos in the event of Soviet aggression of a smaller order.

In the 1970s, when administration officials talked about the vulnerability of the U.S. land-based missile arsenal and the possibility that, by attacking it, the Soviets could "deter our deterrent," they were repeating the Kahn scenario devised twenty years earlier. He did not invent the scenario—it arose from RAND discussions in the fifties—but he systematized and popularized it.

In fact, most of the strategic theories used today are just recycled RAND theories developed years ago by those scientists. Their professional aim was to develop credible plans to fight a nuclear war with the Soviets, often talking about first strike. But they could never devise a winning scenario without imagining the deaths of millions of people. They persisted tenaciously with their theories and still are at it. They spoke, and speak, in strange, esoteric tongues because the terminology allowed them to contemplate ghastly scenarios without permitting these stark facts to penetrate their emotions and their souls. These people taught everyone else how to practice their brand of scientific psychic numbing by eliminating human emotions from the equation of mass genocide. These men were, above all, rational! What a disservice to humanity they performed!

The original villains in the cause of the nuclear arms race were the scientists. Authorized by President Roosevelt to design and construct the first atomic bombs, they did so brilliantly. Some realized their shocking contribution to the world when they watched Trinity, the first-ever bomb, explode in the Alamogordo desert in July 1945. Others were stricken after Little Boy was used on Hiroshima. Still others—people such as Nobel laureate Hans Bethe, Bernard Feld, and Leo Szilard—have been waging a losing battle against the continuous growth of the nuclear arsenals ever since.

Unfortunately, the forces of evil prevailed. After the war, some scientists still were committed to building more bombs. Some were motivated by the intellectual challenge (Oppenheimer called the Teller-Ulam solution to the H-bomb puzzle "technically sweet"). Others, some emigrants from countries overrun by the Soviets, were motivated by fear and distrust of the Soviets. Edward Teller was one of these people. He was the instigator of the hydrogen bomb; indeed, he destroyed the career and reputation of Oppenheimer, who opposed this fearsome weapon because he felt it was unnecessary. Teller has spent his life since World War II promoting the construction of more and better nuclear weapons.

The Los Alamos Lab in New Mexico, which built the first three atomic bombs, continued its work after the war; and nine years later, in 1952, Edward Teller helped found a rival lab, Lawrence-Livermore, in Livermore, California.

These two national laboratories are financed and operated by the Department of Energy under the academic sponsorship of the University of California. This convenient arrangement gives them a degree of independence and neutrality. These labs have designed every nuclear weapon in the arsenal of the United States. Los Alamos operates on a $421 million annual budget and has 7,018 employees; Lawrence-Livermore has a $515 million annual budget with 7,160 employees. The rivalry between the labs encourages design of the best bombs.

Los Alamos has designed two thirds of the weapons in the nuclear stockpile. Its recent products include hydrogen bombs for air- and submarine-launched cruise missiles and the new Pershing II missile. Livermore was an early advocate of the new nuclear artillery shells and short-range-missile atomic bombs for the Army.

Weapons designed by the labs are fitted with fuses and with firing and safety devices by the Sandia National Laboratory, which is operated for the government by Western Electric. This lab, with branches in New Mexico, California, and Nevada, has an annual budget of $738 million and 7,985 employees.

Usually the military asks the scientists to design a specific weapon, but sometimes the labs design the weapons first and present them to the military for approval. As Harold Agnew, former director of Los Alamos Lab, said in reference to his sales pitch, "We used to emphasize cost and practicality until we learned that the 'Gee Whiz, Gosh, Tail Fins, and Chrome Approach' is the best way to go with the military." The scientists are attracted by the intellectual challenge, and the military boys are attracted by the new toys.

The scientists often argue hotly about which weapons are most appropriate to design and build, but never about whether or not to proceed. A dissenting physicist, Hugh DeWitt, who works at Livermore, reports that the labs are "repositories of hawkish views of the world, distrust of the Russians, distrust of arms control, faith in the efficacy of high technology to provide protection, and strong opposition to any measures that might limit nuclear weapons development."

Lab officials say they have no difficulty attracting young scientists to the labs. They offer these ambitious young people a chance to work with similar people and to use excellent equipment such as thirteen CRAY-1 computers, the world's most powerful—all terrific fun. As one scientist, Gerold Yonas of Sandia Labs, said, "I believe weapons are necessary and inevitable. . . . I am not afraid of new technology. Technology is not evil." Robert Thorne, deputy director at Los Alamos, adds, "Most of us believe our efforts will lead to a safer world, one in which arms control will play a part. I don't believe we will ever eliminate nuclear weapons. I don't think we would have a safer or better world if they were eliminated." These men live in ivory towers. They are responsible for the weapons they design, yet they take no responsibility for their ultimate purpose.

Other scientists, such as Herbert York, the first director of Lawrence-Livermore Labs, have misgivings about their pasts. York described the motivations of his former colleagues:

> They derived either their incomes, their profits, or their consultant fees from it, but much more important than money as the motivating force are the individual's own psychic and spiritual needs. The majority of key individual promoters of the arms race derive a very large part of their self-esteem from their participation in what they believe to be an essential—even a holy—cause.

In April 1983, five Nobel laureates and sixty-five other scientists presented a petition to officials at Los Alamos Lab, where they were gathered for the lab's fortieth anniversary. The petition urged a massive international reduction of nuclear arms and went on to say,

> We are appalled at the present level of nuclear armaments of the nations of the world and are profoundly frightened for the future of humanity. . . . The single crucial fact is that the major world powers now possess a sufficiency of nuclear warheads and delivery systems to destroy each other and a significant part of the rest of the world many times over.

But the people working for the labs win out every time because they have access to classified information and are extremely influential within governmental circles. Over the years, these labs have opposed all suggested nuclear arms cutbacks and test-ban treaties. In 1957, Lewis L. Strauss, chairman of the Atomic Energy Commission, and physicists Edward Teller and Ernest O. Lawrence went to the White House to dissuade President Eisenhower from negotiating a test-ban treaty with the Soviet Union. They prevailed with arguments that continued testing was necessary for the development of clean (fallout-free) bombs for battlefield use in Europe and that the Soviets could cheat on any moratorium by testing in underground cavities that would reduce seismic disturbances.

Similar tired arguments are still being used against a complete test-ban treaty, which the Soviets have been ready to sign for several years. In July 1980 they even agreed in principle to voluntary on-site inspection. The labs hold out because they want to continue testing bombs of less than 15 kilotons. They also need to test the hydrogen-bomb warheads for the 17,000 additional bombs the administration plans to build in its "modernization" program. The complete test-ban treaty was, in fact, destroyed in the summer of 1978, when Secretary of Energy James R. Schlesinger; Harold Agnew, director of Los Alamos; and Roger Batzel of Livermore went to see President Carter. Agnew said later, "No question about it. We influenced Carter with facts, so that he did not introduce the [treaty] which, we subsequently learned, he had planned to do. There is no question in my mind that Robert and I turned Carter around, because we incurred so many enemies from the other side."

Sir Solly Zuckerman, a leading scientific adviser to the British government during the 1960s, wrote about these scientists in his book *Nuclear Illusion and Reality*:

> In the nuclear world today, military chiefs, who by convention are a country's official advisors on national security, as a rule merely serve as the channel through which the men in the laboratories transmit their view. For it is the man in the laboratory, not the soldier or sailor or airman, who at the start proposes that for this or that reason it would be useful to improve an old or devise a new nuclear warhead; and, if a new warhead, then a new missile; and, given a new missile, a new system within which it has to fit. It is he, the technician, not the Commander in the field, who starts the process of formulating the so-called military need. It is he who has succeeded over the years in equating, and so confusing, nuclear destructive power with military strength, as though the former

were the single and sufficient condition of military success. The men in the nuclear laboratories of both sides have succeeded in creating a world with an irrational foundation on which a new set of political realities has, in turn, had to be built. They have become alchemists of our times, working in secret ways that cannot be divulged, casting spells which embrace us all. They may never have been in battle; they may never have experienced the devastation of war, but they know how to devise the means of destruction. The more destructive power there is, so, one must assume, I imagine, the greatest chance of military success.

The nuclear bombs developed by the labs are tested continually in the Nevada desert, at the dry Yucca Lake site about 70 miles north of Las Vegas. Each bomb is packed in a box called a "rack" and lowered into a hole 10 feet wide and a mile deep. About every three weeks—18 times in 1981—a bomb is exploded. As of the end of 1984, a total of 412 underground tests had been conducted since the signing of the Partial Test Ban Treaty in 1962; of these, 43 vented radioactive material into the atmosphere. Since the fall of 1983, the administration has returned to an earlier policy of announcing nuclear tests only when they are "significant."

Once the bombs have passed the testing stage, work orders are sent from the Department of Energy to various plants around the United States that produce the weapons' component parts. This huge industrial complex, employing 52,000 people in 10 states, covers more land area than Delaware and Rhode Island combined. The U.S. government owns the plants, and the big corporations run them. Phillips, Exxon, Atlantic Richfield, and other energy giants mine the uranium, the basic raw material for the bombs. General Electric makes electrical components and neutron generators at Pinellas Park, Florida; Rockwell International makes the plutonium bomb triggers at Rocky Flats, Colorado; Bendix Corporation produces electronic components at Kansas City, Missouri; Monsanto works on isotope separation and detonators at Mound Lab, Miamisburg, Ohio; DuPont produces enriched plutonium, tritium, and deuterium at its Savannah River plant in Aiken, South Carolina; and Mason Hanger-Silas Mason puts all the parts together for completion of the bombs at the Pantex plant in Amarillo,

Texas. This listing covers only the production of the warheads themselves. They are then put into various delivery systems: missiles, artillery shells, submarines, airplanes. It takes only 2 percent of the military budget to design and produce new bombs and to maintain about 30,000 bombs.

The push for *Star Wars* weapons came originally from the Lawrence-Livermore Labs. For the past fifteen years, Edward Teller has been encouraging research on defensive weapons systems in the nuclear age, and in the last five years his protégés have been receiving increased funding for this research. Teller calls this defense system the third generation of nuclear weapons—the power of the hydrogen explosion is to be focused and narrowed into direct energy through X-ray lasers or some other device.

Lowell Wood, a protégé of Teller and the head of Livermore's top-secret O Group, is a strenuous promoter of this third generation of nuclear weapons. Teller credits Wood for making the break-through in X-ray laser technology. Apparently the R Group at Livermore, headed by Thomas A. Weaver, has had some success testing such a device, called Excalibur, at the Nevada underground test site. Wood is also very enthusiastic about immobilizing the Soviet missiles by using directed EMP.

There is a profound split in the scientific community about the efficacy of these systems. Most scientists believe they are ridiculous. The most avid proponents are those who work in the weapons labs; they claim to have all the data and hence discredit anyone who disagrees with them. When Wood briefed Hans Bethe on this defensive system, Bethe told *Time* magazine, "I don't think it can be done. What is worse, it will produce a *Star Wars* if successful." Wood's response was that Bethe had not challenged the basic physics but, rather, the feasibility and wisdom of building such a weapons system (the only sane approach, of course).

Outside people are never used to evaluate and assess the lab's scientific work, so there is no adequate debate on whether or not new weapons systems should be built. Hence the genesis of the nuclear arms race is rather like spontaneous combustion. Eisenhower said in his 1961 farewell speech, "Yet, in holding scientific research and discovery in respect, as we should, we must also be alert to the equal and opposite danger that public policy could itself become the captive of a scientific-technological elite."

In September 1982, Teller took his case to the White House and briefed President Reagan on his *Star Wars* concept. Reagan was entranced. Without consulting the normal defense and national security channels and without the active participation of top Pentagon or State Department officials, he wrote his *Star Wars* speech in longhand, basing it in part on the Teller briefing. Reagan's own White House science advisers had already decided, after a year-long study, that antimissile defense was not plausible.

In Reagan's *Star Wars* speech (March 1983), contrary to Eisenhower's warning, he offered an epiphany to the powers of scientific technology to heal all problems, even those it had created. The president has admitted that he really does not understand anything about computers or high technology himself. Yet he said, "The vision is that we embark on a program to counter the awesome Soviet missile threat with measures that are defensive. Let us turn to the very strength in technology that spawned our great industrial base and that has given us the quality of life we enjoy today." His new scheme, according to DOD testimony, could cost as much as $1 trillion.

Within a few weeks of the president's speech, the National Security Council produced National Security Decision Directive 85, with the promising title "Eliminating the Threat from Ballistic Missiles." What started out as ill-defined gleams in the eyes of the president and Edward Teller had been granted an impressive bureaucratic life-support system. Despite massive initial skepticism in the scientific and defense communities, various scientists, research labs, defense contractors, and other entrepreneurs from the military-industrial complex have begun to scramble for first place with a plan for studying and developing the right system to zap incoming Soviet missiles.

Robert Bowman, former head of the Air Force Systems Command Space Division, said of the various *Star Wars* schemes,

> All have staggering technical problems. All are likely to cost on the order of a trillion dollars. All violate one or more existing treaties. All are extremely vulnerable. All are subject to a series of countermeasures. All could be made impotent by a series of alternative offensive missiles and therefore would be likely to reignite the numerical arms race in offensive weapons.

All would, if they worked, be more effective as part of a first strike than against one. Most important, all would be extremely destabilizing, probably triggering the nuclear war which both sides are trying to prevent.

This is one more example of the scientific imperative in the nuclear arms race: Scientific breakthroughs incur new technology, and just when it no longer seems possible, another nuclear weapon or defense system is born.

To their discredit, most large universities are involved in the nuclear and conventional arms race. Although funding was decreased during the Vietnam War because of intense student disapproval, there now seems no limit to the support of campus research by the Department of Defense. Ironically, funding for nonmilitary research has been cut to the bone. Budget analyses by the American Association for the Advancement of Science show military support of universities growing by 7.4 percent in current dollars from fiscal 1983 to fiscal 1984—to $873 million. This represents a cumulative growth of 58 percent since 1981. Most of this money is earmarked by the Pentagon for basic research, which includes categories such as self-contained munitions, electro-optic countermeasures, and low-speed takeoff and landing. This is applied research for killing. From 1983 to 1984, university funding by other federal departments has fallen by 26 percent for Interior, 69.1 percent for Commerce, 6.4 percent for Transportation, 1.5 percent for Energy, and 8.7 percent for Agriculture. In 1982, the Pentagon used 70 percent of the total federal allotment for R&D (if NASA and DOE are included) and funded 13 percent of all university research.

Johns Hopkins, a university founded by a Quaker, receives the largest military research grants in the nation. It is followed closely by MIT, which received a 25 percent increase from 1979 to 1980. Harvard University received a 245 percent increase during the same period.

At Princeton University in 1981, the volume of military research reached such proportions that more than 160 employees, including the president and the provost, held security clearances.

The University of Washington Applied Physics Lab, potentially a major center for research on fisheries and oceanography, has become virtually a wholly owned subsidiary of the U.S. Navy.

Some universities have changed the names of labs so that they are not readily identifiable as military. After students from the University of Wisconsin blew up the Army Mathematics Research Center in 1960, it was moved to a less obvious spot and renamed the Mathematics Research Center. At the University of Michigan, an academic think tank called Willow Run I was moved off campus in the wake of student protest in 1973. Renamed ERIM (Environmental Research Institute of Michigan), its research includes more than $5 million per year from defense contracts for work on optics, lasers, electronic-detection instruments, and a guidance system for cruise missiles.

Many disciplines at universities are involved in military research. The Pentagon has made it easier for researchers to become involved through multidisciplinary, multi-investigator programs wherein researchers from different fields and different institutions work on small parts of a big project. Participants seldom know how their basic research is being used or how it connects with other work.

The Pentagon also jointly sponsors programs with NASA, the Department of Energy, and the National Science Foundation, which gives them an air of respectability and at times confuses the source of the funding. MIT defense-related projects span everything from oceanography to computer science to electronics. A recent graduate, Steve Solnick, said, "I was working on a project for six months before I knew it was funded by the Department of Defense."

Since many areas of research are being neglected, this brain drain may hasten the impending U.S. economic catastrophe. In addition to its huge fiscal military burden, the United States now has a sick domestic industrial structure with little R&D, buses that fall apart, and bridges that collapse. Science and technology are desperately needed to solve the world's problems—among them the scarcity of food, minerals, fuel, shelter, clean air, and clear water.

The beautiful main building at MIT is crowned by the names of history's greatest scientists and thinkers—Archimedes, Socrates, Darwin, Edison, Osler, and many others. What has happened to the long-held tradition of scientists conducting research for the benefit of mankind? The universities have prostituted themselves, using their skilled personnel to work for death. I beg my scientific and academic colleagues to rethink their goals in life.

I constantly ride in airplanes with people who work for the military-industrial complex or war industry (euphemistically called the defense industry). I watch over their shoulders as they pore over their graphs and papers illustrating their latest weapons systems, and occasionally I engage them in conversation if I am not too tired. Almost without exception, I find that they have never seriously considered the logical conclusion of their work: nuclear war. To my surprise, I also find that they are very ignorant about the whole panoply of weapons systems this country has or is building and that they almost always think the Soviets are ahead. We often become involved in heated discussions, but usually I prevail, and in the end they thank me and promise to read my book *Nuclear Madness*. These people, usually very loving parents devoted to their children, admit that they have never really thought about the broader picture before. Sometimes as I fly, I look down from my plane window on large and small towns and ponder the ubiquitous military-industrial complex, which has deliberately placed its factories and work places in almost every community in the United States. The problem sometimes seems so immense that I wonder if we have the power to abort this out-of-control, death-dealing industry.

The "defense budget" of the United States accounts for almost one third of all federal spending. With other military spending, the figure is over 40 percent. These huge businesses are run by men with unique access to government because they are captains of industry and because they manufacture weapons that guarantee "national security." They practice aggressive public and government relations, and because of their tight relationship to government, they have induced a narrowing of the debate on strategic and foreign policy over the years.

The multibillion-dollar defense industries use Washington offices and work out of suites in office buildings all along the Capital (Washington) Beltway, giving rise to the term "Beltway Bandits." The typical Washington office of a large defense contractor employs from forty to fifty people. Not all of them lobby Congress, but they do lobby the Pentagon under the guise of marketing or customer service. Of the top ten contractors, the largest offices are run by General Electric, which employs eighty people, and by Rockwell. The smallest is run by Grumman, with a staff of twenty-four.

The top ten defense companies with major contracts of over $1 billion in 1984 were, in order of size (in billions of dollars):

McDonnell Douglas	$7.7
Rockwell International	$6.2
General Dynamics	$6.0
Lockheed	$5.0
Boeing	$4.6
General Electric	$4.5
Hughes Aircraft	$3.2
United Technologies	$3.2
Raytheon	$3.1
Litton Industries	$2.4

(See the chart on pages 88–90 for their products.)

Half of these companies depend heavily on winning military contracts and on selling weapons to foreign countries.

Since 1970, a total of 3,800 people have gone through the revolving door (more than 1,900 from 1980 to 1983 alone). This mechanism produces a great opportunity for conflict of interest. Executives who leave top jobs in industry often end up in top-level posts at the Pentagon, only to return to their old companies. For example, Paul Thayer, a former deputy secretary of defense, was board chairman of LTV Corporation, a major defense contractor. He left his job in the Pentagon in January 1984 after having been accused of illegally passing along "insider" stock-trading information to others in 1981 and 1982, when he was chairman of LTV Corporation and director of four other companies. (He has since been sentenced to a jail term.)

Because the military pension system allows military personnel to retire after twenty years of service, many of these men transfer straight to defense corporations, taking their inside knowledge and personal contacts with them to benefit the corporations. (In fiscal 1982, a total of 900,000 people of working age with no disabilities were receiving lavish military pensions. One billion dollars a year could be saved by phasing out the pension system for those among these pensioners who have other jobs.) Thomas S. Amlie, formerly technical director at the Naval Weapons Center at China Lake, California, and now a cost analyst at the Pentagon, said,

The military is a closed society that takes care of its own. If a retired general representing a client goes in to see an old classmate still on active duty, he will get a very attentive hearing. The officers on active duty are also thinking ahead.

Fighting the system gets one blackballed, and future employment prospects are bleak. In this way, the industry has come to completely control DOD even more than its political appointees.

Lieutenant General Kelly Burke was once the Air Force's top procurement officer, making yes-no decisions on billions of dollars in business for major defense contractors. When he left in 1983, he teamed up with two of his colleagues—Lieutenant General Thomas Stafford, the former astronaut, who preceded Burke in a top procurement job; and Major General Guy L. Hecker, Jr., who was the top lobbyist for the Air Force on Capitol Hill. They formed a defense consulting firm called Stafford-Burke and Hecker. Six of the ten biggest defense contractors soon became their clients and were advised how to sell to the Pentagon. This is all legal.

In 1983 three Boeing executives were reported to have received a total of $400,000 in severance pay when they left the company in 1981 for high-level Defense Department positions in the Reagan Administration. The three men were Melvyn R. Paisley, assistant secretary of the Navy for research, systems, and engineering; T. K. Jones, deputy undersecretary of defense for strategic theater nuclear forces; and Herbert A. Reynolds, deputy director of the Defense Department's Office of Intelligence and Space Policy. This side of the revolving-door syndrome gives companies access to the executive branch, where the buying is done.

Other prominent people who have been in and out of the Pentagon include Richard DeLauer and John F. Lehman. DeLauer recently retired as undersecretary of defense for research and engineering. From 1943 to 1958, he was an aeronautical engineer and an officer in the U.S. Navy; from 1977 to 1981, with the Defense Science Board; from 1978 to 1981, with the Naval Research Advisory Committee; and from 1960 to 1981, employed by TRW, Inc. Lehman's career has been similarly checkered. From 1966 to 1968, he was in the Air Force Reserve; from 1968 to the present, in the Navy Reserve; from 1969 to 1974, national security assistant to Henry A. Kissinger; in 1974, delegate to the Vienna arms negotiations; from 1975 to 1977, deputy director of the U.S. Arms Control and Disarmament Agency; from 1977 to 1981, a partner in the Abington Corporation (a defense consulting firm) and consultant to Northrop Corporation, TRW Corporation, and the Boeing Company; and from 1981 to the present, secretary of the Navy.

People also leave Congress to work for defense industries. An example: When Congressman Richard Ichord, a Democrat from Missouri, left Congress in 1981 after twenty years there, he joined former Representative Bob Wilson, a Republican from California, to form the Washington Industrial Team (WITCO). Their clients have included eleven of the thirteen largest defense contractors, including McDonnell Douglas, General Dynamics, Boeing, Grumman, Northrop, Raytheon, Westinghouse, United Technologies, General Electric, Rockwell International, and Hughes Aircraft.

At least thirty former congressional staff members, many of whom had key positions with the Armed Services or Appropriations committees, work for defense firms. Most earn their living by buttonholing their ex-colleagues on behalf of defense contractors.

This side of the revolving-door syndrome obviously gives defense firms entry into the legislative process.

These firms lobby mostly in secret, avoiding the press. They entertain important senators, representatives, and their staffers; offer them tickets to sporting events, concerts, and the theater; and play golf with them at the Army-Navy Country Club.

They use PACs to pour money into the campaigns of important House and Senate members, targeting those on key committees. For instance, in 1982, the PACs of McDonnell Douglas and Lockhead Corporation gave money to thirty-six of the thirty-nine members of the House Armed Services Committee who were up for re-election. Recipients included all fourteen members of the subcommittee on procurement. Rockwell, Raytheon Company, and Hughes Aircraft gave to ten members of the House Appropriations Committee.

Nine of the ten leading firms gave more than $1,000 each to Representative Joseph Addabbo, Democrat from New York and chairman of the subcommittee on defense. Senator John C. Stennis of Mississippi, the ranking Democrat on the Armed Services

Committee, received more than $26,000 each from the top ten contractors; and Senator John Tower, Republican from Texas and chairman of the Armed Services Committee, received $13,000 from the top ten in 1981 and 1982.

Powerful House leaders also receive money. Eight of the ten contractors gave $1,000 each or more to House Speaker Thomas P. O'Neill, Jr., Democrat from Massachusetts; and Representative James Wright, Democrat from Texas, received contributions from nine of the ten contractors. Representatives from important defense-related districts also received contributions. Altogether the PACs of the ten biggest corporations gave $1.5 million to federal candidates in the 1982 election. This figure does not include individual contributions by corporation officials, nor does it include money spent on state or local races.

The corporations also gave honoraria for speeches by politicians at company meetings, and some congressmen give services to the PACs.

These contributions do not necessarily buy the weapons, but they do give access to the congressmen's or senators' offices. Washington is run by just such obligations and friendships. Also, many representatives of these contractors serve on fund-raising committees for key House or Senate members.

The Washington office is perhaps the most important part of the whole corporate operation. It conducts what is called "government relations," which involves lobbying and working directly with the Pentagon, DOE, and NASA. The staff monitors relevant issues and attempts to influence legislative, procurement, and appropriations decisions as they move rapidly between the executive and the Congress. The Washington office also coordinates a company's entire political strategy, which ranges from grass-roots organizing aimed at employees and stockholders in local companies, to campaign contributions to members of Congress, to direct contacts with powerful figures in Washington.

These Washington offices accumulate huge amounts of data on government activity, the status of legislation, and key members of Congress, and on procurement policy decisions in the Pentagon, plans and programs for R&D, new regulatory actions, and federal rulemaking. Then they send the relevent information back to the company.

Most of these companies also have direct access to the

president's staff at the White House. The congressional staffs of twenty-three thousand, particularly those of key congressional committees, are extremely important people to influence. The Washington offices work with these people continually and are also engaged in intense lobbying activities both at the congressional level and at the executive level in the Pentagon. The corporations hire lawyers, public-affairs experts and technicians, and outside lobbyists for the lobbying efforts. In fact, a large part of many legal practices represent the company and its sales, as well as strictly legal matters. Thousands and thousands of lawyers in Washington grease the wheels for these corporations. But because giving information and applying pressure are not classified as lobbying, an enormous part of corporate-government relations is never known by the general public.

If Americans wish to survive and save the world for their children, they must rapidly learn how to use their democracy just as these military corporations do.

The men at the top of these industries, extremely powerful and very experienced in handling ties to positions of influence, usually have had many years of service in the industry or government. Some have ties to financial institutions that handle the corporation's business; some hold memberships on boards of companies that supply goods to or are themselves defense contractors. Many of them have served in positions for important institutions, such as chairman of the Defense Science Board, undersecretary of defense for research and development, or counsel to the CIA.

In 1977, a Senate study discussed the dangers posed by such a concentration of power and information in any segment of the economy: "These patterns of director interrelationships imply an overwhelming potential for antitrust abuse and possible conficts of interest, which could affect prices, supply, and competition and impact on the shape and direction of the American economy."

Given the defense budget's increasingly larger role in the expenditures of America, the preceding statement is a very serious warning. Boeing provides an example of interlocking corporate financial and governmental responsibilities: In 1978, Boeing's president, Malcolm Stamper, was among the fifteen corporate officers receiving the highest salaries in the country. Boeing's directors were board members of other firms, which received more than $1 million in Department of Defense contracts in fiscal 1979.

Most of these companies were suppliers of components and petroleum to Boeing.

Four Boeing directors had outside ties that would encourage contact with government or defense policymakers. Former Defense Secretary Harold Brown, a Boeing director, was president of Cal Tech, while Harold J. Haynes, chief executive officer of Standard Oil, was a trustee of Cal Tech. David Packard, deputy secretary of defense from 1969 to 1971, joined the board of Boeing in 1978 and is the chief executive officer of Hewlett-Packard, a major defense contractor. William Reed, a Boeing director, was also a member of the President's Council at Cal Tech when Brown was president; and George Weyerhaeuser was previously a member of the Advisory Council of Stanford Research Institute and of RAND Corporation—both defense contractors.

Trade Associations

Military companies have their own Washington offices, but they are also represented in Washington by trade associations that have been established by the defense industries and the military services specifically to influence buying of weapons. One Pentagon official said of these associations, "As a social unit, they are an incredible force to be reckoned with by the Congress." They overtly encourage increased defense spending, foster specific research and developmental projects, supply information from industry to DOD and NASA, and provide information from federal officials to industry. Senator William Proxmire said they serve as "go-between for ideas and information to flow from the defense industry to the Pentagon."

Most of these trade associations hold at least one convention per year, all of which are attended by military and civilian DOD personnel as well as by Pentagon brass. At these meetings, the associations present a variety of panels and classified briefings and distribute information on upcoming programs, weapons, and policy development. The trade organizations also publish frequent newsletters filled with advertising and articles on defense procurement policies and weapons development. Some people say that these trade associations serve to cement a relationship that is already too close between the buyers and the sellers of weapons. Certainly these associations and the contacts they catalyze totally exclude any opposing views on military affairs, ensuring that the people of the country are not represented in any of these decisions.

Officials of these trade associations regularly testify before Congress and congressional committees on legislative developments that may affect their clients, on specific procurement policies, and on the general level of defense spending. They also work with committees in the Pentagon to influence the Pentagon's attitude toward various weapons systems.

- *The American Defense Preparedness Association,* with 600 members from defense contractors and 40,000 members from industry, campuses, and the Pentagon. It has an annual budget of $3 million and a full-time staff of 27. Members of this organization include the giants in the defense industry, such as McDonnell Douglas, General Dynamics, Boeing, Lockheed, Northrop, Rockwell International, United Technologies, Grumman, Litton, and Martin Marietta. These firms did $37 billion worth of business with the Pentagon in 1983.
- *National Security Industrial Association,* with 313 defense contractors as members.
- *Aerospace Industries Association.* The 47-member companies include most of the aerospace giants, such as McDonnell Douglas.
- *The Air Force Association,* with 181,000 individual and 200 corporate members. Approximately 45 percent of its individual members are on active duty with the Air Force.
- Others include the Navy League; the Association of the U.S. Army; the Armed Forces Communications and Electronics Association; the Shipbuilders Council of America; the Electronic Industries Association; the Society of Naval Architects and Marine Engineers; and the Association of Old Crows, which represents electronic warfare.

The Association of Old Crows publishes the *Journal of Electronic Defense* and has a membership of 12,000 devoted to electronic warfare. Electronic warfare has become a lucrative business—in 1982 worldwide sales of such products reached approximately $7 billion. It involves the manufacture of electronic brains that allow missiles to chase after their targets, render destroyers vulnerable to a single missile, and can turn an opponent's radar against him by making it a homing path for an enemy projectile. Companies involved in this particular form of horrendous warfare are IBM, RCA, Eaton, TRW, GTE Sylvania, Raytheon, Grumman, Hughes Aircraft, Litton, ITT, Westinghouse, Ford Aerospace, Northrop, Lockheed, Boeing, Hewlett-Packard, Motorola, National Semiconductor, Loral Corporation, Watkins-Johnson, Sanders Associates, and E Systems, Inc. Many electronics firms have experienced dramatic rises in earnings, and their stocks are selling at enormous prices. As one Wall Street analyst said, "War is good business again."

The Technical Marketing Society of America held a conference called "New Trends in Missiles—Systems and Technology." Under the heading "Technology and Marketing Imperative," the program read,

> December 1983 sees the deployment of medium range missiles throughout Europe. Despite Reagan's "global limit" of warheads concept, tension is on the increase. The international implication on industry is a worldwide missile market in full expansion. Funding in the U.S. alone has soared to $18 billion. Technological advances in electronics, structures and propulsion are creating new opportunities for autonomous/ multi-mode guidance advanced seekers and sensors, sophisticated tracking and jamming, more kills per mass, kinetic energy weapons, maneuvering missiles, ducted rockets, and the like. At the same time, severe customer affordability problems are creating tougher demands than ever on contractors to reduce costs.
>
> This conference brings together leading experts from government and industry who will discuss new and improved missile programs and systems in all mission areas (strategic, theatre, tactical), plus key technologies for future missile systems: guidance, propulsion, instrumentation and computers. It will provide a unique insight into long-term DOD policy trends, identify and assess emerging programs, and

present the state-of-the-art of crucial missile technologies. It is a must for all scientists, engineers, program and marketing managers who need to formulate realistic business targets and high leverage technology investments.

Defense firms also exert their influence through financial institutions. Their relationship with banks, auditors, insurance companies, and finance companies usually are vested with confidentiality, so most members of the public know nothing about them.

Corporation board members often have significant ties with the boards of financial institutions. If a bank or lending company has lent a firm $1 million, it is then in the former's best interest to lobby for the firm at local, state, and federal levels. Banks are credited with playing a major role in shaping federal policies. As one bank lobbyist pointed out, "The bank lobby can almost certainly stop anything it does not want in Congress." The major government agencies regulating financial matters are often staffed by people who come from or return to the financial world. An informal network links bankers and financial officers to politicians and policymakers, which gives the former group a major role in national policymaking.

Banks supply important services to corporations, including financial and management advice, loans of capital, handling on stocks and bond issues, and management of savings plans and pension funds. They may also be important stockholders in corporations.

Military corporations don't regularly disclose which financial institutions they conduct business with or which ones are large shareholders in the companies. Likewise, investment banks and insurance companies don't provide details on their shareholdings or their role in corporate activities.

Chase Manhattan Bank lends money to Boeing, Grumman, Lockheed, Northrop, and United Technologies, and shares a board member with Lockheed. Citicorp lends to Boeing, Grumman, Lockheed, and United Technologies, and shares directors with Boeing, Lockheed, and United Technologies. Other banks in similar positions are Morgan Guaranty, the Bank of New York,

Bankers Trust, Manufacturers Hanover, Mellon Bank, Wells Fargo, Bank of America, Chemical Bank, Continental Illinois, First National Bank of Boston, and Irving Trust.

This information is frightening. Virtually the whole financial network in America is heavily involved in the weapons industry and is working actively to support and represent it. It will take a highly motivated, well-educated, and incredibly determined movement of American people to shift the whole society toward the life process and divert these unconscious people away from death and suicide.

Accounting firms are also heavily involved in military corporations. The information they choose to recognize or ignore in setting accounting standards and auditing a company's books is enormously significant. They also function as management advisers. Admiral Hyman Rickover has said of these firms, "Companies have great latitude in how they can account for costs and profits for financial accounting purposes. As a result, the figures are susceptible to manipulations and judgments, which can dramatically change reported profits in all—all within the constraints of the so-called generally accepted accounting principles."

Among the accounting firms that represent big defense industries are Arthur Anderson and Company (General Dynamics and Grumman); Arthur Young and Company (Lockheed); Deloitte, Haskins and Sells (Rockwell International); Ernst and Whitney (McDonnell Douglas); Price Waterhouse (United Technologies); and Touche Ross and Company (Boeing and Northrop).

A 1976 Senate report on accounting criticized the way these firms, as auditors, represented the private over the public interests. "It appears that 'the Big 8' [accounting] firms are more concerned with saving the interests of corporate management who select them and authorize their fees, than with protecting the interests of the public, for whose benefit Congress established the position of Independent Auditor." Frequently staff from auditing companies go to work for the defense companies they have audited. Pentagon officials do not check the veracity of the audit statements they receive. One said, "We are ordered to take that information at face value. The presumption is that they are not on the take. If they do something wrong, they'll probably be discovered anyway, and is it really worth it to intimidate these guys?"

Advertising and Organization at the Grass-Roots Level

The military companies conduct large advertising campaigns in the military press and also in the lay press. I am always appalled when I open the op-ed section of *The New York Times* and see a spectacularly beautiful space-age-designed piece of equipment—part of the guidance system of a MIRVed missile—advertised by Northrop. To quote from one of these ads:

> The wonder of the Star Tracker is its ability to focus on the stars during the day. Developed by Northrop's Electronics Division, the Star Tracker is the eye of an airborne astroinertial guidance system so precise it is called upon to check the accuracy of other advanced navigational instruments. Northrop is a pioneer in astroinertial guidance and has earned the worldwide reputation for leadership in precision navigation.

Obviously, most readers of *The New York Times* would not understand what this particular jargon means. What it does mean, of course, is that this is part of a first-strike missile system, using the stars for navigation. This sort of advertising for genocidal weapons is analogous to German industry advertising well-designed parts of its gas ovens in the most prestigious pre-World War II German papers, except that a MIRVed missile could burn and vaporize tens of millions of people in the space of thirty minutes. Corporations often conduct this advertising in the interests of "national security," and very often the taxpayer is subsidizing these costs.

The military press, which is covered extensively by these advertising campaigns, includes publications such as *Aviation Week and Space Technology, National Defense, Armed Forces Journal International, U.S. Naval Institute Proceedings, Army,* and *Air Force Magazine.*

Aviation Week is read by 102,000 subscribers in 132 countries. It often has privileged access to defense information and plays a key role in the nation's public information wars. It publishes sensitive information with a degree of impunity not available to the lay public. Because it is read at the highest levels of government, its frequent advance disclosures may change the balance of power in the world. It keeps the aerospace and defense industries abreast of the latest technical developments, funding, and trends in policy, and it often serves as the industry spokesman to influence policy changes.

Corporations also lobby and advertise in the localities where their manufacturing facilities are based. If they need specific funding for a new weapons system, they mobilize the local constituency and their own factory workers to write to their senators, congressmen, and even the president himself. When a Rockwell plant organized to send a letter to Representative Les Aspin, Democrat of Wisconsin, one worker wrote, "I support the bomber project. OK, OK, I'm really a player just working for Rockwell and they told me to write something." It always amazes me when federal representatives, who receive hundreds or thousands of these letters, don't seem to see through the blatant propaganda.

Research and Development

In 1984, a total of 70 percent of all federal research and development funding went to aerospace and defense programs sponsored by DOD, DOE, and NASA.

The genesis of most weapons systems takes place in the bowels of the military corporations. The government, to a large degree, helps fund this research—and very often the technological inventions become strategic imperatives once the research and development are completed. By the time the new invention is announced, it usually is a political *fait accompli*. The R&D starts years before the weapon systems are made public and is conducted in absolute secrecy in the name of national security—which totally excludes public participation or dissenting views. Typical weapons systems that have emerged from these programs include cruise missiles, stealth technology, high-energy lasers, space-based satellite surveillance systems, precision-guided ammunitions, lightweight fighters, and strategic bombers.

To a considerable degree, this R&D is funded by DOD through the independent research and development (IR&D) and bid and proposal (B&P) programs. IR&D programs are not sponsored by contracts, grants, or other arrangements. B&P describes the company's efforts at preparing and submitting proposals to these government departments. Therefore, a contractor who works on future-oriented defense research and who submits proposal for this work is reimbursed by our tax dollars for part of the cost. The exact amount is negotiated by DOD with each contractor and is dependent on the percentage of the company's total DOD contract work. These funds are *not* scrutinized by the Congress; the public has no idea they exist, although they total nearly $1 billion per year. Moreover, IR&D and B&P programs are focused on the larger firms, which ensures an incestuous, concentrated defense industry. Half this total spending annually goes to the ten top DOD contracting companies.

In a 1976 article from *The New York Times,* John Finney notes,

> Today, policy-making circles in the Defense Department are largely populated by business executives in mid-career, passing through the Pentagon on the way to bigger and better jobs in industry. . . . The trend is particularly pronounced in Dr. Currie's Research and Development office, by far the most important office in the Pentagon for industry because it decides which weapons are to be developed. . . . The roster of Deputy Directors is filled with men who used to work for industry and plan to return to it. As in a game of musical chairs, industry executives rotate in and out of what is known to the Pentagon as the "R&D Cartel."

Of course, this enormously influential R&D corporate community is the nidus of the pathogenesis. If these people, supported by our tax dollars, did not conduct secret research on unbelievably evil killing systems, the arms race would cease.

This R&D and the Pentagon demand for new weapons and equipment are always justified by potential Soviet weapons systems. The CIA and Defense Intelligence Agency calculate the nature and extent of these potential threats. Because major private defense companies have the scientific expertise to evaluate capabilities of Soviet weapons, they are hired as contractors for most of the technical evaluation—for instance, performance of Soviet aircraft and weaponry.

The end result of this activity is, according to a high-ranking Defense Department official, that "the government ends up contracting out to counter an emerging threat to the very people who profit from it." Michael Vahlos, a former CIA analyst now at the Johns Hopkins University Center for Strategic and International Study, said, "Companies that produce the weapons will always inflate the threat to maximize their sales."

Obviously, paranoid thinking about Soviet advances and technology will line the pockets of avaricious American corporations. This whole dynamic must be stopped by the American people.

Interservice Rivalry

James Fallows, in his book *National Defense*, says that the rivalry among the services for appropriations often is more intense than the rivalry and hostility between the superpowers. The latter, of course, is used to justify the former.

Army, Navy, Air Force, and Marines are all represented equally on the Joint Chiefs of Staff. The chiefs are supposed to assess military problems and advise the president. But instead of viewing issues in terms of the broad national interest, each chief tends to view himself as the representative of his own branch of the services and to lobby for programs favored by that particular service. The chairman does not have nearly enough power, according to Air Force General David Jones, former chairman of the Joint Chiefs, to counterbalance the often parochial views of the service chiefs and the civilian defense officials who support them.

In preparing for meetings of the Defense Resources Board, a high-level Pentagon group that is supposed to match available funds with defense requirements, the chairman of the Joint Chiefs has only five staff members to analyze proposals and collect information. Each service chief has thousands of employees to carry out similar tasks.

Because of the strong parochial interests, there is really no central control at all. Former Navy Undersecretary R. James Woolsey wrote, "A gaggle of kibbutzes has formed throughout the government on these questions. . . . For years, the only central voice in defense has been provided by the civilian staff of the Secretary of Defense. Lacking military expertise, it has largely failed."

There are at present all sorts of duplications among the four tactical air forces—one each for the Army, Navy, Air Force and Marines—paid for by the taxpayers. For the most part, each of the services flies different aircraft, which means that few of the thirty production lines run at economical rates.

Each major service (Army, Navy, Air Force) has a civilian secretary and a military chief of staff. Each has its own special think tank (such as RAND for the Air Force), lobbying associations, weapons contractors, and military academy. Consequently, each service tends to view the national interest from the vantage of its own special interests and traditions.

These services are united only through the office of the secretary of defense and through the chairman of the Joint Chiefs of Staff. Both of these positions are relatively weak, and the issues of national defense are now so complicated, given the new technology and incredible numbers and variety of weapons, that it becomes extremely difficult for civilian officials to separate service bias from sound analysis (if, indeed, there can be sound analysis in the nuclear age).

David Jones says that in this sort of atmosphere, "There is good justification for every weapons system. . . . I could develop a rationale for a seven-hundred-ship Navy or ten additional fighter wings. But, that doesn't mean that we ought to do it." Currently the Navy plans to build two additional aircraft carriers (one has just been launched), each with a hundred fighter planes and scores of support ships.

The Pervasive Geographical Grip of the Military-Industrial Complex

Given the dependency of so many states upon the death industry, I feel from time to time that the task ahead of us is enormous. The situation will be changed only when people demand that Congress enact laws to convert the U.S. military-industrial complex from industries creating death to those that will sustain the life process. Such a move will go far toward guaranteeing everyone on earth the right to life, liberty, and the pursuit of happiness, free from starvation, illiteracy, overpopulation, disease, dirty water, polluted air—and military threat.

California is just one example of a state that has become almost totally dependent upon the military-industrial complex. One in eight working Californians is employed directly or indirectly by the military-industrial complex. One in three manufacturing jobs there is related to the aerospace industry (in Los Angeles County, it is one in every two jobs). Almost half these aerospace workers are employed in military projects.

These people often work in beautifully designed, sleek, sanitary buildings, where the stench of death is never present. They are just doing their jobs, working on government or private contracts, making money, thinking about designs and research and fun places to eat and what they did on the weekend. These silver and glass buildings dot the San Diego Freeway in the South and Silicon Valley in the North. In fact, this Californian way of life has become so fashionable that the mores of the Valley Girls have become chic in society.

The military is California's biggest industry. Twenty percent of all U.S. domestic military spending occurs in California. Forty percent of the new strategic systems—big-ticket items such as the B-1, MX, stealth bomber, and cruise missiles—are made in California. In 1984, a total of $40 billion was awarded in contracts to California by the DOD, a figure more than twice the total receipts of the state's farmers.

There are tremendous rivalries among the various California counties for defense dollars, and immigrant workers are attracted to those counties with the biggest defense contracts.

Four California counties—Los Angeles, Santa Clara, San Diego, and Orange—account for 65 percent of every defense dollar spent in California. Many companies are not usually thought of as defense-related. For example, in 1984 producers of paperboard containers and boxes did 12 percent of their business with DOD; fabricated-rubber companies, 36 percent; screw-machine producers, 70 percent; computing machines, 54 percent; machine-shop jobbing and repair, 78 percent; and photographic equipment, 69 percent.

Yet this dependency on defense, even though it helped California during the recession, may actually cost the state jobs. The California state government estimated in 1981 that over the next five years President Reagan's defense buildup would create seven hundred thousand new jobs for California but that another million jobs would be lost because of cuts in domestic spending that had been necessary to finance new military programs.

California's higher-education system provides the necessary scientific and technical pool for growth. Stanford University gives an essential research base as well as the personnel pool for Silicon Valley in Santa Clara County. Since World War II, the University of California has maintained a large number of contracts with DOD, and the university's regents also manage the only two nuclear-warhead-design labs in the United States—Lawrence-Livermore in Livermore, California, and Los Alamos Lab in Los Alamos, New Mexico—under a contract with the DOE.

Because of this strong support from the universities, California has always led in the research and development of weapons. One of three federal R&D dollars is spent in California, and it is exactly this R&D that creates the new weapons systems.

In Washington, D.C., the military firms have metastasized their offices to suburbs surrounding the Pentagon, in Virginia and Maryland. Arranged along the George Washington Parkway and the Capital Beltway, they are nicknamed the Beltway Bandits. Last year the defense-dominated private sector of the Washington area surpassed the federal government as the principal employer in Washington, D.C., and environs.

In the four northern Virginian cities closest to the Pentagon, there are 620 high-tech firms employing 47,000 people, more than 70 percent of whom work on defense-sponsored projects. Ray F. Mitchell, a senior partner in a 35-attorney Virginia law firm, said, "We are a combination of California's Silicon Valley and Boston's Route 128."

As you fly into National Airport outside Washington, D.C., you pass a complex of new office buildings called Crystal City. Crystal City is so dependent upon defense spending that one of its developers suggested calling it Pentagon II. In just one building, there are 19 branch offices for top defense companies, including Rockwell International, General Dynamics, and Newport News Shipbuilding. In 1982, these offices did $11 billion in defense-contract work, or about 10 percent of the prime defense contracts.

Cost Overruns and Pentagon Waste

The number of major defense contractors is very small, and the top companies overwhelmingly dominate the market. In fiscal 1983, ten companies received more than 34 percent of all prime

DOD contracts. With the exception of General Electric, all of these ten previously named companies have the Pentagon as their principal, if not sole, customer. There is rarely any meaningful competition among the defense contractors once a development contract is awarded. About 60 percent of major weapons-system purchases are made on a negotiated, single-source basis. More than 90 percent of all defense-contract dollars are not awarded on the basis of price competition; therefore, there is no incentive to drive down costs. (The Pentagon spends $500 million a day on items ranging from aircraft carriers to paper clips, and only 6 to 7 percent of all prime contracts are bid for in a competitive fashion.) Twenty-five percent of all defense dollars spent on weapons are for contracts awarded on a cost-plus-fee basis, so that the contractor receives all his costs plus a fee—usually 5 percent of the contract value. This policy removes the normal market forces that limit costs.

Because the cost-plus contract is so attractive, many corporations indulge in the practice of "buying in." They submit bids that are less than the actual cost so that they can win the initial R&D contract for a weapons system and then count on recouping the initial R&D loss when they win the production contract. This dynamic is the principal cause of the cost overruns endemic to the defense industry. Obviously Congress and the military buyers find the initial low-cost estimate to get a new weapons system started very appealing. It also enables military buyers to crowd more weapons systems into a total given budget, and it allows more congressmen to extend Pentagon favors to more constituents.

There are other major areas where defense spending is distorted. About 30 percent of the cost of new weapons is caused by defense contractors' slipshod work, which then has to be redone.

The Air Force, because of inadequate management or oversight, may in fact face a $4 billion shortage of spare parts by early 1984. No one is actually held accountable in the Air Force for coordinating this aspect of management. Consider some of the exorbitant prices charged to the Pentagon by contractors and subcontractors:

- A Minuteman II machine screw cost $1.08 in 1982 and $36.77 in 1983—an increase of over 3,300 percent.

- A circuit-card guidance system assembly cost $234.05 in 1982 and $1,111.75 in 1983.
- A tiny electric connector plug for an FB-111 aircraft cost $7.99 in 1982 and $726.86 in 1983.
- Aluminum ladders cost ten times the price they are in a hardware store—$1,676 each instead of $160 each.
- Some defense contractors attempt to charge to their government contracts nondefense items such as office paintings, lavish dinners, tickets to sports events and movie premieres, home swimming pools, and memberships in health clubs.
- The 1982 budget called for $102.1 million to be spent on military bands—a $9 million increase over two years. Only $11 million is to be spent for the National Endowment for the Arts and for local operas, symphonies, chamber orchestras, and other musical programs—a decrease of 12 percent.
- Two billion dollars could be saved by closing unnecessary military bases.
- Four and a half million dollars per year is wasted because enlisted personnel serve as servants to top military officers.
- Navy artists are paid $350,000 to paint portraits for admirals' offices.
- Each year $2 million is spent on government-subsidized meals in Pentagon dining rooms.
- Each year $887,000 goes to promote rifle practice for Boy Scouts, YMCAs, and other youth groups.
- Eight million dollars is spent for stunt shows conducted by the Navy's Blue Angels and the Air Force Thunderbirds and $200 million for the planes.
- Bitter interservice rivalry (each service wants its own planes, missiles, tanks, handguns, and even belt buckles) is very expensive. Different weapons are developed for the same targets.
- Each year $70 million could be saved by consolidating the transport systems for the different military services.
- Each year $400 million could be saved by unifying vehicle and equipment maintenance facilities under a single manager, and $1 billion per year by consolidating support services on military bases in the same geographical area. These include property repair and maintenance, police and fire

services, laundries, utilities, and trash and sewage disposal. In Sacramento there are seven major military bases within a 60-mile area, and they all use separate service systems.

- The DOD spends $300 million per year on recreation facilities, such as golf courses, stables, and marinas.
- Military personnel can retire after twenty years' service, even those who have sat behind desks all their lives. Each year $1 billion could be saved by stopping double-dipping, the practice by which a retired military person receives a pension while simultaneously working as a government employee. Also, $6.9 billion could be saved by delaying full entitlement until after thirty years of service, and by integrating retirement pay with Social Security benefits.
- Contractors had $11.2 billion worth of equipment in 1981 furnished free by the Pentagon.
- The DOD subsidizes foreign governments on weapons, training, and communications to the tune of hundreds of millions of dollars.
- The services now have seven times the number of officers per enlisted personnel as they had in World War II. The number of unnecessary officers in all services could be reduced.

Admiral Hyman Rickover accused several companies of fraud because they submitted cost overrun claims for shipbuilding. For instance, the Electric Boat Division of General Dynamics Corporation submitted $843 million in overrun claims in late 1970. The Navy Claims Settlement Board said they were entitled to only $125 million, but the Navy, rather than face extended litigation, paid the company $484 million. Companies involved in similar cases were the Ingalls Shipbuilding Division of Litton Industries, and Newport News Shipbuilding and Dry Dock Company. And Rockwell International Corporation diverted bills from fixed-price defense contracts (for the B-10 bomber) to its more open Space Shuttle contracts.

Other corporations are also guilty. For instance, Pratt & Whitney, the largest suppliers of military-aircraft spare parts, increased its prices for some items by 300 percent in one year. An Air Force study found that this particular company was making no "significant efforts to control indirect costs or drive costs downward." The current spare-parts shortage is more than likely a result of price increases that far outrun the Air Force's spare-parts budget.

These problems do not involve just the military services and the corporations. The third side of the Iron Triangle—the politicians—also is implicated. In 1982, a subcommittee of the House Armed Services Committee added to the defense budget some $300 million for work at military bases that the Pentagon did not want. About two thirds of these projects were in congressional districts represented by members of the committee.

Many congressmen demand defense spending for their districts as political spoils. Former Representative Jack Edwards of Alabama, then the senior Republican on the House Appropriations Committee's subcommittee for defense, said, "Control of the system has got to be done by the Pentagon with the support of the White House. . . . We are not prone to making the right decisions." Don't forget that these congressmen, even when not swayed by constituent interest, are continually bombarded by lobbyists from defense contractors.

Under a little-noticed government program, inmates at the only federal prison in New England are producing electronic cable assemblies for guided-missile launchers. Defense Department documents show that Federal Prison Industries, Incorporated, in Danbury, Connecticut, received $20.3 million in contracts in 1982 from the Army, Navy, Air Force, and Defense Logistics Agency. Most of the money—$17.7 million—came from the Army, which placed orders for electronic cable assemblies to be used in guided-missile launchers and guided-missile remote-controlled devices.

In 1981, total gross sales came to $128 million for Federal Prison Industries, which was founded in 1934 and now operates 75 plants at almost all the 43 federal prisons in the United States. Of approximately 7,000 prisoners in the program, about 1,135 work in the electronics division. The military does not inform the prison officials of the use for the electronic cable assemblies. A prison official said the primary purpose of the work is to reduce idleness in prisons and to provide vocational training. "The program is open to all inmates, but we have a requirement for basic adult education." I consider this participation in the death-producing program of the federal government a gross exploitation of prisoners.

How Does the System Work in the Soviet Union?

Without the enormous drive for profit, what motivates the arms merchants in the Soviet Union? In Nikita S. Khrushchev's memoirs, he recounts a meeting between himself and President Eisenhower, which is very revealing about the dynamics of the nuclear pathology in both countries:

> "Tell me, Mr. Khrushchev," Eisenhower asked him, "how do you decide the question of funds for military expenses? Perhaps first I should tell you how it is with us."
>
> "Well, how is it with you?" Khrushchev responded.
>
> "It's like this," said Eisenhower. "My military leaders come to me and say, 'Mr. President, we need such and such a sum for such and such a program.' I say, 'Sorry, we don't have the funds.' They say, 'We have reliable information that the Soviet Union has already allocated funds for their own such programs. Therefore, if we don't get the funds we need, we'll fall behind the Soviet Union.' So, I give in. That's how they wring the money out of me. They keep grabbing for more, and I keep giving it to them. Now tell me, how is it with you?"
>
> "It's just the same," said Khrushchev. "Some people from our Military Department come and say, 'Comrade Khrushchev, look at this. The Americans are developing such and such a system. We could develop the same system, but it would cost such and such.' I tell them there is no money; it's all been allotted already. So they say, 'If we don't get the money we need and if there is a war, then the enemy will have superiority over us.' So we discuss it some more, and I end up by giving them the money they ask for."
>
> "Yes," said Eisenhower, "that's what I thought."

In both nations, the armed forces are the biggest consumers of manufactured goods and services. More people are employed in military work than in any other occupation except agriculture, and military research occupies a very high proportion of scientists and engineers.

Both the Soviet military-industrial complex and the American military-industrial complex operate fairly independently of the civilian economy. Each has an artificial system of competition, and each enjoys great political influence. Therefore, in both nations, weapons under development acquire a momentum that carries them into production, regardless of their cost, their efficiency, or their compatibility with the objectives of arms control.

As American aircraft designer and defense expert Pierre M. Sprey told a New York business group:

> You'll realize that our Defense Department buys weapons by almost the same system the Soviets do. That is, we have a very large State bureaucracy that buys weapons from another State bureaucracy, for in most respects Lockheed, Raytheon, Westinghouse, Boeing and Northrop are extensions of the State.

The main difference is that the United States is able to maintain a consumer society and a military-industrial complex simultaneously. The Soviet Union can successfully maintain only the military-industrial complex, while its consumers languish in long lines waiting to buy basic items. This is because the Soviet GNP is half that of the United States, but the Soviets nonetheless spend approximately the same amount on arms as the Americans do. However, America's ability to compete in consumer goods on the open market with Japan, West Germany, and other countries is declining because of the priority given to weapons.

The Soviet Union has integrated its civilian and military production in the same factories. It would be easy for them to switch from military to civilian production. In addition, its weapons tend to be much simpler than the sophisticated weapons produced by the United States, weapons that fewer and fewer people are adequately trained to operate. There is a Russian saying, "Equipment should be designed by geniuses to be operated by idiots."

Reagan and Secretary of Defense Weinberger justify their enormous military buildup by saying that the Soviet Union spent 44 percent more on defense in 1981 than did the United States. However, a recent report by the CIA noted that the 4 percent annual growth rate attributed to the Soviet Union's military-industrial complex may be closer to 2 percent—and the Pentagon's

Defense Intelligence Agency (DIA) has decided to accept the CIA estimate. In fact, according to Franklyn D. Holzman, professor of economics at Tufts University and a Fellow at the Russian Research Center at Harvard University, the NATO spending advantage over the past decade may be at least $600 billion. There is also evidence that the weapons production of the Soviet Union has slowed down since 1977. Senate testimony in 1983 revealed that Moscow had been producing a decreased number of missiles, planes, ships, and vehicles each year between 1977 and 1981, partly because the cost is too high and because it, too, is now indulging in complex weapons technology.

A stupid propaganda battle has been waged between the superpowers over the past five years. In 1981, on Weinberger's instructions, the Pentagon produced a glossy book called *Soviet Military Power*. It is full of illustrations, photographs, and graphs that describe Soviet weapons systems in dramatic and sometimes admiring terms. Less than a year later, the Soviet Union responded with its own version, *Whence the Threat to Peace?*, describing American weapons in equally respectful terms. One Soviet expert said facetiously, "It's like Macy's advertising for Gimbels." Each admires and adopts the trends of the other.

Obviously there is a symbiotic relationship between the U.S. and Soviet military-industrial complexes. As the British historian E. P. Thompson said, "The American missiles prop up the Russian missiles and vice versa."

Pathogenesis: The Pathological Dynamics of the Arms Race

From the beginning, the nuclear arms race in America has been fueled by a mad lust for power, first in the Air Force and later in the Navy; by a fascination with scientific, esoteric, and intellectual pursuits; by clinical paranoia about the Soviets; and by rapacious greed by our military industries.

According to Fred Kaplan, speculation about possible weapons for a Third World War began four months before Germany was defeated in World War II. It was then that Air Force General Henry Arnold said to his top advisers, "We've got to think of what we'll need twenty years from now. For the past twenty years, we have built and run the Air Force on pilots, but we can't do that anymore." He went on to say that he envisioned an age in which intercontinental missiles would dominate warfare and the Air Force would have to change radically to accommodate such new inventions.

Because the Air Force had played a major role in ending World War II by bombing Dresden, Berlin, and Tokyo and by dropping atomic bombs on Hiroshima and Nagasaki, it became the most powerful postwar service in the military. In those days, many people in the Air Force believed that America should threaten to use massive nuclear retaliation in response to any Soviet conventional misdemeanor. The Strategic Air Command (SAC) was a fiefdom created after the war as the first nuclear delivery service. The confidence of the Air Force increased with the arrival of the atomic bomb. They still believed in bombing the enemy flat. In the late

1940s and early 1950s, the Air Force developed a war plan called Sunday Punch—essentially a swift, all-out atomic blow, or spasm, against every target in the Soviet Union. Years later, under the Eisenhower Administration, John Foster Dulles advocated the same plan, then known as Massive Retaliation. At that time, Air Force policy called for the use of atomic bombs in local wars if the situation so dictated. General Curtis LeMay said in 1956, "I see that the Russians are amassing their planes for an attack. I am going to knock the shit out of them before they take off the ground."

The utility of bombing was severely challenged in a postwar study. But the Air Force's own view of things prevailed—with effective lobbying from within by General LeMay and in Congress by special friends, most notably Arizona's Senator Barry Goldwater.

In 1945, a man named Joseph Loftus recommended a counterforce nuclear war, targeting airfields only, and not Soviet cities. He soon realized that the Air Force, and especially SAC, were not interested in mere counterforce but in mass destruction. The first time Loftus went to SAC headquarters in Omaha, he was invited to have cocktails with General Jim Walsh. Walsh, exhorting that the big bomb was meant for big damage, screamed, "Goddamn it, Loftus, there is only one way to attack the Russians, and that's to rip them hard with everything we have, and"—at this point he pounded his fist on top of the Bible—"knock their balls off!"

General Tommy Power, commander of SAC in 1960, exploded after a briefing about counterforce limited nuclear war by William Kaufmann of the RAND Corporation. "Why do you want us to restrain ourselves?" he bellowed. "Restraint! Why are you so concerned with saving *their* lives? The whole idea is to kill the bastards! Look, at the end of the war, if there are two Americans and one Russian, we win!"

From the early days of nuclear weapons, America has reacted like a global big bully. Having been first to build nuclear weapons, it has always intended to use them if necessary. This policy prevailed both before and after the Soviet Union had built enough nuclear weapons to threaten American cities. Since 1945, the United States has threatened or considered first use of nuclear weapons at least nine times:

1. In June 1948, at the beginning of the Berlin Blockade, Harry Truman sent nuclear-capable B-29 planes to bases in Britain

and Germany. Although these particular planes were not loaded, the bluff convinced Harry Truman and his aides of the feasibility of the nuclear threat.

2. In 1950, Truman warned he might use nuclear weapons against the Chinese who surrounded American troops at the Chosin Reservoir during the Korean War. This strategy, of course, would have killed the marines had they not escaped.

3. In 1953, Eisenhower secretly threatened China with nuclear weapons, a strategy that forced a settlement of the Korean War.

4. In 1958, Eisenhower directed the Joint Chiefs to use nuclear weapons against China if it invaded the island of Quemoy.

5. In 1961, after the construction of the Berlin Wall, America threatened to use nuclear weapons first if East Germany prevented the crossing of refugees.

6. In 1962, President Kennedy threatened to use nuclear weapons against the Soviet Union unless it removed its missiles from Cuba; that threat, plus a naval blockage of its ships, persuaded the Soviet Union to remove its missiles.

7. In 1968, America considered using nuclear weapons when marines were surrounded at Khe Sanh, Vietnam, even though such use would have killed the marines.

8. From 1969 to 1972, Nixon threatened (through Henry Kissinger) to use nuclear weapons on North Vietnam. He told H. R. Haldeman: "I call it the Madman Theory, Bob. I want the North Vietnamese to believe I've reached the point where I might do *anything* to stop the war."

9. In 1980, Carter issued a secret Pentagon study that concluded: "To prevail in an Iranian scenario, we might have to threaten or make use of tactical nuclear weapons." This Middle East doctrine, reaffirmed by Reagan in 1981, still is current U.S. policy there.

On only one of these occasions would the United States have risked starting an all-out nuclear war, and that was during the Cuban missile crisis. In other cases America was merely threatening nonnuclear countries with the ultimate genocide in order to get its own way. The U.S. Catholic Bishops Conference has condemned this attitude as immoral.

To my knowledge, the Soviet Union has made only two similar

threats: once in 1956 during the Suez crisis when it had no ICBMs, and once during the Bay of Pigs invasion when it had four ICBMs. It's clear that, for the most part, the use of nuclear blackmail has been a peculiarly American ploy. Nevertheless, even so-called broadminded intellectuals who sat on Reagan's MX commission (the President's Commission on Strategic Forces) in 1983, including Brent Scowcroft, Harold Brown, James Schlesinger, John McCone, and R. James Woolsey, were obsessed in their report with the thought that "if the Russians get ahead of us, they can threaten us or blackmail us." These men are highly intelligent, and all are aware that, according to Pentagon scientist Richard DeLauer, America is years ahead of the Soviet Union in almost every weapon and technological system. This sort of thinking has been common ever since 1945, when the nuclear strategists in RAND and in the Pentagon began to assume the worst-case analysis of the Soviet Union. Despite a lack of concrete knowledge of Soviet capabilities, they projected America's evolving nuclear capabilities onto the Soviets. For instance, the 1960 missile gap was totally fallacious. Everyone who believed in it was acutely embarrassed when the new U.S. satellite discovered that the Soviet Union had deployed only four intercontinental ballistic missiles. Such fantasy thinking, still practiced at the highest levels of government, is overt paranoia.

By definition, a paranoid patient is someone who imagines a certain scenario in his or her own mind, decides (with no objective evidence) that it mirrors exactly what someone else is thinking, and then decides to act on that notion. The paranoid delusions projected onto Soviet leaders come straight from the minds of American strategists. They probably reflect exactly what the Americans plan to do themselves and bear little relationship to the reality of Soviet strategy. The only way to find out what the Soviets are thinking is to ask them.

Soviet policy has been stated on frequent occasions. Because nuclear war would be so devastating, the Soviet Union has pledged not to use nuclear weapons first. But its stated policy is to retaliate against even a small tactical nuclear attack by launching its whole arsenal. The Soviet leaders are vitally concerned about nuclear war. On several occasions within the past few years, Dr. Evgeni Chazov (the cardiologist of Leonid Brezhnev, Yuri Andropov, and Constantin Chernenko) has appeared on national Soviet TV to teach his country's population about the medical and scientific consequences of nuclear war. And once, three American and three Soviet physicians appeared on national Soviet TV for a full hour to discuss the same subject. This uncensored broadcast was seen by nearly two hundred million Soviet citizens. Yet during the program, one of the Americans had the temerity to criticize the Soviet civil defense system, maintaining that it would do no good.

Despite these facts, discussions about Soviet nuclear blackmail prevail in administration circles. The arcane logic goes like this: The Soviets launch a first strike on U.S. ground-based missiles (hard targets), destroying the majority. They use two hydrogen bombs per silo, thus killing between 20 million and 50 million Americans. Such an attack still leaves the United States with 5,142 nuclear bombs in the strategic submarines (minus those destroyed in port) and 3,000 in the intercontinental bombers (those that scramble and take off fast enough not to be caught in the attack). The president now faces a dilemma. Should he retaliate with these remaining weapons—which are accurate enough only for soft targets (cities)—and destroy the majority of Soviet cities, thus exposing U.S. cities to a similar retaliatory attack with the remaining Soviet weapons? Or should he accede to the Soviet global demands, thus saving American cities?

Do the Soviets really think like this, or is the scenario a direct projection of paranoid minds? The Soviet Union cannot be sure that it actually has any first-strike weapons. Although its intercontinental ballistic missiles are becoming more accurate, and its bombs are large, there is no guarantee that they would be accurate enough to hit all the American missile silos.

Furthermore, the U.S. early-warning DSP-647 satellites and radars would detect the attack, and America could well launch its missiles on warning before the Soviet missiles land. The Soviet satellites would detect the U.S. attack and launch the rest of their missiles on warning, resulting in all-out nuclear war. Launch on warning is not official American policy, but many people assume it would be used during an attack.

The event would also trigger the launching of U.S. submarine missiles and strategic bombers. Airplanes would arrive over devastated Soviet territory hours later to bomb the few remaining targets—if they could be identified, because the National Command Authority (NCA) and most communication networks would have been destroyed. (The Soviet Union puts a priority on targeting the command centers in America.)

Even if the Soviets were mad enough to launch a first strike at America's land-based missiles, they would have to understand that America had approximately another 5,000 submarine-based bombs in reserve, invulnerable to a first strike, which could be used to obliterate their own country.

Suppose that the Soviets' first strike worked. What would they do with the terribly radioactive land that is now the conquered U.S.A.? Fifty million people would be vaporized initially, or would die weeks, months, or years later from dreadful radiation-induced diseases. What would the Soviets demand for their blackmail? If indeed they wanted Europe or the Persian Gulf instead of radioactive America, thousands of U.S. bombs would still be available for local use in these territories, or to destroy military, industrial, and civilian targets in the USSR.

American strategic thinkers assume that all would be rational and calm, as U.S. leaders sat waiting in their airborne command posts—assuming they reached them in time—willing to absorb a Soviet first strike without launching on warning. This is not a picture of normal human psychological reaction. People do not function like this under moderate stress, let alone the extreme anxiety and utter panic created in a nuclear war.

To understand the complicated dynamics of the whole pathological system that has produced and still perpetuates the arms race, it is necessary first to understand the new weapons systems that are being built by the Reagan Administration. These weapons are extremely dangerous and destabilizing, and they move the probability of nuclear war into a new realm. They are all an integral part of the Pentagon's 1984–88 Five-Year Defense Guidance Plan, which will give America the "capability" to fight and win a protracted nuclear war over a six-month period. The Soviets do not yet have these particular weapons, but they have announced that they will proceed with construction and deployment if America insists on so doing. This new arsenal will move America away from "parity" with the Soviet Union. The opportunity to obtain a freeze will be lost, because the Soviet Union will not negotiate from a position of "inferiority."

To understand these weapons systems fully, it is necessary to learn the technical terms that describe some of their important functions:

Throw weight or payload: The weight of the nuclear warheads, penetration aids, and the "bus" that carries them after the last rocket motor has separated in flight. Because the United States has miniaturized its bombs, they are smaller and use the available throw weight more efficiently.

Readiness: The number of missiles ready to be launched at any one time. The readiness of U.S. strategic missles is 98 percent, while the Soviet readiness, although hard to verify, is about 75 percent.

Reliability: Percentage of probability that all phases of a missile launch, flight, and impact will work as planned. The reliability of the U.S. missiles is 75 to 80 percent; of Soviet missiles, 65 to 75 percent.

Yield: The explosive power of a bomb expressed as tons of TNT equivalence—1,000 tons of TNT equals 1 kiloton. Soviet bombs are generally bigger.

Accuracy: Measured by "circular error probable" (CEP), which represents the radius of a circle centered on a target. Half the bombs are expected to land within the circle, the other half outside. Until recently, Soviet strategic weapons would miss their mark by as much as 2 nautical miles. Some of the newest Soviet missiles have a CEP of about 0.3 nautical mile. By contrast, recent improvements in U.S. missiles place them within a 0.12 nautical mile radius.

MIRVing: Multiple independently targetable re-entry vehicle. This system was developed by the United States in the 1960s and deployed in 1970. It was not outlawed by the SALT I treaty because only America could MIRV at that time. But the U.S. advantage was short-lived; the Soviet Union started MIRVing its missiles in 1975. When a nuclear rocket or missile is MIRVed, it carries more than one hydrogen warhead, each of which is called a re-entry vehicle, or RV. These separate re-entry vehicles are carried on a "bus," which releases the RVs one by one. It makes preselected changes in speed and orientation so that each hydrogen bomb will land very accurately on target.

Given the missiles' increasing accuracy and multiple warheads, it is possible that a few missiles launched from one side could destroy all the land-based missiles on the other in a surprise pre-emptive first-strike attack. Before missiles could be MIRVed, a pre-emptive attack (provided each missile was extraordinarily accurate) would have required one missile per silo. But now, theoretically, the attacking country need use only a fraction of its missiles to destroy its enemy's MIRVed ground-based missiles before they are launched. It still will end up with many missiles to spare. To destroy a reinforced-concrete missile silo adequately, two hydrogen-bomb explosions per silo are necessary—one landing above the silo and, several seconds later, a second landing near it on the ground. The missile itself will not be destroyed but will be damaged sufficiently to prevent it from being fired. Two missiles, each with ten warheads, could destroy ten missile silos, each of which theoretically could contain ten bombs. Thus, the advantage to offense: Twenty warheads destroy one hundred warheads. Of course, such an attack is suitable only for land-based missiles. It cannot be used against submarines loaded with nuclear missiles or against strategic bombers once they have taken off. But it is a very destabilizing technology nonetheless. Each superpower will continue to wonder when the other might attempt a pre-emptive first strike. Because 70 percent of Soviet strategic weapons are land-based, the United States would benefit from such a move. But the USSR would be crazy to contemplate it: Almost 4,000 hydrogen bombs on U.S. submarines always at sea are ready to destroy the Soviet Union in retaliation.

The origin of MIRVed warheads is interesting. As the Soviets moved to develop ABMs in the late 1960s and early 1970s, the U.S. Air Force supported development of separately targetable warhead "decoys" that would confound Soviet antiballistic missile (ABM) defenses. Inevitably, someone pointed out that having developed the guidance systems, it would now be easy to put a real warhead on each decoy and significantly increase both yield and threat. Hence MIRVing. Five years later the Soviets also had MIRVed warheads. They were not included in SALT I or II because neither the United States nor the USSR wanted to halt *arms development* but merely to limit existing *strategic arsenals*. Neither country has been able to achieve that.

Lethality: The ability of a weapon to destroy a target

or reinforced-concrete missile silo. This is a function of yield in megatons (EMT) to accuracy (CEP) and is expressed as $L = \dfrac{EMT}{CEP}$. Making the warhead twice as accurate has the same effect as making the bomb eight times more powerful. Lethality also increases in proportion to the number of bombs dropped on a target as well as to the size of the bombs. In practice, the area of blast destruction is enlarged by increasing the number of bombs and lowering their individual yield—that is, several small bombs with the same aggregate yield are much more effective spread out over the target area than one large warhead. A 1-megaton yield divided into twenty 50-kiloton bombs has the equivalent destructive power of a 3-megaton bomb.

When the Minuteman II missile was fitted with a single large bomb of 1-megaton yield with a CEP of 0.3 mile, it was given a lethality of 11. But with three warheads, each of 170 kilotons, and each with a CEP of 0.2 mile, the Minuteman III has a total lethality of 23. By MIRVing and increasing accuracy by one third, the United States more than doubled the lethality of its long-range missiles. At the same time, total megatonnage has been reduced from 1 to 0.54. Today, three hundred Minuteman missiles have been fitted with still another warhead: the very accurate Mark 12A. These warheads have a yield of 335 kilotons each and a CEP of 0.1 mile.

The Soviets have many missiles, but few are extremely accurate. They have 308 SS-18 missiles with one, eight, or ten warheads. The largest single warhead is on as many as twenty SS-18 missiles. The yield ranges from 20 to 24 megatons. Other SS-18s are MIRVed, and may have an accuracy equal to that of the Minuteman III.

So far, only land-based missiles have been made very accurate. The submarine-based missiles cannot yet be used for missile-destroying first-strike attacks.

Range of ICBMs: Intercontinental rockets have ranges up to 8,000 nautical miles. This means, in effect, that any place on earth can be hit within approximately thirty minutes by rockets launched from either the American or the Russian continent. (The South Island of New Zealand would have to be targeted, of course, by the nuclear submarines.)

The MX Missile—Alias "Peacekeeper"

Research for the MX began in 1963 with a $166 million program to define a successor to the Titan and Minuteman missiles; the actual MX missile program was initiated in 1974. At that time, it was decided that the Minuteman ICBM silos would eventually become vulnerable to a Soviet first-strike attack, even though the Soviets did not even begin to MIRV their missiles until 1975. This projected supposition was almost certainly based on U.S. activity at the time, to increase vastly the accuracy of its ICBMs, which it had already MIRVed. In 1977, Donald Rumsfeld, secretary of defense, said, "Our calculations indicate that by the early 1980s there could be a substantial reduction in the number of surviving ICBMs should the Soviets apply sufficient numbers of their forces against the U.S. ICBMs in a first strike." Based on these suppositions, he asked Congress for $294 million for MX missile development and testing so that the MX could be operational by 1983—two years ahead of schedule. President Carter originally rejected this proposal, but decided in October 1977 to proceed with full-scale development of the missile. He reversed his decision again in 1978, but in 1979 once again supported full-scale development to ensure that the hawks on the Committee on the Present Danger (whose origins are discussed at some length in "Case History," pages 167 to 201) would agree to SALT II ratification.

Throughout its history, the MX missile has been designed to be a mobile, invulnerable, extremely accurate system, not subject to a hypothetical first-strike attack. Many methods of "basing" the missile have been considered, including placing missile pods in the bottom of ponds or in truck- or railborne capsules, carrying the missile around on highways, hiding it in a submarine, and flying it around in an airplane.

The Pentagon describes the MX as an advanced, high-throw-weight, MIRVed ICBM capable of fulfilling U.S. strategic requirements into the twenty-first century. It is a huge missile, weighing 195,000 pounds (or 97.5 tons) and measuring 7 feet, 6 inches in diameter and 71 feet in length. A four-stage rocket, the MX will be able to carry a payload of 4.5 tons over a 7,000-mile range and will carry ten precision-guided hydrogen bombs in its nose cone, or bus. A new guidance system, called the Advanced Inertial Reference Sphere (AIRS), will enable the rocket to reposition itself as it travels through space, giving it a CEP of better than 400 feet.

The bombs themselves will each yield about 350 kilotons, which is roughly twenty-four times larger than the Hiroshima bomb. It hardly matters whether the bomb is extremely accurate or not with this sort of yield, except for hitting missile silos, which have been "hardened" against hydrogen-bomb explosions by reinforced concrete.

In 1980 and 1981, the Air Force wanted to base two hundred MX missiles in Utah and Nevada on an underground racetrack, shuttling along twelve hundred miles of roadway among forty-six hundred shelters. (The reason for building so many shelters was to increase the number of targets the Soviets would have to destroy while keeping the number of missiles within the SALT II limits.) These two hundred missiles, carrying two thousand hydrogen bombs, would be hidden in some of these shelters, to prevent the Soviets from knowing where they were. To conform to SALT II provisions, the plan called for America occasionally to open the hatches of the shelters to let the Soviet satellites detect and count the missiles, quickly close them, and move the cumbersome missiles to other shelters as fast as possible. By the time the Soviets had a chance to retarget their missiles, the MX missiles would already have been relocated. The ranchers and the Mormon Church, among others in Utah and Nevada, were understandably upset with this particular plan. It would have destroyed the natural beauty of their states, to say nothing of making them a first-strike target and using up enormous amounts of precious water to lay all the concrete.

The system was rejected, but in late 1982 the Reagan Administration came up with a new basing mode called Dense Pack, and the president ironically renamed the MX "Peacekeeper." The new plan called for a hundred missiles to be placed very close together over an area of about twenty square miles. If the Soviets attempted a first strike, the incoming missiles would either explode together and blow each other up, or produce such collateral damage from enormous quantities of radioactive debris that they would be unable to damage the MX missiles in their silos, which had been hardened to withstand such an event. This incredible bomb-damaging scenario is called fratricide (killing a brother)!

Congress did not like the Dense Pack basing mode, and experts didn't think it would work, so the system was rejected in November 1982. But the president, not to be outmaneuvered, created a "bipartisan" panel called the Scowcroft Commission. Its members, old-time professional military people and past secretaries of defense, attempted to devise an acceptable basing mode. All these men had spent their lives involved in various aspects of the arms race. The group concluded that MIRVed missiles are destabilizing because they are targets for a first strike—the Soviets could destroy lots of bombs with a few missiles—and because they are also good for use in a first strike. They then recommended that the United States build a hundred missiles containing a thousand of these first-strike hydrogen warheads and place them in pre-existing Minuteman silos. Their recommendations revealed that they are worried neither about a Soviet first strike after all nor about the "window of vulnerability" that the president's people are fond of discussing.

The Scowcroft Commission also recommended that a thousand small, single-warhead missiles, called Midgetmen, be built to encourage superpower de-MIRVing. These Midgetmen will almost certainly have first-strike accuracy and will be clustered at up to twelve military bases with roads radiating from them. To use the Pentagon's phrase, they "will dash" out onto these roads under nuclear attack. Each missile will be based in an armored vehicle called an armadillo. Under nuclear attack, it can go to the side of the road and anchor itself into the dirt like its namesake. Suckers on its feet will hold it firm while hydrogen bombs are exploding all around it. Then it will emerge "undamaged" after the nuclear salvo and send off a single, very accurate hydrogen bomb toward as yet undetermined targets in the Soviet Union.

This commission of apparently intelligent men thus contradicted itself by recommending construction of the MX missile when it was opposed to MIRVed missiles; it also produced a bizarre and fantasylike weapon that could only have come from the heads of military and scientific child-adults who are desperate to keep the nuclear arms race game going.

If the Reagan Administration has dropped its scare talk of vulnerability, what then does it want the MX missiles for?

Obviously, given its characteristics, the MX is an extraordinarily crafted piece of weaponry designed only for first-strike nuclear war. Once the production lines are cranked up, the United States will not want to stop at 100 missiles. It could well build 200, as previously planned. Two hundred missiles will contain 2,000 thermonuclear warheads, enough to destroy most of the Soviet land-based ICBMs or the majority of its strategic force (2 hydrogen bombs per silo; 1,398 Russian missile silos).

The members of Congress, smitten by this intelligent, bipartisan, presidentially appointed panel and further cajoled and seduced by White House dinner invitations, voted for the scheme in November 1983. They did not analyze this contradiction adequately. One would have to ask: "Do these legislators in Washington represent the good of their constituents—men, women, and children, and the lives of future generations—or have they given up their souls and intellects to be so dazzled by dinner at the White House and gold-medal presidential commissions?" This occurred when three quarters of the U.S. population, on a nonpartisan basis, wanted a bilateral nuclear freeze, which would invalidate the MX.

The MX missile project itself will cost about $30 billion. This figure does not include the cost of the bombs, to be built by the Department of Energy. Actually, because of the MX's admitted vulnerability, military planners have discussed the use of antiballistic missile systems to defend the MX-converted Minuteman silos. Such a move will openly defy the Anti-Ballistic Missile Treaty signed by the Soviet Union and America in 1972 and will cost enormous sums of money. With the MX, the United States will be able to fight a pre-emptive first-strike nuclear war and will flout the ABM Treaty. The fiscal 1980 Arms Control Impact Statement states, "If MX were deployed in substantial numbers . . . the U.S. would have acquired—through both MX and Minuteman improvements—an apparent capability to destroy most of the Soviet ICBM force in a first strike. . . ." Soviet leaders who have their fingers hovering over the button, wondering when and if the United States plans to strike first and destroy their missiles, will almost inevitably adopt a launch-on-warning policy, bringing us all closer to the brink of annihilation.

In the November 1982 congressional election, the MX missile contractors more than doubled their campaign contributions to members of Congress. Twelve of the thirteen biggest MX contractors had contributed $780,000 to congressional incumbents by July 30 (two years before, their total contributions were $455,000). The largest Senate recipients were strong MX supporters in tight races: Howard W. Cannon (Democrat of Nevada) received the most, $21,500; Harrison H. Schmitt (Republican of New Mexico), $17,000; Richard G. Lugar (Republican of Indiana), $12,850; and Henry M. Jackson (Democrat of Washington), $11,000. (Both Cannon and Schmitt lost; Jackson is now deceased; and Lugar is chairman of the Senate Foreign Relations Committee.) In the House, the lineup consisted of Norman D. Dicks (Democrat of Washington), $11,500; John P. Murtha (Democrat of Pennsylvania), $10,950; and David F. Emery (Republican of Maine), $10,050. The twelve contractors were: Aerojet, AVCO, Boeing, General Electric, GTE Sylvania, Hercules, Honeywell, Martin Marietta, Northrop, Rockwell Autonetics, Rockwell Rocketdyne, and TRW.

The day the MX Dense Pack was defeated in November 1982, I was lobbying in the halls of Congress. The halls were full of Pentagon lobbyists and lobbyists from these companies, but I saw no American people or their children.

The saga is not over yet. In March 1985, the House approved funds for twenty-one MX missiles by a six-vote margin. There are many more votes coming up to appropriate funds for the development, production, and deployment of the MX. Since this is a democracy, it is up to the American people to determine eventually the outcome of this debate.

Trident II or D-5 Missiles

There has been noisy and anguished debate about the MX missile for some time, but another equally dangerous missile is being designed and built. Funds for it are being appropriated by Congress with virtually no fuss at all. The Trident II or D-5 missile has no basing problems to upset the public or the politicians. It is designed to be placed inside the new noiseless, invulnerable Trident submarines. Each submarine will contain twenty-four Trident II missiles, and each missile can deliver from eight to ten warheads with a payload of about 475 kilotons each—thirty-eight times bigger

Associate Contractor & Location	Contract Description and Cost (in millions of dollars)
AEROJET SOLID PROPULSION CO. Sacramento CA	Stage II propulsion system. Received $11.0 of $129.4 Stage II. $8.2
AVCO Huntsville AL	Rocket test cell data acquisition and control of testing environment for use in J-4 and J-5 Arnold Engineering Development Center test facilities. Received $2.8 of $7.5
Wilmington MA	Re-entry system integration. Received $0.005 of $3.4 Re-entry system integration. Received $7.7 of $164.3
BOEING AEROSPACE Seattle WA	Redirection of basing concept from vertical shelter to horizontal multiple protective structure. TTD $0.046 of $3.4 Horizontal basing system. TTD $0.101 of $24.9 Blast and shock test program. $4.5
DRAPER LABORATORIES Cambridge MA	Technical support for guidance programs. TTD $0.038 of $16.5
ENERGY RESEARCH CORP. Danbury CT	MX ground power advanced development program.
E-SYSTEMS Greenville TX	Conceal locations of MX missiles. $0.396
FURGO NATIONAL Long Beach CA	Siting and geotechnical investigations. Received $4.6 of $8.3 Acceleration of geotechnical and siting investigations. TTD $0.013 of $5.5
GENERAL ELECTRIC Philadelphia PA	Adaptation of MARK 12 re-entry vehicle for the MX. Received $5.3 of $69.9
GEODYNAMICS CORP. Santa Barbara CA	Geodetic and geophysical support. $2.2
GTE-SYLVANIA INC. Needham Heights MA	Command, control and communications system. Received $10.0 of $325.5
HENNINGSON DURHAM & RICHARDSON Santa Barbara CA	Environmental baseline studies and environmental statements. Received $3.3 of $6.9
HERCULES Magna UT	Stage III propulsion system. TTD $0.084 of $75.3 Nuclear hardness and survivability. TTD $0.087 of $5.2 Engineering development, late exercise of Option D equitable adjustment. $87.4
HONEYWELL INC. Horsham PA	MX ground power advanced development program.
St. Petersburg FL	Specific force integrating receiver. Received $10.0 of $34.0
KARAGOZIAN AND CASE Los Angeles CA	Engineering services.
LOGICON San Pedro CA	Software performance analysis and technical evaluation. Received $0.556 of $9.1
MARTIN MARIETTA Denver CO	Performance of MX weapon system assembly. Received $15.7 of $321.5 Assembly, test and system support, option changes and additions. TTD $0.402 of $49.9
Vandenberg AFB CA	Launcher studies and analysis for MX weapon system. TTD $0.352 of $3.1
NORTHROP Precision Products Div. Norwood MA	Third generation gyroscope program. Received $7.6 of $36.2
Hawthorne CA	Inertial measurement unit. Received $17.5 of $235.0 Inertial measurement unit changes. $6.7
OLIN Stamford CT	Propellants used to support space shuttle, Titan missiles, F-16 aircraft and MX. $40.1
QUESTRON, INC. La Jolla CA	Hardened elecyronics analysis.
R.S. HANSON CO., INC. Spokane WA	Engineering study—construction equipment.
RALPH M. PARSONS CO. Pasadena CA and Luke AFB AZ	Buried trench construction. $6.3
ROCKWELL INTERNATIONAL Autonetics Div. Anaheim CA	Flight computer and integration of components into guidance and control systems. TTD $0.273 of $259.4
Rocketdyne Div. Canoga Park CA	Stage IV propulsion system. TTD $0.203 of $192.8 Redirection of Stage IV. $8.5

SCIENCE APPLICATIONS INC. La Jolla CA	MX software studies.	
SMALL BUSINESS ADMINIS. Washington DC	MX software studies and analysis program.	
SOFTECH, INC. Waltham MA	MX JOVIAL compiler. $1.9	
SYSTEMS, SCIENCE AND SOFTWARE La Jolla CA	Nuclear hardness and survivability studies. $1.5	
SYSTEMS TECHNOLOGY LABORATORY INC. Arlington VA	MX basing study.	
THIOKOL Brigham City UT	Stage I propulsion system. Received $13.6 of $136.5 Stage I and ordnance update. $17.9	
TRW Redondo Beach CA and Norton AFB CA and Vanderberg AFB CA Redondo Beach CA	 Engineering development. TTD $0.033 of $12.1 Systems engineering and technical support. $42.3 Targeting and analysis program for FY80. $5.8 Development of ST/TS of the Advanced ICBM (MC) weapon system.	
ULTRASYSTEMS, INC. Irvine CA and Norton AFB CA	Integrated logistics support.	
WEIDLINGER ASSOCIATES New York NY	Nuclear hardness and survivability analysis.	
WESTINGHOUSE ELECTRIC CORP. Sunnyvale CA	MX Canister. $6.0	

Sub Contractor & Location	Contract Description and Cost (in millions of dollars)	Associate Contractor
AIR RESEARCH MANUF. CORP. Phoenix AZ	Build TVA Actuator.	AEROJET- GENERAL CORP.
BRUNSWICK CORP. Lincoln NE	Manufacture Stage II case.	AEROJET- GENERAL CORP.
ALCOA* Cleveland OH 44105	Aluminum forgings.	AVCO
ATLANTIC RESEARCH CORP. Gainesville VA 22065	Rocket motor.	AVCO
AVCO AEROSTRUCTURES, INC. Nashville TN 37202	Deployment module structure	AVCO
G & H TECHNOLOGY Automation Industries, Inc. Santa Monica CA 90404	Separation connector.	AVCO
GRUMMAN Bethpage NY	20 ship sets of titanium shroud components for MX nose cone. $10.0	AVCO
HONEYWELL AVIONICS DIVISION* St. Louis Park MN 55416	Automatic test equipment	AVCO
O.E.A., INC.* Denver CO 80210	Separation nut/gas generator.	AVCO
TIMEX* Pittsburgh PA 15230	Shroud structure material.	AVCO
UNIDYNAMICS PHOENIX, INC.* Phoenix AZ 85062	Arm/disarm device.	AVCO
COMPUTER SCIENCES CORP. Applied Technology Falls Church VA	MX C3 system.	GTE-SYLVANIA
HAYES INTERNATIONAL Birmingham AL	MX C3 system.	GTE-SYLVANIA
NORDEN SYSTEMS Norwalk CT	MX C3 system.	GTE-SYLVANIA
ROCKWELL Tulsa OK	Interstage integration.	HER- CULES
HYDRAULIC RESEARCH INC. Valencia CA	Thrust vector actuation.	HER- CULES
BDM Albuquerque NM	Preservation and location uncertainty	MARTIN- MARI- ETTA

Company	Description	Prime
CINCINNATI ELECTRONICS Cincinnati OH	Range and safety receivers. $0.940	MARTIN MARIETTA
ENDEVCO San Juan Capistrano CA	Dynamic data measurement system of 750 channels for MX testing.	ROCKWELL ROCKETDYNE AEROJET MFG. CO.
GOODYEAR AEROSPACE CO. Litchfield Park AZ	MX Transportation and handling equipment.	
SCI SYSTEMS INC. Huntsville AL	MX multipliers and power supply verifiers.	
SYSTEMS ENGINEERING LABS Ft. Lauderdale FL	Computers for MX program.	
AMERICAN BERYLLIUM Sarasota FL	Beryllium spheres for MX guidance system	NORTHROP
SYSTEMS ENGINEERING LABS Ft. Lauderdale FL	Computers for MX program.	
HAMILTON STANDARD Windsor Locks CT	Flight coolant system. $4.5	ROCKWELL AUTONETICS
HONEYWELL St. Petersburg FL	Main memory sub-system for MX electronics and computer assembly. $12.0	
SYSTEMS ENGINEERING LABS Ft. Lauderdale FL	Computers for MX program.	
YARDNEY ELECTRIC CO. Denver CO	Guidance and control batteries. $1.0	
AEROJET MANUFACTURING CO. Fullerton CA	Support for Stage IV.	ROCKWELL ROCKETDYNE
BELL AEROSPACE, DIV. OF TEXTRON INC. Buffalo NY	Support for Stage IV.	
ROCKWELL INT'L MISSILE SYSTEMS DIV. Columbus OH	Support for Stage IV.	
OAO CORP. Beltsville MD	Support for MX software studies and analysis program.	SMALL BUSINESS ADMINIS
LOCKHEED MISSILE SYSTEMS CO. Sunnyvale CA	MX Ordnance Initiation sets/flight termination ordnance sets.	THIOKOL
MOOG East Aurora NY	Stage I thrust vector actuation control system.	
HERCULES Bacchus UT	Graphite composite launch tube for MX canister	WESTINGHOUSE

than the Hiroshima bomb. One Trident submarine could destroy most of the major cities in the Northern Hemisphere. This missile will be able to travel over 4,000 nautical miles, an increase of 1,500 miles over the range of the Poseidon missile. (The new Trident I missile, which has already been used to refit twelve of the thirty-one Poseidon subs, has a maximum range of 4,350 nautical miles.)

Why does the Navy want more, and more sophisticated, subs? It already owns thirty-one Poseidon submarines—noiseless, sleek, invulnerable. Over half of them are at sea at any one time. A single Poseidon submarine can deliver from 160 to 224 independently targeted warheads. The fleet has a total patrol area of approximately 2.5 million square miles available in the oceans, because of the 2,500-nautical-mile range of the old missiles. Refitting Poseidons with 4,000-mile-range missiles will give them from 12.5 million to 20 million square miles of patrol area. The new Trident subs also will have this capability, which offers them ten times as much ocean in which to hide.

Deputy Defense Secretary David Packard directed the Navy to begin full-scale development of Trident in September 1971. In 1973, the Navy announced that it would base Trident in the Pacific Ocean with a home port along the Hood Canal, which is in Puget Sound near Bangor, Washington. Construction of the first submarine began in 1974, and one of the first Tridents was launched in 1981. Archbishop Raymond G. Hunthausen of Seattle has described the Trident submarine as the Auschwitz of Puget Sound.

Each Poseidon submarine displaces 8,250 tons of water when submerged. A Trident sub displaces 18,700 tons. It is 560 feet long—over 1½ times the length of a football field. As of 1985, thirteen Tridents have been funded, but final construction will likely call for up to twenty Trident subs. The Navy has refused to commit itself to a final production number.

The Trident II, or D-5 missile, will be capable of striking any point on more than half the earth's surface. Each missile can deliver from eight to ten superaccurate MIRVed hydrogen bombs, each with a first-strike hard-target counterforce accuracy. Trident IIs will be guided by the NAVSTAR satellite system, which will provide accuracies to within 50 feet in all three dimensions, and velocity to within tenths of a foot per second.

NAVSTAR is comprised of twenty-one satellites that will give a true position in three dimensions within 50 feet, and an actual velocity within tenths of a foot per second. The missile's navigation computers will be updated as it flies, and corrections will be made by the bus just before each re-entry vehicle or hydrogen bomb is released. The missiles' navigation computers will be updated by fixing on a star during the boost phase, and corrections will be made by the guidance system on the bus just before each hydrogen bomb is released. The CEP will be better than 400 feet—a first-strike accuracy.

At present, the U.S. Navy is installing an extremely low-frequency (ELF) radio transmitter in Michigan. They have already completed a similar facility in Wisconsin. Miles of cable are run on poles similar to power lines, the ends of which are embedded in the earth. The Michigan and Wisconsin facilities would work as one, constantly pumping millions of watts of electricity into the granite bedrock of Lake Superior to form a giant underground antenna. This electrical energy would radiate a constant signal around the earth and deep into the ocean. ELF would serve as a giant beeper, summoning all the submarines to the surface. According to Robert Aldridge, a former design engineer at Lockheed who worked on the Trident program, once summoned to the surface, "existing communication systems could give them the fire order."

Until this time, submarine missiles could be used only for second-strike, soft-target, "city-busting" purposes because they lacked the necessary accuracy for "silo-busting," hard-targeted capability. Now these Trident subs can be used for a first-strike "winnable" nuclear war. In fact, the fiscal 1980 Arms Control Impact Statement reported:

> The addition of highly accurate Trident II missiles with higher yield warheads would give the U.S. Submarine Launched Ballistic Missile forces a substantial time-urgent hard-target-kill capability for the first time. The counter-silo capability of a [deleted] KT Trident II missile would exceed that of all currently deployed U.S. ballistic missiles. Moreover, the additive effects of two potential advances (Trident II and MX) in U.S. counter-silo capabilities by the early 1990s could put a large portion of Soviet fixed ICBM silos at risk. This could have significant destabilizing effects.

Trident II missiles are even more psychologically destabilizing than MX missiles because they are invulnerable to attack and are totally hidden from the Soviets. Professional nuclear strategists argue that because the Tridents are hidden, they are more stabilizing—presumably the Soviet Union will not be tempted to try to destroy them with its own first strikes. I think this argument is back to front. It more accurately reflects actual U.S. thinking about *its* plans for a strike—another example of projection of one's own thinking onto the enemy.

The Cruise Missile

Cruise missiles are small missiles that incorporate a 200-kiloton hydrogen bomb and a small jet engine. They are being developed by the Air Force for launch from airplanes (air-launched cruise missiles, or ALCM) and by the Navy (sea-launched cruise missiles, or SLCM). Ground-launched cruise missiles (GLCM) are also operated by the Air Force. Cruise missiles are guided by an inertial guidance platform, which is supplemented in turn by a sensor system called TERCOM (terrain contour matching), a brilliant device that can steer cruise missiles to their targets with extreme accuracy. TERCOM gives cruise missiles a 100 percent "kill" probability against military targets that have been hardened to survive nuclear war. It compares the ground over which it is flying to a radar map of the terrain, which is stored in its computer. If the missile deviates from its course, a signal sent by TERCOM corrects the guidance system. Because TERCOM allows the cruise to skim so low over the ground, going over and down hills, across valleys, and around obstacles, it can evade radar detection. It is thought, however, that the cruise missile will be unable to find its way over homogeneous ground that is covered with snow. This is why the U.S. military has been testing the cruise missile over Canadian territory during the winter, in conditions similar to those it would encounter over the Soviet Union.

The cruise missile is very destabilizing for the arms control process. It is extremely small (only 21 feet long) and so can be hidden from satellite detection in haylofts, on trucks, and in sheds on the ground. It will also be dual-capable, able to carry either nuclear or conventional warheads. Therefore, when it is deployed on the ground in the European theater, in the air, or on surface ships and submarines, the Soviets will have no way to determine the number of American nuclear cruise missiles. Because of their extreme accuracy for hard-target "killing" capacity and because they will be undetectable by radar during flight, Defense Secretary Caspar Weinberger has defined them as strategic weapons, even though they travel at only half the speed of sound and will take several hours to reach their targets. These weapons can destroy the strategic arms control process, which depends upon absolute weapons verification and detection by both sides.

Air-launched cruise missiles will be carried by B-52s and B-1 bombers. Ground-launched cruise missiles have been deployed by the Air Force in Europe, starting in Britain in December 1983. Plans call eventually for 464 ground-launched cruise missiles to be placed in Belgium, Holland, England, Italy, and West Germany. Those in Sicily can also be targeted on the Middle East by the United States. Ground-launched cruise missiles fired from mobile launchers anywhere in Western Europe will be able to reach much of the western Soviet Union, with the ability to kill 40 percent of the Soviet population and destroy most of its industry. There are huge movements in each of these countries to prevent deployment.

The Air Force had planned to place 4,348 air-launched cruise missiles in its airplanes. In December 1982, it deployed its first batch of cruise missiles on 16 B-52 airplanes in Rome, New York. The Navy also plans to deploy 3,994 sea-launched cruise missiles, of which 758 will be nuclear-armed on 190 naval vessels—in attack submarines, cruisers, aircraft carriers, destroyers, and refurbished battleships. Any surface ship can be equipped to carry this versatile cruise missile. Neither the United States nor the USSR can know for sure how many will carry nuclear and how many conventional weapons. Already two old battleships have been taken out of mothballs and refitted to carry cruise missiles: The Navy would like to dock one of these ships, the *Iowa*, in an Eastern Seaboard harbor. It had suggested Boston, New York, or Rhode Island for this purpose but decided on New York after the New England congressional delegation influenced a very close MX vote in the House.

In mid-1983, the military curtailed plans to procure air-launched cruise missiles at 1,739 and instead announced that it wants to procure some 1,500 "stealth" cruise missiles. "Stealth" technology involves special aeronautical designs that decrease radar visibility and infrared detection, as well as special construction materials in the missile itself.

The Soviets, who are five years behind the United States in cruise-missile technology, are very concerned about this new weapon. Because cruise missiles could approach their homeland from so many different directions, adequate defense against them would be virtually impossible. They would be extremely difficult to detect because they fly so low and are so small, and if they are launched in large numbers—one plane launching 20 cruise missiles—the Soviet Union would have to deploy vast numbers of surface-to-air defense systems. As the military says, "Air-launched cruise missiles are expected to dilute Soviet defenses, facilitating their penetration, as well as that of manned bombers."

Apparently work also is proceeding on a supersonic, "interhemispheric" cruise missile, which will be capable of skimming the ground at supersonic speeds over long distances.

Pershing II

In December 1983, West Germany began to deploy 108 Pershing II missiles. These weapons are suitable for use in "decapitation," which the Pentagon Defense Guidance Plan describes as strikes at Soviet command centers. The Pershing II is an extremely accurate missile, with a 99 percent probability of destroying a command bunker or missile silo hardened to withstand blast pressures of 2,000 pounds per square inch (psi). President Reagan has said that it is being built to advance "the cause of peace and disarmament." In actuality, it lies at the heart of the U.S. first-strike counterforce system.

The Pershing II program will cost about $3 billion. The missiles are to be placed on modified trucks called "transporter-erector-launchers" (TEL). The Army signed a contract to continue their development before the funds had been approved by Congress.

The missile will be mounted with a single "selectable" nuclear warhead, which will permit the yield or power to be adjusted for varying targets. Yield will range from 10 to 80 kilotons (the Horoshima bomb was 12.5 kilotons). The low range will be used to destroy military or command targets and to limit "collateral" damage—that is, the killing of civilians—to adjoining areas. The Pershing II missile will have unprecedented accuracy and a maneuverable re-entry vehicle (MARV). An onboard computer will compare the target terrain to a reference map, giving a radar picture of the target area. The maps in cruise and Pershing II missiles were developed by the Defense Mapping Agency from highly sophisticated mapping satellites. (Arms experts in Washington generally agree that the cruise missile will deliver its hydrogen bomb to within 100 or 150 feet of the target.) Control vanes will then fly the warhead into the target. The CEP is expected to be 65 to 130 feet. The range of the missile is classified, but it is about 1,100 miles. A modest extension of this range would enable it to reach Moscow from West Germany, a distance of perhaps 1,200 miles. (One can assume that the locations of the command bunkers are known.) The flight time from West Germany to Moscow is very short—from six to eleven minutes. This fact lies at the heart of Soviet fears about the Pershing II. Theoretically it will give the

United States the capability of disrupting and destroying the Soviet National Command Authority, thus immobilizing Soviet ICBM forces until American ICBMs, cruise missiles, and even bombers can destroy them.

Because flight time is so short, detection by Soviet early-warning satellite systems will allow the Soviet command less than six minutes' notice before its command centers are destroyed. Less than six minutes is not enough time for human input into the decision loop. The Soviets have said that if Pershing II is deployed, they probably will use a launch-on-warning system, whereby the decision to launch nuclear war is made by computers. Since we did not elect politicians in November 1984 who would have ceased production and deployment of cruise and Pershing II missiles and removed those few already deployed, our world is technologically out of human control.

Many Europeans have been determined to prevent deployment of both ground-launched cruise missiles and Pershing IIs. But America controls the NATO alliance economically with an iron grip, as it does many Western nations. It is a subliminal policy of the United States to threaten trade with its allies if they do not comply with its military wishes. This is almost certainly happening now. When I visited Europe two years ago, I was shocked to discover that NATO was not really our "Western allies" but was, in fact, controlled and run by the U.S. government. Because the Reagan Administration recognized European concern over deployment, it mounted a public-relations campaign to convince the European people that ground-launched cruise missiles and Pershing IIs are good for them. To this end, Reagan employed Peter Dailey, his 1980-campaign advertising manager, to lead the effort to win backing for these missiles. William Clark, the president's former national security adviser, originally headed a planning group for this project. The group includes Secretary of State George Shultz, Secretary of Defense Caspar Weinberger, Director of the U.S. Information Agency Charles Wick, and Peter McPherson, administrator of the Agency for International Development. This group is intended to ensure better overall coordination of public-information policies to combat what one official called the "Soviet peace offensive" and to react better to such public-relations problems as the nuclear-freeze movement at home. NATO instigated its own public-relations campaign for the missiles in October 1981.

The B-1 Bomber

Ever since World War II, the Air Force has been attached to its strategic bomber force. Yet these planes, which would take from twelve to fourteen hours to reach the Soviet Union, have long been outdated by the ICBMs, which can reach the same targets in thirty minutes. The initial technology of the B-1 was designed in the 1960s, although much of its updated equipment was borrowed from more recent aircraft. At best, critics say, the B-1 is a jumble of military compromises, a flying white elephant that has stayed airborne through sheer momentum. The full flight test of the latest version of the B-1 took place in October 1984; if all goes well, the nation will have an operational fleet of a hundred bombers by the end of 1988. However, most people now agree that the B-1 is a decade late. It is intended to air-launch cruise missiles outside the perimeter of the Soviet air-defense mechanisms and apparently also is to be used as a device for signaling U.S. intentions. But America and the Soviet Union can easily pick up each other's preliminary moves with their sophisticated surveillance systems long before the B-1 has reached the Soviet Union. As one Air Force officer described it: "Sending a bomber to deliver such a message is rather like hand-delivering a telegram two days after the message has been phoned through." The USSR will have had time before the bomber arrives to launch one or perhaps two missile attacks. The B-1 is also to be used to bomb those silos that still contain unfired missiles or to target "cold-launch" silos, which are reloadable after the initial nuclear attack has been launched. In other words, it is a weapon for "postattack strike and reconnaissance."

A four-engine, swing-wing bomber roughly the size of a Boeing 707 and two thirds the size of a B-52, the B-1 is designed to fly at both subsonic and "transsonic" speeds and can reach 1.2 times the speed of sound. Its range without refueling is approximately 6,000 nautical miles, and it can carry twice the payload of the B-52, or twenty-two ALCMs—eight internally and fourteen under the fuselage. (It can also deliver twenty-four nuclear bombs.) It is designed for low-level penetration of enemy air space, from 100 to 300 feet above ground (which is below enemy radar), at high subsonic speeds. It is capable of very quick takeoff, as is the B-52. With sufficient warning, both the B-1 and the B-52 forces could survive a nuclear war by taking off early, but without such warning, they would be destroyed. Within a few years, as Soviet defenses become increasingly sophisticated, the B-1 would be subjected to attack from Soviet air-defense systems as it entered Soviet territory.

In 1977, President Carter canceled production of the B-1 because he decided it was not needed, but the Reagan team has decided to order every weapon on the shelf, including the B-1. It provides a bonanza for the contracting firms: a hundred bombers at a total program cost that could reach $40 billion, according to the Congressional Budget Office. The official cost of building the B-1s does not include replenishment of spare parts or the sophisticated ground-support equipment and training devices necessary to use them. Given its drawbacks, a 1977 Pentagon assessment of the B-1 found it unnecessary and recommended that the B-52 would be good "indefinitely." In the past, the Air Force reinforced its case for the B-1 by canceling improvements to the B-52 fleet and exaggerating the cost of maintaining them, although the improvements are now being made.

Despite these obvious flaws and the huge expense, the B-1 program has survived for twenty-one years because of an enormously intricate complex of contractors, subcontractors, and interest groups that have supported it. Even after President Carter decided to cancel the plane in 1977, Congress voted funds to build and test one more plane.

There has been little independent evaluation of the bomber or its mission since it was first proposed. Much of the "outside" analysis of the Soviet weaponry that the B-1 might have to face has been done by direct B-1 contractors or by think tanks, neither of them eager to destroy a bomber that they or their clients were determined to build.

Early cost overruns on the B-1 were not quickly corrected, and in some cases were reported to Congress only by independent watchdog agencies. Consequently, in 1974, only four years after the first development contract was signed, the General Accounting Office reported that the Air Force had reduced the performance requirements for the B-1 by 20 percent for maximum speed, 25 percent for internal missile payload, and 15 percent for takeoff distance.

After Carter canceled the B-1, he allowed Rockwell to continue to receive R&D funds to keep the "bomber option" alive. So Rockwell stored forty-three thousand pieces of specialized equipment and materials, such as titanium, in Air Force warehouses at government expense until Reagan gave it the go-ahead again. According to a former Rockwell employee, Bobby Witzezak, Rockwell also shaved costs on the B-1 program during the years when it received only R&D funds, by charging bomber costs to its Space Shuttle contract. In 1982, after a three-year FBI investigation, Rockwell had to pay $500,000 in compensatory damages to the government and spend $1 million for a computerized time-keeping system because of allegations that from 1975 to 1978 it had charged other work to its Space Shuttle contract.

In the mid-1970s, Rockwell spent tens of thousands of dollars on information and lobbying activities and on entertaining influential Pentagon officials at its goose-hunting lodge on Chesapeake Bay near Washington, D.C.

Lobbying in Congress over the years has focused on the idea that the B-1 would provide jobs and incomes to many congressional districts. During the lobbying campaign, the Air Force teamed up with the United Auto Workers, who were expected to get a big share of the jobs.

Grant Miller, a retired Air Force colonel who was a chief B-1 lobbyist for a decade, said,

> I had a list of every B-1 contract over $10,000, of the location of the contracts state by state, congressional district and town, and a map showing numbers of dollars and employees. We'd sit down, make assignments, [decide] who we needed to work on. We'd find out who had the most influence with that guy, and we'd get the Air Force Association or somebody to work. It was really an orchestrated effort.

This was only a small part of a huge machine that was supporting the B-1 bomber: Air Force officers whose careers were linked to a successful B-1 program, industry and government researchers and designers, the giant aerospace corporations led by Rockwell, plus all the fifty-two hundred subcontractors spread over forty-eight states, and the politicians in Congress, as well as White House and

Pentagon officials. (With so many different subcontractors making different components for the plane, I doubt that the plane will ever function adequately.)

Rockwell's B-1 revenues are predicted to reach $10 billion by 1987, with pretax profit margins at 15 percent.

The subcontractors include most of the heavyweights: Boeing, TRW, Westinghouse, General Electric, Goodyear, Singer, Sperry, Bendix, Vought, Martin Marietta, Northrop, Litton, IBM, Teledyne, Brunswick, AIL Division of Eaton, United Technologies, Kaman Aerospace, and others. Each of these major subcontractors has a Washington office and its own lobbyists. It can generate powerful coalitions of workers, union leaders, local businessmen, and government officials in home districts to pressure their congressional representatives.

Almost all of the major subcontractors have held seats in the past twenty years on either the Defense Science Board or the Air Force Scientific Advisory Board. These boards help assess the nature of the Soviet threat and help determine what weapons the United States needs in response. For example, Richard DeLauer, formerly top executive in TRW and, until recently, undersecretary of defense for research and engineering, was a member of the Defense Science Board when the B-1 was moving from concept toward production; and Assistant Secretary of Defense Richard M. Paul was a consultant to Boeing. A congressional staff aide who has studied the B-1 program said it is a closed club.

> A few years after a program like this gets started, there comes the consensus that the airplane absolutely must be built. The consensus is held by the believers. It doesn't matter really whether they're in industry or government or flow back and forth. There are two problems with this: One is that the program picks up tremendous forward momentum and probably nobody can stop it for whatever reason. The second is: Everybody wants his favorite widget built into the airplane, so the performance becomes compromised and the cost goes up.

Another former defense official said, "These people aren't disloyal; they just get blinders on and they see in the data what they want to see."

It is widely accepted in congressional and defense-industry

circles that companies often choose subcontractors or sites for new plants with politics or political influence in mind.

Rockwell has been extremely successful in spreading its B-1 subcontracts all over the country. This is not efficient, but it creates enormous lobbying power for jobs, money, etc. For example, of the prototype models already manufactured, the engines were made in Lynn, Massachusetts; the fan blades in Springfield, Ohio; the rudders in Bloomfield, Connecticut; the stabilizers in Baltimore; the actuators in Kalamazoo, Michigan; the wing-control surfaces in Tulsa; the tires in Akron; the parachute escape system in Des Plaines, Illinois; the secondary power subsystem in Melbourne, Florida; the windshields in Garden Grove, California; the avionics integration in Seattle; the radar altimeter in Minneapolis; and the seats in Denver.

In 1973, a list compiled by Rockwell showed B-1 subcontractors beside the names of nearly every member of the House and Senate Armed Services committees and Appropriations committees. This is the epitome of pork-barrel politics, for all these congresspeople feel pressured to vote for this lemon of a plane because of jobs and money in their districts.

Bureaucracy in government, industry, and outside think tanks also is part of this "old boy" supportive network: the analysts who assess the strategic threat, the accounting firms, the technicians who test the aircraft and equipment, and thousands of others. A similar story of intrigue, lobbying, and corruption has supported Lockheed's C-5B transport plane, which recently won acceptance by Congress, and also the MX missile.

The Stealth Bomber

This will be an even more sophisticated plane than the B-1 and is intended to carry gravity bombs and short-range attack missiles, although it still will take twelve to fourteen hours to reach the Soviet Union. It will feature the same kind of radar-evading materials as the stealth cruise missiles.

Competition among aerospace companies for the stealth contracts is fierce. Northrop has the stealth bomber contract (worth an estimated $30 billion); Lockheed has the stealth fighter contract; and General Dynamics has the stealth cruise missile contract. In fact, Lockheed and Rockwell joined forces to try to win the $25 billion contract for stealth aircraft and defeat Northrop. These two companies have already begun designing a stealth version of the B-1 to outmaneuver the Northrop stealth bomber. Northrop then said it would deliver its bombers in 1988, three years earlier than scheduled, to eliminate the need for the Rockwell-Lockheed B-1 stealth. (The first flight test has been set for 1987, but deployment is not scheduled until 1992.)

The last four weapons systems—cruise missiles, precision-guided Pershing II missiles, and B-1 and stealth bombers—are to be used to provide the intermediate links in what the Reagan strategists describe as the "seamless web of deterrence"—falling between conventional-warfare options and "execution of a single integrated operational plan" (SIOP)—that is, full-scale nuclear war.

The sea-launched cruise missiles will not be dedicated to the SIOP plan but will be part of the strategic reserve force and will be available for reconstitution and targeting if necessary during the post-SIOP period—that is, after the nuclear war. According to Admiral Frank B. Kelso, director of the Navy's Strategic Submarine Division, the submarine-launched cruise missiles could have been used as a partial substitute for the ground-launched cruise missiles in a European theater war if the peace movement had prevented GLCM deployment in Europe.

The Neutron Bomb or Enhanced Radiation Weapon

This revolting weapon was designed some twenty years ago by a man named Sam Cohen, who is known as the father of the neutron bomb. It is an ordinary hydrogen bomb with the outer layer of fissionable uranium removed, which reduces the blast but allows a huge flux of neutrons to emerge from the explosion. Typically, it has the explosion force of a 1-kiloton bomb but the radiation flux of a 10-kiloton bomb. It is to be used against invading Soviet tanks on the conventional battlefield. Although it does not destroy as much property as an ordinary H-bomb because of its decreased blast, the neutrons can penetrate structural material (including tanks) to kill people within.

The medical implications of this radiation are horrendous. Soldiers who are not killed initially by the nuclear blast will die from high doses of radiation within forty-eight hours. Symptoms include vomiting, severe headache, high fever, ataxia (inability to walk straight), delirium, stupor, and psychosis, although the victims may have a period of lucidity and normality some hours before death. Those who are farther from the very high dose of radiation will die two or three weeks later from acute radiation illness. They may feel normal for a week or two and then develop lassitude, bleeding spots under the skin and around the gums, vomiting and bloody diarrhea, and hair loss (alopecia), eventually to die days later of overwhelming septicemia or massive hemorrhage. Those on the periphery of the radiation field, some miles from the epicenter, will receive doses that will increase their risk of later developing leukemia or cancer. Babies and children are from ten to twenty times more susceptible to these effects than adults are. And obviously, given the population density on the European battlefield, civilians will be affected in greater numbers than will soldiers.

The Ninety-seventh Congress approved Reagan's decision to stockpile fully assembled "enhanced radiation-reduced blast" weapons for the 8-inch artillery projectile and for the Lance nuclear battlefield missile.

Tritium is the principal material for enhanced radiation-reduced warheads. Because there is a shortage of this radioactive isotope, the government has launched a major program to more than double the production of nuclear material. Since tritium decays at a rate of 5.5 percent per year, the neutron bombs will need periodic upgrading.

The government plans to build 380 Lance neutron warheads and as many as 925 neutron shells. Shells of 155 millimeters in diameter will cost $3 million each (compare this with the cost of $24,000 for a conventional Copperhead precision-guided 155-millimeter artillery shell). Total expenditure for these weapons—including the cost of increased production of radioactive material—could exceed $5 billion.

Enhanced radiation-reduced hydrogen bombs seem to be gaining favor in the nuclear-design community. At present, neutron bombs are but two of the twenty-six warhead types in the nuclear stockpile, but they will represent a larger percentage of the nuclear weapons to be produced in the mid-1980s.

The neutron bomb is a trip wire between conventional and nuclear war. As a battlefield weapon in Europe, it is considered more acceptable than an ordinary hydrogen bomb by some military people. Thus, because it blurs the distinction between conventional and nuclear weapons, it could induce nuclear war. The Soviets do not yet have these bombs; but if one nuclear weapon is used against them, they will retaliate with their entire nuclear arsenal.

New Conventional (Near-Nuclear) Weapons

Conventional bombs that are called "near-nuclear" weapons are now being built. They have the destructive potential of tactical nuclear weapons without the radiation and fallout. This "revolution" in conventional weapons began during the Vietnam War. It is now becoming fashionable as popular demand calls for a decrease in nuclear weapons to be balanced by an increase in conventional arms. Scientists are fascinated by these new projects and, of course, they are most lucrative for the manufacturers. The firms who manufacture these weapons are AVCO; Honeywell; General Dynamics; Vought; Martin Marietta; and French, British, and West German firms.

After the Vietnam War, U.S. and European arms firms developed these more sophisticated weapons for European or Middle Eastern battlefields. Their versatility was recently demonstrated by the French-made Exocet missile, which sank the British destroyer in the Falklands. Because the Nonproliferation Treaty does not apply to conventional weapons, they can and are being sold to countries in the Middle East, Africa, and other volatile Third World areas—for profit, of course.

Proposals call for these weapons to be delivered by Lance missiles and submarine-launched cruise missiles—making it impossible to differentiate nuclear from conventional weapons and thus destroying the prospects for adequate arms control treaties.

These nonnuclear weapons use clustered warheads incorporating large numbers of individually guided "submunitions" or bomblets. These can be dispersed over an area of one square mile or one hundred city blocks. Senator Sam Nunn of the Armed Services Committee stated: "They begin to approach the destructive potential of small-yield 2- to 3-kiloton battlefield nuclear weapons." The bomblets, using smart technology, are capable of seeking out enemy targets and exploding when they are within firing range. To advance the weapons' kill probability, military scientists have developed revolutionary explosives and warhead technologies. The most potent of these, called "fuel-air explosives" (FAE), dispense a cloud of highly volatile fuel—ethylene oxide, propylene oxide, or propane. When ignited, it produces a blast powerful enough to destroy entire city blocks. The Daisy Cutter in Vietnam, described as "the closest thing to a nuclear bomb," was one of these. Another is the "vacuum bomb," which was used by Israel in Beirut. The Pentagon now is producing even more dreadful explosives called "advanced fuel-air munitions." It is also developing self-forging fragments (SFF). These munitions are composed of discs of metal that form conical projectiles from the force of the explosion and that will tear human bodies apart, These weapons have a kill probability of 100 percent. The Defense Department recently sent a circular to many U.S. civilian hospitals, asking them to participate in the Civilian Military Contingency Hospital System (CMCHS). It advised that "Future large-scale war overseas will probably produce casualties at a higher rate than any other war in history."

Submunitions will be loaded onto artillery shells, guided bomb units, and surface-to-surface and air-to-surface missiles with advanced guidance systems. These missiles will deliver the weapons deep into "enemy" territory far behind the front lines. One of the guided missiles, the Assault Breaker, is capable of destroying airfields and tank formations. It is viewed by the Reagan Administration as one of its three top-priority armaments together with the MX and the B-1 bomber.

These dreadful weapons obviously will make escalation to nuclear war *more* likely. The Soviets, who always copy and follow, will build them, too. Any future conventional war fought in Europe is likely to produce such high levels of death and destruction that the other side may feel compelled to retaliate with tactical nuclear weapons. And there will be no way for the Soviets to differentiate between a nuclear or a "near-nuclear" cruise or Lance missile in flight. Many experts believe these bombs violate the Geneva conventions, which ban the use of especially cruel and indiscriminate weapons.

Rapid Deployment Force

Since the Middle East oil crisis, the U.S. military has been preparing the Rapid Deployment Force for use not just in the Persian Gulf but also in the Middle East, Korea, South Asia, Europe, and anywhere else around the globe. To this end, it is expanding at every level. The Army is going from 16 divisions to 18; the Air Force is growing from 36 tactical air wings to 40; and the number of officers in both increased from 279,747 in 1981 to 298,829 in 1984.

These forces plan to use conventional, nuclear, chemical, and possibly biological weapons as necessary in what is called the "integrated battlefield." The units are termed "dual-capable"— nuclear or nonnuclear. To this end, two squadrons of 28 B-52 bombers with refueling and reconnaissance planes have been designated by SAC for Rapid Deployment Force planning. Each B-52 can drop 70,000 pounds of conventional explosives per sortie or a range of thermonuclear bombs. Because these B-52s need a forward operating location, airports are being constructed or expanded by the United States at Diego Garcia in the Indian Ocean, Ras Banas in Egypt, Thamit in Oman, and in Saudi Arabia and Morocco. Also, three carrier battle groups are stationed in the Indian Ocean and the eastern Mediterranean and are loaded with hundreds of various kinds of nuclear weapons allocated to the RDF.

To threaten the use of the Rapid Deployment Force in the Persian Gulf is ludicrous when it supplies only 5 percent of total U.S. energy needs and 13 percent of U.S. oil needs. And the Soviet Union, a net exporter of oil, does not need the Persian Gulf oil. Undoubtedly the U.S. emphasis on "security access" to the Persian Gulf is intended to protect U.S. energy companies in the processing and global marketing of Persian Gulf oil, and European access to the oil. For this, the U.S. military and political leadership may be prepared to start a nuclear war.

The Army has prepared for the RDF a new war-fighting doctrine called Air-Land Battle. This doctrine promotes small nuclear-equipped forces as a rapidly deployable substitute for larger, conventionally armed forces. It says the U.S. forces should conduct "rapid unpredictable violent attacks" and comes close to calling for pre-emptive nuclear strikes. It also recommends that, when using the new near-nuclear weapons (or, in fact, nuclear weapons), targets be struck 75 to 100 miles inside enemy territory. Presumably this will ensure that the radiation and blast effects kill only enemy troops and civilians and spare the U.S. forces. The Air-Land Battle plan describes the Middle East and Southwest Asia as "a land of turmoil, terror, violence, and bloodshed." It suggests that if nuclear weapons are used, they be used early and in depth. Many of the "battlefield" nuclear weapons recommended range from 60 to 400 kilotons. Plans include the use of neutron bombs as well. The commanders are directed to "operate without interruption," even after the enemy launches nuclear or chemical attack, and to fight on even with "contaminated personnel and equipment" despite the "large number of personnel casualties and much damage to equipment, as well as psychological stress on an unprecedented scale." The Army is even talking about "preclearance" for use of nuclear weapons—making it unnecessary to ask the National Command Authority before it uses them.

America is driven to achieve strategic superiority over the USSR through construction of the MX, Trident II, Pershing II, and cruise missiles, and the B-1 and stealth bombers. We are in a position potentially to intervene anywhere in the world with impunity while threatening the Soviet Union with a first strike. Theoretically, the Soviet Union will then not interfere with our global pursuits. But at what cost?

Why It Is Not Possible to Keep a Nuclear War Limited

The basic tenet of a limited nuclear war is itself crazy. Even with careful planning, targeting, and execution, intending to target only military facilities in order to reduce collateral damage (that is, deaths of civilians), is it possible that the attacked country would accept the deaths of only three million people, as opposed to twenty million people? The response of an attacked country could lead to all-out nuclear war. The U.S. 1984–88 Defense Guidance for limited protracted, winnable nuclear war is based on this assumption. The Soviet strategic commentators have *never* seriously considered the possibility of controlled or limited nuclear war. They say any attacks will lead to simultaneous and massive unconstrained attacks upon a wide range of U.S. targets, including the Command, Control, Communications, and Intelligence System (C^3I).

The most fundamental tenet of Soviet strategic doctrine is to deter nuclear war. To this end, they believe the better their forces are equipped to wage a nuclear war, the more effective they will be as a deterrent to a nuclear attack on the USSR.

For thirty-eight years, the nuclear doctrine of the United States has been to attack the Soviet Union first with nuclear weapons if the United States disapproves of any Soviet-invoked international incident or war. Until the late 1960s when the Soviet Union deployed survivable weapons in large numbers, the United States had the nuclear monopoly. Now there is strategic parity or equality in intercontinental killing power.

Soviet targeting doctrine states that as soon as the Soviet Union confirms that a nuclear attack is under way, its bombers and ICBMs will take off even before the U.S. bombs land on their homeland. They will retaliate with massive blows against U.S. military and political administrative resources in order to frustrate and damage U.S. military operations and thus minimize damage to the Soviet Union.

Such a Soviet attack would likely target all C^3I and military installations, which are scattered ubiquitously throughout the continental United States; all government centers and places where political leadership is concentrated; and all major economic and industrial facilities. (Power stations, which obviously include the seventy-nine nuclear reactors, are perhaps the single most important nonmilitary targets in Soviet war planning.) Targets include stocks of strategic raw materials, oil refineries and storage sites, metallurgical plants, chemical industries, and transport operations (railroads and yards, bridges, tunnels, ports, and vessels in the water). Urban centers are not to be attacked in pursuit of some arbitrary minimum level of fatalities, but neither are they to be avoided if they are near military, political, or industrial targets.

The Soviets totally reject controlled escalation and limited nuclear war. Of these ideas Georgi Arbatov, head of the U.S.-Canadian Institute, wrote: "In actual fact, these proposals are an attempt to lull public opinion and to make the prospect of nuclear war more accessible, or, if you like, more digestible."

The very idea of introducing "rules of the game" and of artificial limitations by agreement is based on an illusion. It is hard to imagine that nuclear war, if launched, could be held within the framework of the "rules and not grow into general nuclear war." In 1980, Chairman Brezhnev reiterated these sentiments after President Carter released Presidential Directive 59. They reflect overwhelmingly the bulk of Soviet military literature.

Although the Soviet Union has developed an impressive array of C^3I facilities, these facilities are weakest in the capabilities to control nuclear war fighting—that is, the capacity for timely intelligence, attack characterization, and damage assessment via satellite detection, and retargeting flexibilities.

So what have American scientists and military strategists been up to for the past several decades? They are desperately dreaming up schemes in which they might be able to use their nuclear weapons in some limited way without provoking massive genocide. This is schizoid thinking.

To reduce the CEP of the Minuteman III with a MARK 12-A warhead of 335 kilotons in order to reduce collateral damage or deaths of people is ludicrous thinking. A limited attack on the Soviet oil supply would kill from 836,000 to 1.46 million people and injure up to 3.8 million more. An equivalent Soviet attack on the U.S. petroleum centers could destroy 64 percent of U.S. refining capacity and kill from 3.2 to 5.03 million people.

A Soviet counterforce or first-strike attack against the U.S. ICBM silos would kill from 800,000 to 50 million people. Such an attack would also involve destruction of ballistic-missile submarines, support facilities, C^3I centers, and the 18 SAC bomber bases. A similar U.S. counterforce nuclear war, targeting Soviet military facilities only, would cause 26.5 to 27.7 million deaths. A "comprehensive" U.S. counterattack could well double these numbers.

By way of comparison, all the wars the United States has fought in the past two hundred years have caused fewer than 1.2 million U.S deaths (World War II, 291,557 deaths; Korea, 33,629; and Vietnam, 46,558). The United States has suffered *no* civilian casualties since the Civil War. The Soviet Union lost 20 million people in World War II, not within the first couple of hours, but over a four-year period.

But these estimates are fundamentally inaccurate. The official casualty estimates of nuclear war are based only on blast and fallout and fail to include long-term cancer deaths from fallout, to say nothing of deaths from fire, burns, epidemics, starvation, lack of medical care, ozone destruction, cooling of the temperature of the earth, and many other variables. Consequently, the range of death estimates related to counterforce nuclear war could be twenty times larger. The counterforce attack could well become a countervalue attack—that is, an attack on civilians.

Various U.S. officials have testified that the United States does not target civilian areas but does target "industrial sites that are colocated with population centers." By virtue of associated industrial and military targets, the United States has targeted all of the 200 largest Soviet cities and 80 percent of their 886 cities with populations above 25,000. Many of these cities would receive more than 10 hydrogen bombs. Moscow alone would receive 60, and peak overpressures throughout central Moscow would be so severe (greater than 100 pounds per square inch) that not a building or tree would be left standing.

If the United States were to attack the Soviet Union using all the targets included in SIOP (Single Integrated Operational Plan, which locates 40,000 significant targets in the USSR)—and if it were to avoid population centers per se—it still would ensure the destruction of 50 to 100 million people and the injury of 30 million more. It would destroy up to 90 percent of major Soviet political and leadership facilities, up to 50 percent of other military targets, and up to 90 percent of Soviet manufacturing capacity.

The numbers are obscene. Nuclear weapons explode with the force of the energy of the stars; to imagine that they can be used in a precise and discriminate fashion is fantasy.

As the Department of Defense said in a 1974 report to Congress: "The uncertainties in known nuclear phenomena and weapons system performance, let alone those associated with discoveries which may be made at some future date, must certainly raise serious questions as to the predictability and controllability of nuclear warfare."

Yet the Reagan Administration plans to invest $18 billion to provide a C^3I system that could endure a protracted, winnable nuclear war conducted over a six-month period. One observer on the Reagan staff commented about this scheme, "We've been working on this C^3I problem for five years now and can report that the system might survive fifteen minutes of nuclear war."

Physical Examination

I always cringe when people extol the wonders of high technology as if it is the answer to all our needs. It is obvious to me that most people have absolutely no idea what the term really means. The most creative research in the field is conducted by scientists in universities, weapons labs, and industries that are involved with the military. The technology has become so extraordinarily sophisticated that satellites from space can now photograph license plates on earth. They can also monitor radio, telephone, and other communications in the Soviet Union and elsewhere. The whole world is wired up like a ticking time bomb, ready to explode with only a thirty-minute warning.

One frightening aspect of the high-tech revolution is the video-game industry that has captivated our children. Many of these computer games condition our offspring from a very early age to the prospect of nuclear war. They are particularly attractive to boys of all ages (girls, in general, seem less fascinated).

When President Reagan addressed two thousand high-school students in Orlando, Florida, in March 1983, he praised the use of video games for children. He said to a cheering crowd,

> Many young people have developed incredible hand-eye-brain coordination playing these games. The Air Force believes these kids will be outstanding pilots should they fly our jets. Watch a twelve-year-old take evasive action and score multiple hits while playing Space Invaders, and you will appreciate the skills of tomorrow's pilots.

The military have also echoed these sentiments. Not only are our children being brainwashed to accept the concept of nuclear war, apparently they are also being trained to be able to fight one.

Here is some public-relations copy taken from the pamphlet advertising Star Path video games for children:

> *Communist Mutants from Space:* Your mission: Vaporize the mutant warriors before they overrun your home planet. These Commie Mutants are crazy! Wipe out wave after wave of them, and they keep on coming. The more you vaporize, the meaner they get. Well . . . You've got a few tricks up your sleeve, too. The "Shields" option lets you deflect their bombs with a tug on the joy stick. "Time Warp" lets you gain back lost ground, when necessary. "Penetrating Missiles" and "Guided Missiles" lets you mow them down in style, but the real trick is to keep your planet safe for democracy without using any special features. Up to four can play and the screen keeps track of the highest scores just to make sure the heroes get the recognition they deserve.

> *Killer Satellites:* Your mission: Zap this orbiting junkyard of satellites before they knock your hometown back to the Stone Age. You're the one defender. Test pilot of the only rocket plane that can intercept and outmaneuver this deadly rain of molten metal. Now you're low on fuel and ammo, but watch out when you land. Touch down in an ocean and you're up the creek. And that leaves the Big Apple a pancake.

These games are not wholly fantasy. In 1983, a bill was introduced in Congress, sponsored by Senator Bill Armstrong and Representative Ken Kramer, Republicans of Colorado, called the People Protection Act. It has five major provisions. (1) to turn the new Air Force Space Command into an overall space command for all armed forces; (2) to create an Army command under it for ground-based air and anti-missile defense weapons; (3) to establish a single agency for directed-energy weapons, such as lasers, microwaves, and particle beams; (4) to take military missions of the Space Shuttle away from NASA's responsibility for exclusive Pentagon control; and (5) to order NASA to launch a manned space station as soon as possible (President Reagan suggested this in his 1984 State of the Union address).

The Air Force Space Command believes war in space is inevitable, that fighting in space will be "the decisive form of military power," and that the United States will win if it hurries. In the summer of 1983, the Soviet Union suggested negotiating a ban on military force in or from space. Our administration has ignored this offer. According to Flora Lewis of *The New York Times*, the Space Command planners want to restore "preatomic notions of military superiority" and to "make conflict at the upper levels of military violence [nuclear attack] again thinkable." They think this would be an "invigorating turn of events for the spiritual vitality of the Western democracies."

The success of films such as *Star Wars* also reflects society's insidious acceptance of high-tech war in space. The research and development of high-tech weapons is not far behind these fantasies.

I remember when the first Space Shuttle landed after a successful mission. Thousands of Americans turned out to celebrate its landing, as they once turned out with picnic lunches to gaze at the wonders of atmospheric nuclear explosions. People carried signs reading "We're Number One Again." The Space Shuttle has become a largely military operation, so that now more than one-third of all Space Shuttle flights will be funded by the Pentagon and reserved for military missions. It is used to launch antisatellite platforms and other contributions to war in space—which, of course, is internationally banned by the Weapons in Outer Space Treaty signed by the superpowers. The Space Shuttle crew will be trained to use wire-cutting pliers to remove a satellite's power cells and render it inoperative. Astronauts could also attach a limpet mine to a satellite's hull and use telemetry to detonate it. During a typical seven-day mission, an American Space Shuttle could destroy up to twelve Soviet satellites.

According to White House science adviser Dr. George Keyworth, the Space Shuttle will be necessary for the transportation and integration of a future space-based ballistic-missile defense system. The Space Shuttle has four potential military functions: (1) to carry into orbit the Defense Support Program 647 early-warning satellites, the U.S. Air Force Defense Satellite Communications System's Phase III satellites, the Fleetsatcom Fleet Satellite Communications System satellites, Defense meteorological satellites, long-wavelength infrared surveillance sensors, and even laser weapons; (2) to provide in-orbit servicing and refurbishment of low-altitude military satellites; (3) to retrieve defunct but still highly sensitive satellites; and (4) as a test bed for various new technologies.

In June 1983, President Reagan previewed a new MGM film called *WarGames*, about an adolescent boy who plugs his home computer into the NORAD system and almost sets off World War III. Reagan was discussing his MX policy with a group of congressmen in the White House after the screening when suddenly his face lit up, and out of the blue he started describing the movie. One of the congressmen reported later, "I was sitting there so worried about throw weight, and Reagan suddenly asks us if we have seen *WarGames*. He was in a very good humor. He said, 'I don't understand these computers very well, but this young man obviously did. He had tied into NORAD.'"

In the age of high-tech nuclear war, this lack of knowledge about computers is a most serious admission for the commander-in-chief to have voiced. Ultimate authority for the release of nuclear weapons rests with the president. It derives from his constitutional position as commander-in-chief in accordance with the Atomic Energy Act of 1947. In practice, this authority is exercised jointly by the president and the secretary of defense. They are described as the National Command Authority (NCA). The chain of command for the actual execution of nuclear war should go from the NA through the chairman of the Joint Chiefs of Staff to the executing commander, as defined in 1971. In operations involving strategic nuclear weapons or in a crisis situation, the president may bypass the Joint Chiefs and perhaps even the senior commanders in the field and communicate directly with the commander on the spot. However, the chain must include the secretary of defense and the chairman of the Joint Chiefs of Staff. This arrangement was reconfirmed by Secretary of Defense Schlesinger in the last traumatic days of the Nixon Administration to ensure that Nixon could not mobilize any U.S. military forces without the consent of Schlesinger himself and the chairman of the Joint Chiefs of Staff, General George Brown.

Because the system to control and conduct nuclear war is

composed of the most complex technology that man has ever devised, it would seem mandatory that the person in control have at least a working knowledge of the system.

Caspar Weinberger, secretary of defense, displays a similar lack of in-depth knowledge about nuclear weapons and the supportive technology behind them.

Material for the following section has been obtained from Desmond Ball in *Can Nuclear War be Controlled?* and *A Suitable Piece of Real Estate.*

The Command, Control, Communications, and Intelligence system, known as C^{3}I, will determine the future of life on our planet. The system has two functions. *Intelligence* assesses all aspects of Soviet weapons systems, monitors a Soviet attack, and determines the extent of Soviet damage after a nuclear war. *Command, Control, and Communications* does precisely what its name implies. It controls and communicates with all the U.S. strategic, tactical, and conventional weapons and forces and with all the Allied forces before, during, and after a war.

Command

In the event of the deaths of the president and the secretary of defense, well-defined lines of succession maintain a viable National Command Authority (NCA). From the president, the succession of command follows the constitutional succession of presidential authority: the vice president, the Speaker of the House of Representatives, the president pro tempore of the Senate, and all the members of the Cabinet, from the secretary of state to the secretary of education. In the case of the secretary of defense, the succession proceeds as follows: deputy secretary of defense, secretary of the Army, secretary of the Navy, secretary of the Air Force, director of defense research and engineering, assistant secretary of defense, and the general counsel of the department of Defense (in order of their length of service as such); the undersecretaries of the Army, Navy, and Air Force (in order of their length of service as such). The highest-ranking survivor would continue to run the government, approve the victory or surrender terms, and marshal the surviving resources for a post-attack recovery. Apparently several thousand preselected bureaucrats belong to some thirty federal agencies deemed "essential" and "uninterruptable," which would also be necessary for post attack recovery, according to a series of executive orders dating back to 1969. These include the U.S. Postal Service and the Railroad Retirement Board. This whole effort to ensure the continuity of government (COG) entails saving government officials in the event of nuclear war.

Two agencies are responsible for the bulk of COG planning and financing—the Defense Department and the Federal Emergency Management Agency (FEMA), an institution created in 1979 by consolidating several small emergency-related agencies. More taxpayer money is being invested in this effort than in saving the lives of 220 million taxpayers and their families. The money for this program is allocated under a category called Federal Preparedness, for which the estimated budget in 1983 was $115 million. (In 1981, after President Carter enunciated Presidential Directive 58, ordering redoubled emphasis on the COG program, the budget was only $7 million.) When interviewed in May 1983, Pentagon spokespeople would not discuss COG or its funding, saying it is all classified. There is little congressional oversight of COG programs and funding. The congressional Armed Services committees are involved in the authorization programs. Appropriations are made primarily by independent subcommittees. All of this work is done in closed sessions.

Apparently some government officials are to be protected in a series of underground and aboveground shelters, including a massive bunker that reportedly has two thousand cots near Mount Weather, close to Berryville, Virginia. Yet most of these sites were built more than twenty years ago, and none would likely survive direct or nearby hits.

One might ask, Who authorizes the government to decide who lives or dies in a nuclear war? It seems ironic that those very people who have planned and equipped the nation to fight a nuclear war are themselves planning to survive it. Because a full-scale nuclear war could certainly threaten most human life in North America, let alone the world, this type of survival planning by an elite is, in fact, a form of unintended eugenics. Are they carriers of the genetic material that society would deem suitable to survive? This is a question that begs an answer in a democratic society.

The National Command Authority and its subordinates would be quickly taken to a secret command post near Washington. In 1954, the command facility was located some distance from Washington, at Fort Ritchie, Maryland; this reinforced-concrete-hardened center is known as the Alternate National Military Command Center (ANMCC). In 1961, Secretary of Defense Robert McNamara decided to convert three special communications KC-135 tanker aircraft to serve as the National Emergency Airborne Command Post (NEACP, pronounced *kneecap*). The old planes have since been replaced by four E-4Bs, which are converted Boeing 747s. These airborne command posts bear primary responsibility for providing the link between the NCA and the subordinate commands and strategic forces in nuclear war.

Obviously, neither the White House nor the National Military Command Center (NMCC) in the Pentagon is designed to survive a direct nuclear strike. Any comprehensive Soviet attack would target both these facilities and the underground ANMCC. Therefore, the survival of the NCA depends upon its ability to reach the specially equipped plane and be safely airborne by the time the Soviet hydrogen bombs hit Washington. Until recently, the NEACP plane was based at Andrews Air Force Base in Maryland, ten miles southeast of the White House. Now it is maintained at Grissom Air Force Base in Indiana, which will render this whole scenario impossible.

It is generally assumed that a Soviet attack against Washington and the C^3I centers would involve the use of submarine-launched ballistic missiles, which, if launched from offshore submarines, could take from five to ten minutes to hit their targets. But the helicopter ride from the White House to Andrews Air Force Base typically takes eight minutes, and there usually is not a helicopter based at the White House. In addition, it would take several minutes for the president and his military aide to be picked up. Nor would NEACP necessarily be ready to take off. In the winter, Andrews Air Force Base can be covered with snow (once, when Defense Secretary Brown was urgently called back to the White House from the Middle East during the Iranian crisis, it took four hours to clear a runway there of snow).

Since any dedicated Soviet attack would doubtless include all airports near Washington where a 747 could land or take off, NEACP would obviously be slated for destruction. Dr. William Perry of the Pentagon testified in March 1979: "The availability of this aircraft cannot be unconditionally guaranteed."

The continuity of leadership would be difficult to manage in any case. If the president were killed in a nuclear attack on Washington, many of the most important people in the chain of command, at the White House or the Pentagon or in the immediate environs, would probably be killed, too. Those on vacation or away for other reasons might be impossible to find. As Admiral Jerry Miller, former deputy director of the Joint Strategic Target Planning Staff (JSTPS), testified in March 1976, the United States "might have considerable difficulty in executing a retaliatory strike in the event of the death of the president."

Under the best of circumstances, the execution of a retaliatory strike is unlikely to involve much control. The new American leader is liable to be ignorant of the arguments or arcane logic of nuclear strategy and apt to accept the recommendations of the military leaders. Political judgments and subtlety about the conduct of the war are unlikely to survive the death of the true national leader. This death itself would elicit extreme and probably irrational demands for all-out retaliation if, indeed, they had not existed before.

Control

The means by which the NCA and subordinates direct the U.S. armed forces are provided by the Worldwide Military Command and Control System. This system, known also as WWMCC (pronounced *wimmex*), is a network of command posts, computers, and communications links established in 1962 "to provide the constituted authorities with the information needed for accurate and timely decisions and the reliable communications needed to transmit these decisions to the military forces under all conditions of peace and war."

The number of personnel dedicated to the strategic command and control capability is impossible to estimate precisely, but probably twenty-five thousand to thirty thousand people are involved. The budget to support this activity ranges from $2 billion to $2.5 billion a year.

The WWMCC system currently consists of thirty-five computers at twenty-six command posts around the world. It has six functions:

- assessment of the situation
- tactical warning (warning of impending nuclear war)
- briefing of the NCA, and then selection of options by these leaders
- execution of a selected option of nuclear war
- assessment after the attack of strikes and damage in the enemy country
- termination of a previously transmitted order—that is, stopping the war

Each of these functions requires extensive communication between WWMCC and a wide range of other systems and organizations, including the White House Communications Agency, the NATO Command and Control System, the Tactical Command and Control systems, and various intelligence collection and assessment systems.

One of the most important components of WWMCC is the National Military Command System (NMCS), which consists of the national-level command centers and the communications facilities linking them to intelligence systems and other subordinate command centers. The NMCS has three principal components:

The National Military Command Center (NMCC) is in the Pentagon and occupies seventy-eight thousand square feet of the second and third floors. It is the hub of both routine and crisis command capability, including the event of strategic nuclear war. The "hot line" between Washington and Moscow is housed here, but no special measures have been taken to protect the NMCC, and the House Armed Services Committee concluded in 1977 that "there is little possibility that the NMCC would survive a nuclear attack directed against it."

The Alternate National Military Command Center (ANMCC), underground at Fort Ritchie, Maryland, is seventy-five miles from

Washington. Because this center would not survive a "dedicated" nuclear attack, a backup for ANMCC has been built at the Federal Civil Defense Administration's main relocation site at Mount Weather, Virginia, but it is no less vulnerable than Fort Ritchie. All communications from the NMCC to the worldwide forces are routed through the ANMCC to permit spontaneous control at Fort Ritchie, if necessary—that is, if the Pentagon is destroyed and Fort Ritchie is not.

The National Emergency Command Post (NEACP) consists of several E-4Bs Advanced Airborne National Command Post aircraft at Andrews Air Force Base, Maryland, as previously described.

The NMCS is backed by the National Military Command System Support Center, also in the Pentagon. This facility, which is also unprotected against a nuclear attack on the Pentagon, supports the automatic data processing, computer display, and display distribution systems for the operation of the NMCS and prepares and disseminates appraisals and analyses of attack hazards and of the vulnerability of forces and resources on a worldwide basis.

Effective, efficient command and control depend totally upon surveillance, warning, and assessment systems, which provide data and intelligence information to the command systems. The systems have various components:

Satellites: The Defense Support Program (DSP) is the most important component of the early-warning system, designed to detect a ballistic-missile attack from the Soviet Union itself or its submarines. The DSP consists of three Code 647 satellites in geostationary orbit (that is, the satellite's orbital speed matches the speed of the earth's rotation, allowing it to "hover" over one area of the earth).

These satellites provide full coverage of all potential areas of ICBM and SLBM launchings. One is stationed over the Eastern Hemisphere to provide first warnings of a Soviet or Chinese missile launch, and two are stationed over the Western Hemisphere to monitor submarine-launched ballistic missiles off the East and West coasts of the United States. These satellites would give a twenty-five- to thirty-minute warning of an ICBM attack, and a ten- to fifteen-minute warning of a submarine-launched ballistic-missile attack. The warnings are relayed from satellites to ground stations in Australia and Buckley, Colorado; to NORAD; to SAC headquarters near Omaha, Nebraska; to the NMCC in Washington; and probably to the Situation Room in the White House.

The satellites' principal mechanism for detaching a missile launch is a 1-meter Schmidt infrared telescope, which can sense the energy emitted by ballistic-missile exhausts during the flights' powered stage. The satellites also carry detonation detectors, as well as ultraviolet sensors, which can identify the fluorescence from gases surrounding the boosters or nose cones during ballistic flights.

To complement the infrared and ultraviolet sensors, the 647 satellite also carries a visible-light sensor—a television-camera device that enables observers at ground stations in Australia and the United States to observe the plumes of ICBMs as they are launched and rise above the atmosphere. In addition to its early-warning function, the infrared equipment on the 647 satellite can be used for postattack intelligence information by monitoring warhead impact points in the Soviet Union, China, or elsewhere.

Velas, a separate class of satellites, are equipped with sensors that can detect and assess nuclear explosions by monitoring nuclear particles, gamma rays, X rays, and electromagnetic pulses. This equipment is designed to monitor and gather specific data on Soviet, Chinese, and French nuclear tests and to assess damage after nuclear war.

Radar: Verification of a satellite early warning would be provided ten minutes later by (1) the backscatter, over-the-horizon (OTH) radar system, located on the East Coast and at two West Coast sites; (2) the Ballistic Missile Early Warning System (BMEWS) at radar stations in Thule, Greenland; Clear, Alaska; and Flyingdales, England; (3) Perimeter Acquisition Radar Characterization System (PARCS), the upgraded Safeguard antiballistic missile radar at Grand Forks, North Dakota; and (4) Cobra Dane, a large-phased radar at Shemya Island, Alaska, near the end of the Aleutian Islands chain.

These radars can track the missiles and can help predict impact points. To detect submarine-launched ballistic missiles, the early-warning DSP satellites in the Western Hemisphere are complemented by PAVE PAWS phased-array radar stations on Cape Cod in Massachusetts, at Beale Air Force Base in California, at Eglin Air

Force Base in Florida, and at two other facilities under construction—Robins Air Force Base in Georgia and Goodfellow Air Force Base in Texas.

Intelligence Monitoring: Some early warning and attack assessments could be provided by Signals Intelligence sources, which include some 2,000 signals-intercept ground stations around the world, electronic intelligence and communications intelligence satellites in low orbit, and Signals Intelligence derived from the Rhyolite electronic intelligence geostationary satellites. These sources could detect and provide early warning of launch commands for ICBMs in the Soviet Union or China, scrambling orders for strategic bombers to take off, or communications related to attack preparations.

Most of these data and intelligence related to early-warning, midattack, or postattack activities are relayed to NORAD, SAC headquarters, the NMCC in the Pentagon, and the Situation Room in the White House.

Communications Systems

In order to transmit the vast amount of data from the systems just discussed to the Command and Control centers, an enormous and extremely vulnerable network of global communications has been established under the Defense Communications Agency (DCA). It is all controlled by the WWMCC system, which integrates some forty-three different communications systems and enables any emergency action message to be sent from the NMCC in the Pentagon to U.S. military forces. The communications network includes underwater cables, land lines, satellite relay systems, and radio systems across the entire radio-frequency spectrum from extremely-low frequency (ELF) to ultrahigh frequency (UHF). Much of this network is part of the Defense Communications Systems (DCS), which includes six hundred facilities, dozens of satellites, more than a hundred satellite ground terminals, and well over fifty-thousand individual circuits measuring thirty million miles.

The 494-L Emergency Rocket Communication System (ERCS) is intended for use after most communications methods have been destroyed. Apparently ten Minutemen II missiles are equipped with UHF radio transmitters instead of warheads; when all other communications with the forces have been destroyed, these missiles will be launched. During their thirty-minute trajectory they will communicate with TACAMO aircraft, which will communicate in turn with the submarines (but only if the submarines trail a radio receiver just below the water, exposing them to detection and attack). The only message these radios are programmed to give is to launch everything left. This final backup system is actually placed in the most vulnerable part of the ICBM force. It has no part to play in a controlled escalation and can only order a massive, last-ditch response.

Control of the weapons systems on ICBMs, bombers, and submarines is maintained by a very complex system of technical safeguards, organizations, and operational procedures. These are designed to ensure that a command to launch missiles or bombers will be received, authenticated, and acted upon promptly and responsibly and that nuclear war cannot be launched accidentally or without proper authority.

Checks and safeguards are inherent in every strategic system. Throughout the chain of command, from top to bottom, two or more men are always required to communicate about and cooperate in giving and receiving launching signals. In theory, this ensures that no one person could launch a nuclear war. Yet a retired admiral recently told me that no system is so fail-safe that an intelligent person could not bypass it in order to start a nuclear war.

The control system includes:

Long-Range Strategic Bomber Force: In order to activate this force, the attack and targeting order from the National Command Authority has to be authenticated by several levels of command at SAC headquarters before being given to the bomber crew. All commands must be positive; if at any stage of the attack the crew does not receive appropriate orders, radio signals, or other communications, it must return to base. From the outset, each part of the operation must be carried out carefully by two men, usually working independently of each other.

ICBMs, Minutemen: These missiles are assigned to strategic missile wings made up of strategic missile squadrons. The squadrons, each of which is allocated 50 missiles, are then divided into flights of ten missiles. Each flight is controlled by a launch-control facility manned by two officers working underground. They monitor the day-to-day operational status and security of the ten missiles, and they will take action when they receive a launch order. After they receive the "go code," the two officers check the validity and authenticity of the message and prepare the missiles for launch. To fire, each officer must insert a key into his own launch console. The consoles are separated by several feet, and both keys must be turned simultaneously and held in position for several seconds. Before the missiles can be launched, two other launch-control officers at another center have to insert their keys as well. Any launch-control center can nullify a launch entered by a single launch-control center acting independently of the squadron.

Submarine-Launched Ballistic Missiles: The operational control of submarines in the Atlantic is administered by the commander-in-chief of the U.S. Atlantic Command headquartered in northern Virginia. This authority passes down through the commander-in-chief of the U.S. Atlantic Fleet to the commander of the submarine forces, U.S. Atlantic Fleet, for administrative control. The operational control of Pacific submarines is administered by the commander-in-chief, U.S. Pacific Command, in Hawaii. His subordinates parallel those of the Atlantic command.

As with bombers and ICBMs, two men at each level are required to launch the submarine-launched ballistic missiles. The submarine has a two-man message-verification team (made up of commissioned officers) that confirms receipt of a launch message. Once a verified message has been received, the captain will open the lock on a red "fire button," thus beginning a carefully coordinated launch sequence that would involve several different individuals at various stations on the boat. To launch an SLBM, four officers in different parts of the submarine have to turn keys or throw switches—the navigation officer, the captain, the launch-control officer, and the missile-launch officer. Each switch indicates "Ready to Launch" and does not imply permission. But if, in time of emergency, the submarine cannot communicate back to NORAD or the NCA, no physical reason prevents a submarine commander from launching his missiles alone.

Intelligence

Intelligence obtained from satellites and relayed to ground stations is used to identify Soviet military movements and production of weapons, to obtain detailed information from observing weapons testing and launch orders, and to observe Soviet territory after a nuclear war. The agencies involved in gathering and interpreting this information are the CIA, the National Security Agency (NSA), and the National Reconnaissance Office (NRO).

The NSA, an arm of the Defense Department, was created by a classified executive order signed by President Truman in 1952. An electronic spying operation under the direct command of the CIA director, the NSA operates a massive bank of the largest and most advanced computers available to any agency in the world—computers that break codes; direct spy satellites; intercept electronic messages; recognize target words in spoken communications; and store, organize, and index this information. At the heart of this technology are the digital computers made by IBM, RCA Corporation, and Sperry Rand, underwritten by the NSA.

Although the Constitution of the United States demands an open government operating according to precise rules of fairness, the NSA is an unexamined entity. Its annual budget and staff far exceed that of the CIA or the FBI. No specific federal law defines the NSA's obligations and responsibilities, nor is it subject to any congressional review. The agency is based at Fort Meade, about twenty miles northeast of Washington. Because there is tremendous secrecy surrounding the agency and because it operates in a highly technical field, it is free to define its own goals, which apparently are twofold: (1) It aggressively monitors international communications links, searching for "foreign intelligence," intercepting electronic messages and signals generated by radar or missile launchings; and (2) it prevents foreign penetration of links carrying information bearing on "national security."

A recent unpublished analysis by the House Government Operations Committee reports that the NSA may have employed sixty-five thousand people in 1976 (the FBI had one employee then for every six in the NSA) and operated two thousand overseas listening posts, with an annual expenditure greater than $10 billion. The bulk of its work is done by its three service components: the Army Security Agency, the U.S. Air Force Security Service, and the U.S. Naval Security Group.

From 1952 to 1974, the NSA developed files on seventy-five thousand Americans—civil rights and antiwar activists, and congressmen and citizens who lawfully questioned government policy, as well as those who threatened national security. The CIA had access to all these files.

In 1975, the Senate Intelligence Committee investigated the NSA and expressed great concern about its activities and the failure of Congress and the federal courts to comprehend these activities. The report said:

> The watch-list activities and sophisticated capabilities that they highlight present some of the most crucial privacy issues now facing this nation. Space-age technology has outpaced the law. The secrecy that has surrounded much of the NSA's activities and the lack of Congressional oversight have prevented in the past bringing statutes in line with the NSA's capabilities. Neither the Courts nor the Congress have dealt with the interception of communications using the NSA's highly sensitive and complex technology.

Apparently, by using this highly sophisticated technology for decoding computer-based material, the NSA can investigate data used for statistical purposes; employment records; and credit card, banking, and other operations essential to American life. These data bases are "electronic windows" into the most intimate details of people's lives.

Two thousand permanent intercept stations are based outside the United States, in Great Britain, Australia, Taiwan, Japan, South Korea, Turkey, Morocco, West Germany, Spain, the Azores, Italy, Greece, Cyprus, Diego Garcia, South Africa, Thailand, the Philippines, Norway, and scores of other places.

In Australia, the NSA works with the defense signals director of the Australian Department of Defense Signals Internal Organization. There are three main sites of operation—at Northwest Cape in Western Australia, at Pine Gap in the middle of Australia near

Ayers Rock, and at Nurrungar in South Australia. Below the U.S. Embassy in Canberra, there is also an NSA facility that apparently is capable of monitoring Australian diplomatic traffic, although such activity is internationally illegal.

When Pine Gap was installed in the 1960s, the Australian government was told it was operated by the U.S. Department of Defense. During the mid-1970s, the Labor prime minister, Gough Whitman, learned that Pine Gap was in fact a massive CIA installation that used the Defense Department as a cover. The CIA responded to his discovery by organizing a campaign to overthrow his government. Victor Marchetti, former executive assistant to the deputy director of the CIA, and coauthor of the secret Pine Gap agreement, described this operation as a "mild Chile." Much of the CIA overthrow is described in a book and subsequent film called *The Falcon and the Snowman* and in an Australian documentary called *Home on the Range.*

The CIA program at Pine Gap is called Rhyolite and uses satellites developed by TRW. The Rhyolite satellites are 35,900 kilometers (22,312 miles) above Borneo. Like a vacuum cleaner, they suck up a wide spectrum of Soviet and Chinese military communications and radar emissions and beam them back to Pine Gap. They also monitor telemetry data from Soviet ICBM tests, which lets the United States know exactly what the Soviets are doing. These satellites are also capable of monitoring all Australian domestic communications.

Pine Gap also used to be the site of a Pyramider project, which allowed the CIA to indulge in covert activities. It communicated with foreign agents using sensing mechanisms placed in strategic locations around the world, and backup communications for overseas systems. The Pyramider program was supposed to ensure "maximum undetectability."

One of the stations at Pine Gap receives for, and controls, orbiting photographic-reconnaissance and electronic-intelligence satellites run by the National Reconnaissance Office. This office was established in 1960 as a coordinating office for the U.S. Air Force, CIA, and NSA spy-satellite program, and is run by the office of the secretary of the Air Force in the Pentagon. There are three kinds of satellites involved in this spy operation—KH-8; KH-9 ("Big Bird"); and KH-11, which can take pictures from an altitude of 150 kilometers (93 miles), with a resolution of about six inches. A film is sent back to earth in a capsule, or the KH-11 uses "advanced sensor and data transmission techniques" in spy-satellite programs.

U.S. reconnaissance systems, including Big Bird and KH-11, use infrared and multispectral photography that can detect underground silos. By noting graduations in temperature between the facility and the surrounding atmosphere, this technology provides a means, however limited, to monitor the production of nuclear weapons.

Big Bird and KH-11 satellites are the chief means of monitoring Soviet compliance with the SALT treaty. During U.S. involvement in Vietnam, they were also used in a large operation to pinpoint targets for the secret bombing of Cambodia. The satellites monitored the outbreak of the Yom Kippur War in 1973 and detected the Indian nuclear tests in 1974. Yet B. M. Jasini, in *Outer Space 14*, stated: "It has been noted that this use of reconnaissance satellites is not the accepted use stipulated in the SALT agreement."

If Australia is being used in this way, surely many other nations' sovereign rights are being similarly violated by the U.S. military and intelligence operation.

Australia also is used for other U.S. military purposes. A large facility built in 1967 by the U.S. Navy at Northwest Cape in Western Australia is now one of the most important links in the U.S. global defense network. This facility transmits very-low-frequency (VLF) radio waves that can penetrate ocean layers to a depth of up to fifty feet. American nuclear submarines can receive the VLF radio waves from below the fifty-foot depth by trailing submerged antennae, attached by wire, which float up to the fifty-foot depth.

The Northwest Cape is the largest and most powerful of the three main VLF stations in the U.S. submarine communications system. It covers the western and southern Pacific and Indian oceans. Other VLF stations are at Jim Creek, Washington (which covers the eastern and northern Pacific, the Bering Sea, and part of the Atlantic Ocean), and at Cutler, Maine (to cover the North Atlantic, the North Sea, the Arctic, and the Mediterranean).

Classified messages to submarines in the Indian Ocean are sent from Northwest Cape. The submarines enter the Indian Ocean through the Indonesian straits (Lombok and Ombai-Wetar) under a secret agreement between the U.S. and Indonesian governments. Because of the strategic significance of these straits and to maintain friendly interests in the area, the United States condoned the Indonesian massacre of approximately 250,000 people in East Timor.

There is also a U.S. high-frequency transmitter at Northwest Cape, used by America during the mining of Haiphong and other North Vietnamese harbors in 1972. More recently, a new satellite ground station was installed at Northwest Cape without the knowledge of the Australian government. The station will greatly improve the facility's importance to the U.S. military operation by enabling Northwest Cape to participate fully in global events in Europe. The facility will be used by the U.S. Army, Navy, and Air Force. Northwest Cape also is used by the NSA for electronic intelligence receivers that monitor Soviet naval communications from Vladivostok, Khabarovsk, and other Soviet bases.

The Australian government must pay the United States $1 million per year for limited use of the Northwest Cape facility by its military personnel.

In October 1973, the Northwest Cape was put on alert and was used to communicate a general nuclear alert on October 25 to U.S. military forces in the western Pacific and Indian oceans. The Australian government was not informed.

Northwest Cape, Pine Gap, and their sister station Nurrungar obviously are vital Soviet nuclear targets. Yet Australia did not consent to become a nuclear target. Many of her citizens feel that she has signed a mutual suicide pact with America by allowing some twenty to thirty American military installations into the country. Indeed, some studies suggest that Australian cities and major industries also are targeted in the event of nuclear war.

A facility called TRANET in Smithfield, South Australia, is part of an international network used by the U.S. Navy to track its navigational satellites, which were developed to provide the Polaris missile submarines with high-accuracy navigational capabilities. The other purpose of these satellites is to obtain geodetic information—that is, the measurement of the earth's exact size and shape and the study of variations in the earth's gravitational field. Such geodetic information, together with the extraordinary mapping capabilities of the Big Bird and KH-11 satellites, provide the accuracy required for U.S. missile attacks on "pinpointed targets" such as USSR ICBM silos and command and control centers. This sort of information is needed to prepare for a pre-emptive first-strike nuclear war, as stated in the Pentagon's Defense Guidance Five-Year Plan.

Another important U.S. military installation, about which the Australian public knew nothing, is the Omega station in East Gippsland, Victoria. It is part of an international network of eight stations (the others are in Argentina, Japan, Liberia, La Réunion—a French island off the eastern coast of Madagascar—Norway, North Dakota, and Hawaii). These stations emit radio signals independently, each in turn in a precisely timed sequence, each repeated every ten seconds. Omega is an all-weather, worldwide, continuous, very-low-frequency radio navigation system for aircraft, surface ships, and submarines. It is the only radio navigation aid that can be used by a fully submerged submarine in midocean. The VLF radio waves are received by trailing antennae at a depth of from 12 to 30 meters (39 to 98 feet), so the submarine can operate at a depth of 600 meters (1,969 feet).

Omega is used by the fleet ballistic-missile submarines, all U.S. Navy surface ships, most U.S. Navy aircraft, most U.S. submarines, many U.S. Air Force planes, and some U.S. Army weapons systems. U.S. Omega receivers have been produced by Northrop, Canadian Marconi, Dynell, Litton Industries, Rockwell, Tracor, Hoffman Electronics, and II Avionics.

The U.S. nuclear-powered hunter-killer attack-submarine fleet uses Omega receivers. These submarines carry a variety of nuclear weapons, including the Tomahawk cruise missile and the SUBROC nuclear antisubmarine missile. These submarines are targeted on Soviet fleet ballistic-missile submarines, which makes them part of the counterforce first-strike scenario. Because they threaten the Soviet Union's second-strike capabilities, they are inimical to stable deterrence. The United States has ninety-four hunter-killer submarines and is building more. Since the Soviet Union is constrained by the SALT treaty to sixty-nine strategic nuclear submarines, it seems obvious that they are concerned about the viability of their deterrent force.

The Omega system also is used by British submarines and by a West German submarine. The whole of the Western world's navy surface fleet is being equipped with these receivers to increase efficiency in naval maneuvers, blockading, convoying, searching, patrolling, rendezvousing, and station-keeping. Omega is to be used by many of the U.S. Air Force planes and was specifically developed for use as a guidance input for the glide bombs used in the Southeast Asian air war.

The C^3I system has a force multiplier effect. Because it allows the potential of nuclear weapons to be used more effectively, it enhances their efficiency by a factor of two to four. In some ways, the nuclear weapon force can be made more efficient by retargeting the missiles after either first- or second-strike nuclear war. The intelligence satellites review the Soviet landscape (this is called postattack reconnaissance) and relay the information back to the central command (if they have survived). They then communicate with missile silos from their airborne command post to order retargeting to new areas (if the satellites have survived the EMP from the nuclear attack).

The rapidly advancing technology of the C^3I system allows navigational satellites to provide midcourse internal guidance to the SLBMs, making them extremely accurate and bestowing upon these once contervalue city-busting missiles a hard-target counterforce potential for a first-strike nuclear war. Trident II missiles will have this capability.

The massive pre-emptive first-strike doctrine of the early 1950s, according to which nuclear weapons were to be used against the Soviet nation in retaliation for unwanted Soviet conventional moves, required only a minimal command and control system. The massive retaliation and assured-destruction second-strike doctrine required four hundred survivable strategic nuclear weapons to reach the Soviet Union after America was hit by a first strike. It required only that the command and control systems survive to guarantee communication and implementatioin of the response order for a second strike. The scenario of flexible response, damage limitation, nuclear war fighting, and controlled escalation was first introduced by Robert McNamara, President Kennedy's secretary of defense. This doctrine has evolved to such a complicated degree that it is virtually unworkable.

The C^3I system must be durable enough to survive successive nuclear strikes over months. It must continuously allow political decision makers to select targets, determine firing rates, communicate with the enemy to clarify confusing events, and provide for negotiations and the control of escalation. This, of course, is a fairyland fantasy in the minds of the war planners. In the midst of nuclear war, nothing and nobody would work according to plan.

The C^3I system would also have to provide reliable warning of each strike on the United States as well as assessment of damage to the Soviet Union, and subsequent retargeting of missiles on worthwhile Soviet targets so as not to waste bombs. It would, finally, have to ensure that strike targets of equivalent value to those just hit in America are chosen. Of course, adequate communication between the NCA and the strategic forces must survive to ensure that all this happens.

A natural corollary of the "damage limitation" doctrine is to maintain the ability to terminate a nuclear war if desired. Unfortunately, most of the R&D effort has been focused on the beginning and early phases of nuclear war. Missiles once launched cannot be recalled or aborted, and it is impossible for the NCA to communicate with the SLBM submarines or low-flying B-52s over Soviet territory. At the moment, the only available way to stop a nuclear war is to use the hot line. Strangely enough, it has not been protected against nuclear war.

Much of the technology that has been developed for the C^3I system is both oversophisticated and unnecessary. Yet it is almost impossible for industry, politicians, or the military to reject it. They have become captives of the scientific imperative of this new "fun" technology.

In March 1974, Secretary of Defense James Schlesinger testified that the command and control systems necessary to support the "new targeting doctrine" came to $300 million, of which $186.7 million had already been committed. On the same day, he asked Congress for total obligational authority (TOA) for $6.646 billion for intelligence and communications for fiscal 1975.

There is also a lethal trade-off inherent in this surprisingly sophisticated technology. Should the safety mechanisms to prevent accidental or inadvertent firings be so strict as to inhibit a "readiness and reliability" in time of emergency? Actually, the military has resisted installing safety devices such as self-destruct mechanisms (radio antennae on ICBMs and SLBMs, for example) because they would increase missile weight, and generate reliability problems, and increase the possibility of Soviet jamming and "spoofing." The antennae would increase the missiles' vulnerability to EMP and other nuclear effects. This sort of thinking is hardly conducive to world safety. Once the military was deployed by a nation to protect its citizens; now it is more concerned with protecting its missiles.

The command and control centers themselves are the most vulnerable points of the C^3I system. If one of the functions of the C^3I is to produce a force-multiplying effect of 20 or 30 percent of the strategic force, its adversary would obviously try to destroy first the command, control, and communication centers. But since the C^3I produces the force-multiplying effect only as long as the system is functional, pressures to use the system before it is attacked in the first strike would be overwhelming. As the C^3I system grows more sophisticated in its force-multiplying potential for controlling the timing and limitations of attacks over a protracted period of time, greater pressures are generated for early and massive use of strategic arsenals. Apparently this scenario is most realistic for Western Europe, where the control systems for tactical nuclear weapons are particularly vulnerable.

Any scenario for fighting "controlled" nuclear war depends upon the invulnerability of the C^3I systems. A chain of command is only as strong as its weakest link. In this case, it is the communications link with the command posts. Apparently current U.S. policy calls for the command and control systems to be able to operate for six months from the beginning of a strategic nuclear war. They are also meant to operate for an additional period during which they support restitution of the residual strategic forces—presumably to be ready for another nuclear war.

The C^3I system's most vulnerable parts are the radar dishes, cables, microwave towers, radio and radar antennae, early-warning apparatus and power supply, VLF and Omega communications systems for the submarines, and the satellite control system. Like cities, these are "soft targets."

There are numerous ways in which the C^3I system is vulnerable to damage. The blasts from a nuclear explosion, for example, can create extraordinary overpressures, followed by winds exceeding five-hundred miles per hour. These can destroy everything in the vicinity except hardened facilities, and even these are destroyed by direct hits.

Three types of radiation can damage the C^3I system:

1 A high-altitude explosion can cause ionization of the atmosphere. By seriously disrupting VLF transmissions, the atmospheric effect can destroy communications with the fleet ballistic-missile submarines.

2. Transient radiation effects on electronics (TREE) is a combination of the deleterious effects of X rays, gamma rays, and neutrons on materials used in electronic systems such as radio and radar sets, gyroscopes, inertial guidance devices, and computers. Solid-state systems—diodes, transistors, and integrated circuits—and vacuum and gas-filled tubes can be destroyed by these effects.

3. The effects of electromagnetic pulse (EMP) have been described previously. The most effective collectors of EMP in the C^3I system are long runs of cable, piping, or conduit; large antennae and their feed cables; guy wires and support lines; overland power and telephone lines; long runs of electrical wiring; railroad tracks; aluminum aircraft bodies; computers; power supplies; alarm systems; intercoms; life-support control systems; transistorized receivers and transmitters; base radio stations; and some telephone equipment. A single bomb exploded two-hundred miles above the continental United States probably could knock out most of these systems in the United States, Canada, and Mexico. Fewer than five such explosions would blanket the United States with as much as one hundred thousand volts per meter. The military has attempted to protect this equipment from EMP, but without much success.

Of course, it is impossible to guard thousands of miles of cable, land lines, antennae, guy wires, towers, and the like from the possibility of willful sabotage.

Nonnuclear "smart" weapons such as the Exocet missile could easily destroy antennae farms, satellite ground stations, radar facilities, and field command posts.

Natural phenomena such as solar-induced ionospheric disturbances and the aurora borealis can seriously disrupt high-frequency radio communications. Changes in the earth's magnetic fields and bad weather can adversely affect the accuracy of ICBMs. All the talk about accuracy and first strike is seriously challenged by the fact that ICBMs have never been launched over the gravitational fields of the North Pole. These magnetic forces could considerably disrupt a missile's flight path.

The C^3I system frequently breaks down. The Honeywell 6000 series of computers, built in 1964, still is the basis of the WWMCC. An exercise conducted in 1977 showed that when the computers were tested, they worked only 38 percent of the time.

Jamming: The Soviet Union and America often jam each other's communications and frequencies of similar wavelengths. This is called electronic warfare.

Finally, there is always the factor of human error. Controlling a nuclear war would be one of the most complicated operations ever undertaken by a government and one that cannot be rehearsed. The slightest breach of discipline or departure from set procedures could be disastrous; yet imagine the psychological state of humans at the control post just before and during a nuclear exchange. The most important lesson of past conflicts and crises is that command and control procedures never work as predicted in manuals, and that communications systems and procedures often fail—frequently at the most inappropriate times—because of human error. To control a nuclear war, the entire sequence of events must work to perfection the first time. "The simple human mistake of entering a single erroneous digit into a launch control computer could be catastrophic, since it could spell the difference between the destruction of the intended target—an ICBM silo or a remote oil field refinery and that of the wrong target—Moscow." Such an error induced the aberrant course and subsequent destruction of the KAL passenger jet shot down over the Soviet Union.

According to Dr. William Perry of the Pentagon (in June 1979 testimony), "Nearly all of the command and control systems will be lost during a nuclear attack, and we would be totally dependent upon our airborne command and control forces at that time." Let us assume that the president or his designated surviving deputy reaches the airborne command system in time and that it takes off before the bomb lands. This NEACP plane is designated to fly above the exploding bombs—if, indeed, it can evade high-air bursts of the hydrogen bombs and is not damaged by EMP, both very unlikely. It must maintain communication with the strategic forces, ICBMs, and satellites by trailing a five-mile-long copper wire—VHF antennae and other sorts of antennae to monitor different frequencies from satellites. Of course, these wires will be damaged by EMP and other effects.

There is a second set of alternative airborne command and control planes based near Omaha at Offutt Air Force Base, which has maintained constant airborne control for SAC bomber and missile forces since February 1961. One set is always in the air, flying eight-hour missions at 26,000 feet in a random pattern, 175,000 square miles around Offutt. These planes are directly linked to SAC, NORAD, the NMCC, and the AABNCP. These also trail wire antennae, two miles long. These planes can actually program and launch the Minuteman force from the air.

The Navy has an equivalent set of planes called TACAMO (Take Charge and Move Out)—two squadrons of EC-130 planes that provide continuous airborne VLF communications to the fleet ballistic-missile subs. One aircraft is airborne at all times over the Atlantic, and one over the Pacific. They can pass communications only one way—from the NCA to the subs and other strategic forces. These planes use a five-mile-long trailing wire antenna and drogue. With the plane flying in a continuous tight turn, the antenna hangs vertically, becoming a relatively efficient VLF radiator.

These command planes could remain in the air for only a few days—seventy-two hours at most, provided they are supplied with refueling planes—until they run out of engine oil and crew fatigue takes over. The TAMACO planes can stay aloft only ten hours, since they have no refueling capacity. Where then would they land after they have conducted the nuclear war? Most airports will be targeted and thus almost certainly destroyed.

Satellite-borne infrared sensors may soon be able to detect these planes in flight. And the powerful communications they emit will make them beacons in the sky to smart weapons and also vulnerable to radio interception and direction-finding by Signal intelligence sources. Further, a nuclear weapon exploding above or below such a plane would rip off the wings by shock waves, while a blast at the same altitude would tear off the vertical tail. Bombs would destroy all aircraft in the relevant operating areas.

These airborne command and control posts are far less effective and more dangerous than ground posts for executing and monitoring nuclear war. They can give only one-way communications to the ICBM silos. Moreover, a single plane can launch an ICBM, whereas ground control requires backup concurrence by a second facility. Because the commanders are on a kamikaze mission, one recent review concludes: "The predicament of being trapped in an aircraft that cannot return to the ground without inviting destruction almost guarantees that the general will order attacks with everything in his power before landing." The hot line between Washington and Moscow, most needed after a nuclear war has started, will almost certainly have been destroyed and therefore will not be available to the NEACP plane.

Satellites and their ground stations are "the most important" of all systems maintained by the United States for early warning of ballistic-missile attack. Both Soviet and U.S. satellites are vulnerable to antisatellite (ASAT) warfare by killer satellites, laser destruction, EMP from weapons exploded in space, and destruction of ground stations by nuclear war. Our early-warning satellites are terribly vulnerable because they depend on only two ground stations—Nurrungar in Australia and Buckley Air Force Base in Colorado. Although these ground stations can allegedly withstand five pounds per square inch of blast pressure, their ability to withstand only one or two pounds per square inch is more likely. The USSR has a rudimentary ASAT system, designed fifteen years ago, which consists of space mines, but they are clumsy and inefficient and represent no substantial threat to U.S. satellites.

In August 1983, the Soviet Union proposed that the United States and the USSR agree to a complete ban on antisatellite weapons. The administration ignored this offer, and in January 1984 tested an extremely sophisticated ASAT weapon—a rocket fired from an F-15 fighter. This system, if developed fully, could conceivably strike hundreds of targets every twenty-four hours; and because it is easily hidden from satellite detection, it is unverifiable. It would take the Soviet Union more than a week to mount a comprehensive attack using its current system.

The original hot line linking Washington to Moscow went in to service on August 30, 1963. Originally a radio and cable link, it has been accidentally disrupted six times. A thief snipped out a twenty-foot section in Helsinki in 1964; a thunderstorm damaged an integral power station in southern Finland in 1964; a fire in a manhole in Rosedale split the circuit in 1965; a farmer in Finland plowed the cable in two in 1965; a Finnish postal workers' strike disrupted the circuit in 1965; and a Soviet freighter severed the cable when it ran aground in Denmark in 1966. The hot line communicates with a telex machine in the basement of the Pentagon. The messages come through in Russian and must be translated into English for relay to the White House. This clumsy system of communication is open to misinterpretation.

In September 1971, the hot line was converted to a satellite communications system with ground stations in Etam, West Virginia; Fort Detrick, Maryland; Vladimir; and Moscow. (It was further updated in 1984, providing faster and more effective transmission.) The new system is even more vulnerable to damage from nuclear war—the ground stations from direct attack, the satellites from EMP, and so on.

The American submarine fleet carries 5,728 bombs—almost half the strategic weapons of the United States. Because the U.S. nuclear submarines are so quiet, they cannot be tracked by Soviet hunter-killer subs. Very-low-frequency sound waves can reach them near the surface of the water with one-way communication to the submarines' commanders, but ground stations that transmit VLF will almost certainly be destroyed early in a war. VLF gives relative navigational accuracy. Satellites can give good navigation, but they transmit in VHF and UHF. VHF can be received only if the submarine projects an antenna above the water for three or four minutes, thereby exposing the sub's position. Ultrahigh-frequency reception requires exposure of a mast-mounted dish antenna, which is even more difficult to camouflage. To bypass these problems, the Navy has begun construction on an extremely-low-frequency transmission system, which will be able to penetrate several hundred feet through the water. The system consists of eighty-four miles of antenna cable strung along towers above ground, its ends buried in the earth in Michigan and Wisconsin. Although the Navy considers the TACAMO plane the only reliable system for communicating an emergency-action message to the subs, it's hardly a feasible system. Fourteen backup planes are needed to keep only one continuously in the air over the Atlantic or Pacific, and the home-base airfields at Bermuda and Guam obviously are prime targets. Communications could be sent only one way, from the

NCA to the submarines, and all methods of communication would doubtless be destroyed very early in a nuclear war. Therefore, the only real use for the fleet ballistic-missile submarines (the most survivable part of the triad) is for first strike. They cannot be used for controlled or prolonged nuclear war because the commanders won't know the locations of remaining Soviet targets and so will be unable to target their missiles accordingly. Also, although one Trident submarine carries at least 160 bombs, as soon as a couple of missiles have been launched, the position of the submarine becomes known, exposing it to attack from antisubmarine warfare.

The incident in which a Korean jetliner was shot down over the Soviet Union on September 1, 1983, sabotaged the tenuous relationship that existed between the Soviet Union and the United States. U.S. intelligence had evidence confirming that the Soviets still thought they were tracking an RC-135 spy plane when they shot down the passenger jet. Yet President Reagan, addressing the United Nations, called the Soviet leaders barbarians.

Since that time, international events have continued to push the world toward the nuclear abyss. The presence of the U.S. "peacekeeping" force in Lebanon exacerbated tensions that have existed for centuries between feuding sects. The U.S. Marines were used to support the Christian Falange government of President Amin Gemayel, a government that is not representative of the majority of the Lebanese people.

On October 23, 1983, a total of 240 young American men in Beirut were killed by a suicidal car bomber while they slept. Since that dreadful event in Lebanon, President Reagan reaffirmed his commitment to play a major role in the direction of that fateful country. To that end, he negotiated an agreement with Israel for increased military cooperation.

The Reagan Administration decided to confront the Syrian government in Lebanon because it was supported by Soviet troops and military technology. Lebanon thus became a site for political superpower confrontation, with U.S. Marines placed fifty miles from Syria and the Soviet troops.

These marines are part of the Rapid Deployment Force, which is armed to fight in the "integrated battlefield" (simultaneous use of conventional, chemical, and nuclear weapons). It is, therefore, possible that the marines in Lebanon were armed with tactical nuclear weapons. There are seven-thousand Soviet troops in Syria. The Syrians were equipped with Soviet "smart" missiles (similar to the French Exocet missile that sank the British destroyer in the Falklands). Two U.S. aircraft carriers and one battleship, the *New Jersey*, all armed with nuclear weapons, patrolled off the Lebanese coast. What would President Reagan have done if the Syrians used a Soviet missile to sink an American nuclear-armed ship?

Several days after the marines were killed in Lebanon, America invaded the tiny island of Grenada, a member of the British Commonwealth and with a population only slightly over the capacity of the Rose Bowl. By this act of war, the United States simultaneously violated international law and deeply offended the people of Great Britain. This event aroused instant jubilation among the U.S. population. For the first time since their humiliating defeat in Vietnam, they felt vindicated.

Such patriotic fervor can be dangerous indeed. As I traveled the United States in the weeks following these events, observing the flags flying at half mast, I felt an increasing sense of anxiety. This is the stuff that wars are made of.

As these international events were unfolding, the unilateral U.S. zero-option proposal was rejected by the Soviets. Cruise and Pershing II missiles began to be deployed in Great Britain, Italy, and West Germany, and the Soviet Union walked out of the INF talks. A week later, the Soviets announced they were also withdrawing from the Strategic Arms Reduction Talks (START) negotiations. They said they would deploy medium-range missiles in East Germany and Czechoslovakia and additional submarine-based missiles off the Atlantic coast—missiles that could hit Washington from six to ten minutes after launching (to match the Pershing IIs). Reagan had maintained that the Soviets would negotiate only if America played from a position of strength. And so continues the deadly arms race, fueled by men who do not understand conflict resolution. Averell Harriman, former U.S. ambassador to Moscow, charges the Reagan Administration with "three years of nuclear irresponsibility." He says that "negotiations have been treated as a forum for propaganda, an occasion for invective, a mask to cover new deployments and as an arena to gain advantage—rather than as a path to human survival on this planet."

Because of the serious potential for superpower confrontation in the Middle East, the Persian Gulf, and Central America, together with the qualitative increase in the arms race and the disastrous relationship between the superpowers, the years ahead promise to be among the most frightening in the history of the world. We must elect a Senate, a Congress, and a president who are serious about the salvation of the planet. To this end, the American people must understand the data about nuclear weapons, delivery systems, and the C^3I system that controls them.

We must educate the politicians about these subjects and hold them accountable to us as they continue to vote for more and more grotesque weapons systems.

As I became more and more concerned about the earth's fate, I developed a hunger for concrete facts about nuclear war. Armed with information, I could maintain my credibility and intelligently debate with any person who believed in deterrence, *Star Wars* defense, winnable nuclear war, and/or the arms race.

There are approximately 50,000 nuclear weapons in the world today. America and its allies own 31,000 (about 26,000 U.S. nuclear weapons are in the active inventory and 4,000 more are in inactive storage). The Soviet Union owns 20,000; China, from 225 to 300; India may have several; Israel, as many as 80, according to CIA estimates; South Africa probably has tested 1. By the year 2000, it is predicted that Egypt, Saudi Arabia, Iraq, Iran, Pakistan, South Korea, Taiwan, the Philippines, Japan, Mexico, Brazil, Argentina, West Germany, Sweden, Italy, Spain, Canada, and Australia could have nuclear weapons. Nuclear war between the superpowers could occur at any time, triggered by computer accident or by design, as the Cold War escalates. It would take between thirty minutes and several hours to complete. At least one billion people would be dead, with one billion more seriously injured.

President Reagan, in his third year in office, started to revive the idea of constructing defensive measures against nuclear war. He devised the "Buck Rogers," or *Star Wars* plan after talking to Edward Teller, one of his chief advisers on nuclear weapons. Teller's system reflects a "third generation" of nuclear weapons for which he was responsible, preceded by atomic bombs and hydrogen bombs. This system was intended to operate from platforms in space. X-ray laser beams generated by nuclear explosions in space would be focused on

Soviet missiles and warheads as they zoomed by at twenty times the speed of sound. In a full-scale nuclear war, as many as seventy-five hundred Soviet nuclear warheads would have to be destroyed in such a manner, all within minutes. Other people advocate laser and particle beams (directed energy), which would need to be focused on each incoming warhead for many seconds (depending upon the energy level) to achieve the desired debilitating effect, but the X-ray beam would be instantaneous. However, the warheads can be protected from such destruction by shielding, spinning, or decoys. According to critics, complete destruction of incoming warheads would be impossible to achieve, so even if only 75 bombs (or 1 percent) of the seventy-five hundred escape destruction, and if they are targeted properly, it would be sufficient to destroy the seventy-five major cities in the United States.

Both the United States and the USSR have been working on this space-based antimissile technology, but both are at least twenty years from achieving any practical application. Further, this new strategy openly violates the Anti-Ballistic Missile Treaty, as well as a 1967 agreement not to deploy weapons of mass destruction in space. The Soviet Union considers a massive missile defense effort, along with a buildup of new and more accurate cruise and ballistic missiles, preparation by the United States for a first-strike nuclear war. It will respond by working harder on defensive mechanisms—which may never work—and it will generate new offensive systems to overcome the new U.S. defense.

Obviously, this new Reagan-Teller strategy does not attempt to define protection for Europe. To destroy Europe, the Soviet Union could simply use short-, medium-, or intermediate-range tactical nuclear weapons, which do not need to travel through space to reach their targets. An article in *Science* magazine in November 1982 quotes Hans Bethe, Nobel laureate and longtime colleague of Teller during the Manhattan Project:

> Everybody recognizes that Teller, more than anyone else, contributed ideas at every stage of the hydrogen bomb program, and this fact should never be obscured; but, 9 out of 10 of Teller's ideas are useless. He needs men with more judgment, even if they be less gifted, to select the 10th idea, which often is a stroke of genius.

It astonishes me that Teller now is a member of the White House Science and Advisory Committee, informing President Reagan about nuclear weapons. One of the main architects of the arms race, Teller destroyed Robert Oppenheimer in a vindictive competition in order to build his "super" or hydrogen bomb.

Throughout his presidency, President Reagan has reiterated his fear that the Soviet Union is ahead of the United States. Let us examine these assumptions, starting with the following quotes. General John W. Vessey, Jr., chairman of the Joint Chiefs of Staff, appeared before the Senate Armed Services Committee on May 11, 1982.

> SENATOR CARL LEVIN: "I am wondering whether or not you would swap U.S. military capability overall, with everything that is included in that phrase, for that of the Soviets?"
>
> GENERAL VESSEY: "I would take some of the things that the Soviets have for their forces in terms of numbers, and give them to our forces."
>
> LEVIN: "But overall, would you trade with Marshal Ogarkov [chief of the General Staff of Soviet armed forces]?"
>
> VESSEY: "Not on your life; not to live there or have his job or his responsibilities or to have his forces in comparison to ours."
>
> LEVIN: "I appreciate your answer. Just focusing on the military capability aspect, is your answer that you would not trade?"
>
> VESSEY: "I would not trade."

And the following exchange took place before the Senate Foreign Relations Committee on April 29, 1982:

> SENATOR CHARLES PERCY: "Would you rather have at your disposal the U.S. nuclear arsenal or the Soviet nuclear arsenal?"
>
> DEFENSE SECRETARY CASPAR WEINBERGER: "I would not for a moment exchange anything because we have an immense edge in technology."

The Pentagon's Undersecretary of Defense for research and engineering recently reported that the United States is superior or equal to the Soviet Union in all of twenty basic technologies that will influence the balance of power during the next ten to twenty years. He also said that the quality of U.S. weapons is equal or superior to the quality of Soviet weapons in twenty-five of thirty currently deployed systems, including land-based nuclear missiles, submarines, and bombers. The United States leads in the areas of computers, electro-optical sensors, microelectronics, guidance and navigation, optics, propulsion, radars, signal processing, computer software, stealth technology, structural materials, submarine detection, and telecommunications. The Soviets are judged equal to the United States only in aerodynamics, conventional warheads, directed energy, nuclear warheads, and mobile power sources.

What follows is a breakdown of the nuclear weapons possessed by the superpowers. Keep in mind that a distinction between strategic and tactical nuclear weapons is highly artificial and is determined only by the mode of delivery of the nuclear bomb.

The Arsenal and Arms Control

Strategic (Long-Range) Weapons

Strategic, or long-range, weapons are capable of being exploded on the enemy's homeland. The United States has more than 13,000 nuclear weapons it can drop on the Soviet Union; the Soviet Union has almost 9,000 destined for the United States. Five hundred 1-megaton Soviet bombs aimed at the 70 largest metropolitan and industrial centers in the United States would kill from 70 million to 90 million people and destroy from 60 to 75 percent of the total industry. Three hundred three 1-megaton American bombs aimed at the 200 largest metropolitan and industrial areas of the USSR would kill 75 percent of the population—or approximately 180 million people—and destroy 62 percent of the total industrial structure.

Of the 13,500 weapons in the U.S. arsenal, about 1,700 are "tactical" nuclear bombs deliverable by F-111s, F-4s, A-6s, A-7s, and other "tactical" airplanes, which could fly to the Soviet Union from Europe or Asia, or from aircraft carriers nearby. The other 11,500 are on land- and submarine-based missiles and on strategic bombers.

Of the 8,800 Soviet strategic bombs, 260 are on the limited Backfire bomber, which can fly to the United States but cannot return unless it is refueled. The remaining 8,540 are based in land and submarine missiles and in bombers.

Submarines: America maintains half its strategic warheads on 37 invulnerable submarines. Roughly 60 percent of the submarines (20 or so) are at sea at any one time. This means that almost 3,500 hydrogen-bomb warheads are constantly targeted on the Soviet Union from under the sea. Because America has two long, uninterrupted coastlines and an additional submarine base in Scotland, it has greater access to port facilities and global oceans than does the Soviet Union. One Poseidon submarine with 16 MIRVed missiles (each fitted with 10 hydrogen-bomb warheads) can destroy 160 separate targets. The 160 bombs carried by the Poseidon have a total explosive yield of 6.4 megatons—greater than that of all the bombs dropped in World War II (and still it is a few thousandths of the megatonage in either the U.S. or Soviet arsenals). Because of their staying power underwater, the U.S. submarines could wage a protracted nuclear attack on the Soviet Union lasting as long as three months.

The Soviets have 62 modern submarines carrying strategic nuclear weapons. They are noisier and easier to track than the U.S. submarines. Because the USSR lacks midocean stations and an extensive coastline, only 15 percent are maintained at sea at any one time. Thus they must rely on the long transit time from their very few all-year ports. The Soviet submarines carry 2,000 nuclear weapons, but because so few are at sea, only about 300 of these are targeted on the United States at any one time. These missiles take from 15 to 30 minutes after launching to hit coastal U.S. targets (they are faster than ICBMs because of their "lower trajectory" and because of the shorter distance they have to travel).

Strategic Bombers: America has 263 B-52 bombers, which, although 20 or more years old, have been constantly refitted and upgraded with new armaments and millions of dollars' worth of antiradar and missile-baffling devices. Although they are high-speed jet aircraft, the planes will not arrive at the targets until after the U.S. missiles, which have a 30-minute transit time, have destroyed the Soviet air-defense bases, radars, and communications systems. Thus bombers will be used for "postattack reconnaissance."

They will drop hydrogen bombs on the few remaining undamaged targets. Altogether, the United States has 324 operational strategic bombers and 264 in storage. The operational planes carry a total of more than 3,600 large hydrogen bombs and missiles. One of the great advantages possessed by the United States is its 600 KC-135 aerial tankers used to refuel the bombers in midair and extend their range. The USSR has only 30 such long-range tankers. America soon will add 60 new KC-10 tankers to its arsenal and re-engine 384 KC-135 tankers.

The Soviet Union has 170 old bombers, almost three quarters of which are propeller-driven. These planes carry 440 large hydrogen bombs and cruise missiles. The paucity of Soviet bombers is a result of a shortsighted and rigid military and political bureaucracy and reflects the dominance of the Army and its land-based missile command.

Land-Based Missiles: The Soviet Union has concentrated on land-based systems—68 percent of its warheads are land-based, 24 percent are submarine-based, and 8 percent are on old bombers.

It has 1,398 ICBMs, which carry 6,012 nuclear bombs. Although these bombs are bigger than their American counterparts, the missiles are less accurate and their systems more clumsy. Ninety-six percent of Soviet ICBMs are old-fashioned and liquid-fueled, and their warheads are large, partly to compensate for inaccuracy. Because liquid-fueled rockets take longer to be readied for launch than those driven by solid fuel, many of the Soviet missiles are as yet unsuitable for quick launch-on-warning strategy.

America has 1,027 land-based missiles containing 2,127 hydrogen bombs. All but 27 are fueled with solid propellant and can be launched against the Soviet Union, should it try to strike first, within the 30-minute flight time of its missiles. This plan, known as launch-on-warning, ensures that the Soviet missiles would hit empty silos. The U.S. ICBM force maintains an alert rate of 98 percent; the Soviet ICBM alert rate probably is much lower. It is now possible to launch 200 of the U.S. ICBMs from an airborne command post if ground command centers are destroyed during a nuclear war.

President Reagan is fond of showing charts demonstrating the large numbers and larger sizes (called throw weight) of Soviet missiles. American missiles, in comparison, seem to be fewer, smaller, and "older" in design. This always suggests to me that the American officials suffer from a case of acute missile envy. In fact, America has continually modified and improved its existing missiles, a policy that has proven cheaper, while the Soviet Union has introduced entirely new models each time it has wished to upgrade its missiles. The United States modified 300 Minuteman III missiles with a very accurate Mark 12A warhead at a cost of $155 million, whereas the Soviet Union, attempting the same thing, had to design three new missiles (SS-17, SS-18, and SS-19) at an estimated cost of $28.5 billion. American missiles are much smaller than Soviet missiles because years ago America learned how to miniaturize hydrogen bombs—that is, to make small bombs with the same yield as large ones. Either the president does not understand these issues or is intentionally misrepresenting the facts.

Tactical Nuclear Weapons

Tactical nuclear weapons are meant to be dropped from airplanes or used in land mines, artillery, and surface-to-surface or surface-to-air missiles. The United States has a total of approximately 20,000 tactical nuclear weapons: 6,000 in Europe (many near the front lines of East and West Germany), 700 land-based in Korea, 1,000 elsewhere in Asia, and as many as 5,000 other forward-based tactical nuclear weapons aboard aircraft carriers, missile cruisers, and other surface ships. The United States has 400 fighter bombers in Europe, which can deliver nuclear weapons on all Warsaw Pact countries, and 180 medium-range Pershing 1A missiles based in West Germany. It also deploys nuclear weapons at over 200 sites in 11 countries outside the United States: Belgium, Canada, Greece, Guam, Italy, the Netherlands, the Philippines, South Korea, Turkey, Great Britain, and West Germany.

France and Britain together have more than 500 nuclear bombs that they can explode on the USSR, including 18 French intermediate-range missiles, 34 French strategic bombers, and 6 French nuclear submarines, each equipped with 16 missiles. According to the Stockholm International Peace Research Institute's "worst-case analysis," Britain and France together could possess 1,600 warheads by 1990—an increase of more than 220 percent.

For 20 years, the Soviet Union had approximately 600 SS-4 and SS-5 medium-range missiles, of which about 200 SS-4s now remain. The United States decided not to counter these with its own ground-based intermediate-range missiles but rather to use 40 strategic missiles on submarines allocated to NATO in the Atlantic, and bombs in forward-based planes placed in Britain. That balance shifted in 1977, when the SS-20 began to be deployed by the Soviet Union. The 414 medium-range SS-20 missiles are mobile and presumably more threatening because each is MIRVed with 3 warheads. One third have been placed along the Sino-Soviet border, aimed at China, Japan, and Korea, and two thirds—that is, 276 missiles with a total of 828 warheads—are aimed at Europe.

President Reagan and his team discriminate against SS-20s, SS-4s, and SS-5s by saying they can threaten Western Europe, but Europe has no medium-range missiles with which to threaten the Soviet Union. Yet the 11,500 U.S. *strategic* weapons deployed in the United States and on submarines could reach the Soviet Union within hours (some can arrive within 15 or 30 minutes); and the Soviet Union, if it wished, could target its strategic missiles on Europe. Thus a new and patently *artificial* distinction between *tactical*, medium-range European weapons and *strategic* weapons is being made.

Further, the Reagan proposal on Intermediate-Range Nuclear Forces (INF) totally ignores all the U.S., British, and French bombs that can hit the USSR and demands that the Soviet Union remove all its SS-4s and SS-20s, including those targeted on China. (These were excluded in a modified U.S. proposal late in 1983.) This is called the zero-zero option. Assistant Secretary of Defense Richard Perle, who engineered the Jackson-Vanick Amendment (Perle worked for the late Henry Jackson) and who helped destroy the SALT II treaty, also drafted, promoted, and defended the U.S. proposal at the INF talks. In the summer of 1982, INF negotiators called for what is now known as the Walk in the Woods proposal, which held that the Soviet Union reduce its 3-warheaded SS-20s to 75 in exchange for 300 single-warheaded cruise missiles and no Pershing II deployment. The State Department, the White House, the Pentagon, and the Joint Chiefs of Staff were favorably inclined.

Perle, who was on vacation at the time, returned to sabotage this informal agreement by demanding that America be free to deploy some Pershing IIs. Before the talks resumed, word got to Moscow that Washington had rejected the compromise, and the proposal collapsed. I consider the INF proposal a very shortsighted and rather unintelligent view of the European situation and one which is bound for failure. If the Reagan Administration were serious in its intent to reach a negotiated agreement on intermediate-range weapons, it would have included American forward-based systems in the airplanes, American missiles in the submarines, and the French and British forces. A bomb is a bomb is a bomb, and to the Soviets it will not matter where the hydrogen bombs originate when they explode on their cities. America could lose 90 percent of its nuclear bombs and still be able to destroy the Soviet Union several times over—if, indeed, that is the conscious intention of a country whose Constitution is deeply rooted in the Judeo-Christian tradition.

It is thought that the Soviet Union maintains approximately 12,000 tactical warheads within the Warsaw Pact countries and within the USSR itself. Three thousand of these tactical weapons are maintained for European use.

In 1982, President Reagan made a proposal to the Soviet Union called the Strategic Arms Reduction Talks (START), which addresses only the strategic weapons and ignores the tens of thousands of tactical nuclear warheads. In this proposal he called for an equal level between the superpowers of 2,500 land-based missile warheads, with a total of 5,000 strategic-missile weapons on both sides. Because the Soviet Union has concentrated on land-based bombs, it had 68 percent, or 6,012 of its strategic weapons on land; under this proposal it would have to disassemble more than half its land-based force. The United States has 2,127 land-based warheads and would, in fact, be allowed to build more under this proposal. Because the United States also has 5,728 nuclear bombs in its submarines (the Soviet Union has only 2,082), America obviously will have to dismantle approximately 2,000 of its antiquated submarine weapons. In his claim that each side have only 7,500 strategic weapons, Reagan counts only land- and submarine-based missile warheads. But he has ignored the fact that America has more than 3,000 hydrogen bombs on strategic airplanes, while the

Soviet Union has over 400 bombs in its strategic planes. He also fails to include the 1,700 tactical, or so-called Euro-strategic, nuclear weapons, which could be flown from Europe to the Soviet Union in a short time.

The START proposal originally did not include cruise missiles (each armed with a single warhead), almost 8,000 of which are to be deployed by the United States. Yet cruise missiles are considered strategic weapons by Defense Secretary Weinberger. The proposal also implies that if the Soviet Union is to be legitimately equal to America, it must make a huge investment in MIRVing its submarine missiles to compensate for the loss of those ground-based bombs and missiles implicit in the treaty.

In order to placate the almost universal mandate from the American people (86 percent in October 1983 wanted a bilateral nuclear weapons freeze), the administration offered a "builddown" proposal in late 1983—dismantle two old nuclear weapons for each new one. This still allows for the modernization program and is totally consistent with the Defense Guidance's first-strike winnable nuclear war. Both the START and builddown proposals are unfair and totally unacceptable for the Soviet Union and are designed for failure, as is the INF proposal. Both were designed to a large degree by the people from the Committee on the Present Danger. When will the American president approach arms control talks with a serious intent and motivation? Both superpowers go to war in their arms control talks, each wanting to come out stronger than the other. This *macho* zero-sum-game mentality is anachronistic, self-defeating, and ultimately suicidal in the nuclear age. In fact, years of arms control talks have only legitimized new generations of nuclear weapons by both superpowers.

Conventional Weapons

Both the Soviet Union and the United States spend about 80 percent of their military budgets on conventional weapons. It is often said that the Soviet Union is stronger than America in conventional arms. Let us again look at the facts.

Troops: NATO has a total of 5.3 million troops, the Warsaw Pact nations 4.8 million, and China 4 million. The Soviet Union deploys 1 million troops on the Chinese border. In 1980, Secretary of Defense Harold Brown described the manpower situation as follows: "In the central region of Europe, a rough numerical balance exists between the immediately available nonnuclear forces of NATO (including France) and those of the Warsaw Pact."

Tanks: NATO has 29,400 tanks; China has 11,400; the Warsaw Pact nations have 63,700 in place in Europe. A war between the Soviet Union and NATO could well involve China, and the Soviet Union would then have an impossible two-front war to fight, which would almost certainly become nuclear. NATO deploys about 500,000 antitank devices, most of which are "smart" weapons—precision-guided, heat-seeking, and extremely accurate. Weapons of similar design destroyed many Israeli tanks in the Yom Kippur War in 1973, and the Exocet "smart" missile sank the British destroyer in the Falklands. Because these antitank weapons are extremely efficient, the numerical superiority of the Warsaw Pact tanks becomes meaningless.

Potential Use of Superpower Conventional Forces

Let us now examine the total conventional forces of the superpowers and their uses. Randall Forsberg, director of the Institute for Defense and Disarmament Studies, has provided an analysis that shows that of the total U.S. conventional forces, half are allocated to help Western Europe in the event of a war with the Soviet Union. This hardware includes the Army's armored and mechanized divisions, heavily equipped with tanks and artillery that require an extensive road network and industrial infrastructure. The U.S. Navy sends seagoing convoys to Western Europe with supplies of tanks, artillery, ammunition, and oil. To prevent the U.S. and NATO forces from being able to replenish supplies during a U.S.-USSR war in Europe, the Soviet Union has developed a very large force of antiship submarines designed to sink the supply convoys during such a war and to defend their own missile submarines and coast. In response to this Soviet submarine force, the United States and its allies have developed extensive antisubmarine-warfare capabilities, which form the main part of the Navy's "sea control" component. This equipment includes: (1) attack submarines—to destroy other submarines; (2) antisubmarine patrol aircraft; and (3) surface ships—cruisers, destroyers, and frigates—that escort the convoys and provide antisubmarine and antiaircraft point defense in case Soviet submarines and antiaircraft penetrate the outer barriers of the convoy's defenses. The antisubmarine-warfare system also is being designed and built to be used against Soviet strategic submarines (those carrying strategic nuclear missiles).

The other half of the U.S. conventional forces is designed to fight in Third World countries rather than to defend Western Europe against the Soviet Union. These forces include the Marines and the Army's infantry, airborne, and air assault (helicopter) divisions. Compared with European divisions, these ground troops are equipped more lightly and can fight in difficult mountainous, desert, or jungle terrain, where there are few roads. Although ill prepared to fight against Soviet tanks, they are well prepared to fight against the weaker and more poorly equipped forces of developing countries such as Vietnam, Cambodia, El Salvador, and Nicaragua.

The Navy has a considerable investment in these missions. Its "power projection forces" are designed to project or to use U.S. military power in distant parts of the world. These forces are organized around two kinds of ships.

Aircraft carriers are large floating airfields with crews of five thousand each. They carry up to a hundred military aircraft, including sixty fighter and attack planes. The attack planes are designed to bomb shore-based or naval targets, and the fighter planes will be used to fight off enemy aircraft. The United States owns thirteen such heavy aircraft carriers; the Soviet Union has none. Each carrier is surrounded by groups of surface ships to give the carrier antiaircraft and antisubmarine defense. The carriers are also supported by "underway replenishment ships," which have their own escorts to provide antiaircraft and antisubmarine defense. Therefore, each carrier with the ability to place up to a hundred planes in any remote region of the world takes with it a task force of eight to ten ships built at a total cost of up to $15 billion. Because it is the wealthiest nation in the world, the United States is the only country that can operate a fleet of aircraft carriers with modern supersonic aircraft.

The amphibious assault ship can land Marines and their equipment. As with aircraft carriers, these assault ships give the United States the ability to sit offshore and launch ground troops onto a beach in an attack on a country where the United States may not have enough popular support for these troops to use a ground base or harbor. The carriers can support such an assault by aerial bombing. The United States has twelve amphibious assault ships, which are the size of small carriers and carry a total of twenty thousand troops. They weigh forty thousand tons and carry thirty helicopters and eight vertical takeoff and landing (VTOL) planes. The United States also has more than fifty amphibious landing ships. Each weighs more than ten thousand tons and carries between three hundred and one thousand marines.

The two largest amphibious ships possessed by the USSR are one fourth the size of the biggest U.S. assault ships. These are the only Soviet ships that can project troops overseas. The smaller ships, which possess only limited combat capability, are designed to operate in the landlocked seas near the Soviet Union—the Baltic and Mediterranean seas, the Sea of China, and the Sea of Okhotsk. Altogether the Soviets have one hundred landing craft. In theory, these ships could carry the total number of Soviet naval infantry (marines)—16,000. Since the Soviet Union does not own large carriers and large amphibious assault ships, it cannot launch a large-scale successful attack as can the United States against a developing nation in South Asia, Africa, or Latin America.

To make up for its deficit vis-à-vis the United States, the Soviet Union recently has started building smaller carriers—the Kiev class. They now have three. Roughly half the size of U.S. amphibious assault ships, they carry twenty-three helicopters and 12 vertical takeoff and landing planes that fly at subsonic speeds. We presume these carriers are to be used mainly for antisubmarine warfare.

The Soviet Union thus has far less offensive power-projection capability than the United States, which is free to intervene militarily in any part of the world. Large-scale Soviet military operations tend to be overt and constrained to areas contiguous to Soviet borders (Iran, Afghanistan, North Korea). The USSR, in short, does not maintain any swing forces for large-scale intervention in the Third World. Instead, the Soviet Union supports nationalist, socialist, and Communist revolutions in developing countries only through the flow of funds, arms, and training.

Of course, this type of small-scale indirect intervention is paralleled by military aid and arms supplied from the West to the Third World. The United States has a longer history of major direct intervention in developing countries—for example, Korea and Vietnam, which together involved approximately five hundred thousand U.S. troops. The Soviet Union, which has traditionally been prepared to intervene on a relatively large scale only in Eastern Europe (Hungary in 1956 and Czechoslovakia in 1968), took an unprecedented step by intervening in Afghanistan. Since one third of Soviet ground and air capabilities are intended for use in Europe, and since one third are deployed along the long Chinese border and in other Far East sites, the one hundred thousand men in Afghanistan had to be taken from other fronts.

Ending the whole arms race obviously will be the only way to prevent the Soviet Union from obtaining such a worldwide capability in the future.

Power Projection

Many Americans tell me about Soviet expansionism as justification for any sort of U.S. military behavior. But outside Eastern Europe and possibly Afghanistan, the Soviet Union has no foreign military bases in the same sense that the United States does. The Soviet Union controls none of these foreign military facilities and merely is allowed access by the host country. It must ask permission to use these stations, and very few Soviet forces are permanently or even regularly stationed there. Even those nations closest to the Soviet Union, such as Cuba, Vietnam, and South Yemen, have stated that they would not allow Soviet bases on their soil. Indeed, Soviet access is limited to seven nations: Afghanistan, Angola, Cuba, Ethiopia, South Yemen, Syria, and Vietnam. The number of personnel is extremely small in each—fewer than 3,000, except in Vietnam, which has 4,500. On the other hand, America controls most of its foreign bases and pays rent for them to the tune of hundreds of millions of dollars, often in the form of foreign military aid. It enjoys unhampered use of the facilities and frequently maintains large military forces and equipment on the bases. America runs 360 large military installations around the world in 21 foreign countries and 8 U.S. territories, plus hundreds of smaller military installations in many other countries.

The number of U.S. bases has increased from 323 ten years ago to 360 today. These bases are used as part of the American power projection around the world. Their locations are illustrated in the table on page 156. The number of American personnel maintained at these bases is extremely large in most instances.

The U.S. base in the Philippines is a typical example. This country serves as headquarters for the thirteenth Air Force at Clark Air Force Base, which is the logistical hub of the U.S. military air traffic in the western Pacific. Subic Naval Base, a nuclear submarine port in the Philippines, is also a major ship-repair facility for the Seventh Fleet. Seven other military installations perform important military communications and surveillance functions. These bases support more than 15,000 military personnel, supplemented by 9,000 Seventh Fleet sailors in port at any one time. The bases cover 192,000 acres of arable land, so important to the malnourished of the Philippines. This base complex is "a state within a state," and Clark Air Force Base is larger than the whole state of Singapore.

Clark was established 80 years ago by General Arthur MacArthur (Douglas's father), chief of the then colonial army that subjugated the Philippines. MacArthur said at that time,

> Its strategic position is unexcelled by that of any other position on the globe. It affords a means of protecting American interests which, with the very least output of physical power, has the effect of a commanding position in itself to retard hostile action.

In the intervening years, these bases have been used as springboards for U.S. military intervention in Korea between 1950 and 1953, in the islands between Taiwan and the People's Republic of China in 1958, and in Vietnam and Cambodia between 1965 and 1975. They have also served as staging areas for U.S. displays of force and military war games in many parts of East Asia, South Asia, and East Africa.

The Philippines is governed by a dictator, Ferdinand Marcos, and his powerful wife, Imelda, both backed up and supported by the United States. They live lavishly, and they spend enormous amounts of their country's money on art, showcase medical

INSTALLATIONS

	Army	Navy	Marine Corps	Air Force	Total
U.S. TERRITORIES					
Canton & Enderbury Is.				2	2
Gilbert & Ellice Is.				2	2
Guam		9		1	10
Johnston Atoll				1	1
Midway Islands		1			1
Puerto Rico	2	3		1	6
Trust. Terr. of Pac. Isl.	1			1	2
Wake Island				1	1
Total U.S. Territories	3	13		9	25
FOREIGN AREAS					
Antigua		1			1
Australia		1		1	2
Bermuda		3			3
Belgium	1				1
Canada		1			1
Cuba		1			1
Diego Garcia		1			1
Germany, Federal Rep. of	177			11	188
Greenland				2	2
Greece		2		2	4
Iceland		1			1
Italy	2	5		2	9
Japan	14	10	4	3	31
Korea, Republic of	36			4	40
Netherlands				1	1
Panama	1	3		2	6
Portugal				1	1
Philippines		8		3	11
Spain		3		3	6
Turkey	1			6	7
United Kingdom	1	4		13	18
Total Foreign Areas	233	44	4	54	335

facilities, and big parties, while the majority of their people live in a state of abject poverty and malnutrition. Their regime is widely regarded as among the world's worst human rights violators. American troops take their R&R here. Consequently, approximately 3,000 women, some of whom have not yet reached their teens, become receptacles for their pleasures. A whole culture of prostitution and degradation has been established. An additional 12,000 prostitutes service the 9,000 sailors of the Seventh Fleet.

The Pentagon has admitted on numerous occasions that "there is no identifiable external threat to the Philippines," but the bases have recently acquired a special significance because of their possible role in the Pentagon's secret 1984–88 Defense Guidance, which outlines American ability to fight a protracted conventional or nuclear war simultaneously on different fronts throughout the world. Because of the Philippines' strategic location, the bases serve the following functions in U.S. interventionist strategy:

1. To project U.S. military power to the mainland of Southeast Asia.
2. For critical backup of U.S. forces in South Korea.
3. To deploy naval units and fighter bombers to East Africa and to serve as an alternate supply line to Israel if there are hostilities in the Middle East.

Early in 1983, the United States agreed to give the Philippines $900 million as rent for the bases. Most of this money will be given in the form of military aid to Marcos. Yet the U.S. Foreign Assistance Act of 1961 as amended, Section 502B, states that "no security assistance may be provided to any country, the government of which engages in a consistent pattern of gross violations of internationally recognized human rights." Also, part of the U.S. bases agreement signed under the Marcos regime allows the United States to conduct intelligence activities virtually anywhere in the Philippines for U.S. security needs.

In July 1983 the United States paid Greece $500 million in military assistance for the right to maintain more than two dozen military facilities in that country (only 4 are part of the 360 major bases previously mentioned). The facilities consist of airfields, weapons depots, radar stations, communications centers, intelligence-gathering outposts, and 2 large anchorages. They greatly facilitate the U.S. presence in the eastern Mediterranean and serve as listening posts for southeastern Europe, the Middle East, North Africa, the Black Sea, and beyond.

Australia also is an unwitting host to 20 to 30 U.S. military installations put there without the knowledge of the Australian people. Only 2 are part of the 360 mentioned earlier.

Obviously the U.S. bases expose all of these 21 countries to Soviet attack in the event of nuclear war. By signing so-called defense agreements with the United States, these countries have signed mutual suicide pacts—not what most people in the nuclear age would call defense.

One of the saddest examples of the abuse of the host country is the saga of the Marshall Islands. These Pacific islands were allocated to the United States after World War II as a U.N. trust territory. The U.N. trusteeship agreement allows the United States in its administration of the islands to bypass the U.N. General Assembly and report directly to the Security Council, where America retains veto power.

The U.N. mandate directed the United States to develop the islands toward self-sufficiency and to "protect the inhabitants against the loss of their lands and resources."

During a twelve-year atmospheric nuclear testing program, America exploded thirty-three hydrogen and atomic bombs over the Marshall Islands. Six islands were blown off the face of the earth, while many others were rendered radiologically uninhabitable by the fallout.

During the 1950s, the CIA operated a secret counterinsurgency base on Saipan, one of the islands, training Chinese Nationalists to retake the Chinese mainland. And since the early 1969s, the Kwajalein group of islands has been used to test all the U.S. long-range intercontinental ballistic missiles. Once the islanders were self-sufficient, living off their fish, coconuts, and other produce, and enjoying their own culture. Now they are dependent upon America for 90 percent of their resources. There have been efforts by these people to move toward independence, but America always quashes them. Military civic action teams are used to promote "friendship," but as Roger Gale, former director of Friends of Micronesia, said,

An interesting pattern developed. Army engineering teams became responsible for civic action in the Marshalls, where antiballistic missile testing is done. Navy Seabees work in the Carolines, where naval port facilities and marine training sites are planned, and Air Force teams operate in the Marianas, where reconstruction of World War II air bases on Tinian and Saipan are in the cards.

The United States has also been working to ensure military control of Micronesia. In 1973, Secretary of State Henry Kissinger directed the CIA to "assess the possibility of exerting covert influence on key elements of the Micronesian independence movement where necessary to support U.S. strategic objectives."

The island of Palau is a matriarchal society where women receive the landholdings and choose the tribal chiefs. Despite the fact that the United States has been teaching the ideals of democracy to the people of Palau for thirty years, it is actively undermining the world's first nuclear-free independent constitution in Palau. This has been passed by popular plebiscite on three different occasions by large majorities. Instead, the United States is pushing for the Compact of Free Association, which calls for extension of an airstrip, use of thirty-two thousand acres for jungle warfare and guerrilla training, and the use of beach areas for landing tanks and other equipment. The pact also demands freedom of activity for off-duty soldiers, storage and ocean dumping of nuclear waste, and storage of nuclear weapons. The women of Palau are leading the battle against this invidious development.

Naval Commander David Burt said during a 1976 visit to Palau, "There are millions of people in Japan and only fourteen thousand in Palau. It may be necessary to sacrifice the fourteen thousand."

Many people from the Kwajalein atoll have been displaced from their islands, and eight thousand people are packed onto a tiny seventy-eight-acre island called Ebey amid appalling sanitary conditions so that America can operate its Kwajalein missile range— which is a convenient forty-two hundred miles from California's Vandenberg Air Force Base—to test the MX and other exotic delivery systems. MIT and Draper Labs, where the guidance systems of the missiles are designed, have a direct telephone line to the Kwajalein missile range. The military has severely restricted the access of these people to a nine-thousand-square-mile lagoon, which they used to use for fishing, and to their ninety-three islands, which they used for agricultural purposes.

In 1978, more than 50 percent of the Ebeye population was under fourteen years of age; yet there is no high school on the islands. The Kwajalein high school, three miles away, is for American children only. The indigenous parents who want an education for their children must send them hundreds or thousands of miles away to schools in Majuro, Guam, or other parts of Micronesia at great personal expense, but these people are destitute. All the food is imported to this island, and the prices are 100 percent higher than for inexpensive food on Kwajalein. These people have very few recreational facilities—a volleyball and basketball court and one baseball field for eight thousand people. In contrast, three thousand Americans on the main island of Kwajalein have a golf course, bowling alley, basketball and handball courts, baseball fields, swimming pools, free movies, and other amenities. The Marshallese are employed in low-paying jobs to serve the Americans as maids, gardeners, cooks, and so forth, and they must have passes, issued in limited numbers, to travel to their own islands for purposes such as banking or airline business.

Sanitary conditions are appalling. Raw sewage is routinely flushed into the Ebeye lagoon, where pollution levels are 25,000 times higher than the level set as safe by the World Health Organization. In 1963, a severe polio epidemic occurred on Ebeye and others of the Marshall Islands. More than 190 people became severely paralyzed at a time when polio vaccines had been available in the United States for eight years. Dr. Konrad Kotrady, a Brookhaven National Laboratory resident physician on Kwajalein, told a U.S. congressional committee investigating the problems of Ebeye:

> The picture I would like to paint for Kwajalein regarding Ebeye's health care system is that Kwajalein [U.S. administration] has an attitude of indifference and apathy to what occurs on Ebeye. The Army's position was summed up for me one day when a high-level command officer at Kwajalein remarked that

the sole purpose of the Army at Kwajalein is to test missile systems. They have no concern for the Marshallese and it is not of any importance to their being at Kwajalein Missile Range.

U.S. Representative John Seiberling (Democrat of Ohio) said in August 1982,

> I think the actions of the military are hardly becoming of a nation that is a great power. Here we have a bunch of people who are our wards. We are occupying their land and are denying them the right to peacefully assemble and petition for redress of grievances that our Constitution guarantees to our own citizens, and yet we are in their country. I think it's a pretty sad spectacle.

The Marshallese made the following statement to the U.N. in 1956:

> Land means a great deal to the Marshallese. It means more than just a place where you can plant your food crops and build your houses, or a place where you can bury your dead. It is the very life of the people. Take away their land and their spirits go also.

On October 20, 1982, the Kwajalein islanders signed an agreement with the U.S. Department of Defense to extend the Kwajalein Missile Range (KMR) agreement through to September 1985. The negotiations brought changes of (1) reducing the maximum term of lease for the KMR from fifty to thirty years, (2) establishment of a $10 million fund to improve living conditions on Ebeye over the next three years, and (3) a return to unrestricted use of six other islands in the atoll.

When President Reagan was in London in June 1982, he introduced a new American plan called Project Democracy, which was designed to promote "democracy" around the world. It will be administered by the U.S. Information Agency at a cost of $85 million. Charles Wick, who illegally taped telephone conversations for the first three years of the Reagan Administration, is the director of the U.S. Information Agency. It was to have been coordinated by William Clark, former national security adviser, who is extraordinarily ignorant about international affairs. (At his Senate confirmation hearings he did not even know the leaders of Zimbabwe or South Africa.) The project has four components—information sources, political involvements, covert activities, and a quasi-governmental institution. Initially the CIA and the National Security Planning Group were to be responsible for the covert component, but the CIA was pulled out because people thought its past invidious activities would create a bad public image for Project Democracy. This project apparently will be used by the United States to train young leaders in other countries and to foster the growth of labor unions, political parties, news outlets, businesses, and universities in countries where democracy is not permitted.

Will Project Democracy be used in the Philippines, South Africa, El Salvador, Guatemala, Brazil, Chile, and other oppressive dictatorships that are propped up and often have been installed by the United States? It is time that neither America nor Russia be allowed to intervene internally or externally in the affairs of any other country. Most Third World countries are struggling for their independence as America once did, and it is absolutely not indicated for the United States to determine the future of any other country in the world. Such behavior openly flouts the principles enunciated in the Declaration of Independence.

Comparison of World Military Spending on Conventional and Nuclear Weapons

Randall Forsberg's analysis of the purposes of military spending shows that only about 20 percent of the U.S. military budget is used for nuclear weaponry—to design, develop, and manufacture the weapons as well as to field and train personnel to operate the nuclear forces. Conversely, 80 percent of the U.S. military budget is for conventional weapons and for ground troops, naval forces, and tactical air forces. It is thought the same breakdown is true for the Soviet Union.

On a worldwide basis, only about 12 percent of military spending is allocated to the nuclear arms race. Another 10 percent of total global military expenditures are made by developing nations for conventional weapons—countries in Latin America, Africa, the

Middle East, South Asia, and the Far East (excluding China and Japan). Eighty percent of world military spending is for conventional weapons and forces by the industrialized nations of the Northern Hemisphere—the European countries, the USSR, China, Japan, and the United States.

The Role of Conventional Weapons and Armed Forces

1. One purpose of conventional weapons is to deter a conventional war—for instance, between the superpowers in Europe. In addition, as the nuclear disarmament movements grow, there are calls to increase conventional forces in Europe to prevent a *nuclear* war. (The rationale here is to use conventional forces to deter a conventional war that might escalate into a nuclear war.) At the same time, however, nuclear weapons are also being built and deployed in Europe to deter or prevent a *conventional* war from occurring.

2. Conventional weapons are used by the superpowers for internal repression—for instance, by the Soviet Union in Eastern Europe. (There were some past suggestions by Henry Kissinger and others that should Socialist or Communist parties in Italy or France appear to be winning elections, the West should be prepared to use military force to oust them. So the United States has threatened to use conventional forces for the internal repression of its allies.)

3. Conventional forces are used primarily by the United States but also by the USSR to intervene in conflicts in the Third World for political, economic, or ideological purposes. What is significant about the role of conventional weapons in U.S. national security is that none of these missions has anything to do with defense of the United States. Rather, they are intended to defend U.S. interests abroad. For the United States, the first category is to help its allies; the second is for interference in the affairs of its allies; the third is for pure aggression.

The Role of Nuclear Weapons

Nuclear weapons are intended to deter nuclear attack by either superpower upon the other. Deterrence itself is a vague, esoteric theory that holds that the mere possession of nuclear weapons will prevent nuclear war. This argument is frequently presented to me as a reason why war has not occurred in Europe for forty years. I am often reminded of a patient who appeared in the casualty department of a hospital some twenty years ago. An old man who said he had been driving all his life and had never had an accident, he appeared that night with a broken neck sustained in a car crash. There is always a first time.

Nuclear weapons are also intended to back up the use of conventional armed forces in the roles previously described. The United States has used this policy against the Soviet Union for years. Although the nuclear weapon used on Hiroshima was said to have ended the war with Japan, the bomb on Nagasaki was used to intimidate the Soviet Union. It implied that America had a nuclear monopoly and was prepared to use it if the USSR used its conventional forces in a manner objectionable to the United States. Right from the start, nuclear policy was inextricably intertwined with conventional war, power politics, and "massive retaliation"—that is, Soviet conventional forces were to be deterred by the U.S. nuclear threat to obliterate major Soviet cities— appropriate as long as the United States had a nuclear monopoly.

Even after the Soviets developed the bomb, the United States enjoyed overwhelming nuclear superiority until the mid-1960s. And so the policy of massive retaliation remained, although the theory of "flexible response" was developed during the Kennedy Administration in the Single Integrated Operational Plan (SIOP) of 1963. It was augmented by a threat to use tactical nuclear weapons first against invading Soviet conventional forces in Europe.

America developed its strategic missile forces between 1960 and 1967, and the USSR developed its missile forces between 1965 to 1971. Therefore, only in the past fifteen years has America become vulnerable to a massive Soviet retaliation in which most U.S. cities could be destroyed within thirty minutes. From 1945 to 1971, America acted as a global nuclear bully, threatening total death and destruction to hundreds of millions of Soviet people. From 1971 to 1981, both sides accepted the fact of second-strike "parity"—each side would retain enough nuclear weapons after a first strike against it to obliterate the other side in the second strike.

But U.S. response to parity has been to try to recover its lost position of nuclear superiority by building and deploying more modern and more accurate new weapons. Thus a plan for a "winnable" counterforce first-strike nuclear war was enunciated by the Pentagon in 1982. If the United States builds these new weapons, parity will be lost, along with the opportunity to stop the arms race bilaterally through a nuclear weapons freeze. The Soviets have frequently stated that they, too, will build such missiles, and the arms race will then careen totally out of control.

The rationale for these new nuclear forces is once again to end parity and to reach for U.S. strategic superiority. This will be used to reinforce American use of conventional force overseas to defend U.S. interests. To stop the nuclear arms race effectively and to move rapidly to bilateral nuclear disarmament, several simultaneous steps need to be taken: (1) a nuclear weapons freeze; (2) a nonintervention treaty signed by the superpowers, which will end military intervention in developing countries and in superpower satellites; (3) a reduction in the huge conventional forces of NATO and the Warsaw Pact and in the conventional forces of Japan and China; and (4) an end to the massive international arms trade to Third World countries, which would be destabilizing in itself, even if the superpowers ceased their interventionist tactics; (5) an end to innovation and development of conventional weapons—developments in fighter planes, tanks, ships, and missiles create instability and uncertainty about the future; and (6) at the same time, a move toward rapid bilateral nuclear disarmament.

There would then no longer be a tremendous preponderance of military superiority in the Northern Hemisphere, and tension would decrease throughout the world. Only if the superpowers engage in serious nuclear disarmament will they have any moral authority to police other potential (or actual) nuclear nations. France has already stated that should the superpowers act in this fashion it would have no rationale to continue its *force de frappe*—now known as *force de dissuasion*. China has made similar intimations.

Eventually, conventional weapons should be used only for national defense—that is, to defend a nation's shores and boundaries. Nuclear weapons will be eliminated.

Wars can no longer be fought. We have opened Pandora's box, and the fissioned atom means that we can fight wars no longer. For example, if World War II had been fought today with conventional weapons, Europe would still be radioactively uninhabitable because of the destruction of the many nuclear reactors that dot its landscape. America is in a similar position with its seventy-nine large power reactors plus many military and research reactors and huge vats of radioactive waste scattered ubiquitously across the country.

Any war in the world—in Lebanon, in Iran or Iraq, in Central America or Grenada—could flare into a superpower confrontation and nuclear war. The American people must rapidly comprehend that war is anachronistic in the nuclear age. We must understand in our hearts and minds what Albert Einstein meant when he said, "The splitting of the atom has changed everything save man's mode of thinking; thus, we drift toward unparalleled catastrophe."

Case
History

How did we get ourselves embroiled in this potential nuclear disaster? Why are the Soviet Union and America such bitter enemies? Why were these bombs built in the first place, and why are they still being made?

I am interested in this enmity between the superpowers because I come from another country. As a neutral observer, I cannot understand America's passionate hatred for communism in general and for the Soviet Union in particular. The problem is not really communism—China, the world's largest Communist nation, is now an ally and a major trading partner of the United States. It is more likely the age-old competition between two powerful nations, each seeking supremacy and nationalistic world hegemony.

America's seemingly implacable hatred of the Soviet Union fills me with intense fear. If this enmity is carried to its logical conclusion, we will all be destroyed. The roots of the problem must be dissected from the historical perspective and understood; only then can pragmatic and constructive solutions be implemented.

Often, after describing to an American audience the almost unimaginable medical consequences of a nuclear war, the first question is, "But what about the Russians?" Of course, in the event of a nuclear war, it is Soviet bombs that will kill us. But the thought behind the question has much deeper and more complicated implications. America's preoccupation with anti-Soviet sentiment is symptomatic of the mechanism of psychic numbing. By blaming the Soviets, one needn't disintegrate emotionally as one contemplates the end of the earth. Even so, a more appropriate response would be: "How can we prevent the Soviets from killing us?"

Early Warning Signs*

As with disease in an individual, a nation's pathological reactions are rooted in the past. Obviously, the ideology and perspectives of American people have a characteristic logic derived from America's historic expansion and ascendancy to world political and military power. Let us examine the historical context of this dilemma.

During my fourteen years of intermittent residence in the United States, I have been trying to understand the nationalistic attitudes of its people. Just when I begin to feel that we share a common understanding about the world, a national crisis emerges, like the one in Iran. People's self-righteous, paranoid, warlike sentiments frighten me. But I also like Americans very much and know that they are kind, loving people who want desperately to do the right thing.

The Declaration of Independence states that men

> are endowed by their Creator with certain unalienable Rights, that among these are Life, Liberty, and the Pursuit of Happiness . . . whenever any Form of Government becomes destructive of these Ends, it is the Right of the People to alter or to abolish it, and to institute new Government, laying its Foundation on such Principles, and organizing its Powers in such Form, as to them shall seem most likely to effect their Safety and Happiness.

So pleased were the Founding Fathers with their new government that they felt all the world deserved a similar one.

These sentiments were reinforced by a strong Protestant ethic, dating back to the early colonists, that God was always on America's side. Indeed, God was, and has been, invoked in every American confrontation—with the French, the black Catholics of Latin America, the infidels in Turkey, Islam in Asia, and the atheistic Reds of modern times.

---

* (Material for the following section has been obtained from William Appleman Williams, Thomas Boylston Adams, and Henry Steele Commager.)

In 1850, Herman Melville wrote, "We Americans are the peculiar chosen people—the Israel of our time: We bear the ark of the liberties of the world. God has predestined . . . The rest of the nations must be in our rear." And during the same period, Orestes Brownson wrote that reforming America was a preliminary step in claiming the rightful "hegemony of the world." So, very early in their history, Americans felt they had the right to determine the fate and political direction of other nations, whether or not such intervention was welcomed.

America's founders experienced an almost holy sense of mission together with a strong feeling of isolation from the rest of the world. They felt that the past was of little value, and the future threatening. By preserving and expanding the present, American upper classes maintained an inequitable political structure in their favor. And their commitment was supported by the lower classes. Poor people were inhibited from demanding equality because they were promised, in theory, future riches by the expanding capitalist economy.

In his 1789 work *The Wealth of Nations*, Adam Smith propounded the theory of capitalism and its moral justification. He maintained that through the invisible hand of the marketplace, everyone will eventually achieve everything he desires. This philosophical justification, logically and morally contradictory, has failed: Some people achieve everything they materially desire, and some do not.

During the early years of the French Revolution, America was initially supportive in the name of self-determination. But it soon became uncomfortably apparent that the French lower classes were demanding equal rights with the upper classes, a general denunciation of private property, and the abolition of slavery. American support vanished. America attacked the French for utopianism with this surprising statement: "Empire was the key to property, and property was the foundation of the good American presence."

Ironically, the United States has always viewed itself as the savior of mankind, even as it maintains a commitment to expansionism. Its Founding Fathers saw their country as an endlessly expanding frontier, but they were also motivated by greed. As the marketplace enlarged, so did "the American form of freedom in the world."

Early in the 1800s, the desire to expand America's commerce was very strong. Back in 1786, Jefferson had said that he hoped circumstances would allow the United States to bring the South American Spanish territories "piece by piece" into an American system. Another commentator viewed Latin America as the key to the "future prosperity, commerce, and security" of the United States. And in 1823, President James Monroe proclaimed the "Monroe Doctrine," to which U.S. interventions in Western Hemisphere nations are usually ascribed.

According to Thomas Boylston Adams, the Monroe Doctrine states clearly that the true policy of the United States is to leave the nations of South America to decide their own destinies and that the United States would neither interfere itself nor permit any new colonization by any other power.

But for this enlightened policy, Theodore Roosevelt later substituted a proclamation of new imperialism:

> If a nation shows that it knows how to act with decency in industrial and political matters, if it keeps order and pays its obligations, then it need fear no interference from the United States. Brutal wrongdoing, or an impotence which results in a general loosening of the ties of civilized society, may finally require intervention by some civilized nation, and in the Western Hemisphere, the United States cannot ignore this duty.

His statement overlooked the fact that people with diverse views, traditions, habits, and aspirations—not necessarily North American or European—would not be concerned with these admonitions. Any doubts about U.S. intervention anywhere in the southern portion of the Western Hemisphere Roosevelt dismissed with the remark, "It will show those Dagos that they will have to behave decently. They will be happy if only they will be good."

America expanded its frontiers by conquering the western territories. The annexation of Texas in 1845 and northern Mexico in 1848 were justified by altruism. The phrase "manifest destiny" was used to proclaim America's historic role in world history—to "civilize" and to develop a cohesive empire under the mantle of capitalist democracy.

In the years before the Civil War, America opened up the West by developing new methods of transportation, which offered outlets and incentives for investment. Business interests were encouraged as steam navigation advanced and as the land-grant railways enlarged. But in 1860, the Confederate secession plunged the country into a wrenching internal conflict.

When the Civil War was over, the balance of power in America had shifted from southern landowners to the burgeoning industrial North. The defeat of slaveowners enhanced the progress of industrial capitalism and helped to destroy faith in representational government. A steady stream of European immigrants enlarged the population by over 7.5 million from 1850 to 1880, fulfilling the growing need for a labor supply for American industry. So the growth of industrialism, mechanized production, and national income provided a material basis for further national aggrandizement.

People who supported the future of America as a world empire, such as John Fiske, Josiah Strong, and Admiral Alfred T. Mahan, were confident about the future. Mahan pressed for increased naval strength, arguing in the popular press that war, far from being the worst resort, functioned as a means for the ascension of mankind. It was, he explained, a way of exercising right by force according to the power that God ascribes to man. He also stated that America's moral duty was to protect its colonial possessions, such as Puerto Rico and the Philippines, and to drive European nations (such as Spain) out of the Americas through naval power. Obviously, the commercial advantages of such a strategy were considerable, but a semblance of responsibility had to be maintained. As a popular philosopher of war and imperialism, Mahan once said, "Peace, indeed, is not adequate to all progress; there are resistances that can be overcome only by explosion."

This attitude justified the dispatch of marines to Panama to quell an insurrection in 1885, and further military campaigns in Chile, Peru, and Brazil to destroy incipient revolutions against semifeudal ruling aristocracies.

In 1880, the United States was heavily involved in the Cuban economy, particularly in sugar. One American financier wrote in 1895, "It makes the water come to my mouth when I think of the state of Cuba as one in our family." America's investment in Cuba was continually threatened by the Cuban people's moves against Spain for revolution and self-determination. So in 1898, America "liberated" Cuba from Spain in the Spanish-American War. The United States also moved into the Congo to support Belgium, which meant another market for American goods. It divided Samoa with Germany and Britain in 1887. In 1891 and 1892, America campaigned to control Chile and Peru, and it intervened in Brazil to defeat revolutionaries opposed to economic penetration by American corporations.

The Monroe Doctrine asserted American supremacy in the Western hemisphere, while in China, the Open Door policy of free and unencumbered trade legitimized eastern U.S. economic and political expansion. These policies have vitally affected present U.S. relationships with the rest of the world. Under a deceptive umbrella of responsibility and goodwill, they have created a vast military armada that reaches out to touch every corner of the world.

The Birth of the American Military-Industrial Complex

The American military industrial-complex was spawned before World War I, when links were forged between the big steel companies, such as Bethlehem and Carnegie, and the U.S. Navy. The superpowers of the "Age of Imperialism"—Great Britain, France, the United States, Germany, Russia, and Japan—were all seeking ways to build navies commensurate with their quests for global advantage. The United States perceived itself as a nation with political and economic requirements to compete in a hostile international environment. This was an era of transition from the "militia" processes of the Civil War to an integrated military production system designed to meet the needs of both an expansionist nation and its largest industrial manufacturers. To this end, connections were made among the captains of industry, admirals of the Navy, and politicians. By 1882, steel company executives were viewing with keen anticipation the profits and markets to be gained from the construction of armaments.

New shipbuilding technology heralded a shift from wooden to steel vessels. Additional ties were established among the steel industries. Their mutual dependence undercut the traditional laissez-faire dictum separating government and private enterprise. Under these conditions, the characteristics of the modern military-industrial relationship—political deals, kickbacks, cost overruns, favoritism—began to emerge. By 1887, faced with a slump in railroad orders and sinking profits, the steel firms looked increasingly to the U.S. Treasury to bolster their fortunes. President Cleveland lauded these military construction programs as devices to help alleviate serious domestic economic problems—those associated with unemployment and social unrest. The Navy was eager to pay any amount to get the steel necessary for naval expansion in 1899. According to naval historian Benjamin Franklin Cooling, "The proliferation of defense-related industries became inevitable once American industrial capacity and the needs of security became synonymous in the minds of policymakers and entrepreneurs alike. Each crisis—real or imagined—opened another stage in the process."

Fortified with an imperialistic ideology and the sustaining life of a global "free market," America hobbled into the twentieth century with its working class increasingly vulnerable to severe economic depressions.

President Theodore Roosevelt fed the American national ego with his vigorous foreign policy, boldly proclaiming that the semibarbarous peoples of the world must be disciplined by an international police force for the welfare of mankind. A tireless campaigner for American military and economic strength, Roosevelt succeeded in "taking Panama," as he put it, and subjugating nationals of Central America to construct the Panama Canal for the purposes of U.S. trade access. He once asserted to President Drago of Argentina that only those countries in conformity with certain standards of political and economic behavior could rely on U.S. friendship. In building up the Navy, Roosevelt compelled international recognition of America as a significant force.

The U.S. economy recouped after the slumps of the 1890s, primarily through the consolidation of large corporations. A leading role was played by investment banking houses—notably J. P. Morgan and Company, which dominated the railroad industry and later influenced the creation of General Electric Company, American Telephone & Telegraph, Western Union, and International Harvester. Eventually, aroused popular outcry against the big trusts mobilized around the candidacy of Woodrow Wilson, who opposed monopolies and favored state interventionism in the public interest.

In foreign policy, Wilson promoted an explicit role for American power—"to prevent revolutions, promote education, and advance stable and just governments." Adamantly opposed to popular attempts at revolution, he utilized American military forces to put down rebellions—in China, in Haiti in 1915, and in Mexico in 1917—that advocated communal ownership of productive assets.

It seems clear that in its relations with other countries, the United States has pursued an aggressive, often antidemocratic policy, more intent on opening the doors for resource and labor exploitation than on implanting democratic norms and political practices. Wilson himself abjured the uses of national power on behalf of corporate interests, saying, "It is a very perilous thing to determine the foreign policy of a nation in terms of material interest. It not only is unfair to those with whom you are dealing, but it is degrading as regards your own action."

Regardless of these sentiments, Wilson justified sending forces to dominate Nicaragua and Mexico. Despite their antidemocratic characters, he dubiously distinguished between "good" and "bad" revolutionists. Ironically, this convoluted logic prevails today, reflecting the tolerance of the U.S. State Department for pro-Western "authoritarian" regimes, as distinguished from socialistic "totalitarian" ones.

Wilson's ideas were opposed by Herbert Hoover, who was president from 1929 to 1933. A Quaker who considered the Bill of Rights to be "the heart of the Constitution," Hoover opposed the use of force, except in self-defense, and "absolutely disapproved" of global crusades and of Dollar Diplomacy, claiming the latter was "not a part of my conception of international relations." He warned Wilson against destroying revolutions that would only allow the rich to dominate the poor. "We cannot slay an idea or an ideology with machine guns," he said. "Ideas live in men's minds, in spite of military defeat." Hoover honored his commitment to self-determination. He saw national security as requiring only enough force to prevent any foreign soldier from landing on American soil: "To maintain forces less than that strength is to destroy national safety, to maintain greater forces is not only economic injury to our people, but a threat against our neighbors, and would be a righteous cause for the ill will amongst them." Is this not a prophetic statement for today?

*Emergence of a Rival**

America's adversarial relationship with Russia (later the Soviet Union) began during the rule of the czars. Yet only after World War I did the United States begin to perceive the Soviet Union as the "spokesman" for a world view that would challenge America's newfound status as a global power.

Russia's two revolutions in 1917 were seen by America as more relevant to World War I and the Germans than to internal Russian events. The first revolution, early in 1917, involved the fall of the czar and his replacement by a liberal democratic regime, which opposed the pro-German imperial Russian court. This was welcomed by America as support for the Allied war efforts. The second revolution, by the Bolsheviks in November 1917, was misunderstood; Americans seemed to believe that the Bolshevik leaders were merely pro-German agents.

Only after the war was Russian communism seen as a true political reality. From 1918 to 1920, during the Russian civil war, America intervened, sending troops to two areas of the Soviet Union: to Arkhangelsk (Archangel) on the White Sea in northern Europe and to eastern Siberia.

It was difficult for America to accommodate to the new Soviet regime. Although it did not declare war on the United States, it was committed by its strongest beliefs to the dismantling of those political and social traditions common to the American ethic. This threat was especially monstrous in the eyes of Americans because it struck right at the heart of the ideological beliefs of capitalism, free enterprise, and God. It could be viewed as a religious dispute, in that communism denied the existence of God. Yet communism in unadulterated form really represents the good and well-being of all people. And America's Judeo-Christian tradition also recognizes the quality and goodness of humanity. Hence the basic American ethic is almost socialistic in its call for government of the people, by the people, and for the people.

In the Soviet Union, theoretically, all people were considered

*Material from this section has been obtained from George Kennan.

equal and worked for each other's good. They were organized by a state bureaucracy, which should come from the people, and there was no recognized God. In America, theoretically, all people had equal opportunities to look after themselves. There was no built-in mechanism that cared for everyone equally, and a belief in God was dominant. The concept of religion was eliminated in the Soviet Union because of the Church's corrupt role in supporting the czars during years of gross inequality. Over the years, the Soviet ideological ethic became more "a rhetorical exercise than a guide to policy." But another circumstance had concerned and alienated America: the lack of commitment by the new Soviet government to repay debts owed by the czars to the United States.

The American government remained resistant to the new regime for thirteen years. Finally, in 1933, Franklin Roosevelt established formal diplomatic relations between the two countries. The debts, never repaid, were quickly forgotten. During the 1930s, Stalin began to implement his repressive policies within Soviet society, murdering millions of Soviet citizens; and by the end of the 1930s, belief in Lenin's idealism had been, for the most part, extinguished.

In 1933, Hitler became chancellor of Germany. For six years, he and his Brown Shirts instigated the persecution of Jews, eventually evolving "the final solution." Those United States newspapers that supported Hitler did so because of his anti-Bolshevik policies; only after Kristallnacht in 1938, when the Jews all over Germany were overtly attacked, did U.S. newspapers begin to report the Nazi atrocities.

Although official U.S.-Soviet relations improved during this period, Red-baiting and other anti-communist tactics were used by U.S. corporations to break unions and undermine their growth. Corporations stocked munitions and killed workers to end strikes. By 1983, only 20 percent of American workers were unionized. (In Australia, the figure is closer to 75 percent.)

In 1939, Germany and the Soviet Union signed a nonaggression pact; in June 1941, the USSR was invaded without warning by Hitler. Suddenly the Soviet Union became a close ally of the United States. All previous hostilities were forgotten during those fateful days of World War II. (When Germany turned its might on the USSR, my Australian mother heaved a sigh of relief and said, "Thank God, we're saved.")

The First Missile Gap

During the years of World War II, the structure of the world changed. Man learned to fission the atom. Overnight our concepts of good and evil, and our previously acceptable standards of international behavior, became old-fashioned. In 1939, the physicists Albert Einstein, Leo Szilard, and Edward Teller, and the banker Dr. Alexander Sachs wrote a letter to President Roosevelt. They believed Hitler was developing nuclear weapons and suggested that America do the same thing. Roosevelt, convinced by the letter, instituted the Manhattan Project—the largest scientific operation ever undertaken. Run by General Leslie Groves and the brainchild of a brilliant physicist named Robert Oppenheimer, it was conceived and executed in total secrecy at a private boys' school named Los Alamos, deep in the mountains of New Mexico. The project quickly grew to incorporate thousands of brilliant scientists and technicians and was in operation for three years.

When Hitler was defeated some months before the bombs were due to be completed, the *raison d'être* for the nuclear force disappeared. One of the scientists called an emergency meeting to plan an agenda. Oppenheimer did not attend. Eventually, they decided to proceed with the work. A documentary film, *The Day After Trinity*, confirmed that the scientists could not stop themselves from working on these fascinating technical problems.

The first bomb, named Trinity (code-named the Gadget), was scheduled to be tested in the New Mexico desert at Alamogordo in July 1945. There was great uncertainty about whether the bomb would explode at all and, if it did, what its yield would be. There was also an outside chance that the earth's atmosphere would be rendered critical and the globe enveloped in fire. One astonished junior technician was amazed to hear the brilliant physicist Enrico Fermi taking side bets, as the Gadget was hoisted to the top of its tower, that New Mexico would be incinerated.

The night was wild and stormy. Lightning bolts split the sky, and the scientists were worried that they might explode the bomb prematurely or disturb its functions. However, Trinity exploded on time. As the scientists crouched in their shelters some miles away, they were amazed at what they had done. The desert suddenly became tiny as it filled with a violent blue light. A sound like thunder seemed to last forever, and a huge cloud of radioactive debris appeared and hovered overhead. But at just the right time, the wind changed and the cloud blew away, sparing the scientists from fallout contamination. Robert Oppenheimer, witness to the first atomic explosion of Trinity, quoted from the *Bhagavad Gita:* "I am become death, the shatterer of worlds."

That night the scientists held a party to celebrate their success.

The next bomb, code-named Little Boy and equivalent to 12,500 tons of TNT, was dropped from a plane called *Enola Gay* at 8:15 A.M. on August 6, 1945, over a city called Hiroshima. The population had responded to an earlier air-raid siren, but had emerged from the shelters just before the bomb exploded. Approximately 130,000 people were dead by November. Hiroshima disappeared.

People there exposed to heat equal to that of the sun at the instant of the explosion were vaporized—they left only their shadows on the pavement behind them. Children were seen running along the streets with their skin falling off their bodies like veils. A woman lay in the gutter with her back totally burned, and as she died, her baby suckled at her breast. A man stood acutely shocked, holding his eyeball in the palm of his hand. Bodies lay in all areas. Swollen tongues protruded from mouths; eyes that had been eviscerated from the blast hung on cheeks. To quote a survivor: "In one small space amid a pile of bricks, a young woman's head faced toward me, and a look of innocent beauty still remained on her face."

That night the scientists held another party. One man said he could not go because he was so depressed and physically nauseated. When the scientists were planning and designing the bombs, he explained, they never calculated people as matter. In other words, although they had designed bombs to kill people, they had not extrapolated their calculations to determine how the enormous forces they had unleashed would affect the human body.

Some people survived Hiroshima and ran away to the only Christian center in Japan—a very old port called Nagasaki. They arrived just in time for the second atomic bomb, code-named Fat Man. Between 60,000 and 70,000 people were killed instantly. The Atomic Age had begun.

Roosevelt died some months before the bombs were used, and Harry Truman came to office with little knowledge of foreign affairs. Just before Roosevelt died, Szilard, Einstein, and others had written a letter to the president advising him that the bomb should not be used on population centers. The letter lay unopened on his desk when Truman acceded and was not read until after the war. By the time the bombs were dropped, the Japanese had already opened peace negotiations through the Soviet Union. But the American government, which knew about these peace initiatives, nonetheless proceeded. Truman said of the Soviets on the eve of the first atomic test, "If it explodes as I think it will, I'll certainly have a hammer on those boys."

It is said that those bombs saved 500,000 American lives that would otherwise have been lost during the invasion of Japan—obviously a fallacious argument because of the ignored peace proposal. At the same time, the Soviet Union—a professed ally that had shouldered an enormous burden during World War II—was being branded as an enemy by the American president. Why were the bombs really used?

Americans had been told during World War II that Soviet-American collaboration assured the future peace, but this obviously was not to be so. Only after the end of the war did the behavior of the Soviet Union become overtly suspect. It left modern mechanized military units in the Eastern European countries. Although Soviet equipment was inferior to that of the Western armies, its presence nonetheless threatened both Europeans and Americans. But the move represented little change from previous Russian policy. For centuries, Russian rulers had customarily maintained ground forces much larger than necessary even in times of peace.

Furthermore, Soviet troops often were brutal in the countries they overran. Although inexcusable, their behavior could arguably be a reaction to the sheer brutality they had suffered under the Nazis. It soon became clear that democracy was not to be practiced in countries occupied by the Soviet Union—Germany, Austria, Hungary, Bulgaria, Romania, Poland, and Czechoslovakia. In addition, the Soviet government remained secretive, continuing to issue propaganda statements about the destruction of capitalism. American anxiety increased.

At the end of the war, America—the only nuclear nation on

earth—still had one bomb in its arsenal. There was one clumsy, and ultimately unsuccessful, attempt to internationalize nuclear energy. Called the Baruch Plan, after wealthy businessman Bernard Baruch, it was initially conceived by Secretary of State Dean Acheson and David Lilienthal, chairman of the Atomic Energy Commission. The plan was as follows:

A proposed International Development Council would receive the nuclear warheads from America only if the Soviet Union immediately relinquished control of its uranium mines and production facilities to an international authority. Meanwhile, America could continue making bombs and conducting research on new weapons until it was satisfied with the international procedures for inspection and control. A nation that failed to abide by the agreement would receive punishment at the behest of the U.N. Security Council, which was dominated by the United States. The Soviet Union would also have to surrender its veto power.

Because the Soviet Union rejected the plan, the United States continued to build nuclear weapons.

Anti-Soviet feeling in the United States immediately after the war seemed to be almost as intense as anti-Nazi feeling had been there during it. In 1946, Eugene Rostow (director of the first-term Reagan Arms Control and Disarmament Agency) circulated a memo among people at the Office of Strategic Services proposing that Stalin be given an ultimatum: Democratize your society or we will obliterate your cities with nuclear weapons.

Before World War II, the USSR had been seen by America as a revolutionary political force. After the war, it became the traditional great military power poised on the edge of America's newly acquired sphere of political-military interest in Europe.

At the end of the war, the United States was left with a huge military superstructure and an expanded apparatus for military planning. With Germany and Japan defeated, a new military opponent seemed necessary in order to maintain the American military status quo. The Soviet Union was the obvious candidate. Soviet leaders were partially confused by American pro-Soviet support during the wartime years and by Western agreement to extension of Soviet borders after the war. They thought that American forces would probably withdraw from the European continent after the war, and they had hoped to penetrate the

European vacuum that would result. They had not intended to use force but rather to ally themselves with the French and Italian Communist parties, to exploit Soviet military-controlled powers in Berlin and Vienna, and to penetrate the Western labor unions' intellectual and student movements. However, Soviet dreams of political takeover in Western Europe were frustrated by the Marshall Plan, which helped to restore the shattered Western European economy. Some think that the crackdown in Czechoslovakia and the Berlin Blockade in 1948 were essentially defensive in nature—attempts by Moscow to play its last political cards in anticipation of a new division of power on the European continent. Had the Marshall Plan continued to improve European recovery, Stalin might have been forced to concentrate on building economic strength within the Eastern Bloc countries. But America, already conditioned by anti-Soviet thinking, interpreted this international tension as the forerunner of war. Thus, in 1949, the North Atlantic Treaty Organization (NATO) was established. Because it was a military alliance, its existence obviously exacerbated the tensions within Europe.

By indulging in a fantasy of nuclear strength, America had sown the seeds for its own suicide. It had initiated the nuclear arms race; the USSR, anxious to be a viable superpower, followed. Until the Soviet Union developed a large, deliverable nuclear arsenal, America was totally invulnerable. Today it can be virtually obliterated within several hours.

The Arms Race Begins

By 1949, the Soviet Union had learned how to fission the atom and had exploded its first atomic bomb. That same year, America "lost" China to Mao's Communist revolution. Although blamed on the Soviets, it was in fact an internal civil war supported by a majority of its six hundred million people. Throughout the Chinese Revolution, the only major American reporting came from Theodore White, a brilliant young *Time* correspondent stationed in China. Henry B. Luce, the owner of *Time* magazine, had been born in China to missionary parents. Because he reviled the revolution and supported deposed leader Chiang Kai-shek, Luce altered most of the dispatches he received from White. Consequently, America was given a woefully biased account of the happenings in China;

thus began the Two China policy, which led to such bitter acrimony between the two nations.

In 1949, the General Advisory Committee met to decide whether America should proceed with the construction of a hydrogen bomb—the brainchild of Edward Teller. The committee, chaired by Robert Oppenheimer, recommended against it on the grounds that its unlimited potential for destruction would endanger humanity. But Teller, pushing for his "super bomb," prevailed against Oppenheimer, and Truman decided on a crash H-bomb program. The first H-bomb was exploded on Eniwetok atoll in 1952; an improved model was detonated at Bikini in 1954.

In 1950, soon after the explosion of the first Soviet atomic bomb, another source of conflict emerged: the war in Korea. Viewed by the United States as an attack by the Red Army across international borders, it was, in fact, a conflict inspired overwhelmingly by local problems related to the Manchurian-Korean area.

By 1951, America (which had many more nuclear weapons) had the USSR ringed by air bases in Greenland, Iceland, Okinawa, Japan, Alaska, Spain, Saudi Arabia, Tunisia, Morocco, and Turkey. Planes from these locations could all deliver nuclear weapons. Because it is cheaper to deploy nuclear weapons than military troops, the United States had cut back manpower. But by 1955, the Soviets, no doubt responding to America's nuclear arsenal, had a huge standing army of six million. From the beginning, NATO has always maintained the right to use nuclear weapons first if provoked by political or conventional military considerations. This doctrine is known as "first use." In 1954, the United States decided to rearm West Germany and to include it in NATO. The decision upset the USSR because of its recent conflict with Germany. At that time, the Soviet Union announced the formation of the Warsaw Pact, also a military alliance.

The Eye of the Beholder

The American statesman George Kennan says:

When a military planner selects another country as the leading hypothetical opponent of his own country—the opponent against whom military preparations and operations are theoretically being directed—the discipline of his profession obliges him to endow that opponent with extreme hostility and the most formidable of capabilities. In this way, not only is there created, for planning purposes, the image of the totally inhuman and totally malevolent adversary, but this image is reconjured daily, week after week, month after month, year after year, until it takes on every feature of flesh and blood and becomes the daily companion of those who cultivate it, so that any attempt on anyone's part to deny its reality appears as an act of treason or frivolity. In this way, the planner's hypothesis becomes imperceptibly the politicians' and journalists' reality, upon which a great deal of American policy and of American military efforts come to be based.

The "enemy image" that a nation adopts is notoriously fickle. In 1942, Americans responded to a poll by describing the German-Japanese enemy as warlike, treacherous, and cruel. None of these adjectives appeared in describing the Soviet allies. By 1966, the mainland Chinese were warlike, treacherous, and sly; but the Germans and Japanese were by then considered hardworking allies. Now the Soviets had become warlike and treacherous. In American eyes, the "bloodthirsty, cruel, treacherous, slant-eyed, buck-toothed little Japs of World War II [had] become a highly cultivated, charming, industrious, and thoroughly attractive people." Since 1966, the American attitude toward the Chinese has softened. Yet they are still hard-line Communists armed with nuclear weapons.

The present enemy image is that of the Soviet Union. The American nuclear arms race has reinforced itself with that enemy image as well as with suspicions and inadequate information. As Jerome Wiesner, president emeritus of MIT and former science adviser to President Kennedy, said recently, "For years, America has been holding an arms race with itself."

The War Blows Hot and Cold

Since 1945, American perceptions of the Soviet Union have been determined largely by internal domestic affairs, often divorced from the reality of international events.

The period from 1945 to 1952 was one of intense Cold War

rivalry. President Truman, not well versed in international affairs, was open to manipulation. Harry Hopkins, a trusted adviser, was sent by Truman to Moscow in 1945 and found Stalin to be a reasonable man, interested in cooperation and even willing to compromise on Poland. Secretary of State James Byrnes, in Moscow in late 1945, negotiated a compromise with Stalin over Eastern Europe and won agreement for a U.N. Atomic Energy Commission. Diplomacy with the Soviet Union obviously was possible.

But a faction of old hard-liners in the State Department, who were notoriously anti-Semitic, tolerant of Hitler, and ultrareactionary, persuaded Truman to adopt a hard-line posture toward the Soviet Union. Their attitude was reinforced by some liberals in labor unions who sought to gain respectability against some of their more radical opponents, and by those liberal politicians who saw a strong anti-Soviet stand as an opportunity to placate more conservative politicians. In addition, an adversarial posture toward the Soviet Union promulgated high military budgets, which were thought to be conducive to postwar economic recovery. All these factors combined to create an ideological offensive against the Soviet Union.

In 1952, the American people elected a president who was more moderate in his interpretation of the Soviet threat. Eisenhower, fiscally conservative, was not prone to vast increases in weapons expenditures. Although John Foster Dulles, secretary of state, was a zealous anti-Communist, he seemed more hostile to the Chinese than to the Soviets. By mid-1958 he became more flexible, exploring partial American military disengagement in Europe and apparently endorsing reduction of tensions with the Soviets.

The American right wing, increasingly frustrated by Eisenhower's policies, mobilized from 1957 to 1963. Its "Gaither Report" described a fallacious missile gap between the United States and the USSR. Former Army Chief of Staff Maxwell Taylor wrote a book, *Uncertain Trumpet*, calling for a buildup of conventional arms, and Henry Kissinger produced a study outlining the advantages of a U.S. strategy based on limited nuclear war. Some ambitious Democratic presidential contenders—Stuart Symington, John Kennedy, Lyndon Johnson, and Hubert Humphrey—were attracted to this anti-Soviet rhetoric and used it to criticize Eisenhower's complacency. Upon his election, President Kennedy increased the defense budget, supported the Special Forces, encouraged counterinsurgency warfare around the world, and intimated that he would welcome a confrontation with the Soviet Union. He was assisted by the verbally belligerent Nikita Khrushchev, who sought to maintain Soviet control over Eastern Europe and attempted to curry favor with newly independent nations in the Third World. But the USSR still was far behind in military strength.

After the Cuban missile crisis, Kennedy did reach out toward the Soviet Union, negotiating a partial test-ban treaty. But both Kennedy and Johnson, determined not to be seen by the American right wing as "soft on communism," escalated an internal political struggle in Vietnam into a major confrontation with China and the USSR. The war was not welcomed by either country. China is an old enemy of Vietnam, and the Soviet Union did everything it could to bring the conflict to an end. The Soviets also negotiated SALT I and the ABM Treaty during this traumatic time, even as America broke international law by secretly bombing Cambodia.

Both Nixon and Ford were more domestically secure in their anti-Communist stance and therefore less inclined to play the domestic anti-Soviet line. They were pragmatic about international big-power politics, and they recognized China and established détente with the Soviet Union. The defense budget, as a percentage of the GNP, fell. Tensions between the superpowers relaxed.

Then, during the Carter Administration, the Committee on the Present Danger mobilized to counteract the effects of détente—again influencing a liberal Democratic administration to develop hard-line, anti-Soviet policies. President Reagan, contrary to most previous Republican administrations, has continued and even exaggerated the anti-Soviet stand.

The Reality of the Soviet Threat

The Soviet "menace" has been used by Democratic administrations since 1945 to bolster their more progressive domestic policies and to support themselves against attack from right-wing Republicans who disapprove of liberal social programs. Thus the Soviet threat has assumed a magical political quality. It placates the right wing and allows liberals to be liberal at home. It has also been used extensively by the U.S. armed forces to promote interservice rivalry and by the military-industrial complex to support military and economic growth. This self-fulfilling enemy image has been so successful that between 1949 and 1968 not a single military appropriations bill was denied in the House or Senate.

In 1950, the United States had 150 nuclear bombs—the only nuclear weapons in the world—and some 500 strategic bombers. By 1953, the United States had about 1,300 nuclear weapons and the USSR 300.

In 1955, during Moscow Aviation Day, the Soviets repeatedly flew 10 Bison bombers past the reviewing stand. Because of this trick, American officials thought the Soviet Union had many more planes than they actually had and estimated that they could build 600 by the year 1957. Responding to this misperception, by 1959 the United States had expanded its bomber force to 500 B-52s and 1,350 B-47s. In fact, the Soviet Union never had more than 150 long-range bombers until they began to build more Bear bombers in 1983. (They now have about 170 heavy bombers.)

By 1960, the Soviet Union had acquired the means to deliver nuclear weapons to the United States. It had 150 intercontinental bombers and 500 short-range bombers that could reach Western Europe. It also had about 10 intercontinental ballistic missiles (ICBMs). But President Kennedy campaigned in 1960 on a fictitious missile gap, claiming that the Soviet Union had many more nuclear weapons and missiles than did the United States. Consequently, by 1962, America had built 224 ICBMs, 144 submarine-based Polaris missiles, 105 Thor and Jupiter nuclear missiles placed in Europe, 1,500 long-range bombers, 300 carrier-based fighters, and about 1,000 supersonic land-based fighters—all aircraft capable of carrying nuclear weapons.

Soon after his election, President Kennedy learned from a spy satellite that the missile gap was fallacious. Yet the Defense Department decided to build 1,000 new intercontinental missiles (Minutemen) and 656 submarine-launched Polaris missiles.

The arms race has continued in this fashion to the present day. The chart on page 187 illustrates that on only three occasions has the Soviet Union surpassed the United States in nuclear weapons developments. And one—the antiballistic missile system—did not work.

So between 1960 and 1967, the main force of U.S. missiles was deployed both on land and at sea in submarines. At that time, the Soviet Union was relying only on its few intercontinental bombers and about 300 intercontinental ballistic missiles. However, in 1965, partly as a response to the Cuban missile crisis, the Soviet Union began developing missiles that were placed in reinforced-steel underground silos—invulnerable in the event of a large-scale nuclear war. From 1965 to 1971, the Soviet Union deployed 1,400 intercontinental ballistic missiles in hardened silos and began deploying submarine-based missiles within range of the United States—62 strategic submarines between 1967 and 1977. Only within the past 20 years or so have United States cities become vulnerable to a Soviet missile strike that could take place within 30 minutes after launching. This is because the United States failed to stop the arms race in 1960, when it started deploying its first intercontinental ballistic missiles.

Action	Initiated by	Date	Reaction by	Date
Sustained nuclear chain reaction	U.S.	1942	USSR	1946
Atomic bomb	U.S.	1945	USSR	1949
Intercontinental bomber	U.S.	1948	USSR	1955
International military pact (U.S. NATO; USSR Warsaw Pact)	U.S.	1949	USSR	1955
Tactical nuclear weapons deployed in Europe	U.S.	1954	USSR	1957
Nuclear powered submarine	U.S.	1955	USSR	1959
ICBM	USSR	1957	U.S.	1958
Satellite launching	USSR	1957	U.S.	1958
Supersonic bomber	U.S.	1960	USSR	1975
Submarine-launched ballistic missile	U.S.	1960	USSR	1968
Solid fuel missiles	U.S.	1960	USSR	1968
Accelerated ICBM build-up	U.S.	1961	USSR	1966
Multiple reentry vehicles (MRVs)	U.S.	1964	USSR	1968
Penetration aids on missiles	U.S.	1964	USSR	none yet
ABM system	USSR	1968	U.S.	1972
High-speed warheads	U.S.	1970	USSR	1975
MIRVs	U.S.	1970	USSR	1975
Computerized missile guidance	U.S.	1970	USSR	1975
Neutron bombs	U.S.	1981	USSR	none yet
Long-range cruise missiles	U.S.	1982	USSR	1985

During the 1960s, physicist Theodore Taylor developed a method of miniaturizing nuclear weapons. His work enabled the United States to nuclearize all forms of conventional weapons—torpedoes, land mines, and surface-to-surface and surface-to-air missiles—even small nuclear weapons on recoilless rifles (called Davy Crocketts) that people could carry on their shoulders. And since 1950, large numbers of tactical nuclear weapons have been deployed throughout the world. There are approximately 6,000 short-range tactical nuclear weapons deployed in Western Europe, many very close to the border of East Germany. In the event of a Soviet invasion of West Germany, U.S. military doctrine prescribes a policy of first use. If NATO were losing a conventional war with the Soviet Union, it would use tactical nuclear weapons first to stop invading Soviet tanks, on the theory that the USSR would not be crazy enough to retaliate with a nuclear weapon and risk an expanded nuclear war. To quote Morton Halperin, former deputy assistant secretary of defense, "The NATO doctrine is that we will fight with conventional forces until we are losing, then we will fight with tactical nuclear weapons until we are losing, and then we will blow up the world." Soviet policy is exactly the reverse.

Over the years, Cold War politics and enemy image have been used to justify the momentum of the nuclear arms race. Yet Sir Solly Zuckerman, a British scientist who was involved in the Manhattan Project, identifies scientists as the driving force behind the arms race. Politicians obviously use the threat of Communist menace to enhance their political prestige and power. Historically, at every election and at appropriations time for nuclear weapons, the same threat has been dragged out of the closet to justify either personal or political ambitions or new weapons development.

Relationships between the superpowers are now almost totally controlled by military thinking—political considerations have, in effect, ceased to exist. The Pentagon and the secretary of defense seem to determine the direction of international affairs. Just as weapons are invented, so political doctrines and rationales for their use are devised. Political thinking always lags five to ten years behind scientific development. In a way, politicians are almost innocent bystanders. They watch the mad technological momentum emanating from the scientific community, which always assumes the worst possible case for Soviet motivations and weapons development. Over the years, the strategic doctrine of American nuclear thinking has changed to accommodate the new weapons systems.

The Collapse of Détente*

The Cold War came to an end when détente was established by a hawkish Republican president in the early 1970s. President Nixon and his secretary of state, Henry Kissinger, also established diplomatic relationships with China, for years a bitter enemy.

Soon after his inauguration in 1969, Nixon moved to end the Cold War with the Soviet Union. SALT I was negotiated with the Soviet Union and ratified in 1972, together with the Antiballistic Missile Treaty at the Moscow summit in 1972. The United States had just learned how to MIRV missiles, and since the Soviets had not yet mastered the technology, MIRVing was not included in the SALT I treaty. The United States continued to increase its arsenal of nuclear warheads by MIRVing its missiles; the Soviet Union began to catch up only in 1975, when it learned to MIRV. This situation has created an enormous bilateral momentum in the arms race; Kissinger has said that he rued the day that MIRVing was not outlawed in SALT I.

After Nixon's resignation, President Gerald Ford and General Secretary Leonid Brezhnev met in Vladivostok in November 1974. They intended to establish a limit on all strategic weapons systems, to extend for ten years. At that time, the USSR agreed not to include in the strategic balance French and British strategic forces or U.S. medium-range nuclear bombers (forward-based systems) in Europe and Asia. This was a quid pro quo for abandonment of U.S. insistence on a cutback in Soviet heavy ICBMs. But Senator Henry "Scoop" Jackson, Democrat from Washington and one of the most powerful senators in military affairs and national security, disapproved of the SALT I treaty and falsely suggested that it gave the Soviet Union a strategic advantage. He moved quickly to destroy the pending U.S.-Soviet trade bill by attaching the Jackson-Vanick

* Information for this section was taken from *Russian Roulette* by Arthur Macy Cox and from *With Enough Shovels* by Robert Scheer.

Amendment to the bill. The amendment called for withholding most-favored-nation status from the Soviet Union unless it granted the right of emigration to its Jewish citizens. In December 1974, Congress was persuaded by Jackson and his young staffer Richard Perle to vote for the amendment. The Soviet Union immediately rejected the amendment, unwilling to submit to manipulation and humiliation by the United States. Jewish emigration fell from thirty-five thousand to less than ten thousand per year, and the USSR lost the trade bill it so desperately desired. And, partly in response to the U.S. forward-based systems and the British and French strategic forces, the Soviet Union announced that it would modernize its medium-range SS-4 and SS-5 missiles targeted on Europe. To this day, the Jackson-Vanick Amendment remains a source of friction between the superpowers. Senator Jackson was a long time advocate of both U.S. military superiority and the Boeing Company, which manufactures the B-52 bomber, the Minuteman missile, the cruise missile, and the Trident submarine. Only by establishing good trade relationships with the Soviet Union can the United States ever hope to defuse tensions.

During the years of détente, a group of neoconservative Democrats—the Coalition for a Democratic Majority—always rejected the détente concept. They were hawks who preferred to compete with the Soviet Union by building more hydrogen bombs and missiles rather than by reducing tensions and weapons. Among them were Henry Jackson, Daniel Patrick Moynihan, Ben Wattenberg, Eugene Rostow, Norman Podhoretz (editor of *Commentary*), and Irving Kristol (editor of *The Public Interest*).

President Ford's first secretary of defense, James Schlesinger, was another hawk who had been highly critical of SALT I because it gave the Soviets greater "throw weight." He said that the Soviet missiles, bigger and heavier than those of the United States, were superior. But the United States has always chosen to build smaller, more accurate missiles than the Soviet Union, because accuracy increases killing power and because, at that time, America was far advanced in MIRVing. A Schlesinger report to Congress in 1974 audaciously compared the American military arsenal—the most lethal in history—to that of impotent Britain in the 1930s and used Neville Chamberlain, with his pathetic performance in Munich, as an example of the type of appeasement the United States might have to follow in dealing with the Soviet Union. This totally inappropriate position became a regular theme song of the hawks during the 1970s and into the Reagan presidency.

In November 1975, George Bush, with no previous intelligence experience, was appointed head of the CIA. The hawks saw their chance. Bush quickly appointed a handpicked committee called "Team B" to compare U.S.-Soviet military spending (although the CIA already had "Team A," a group of professional intelligence officers who were paid to do the same work in an unbiased way). Team B was stacked with hawks, many now appointees in the Reagan Administration. The committee was chaired by Richard Pipes, a Polish immigrant and a professor of eighteenth-century Russian history at Harvard, later to be Soviet specialist on the Reagan National Security Council, and a notorious anti-Soviet hard-liner. Other members were Paul Nitze, later chief of the U.S. delegation to talks on intermediate-range nuclear weapons in Geneva (which were ended in December 1983 by a Soviet walkout); William R. van Cleave, later head of the Reagan transition team for the Department of Defense; Paul D. Wolfowitz, now chief of policy planning in the State Department; Seymour Weiss; Daniel O. Graham, retired Army lieutenant general and former director of the Defense Intelligence Agency, now director of the High Frontier Foundation, a *Star Wars* lobbying group; Foy D. Kohler, a think-tank associate of General Graham; Thomas Wolfe, a specialist on Soviet military affairs at the RAND Corporation, a think tank substantially funded by the U.S. Air Force; John W. Vogt, Jr., retired Air Force general; and Jasper A. Welch, Jr., Air Force brigadier general, assistant Chief of Staff, who has helped prepare SALT positions for the Joint Chiefs of Staff.

The team used new evidence and reinterpretation of old information to produce a revised estimate of Soviet military spending. The still-classified report, published in October 1976, showed that Soviet military spending, as a percentage of gross national product, had increased from between 6 and 8 percent to between 11 and 13 percent, whereas America held firm at 6 percent—apparently overwhelming proof for Team B that the USSR was ahead in the strategic nuclear race.

It is important here to understand how the CIA estimates Soviet military spending. They calculate the projected cost of Soviet materiel if built in the United States, at U.S. prices. They also estimate Soviet military pay as equivalent to American military pay, although, comparatively, the USSR pays its soldiers a mere pittance. Every time the American military receives a pay raise, estimates of Soviet military spending increase.

What the new estimates really showed was that an error had been allowed to stand for years in previous CIA estimates. In fact, the Soviets were far less efficient at producing weapons than had previously been thought. (America has known for years the size of the USSR conventional and nuclear arsenals.) To place these new figures in perspective, it is necessary to understand that the Soviet gross national product is half that of the United States. Consequently, Soviet-American expenditure levels are approximately equal, allowing for all contingencies I have just discussed. And no mention was made of NATO-Warsaw Pact spending. For example, in 1971 and 1972 the NATO allies outspent the Soviets' Eastern European allies by five to one.

The Team B report concluded that the USSR had rejected the notion of parity and mutually assured destruction (MAD) and was aiming instead for nuclear superiority. This erroneous conclusion was derived solely from the false estimate of increased defense spending. (The Team B people also concluded that the Soviet Union expected not only to survive but also to win a nuclear war.)

According to Team B spokesman General Daniel Graham, adequate civil defense is necessary to fight and win a nuclear war. Studies on Soviet civil defense had been performed by Thomas K. Jones, now deputy under secretary of defense for research and engineering, strategic and nuclear forces, in the Reagan Administration. Before he worked in the Defense Department, Jones was employed at Boeing and had extensively studied the Soviet civil defense manuals, which enthusiastically suggested twenty to thirty designs for digging holes in the ground where people could shelter from nuclear attack. Jones had also practiced covering factory machinery with dirt and then detonating large TNT explosions above the machinery. From these experiments he had deduced that the Soviets could protect much of their industrial plant from the effects of nuclear war. T.K. (as he likes to be called) also estimated

Soviet nuclear war casualties by theoretically spacing the Soviet people equidistant from one another over the whole Soviet subcontinent and then dropping bombs on selected military and civilian targets. These data have been interpreted by Richard Pipes to mean that the Soviet civil defense program would permit "acceptable" casualties of about 20 million, which, as he likes to point out, is similar to the numbers of their dead in World War II. He concluded that because this had happened before, they could well tolerate a repeat scenario in a nuclear war. Pipes estimates the current probability of nuclear war as 40 percent. Jones estimates that recovery from nuclear war could occur within four years.

The whole Reagan nuclear rearmament program is based upon the assumptions of Team B and T. K. Jones. This is why the president repeats again and again that the Soviet Union has engaged in a massive military buildup over the past decade, that they are preparing to fight and win a nuclear war, and that we have to catch up.

The Team A-Team B process was slated to end in February 1977, but when Jimmy Carter was elected president in 1976, the Team B report was leaked to the *Boston Globe.* In an unprecedented interview with *The New York Times,* CIA head George Bush said the Soviet military buildup was much greater than previously had been assumed by the CIA. (Former CIA directors had always refused to be interviewed by the press concerning top-secret national intelligence reports.) Herbert Scoville, Jr., a former CIA deputy director for science and technology, said,

> I think this whole thing was clearly an attempt to leave a legacy for the new Administration, which would be very hard to reverse. . . . Now that the integrity of the estimating process has been questioned, it is extremely difficult for the CIA regulars to stand up to the pressure of a biased point of view when the people at the top want to prove something.

The Committee on the Present Danger

In 1976, Secretary of State Henry Kissinger found himself surrounded by tough, dedicated hawks in the Pentagon, in the Arms Control and Disarmament Agency (ACDA), and in the Senate Armed Services Committee. Some of the hawks were Henry

Jackson; his assistant Richard Perle; Paul Nitze; Eugene Rostow; Fred Iklé, director of ACDA; and John Lehman, deputy director of ACDA. Because James Schlesinger, former secretary of defense, was working with Henry Jackson to destroy the SALT II concept based on the Vladivostok agreement, President Ford fired Schlesinger.

After his dismissal, Schlesinger met with Eugene Rostow and Paul Nitze. Together they decided that a private national committee was needed to influence public opinion about the "danger" of détente and the need to increase U.S. military power. (Rostow later was appointed head of the Arms Control and Disarmament Agency by President Reagan.) Thus the Committee on the Present Danger was born at a luncheon at the Metropolitan Club in Washington in March 1976. Nitze's involvement with these issues began in 1950, when he drafted a document, NSC-68, commissioned by the Department of Defense and Department of State. His report contrasted the "Soviet desire for world domination with the U.S. desire for an environment in which free societies could exist and flourish." It compared Soviet global intentions to the totalitarianism and aggressiveness of Nazi Germany, even though theirs were different social systems. NSC-68 never was officially adopted by the Truman Administration, but it is generally regarded as a crucial turning point in American policy because it provided a rationale for two major transformations. It called for programs that would triple the defense budget, and it gave the American people a special interpretation of the Soviet threat. Paul Nitze also was an influential member of the Gaither Committee, established in 1957 by President Dwight D. Eisenhower. This group's report concluded that by 1959 the Soviets would have an ICBM force capable of destroying the U.S. strategic bombers. This claim was known as the fictitious missile gap. Nitze also said, during the Berlin Blockade in 1949, that the United States should evacuate its cities and put the Strategic Air Command on full alert.

Many of the people on the Committee on the Present Danger were transferred into the Reagan Administration after his election. All strident critics of SALT II, they defeated this agreement. Some of the members of the committee were: Henry Fowler, former secretary of the treasury under Johnson; Lane Kirkland, president of the AFL-CIO; David Packard, former deputy secretary of defense under Nixon; Paul Nitze, negotiator for intermediate nuclear forces in Europe; Eugene Rostow, former head of the Arms Control and Disarmament Agency; Richard Allen, former national security adviser to President Reagan; Richard Pipes, former adviser on Soviet affairs to President Reagan; Geoffrey Kemp of the National Security Council; Fred Iklé, undersecretary of defense for policy, and his deputy, R. G. Stillwell; Richard Perle, assistant secretary of defense for international security policy; William van Cleave from the General Advisory Committee; William Casey, head of the CIA; John Lehman, secretary of the Navy; Jeane Kirkpatrick, recently retired ambassador to the United Nations; Colin Gray, Arms Control Agency Advisory Committee; George Shultz, secretary of state and a founding member of the Committee on the Present Danger; and W. Allen Wallis, top assistant to Secretary Shultz.

After President Carter was elected, he attempted to bring the right and left factions of the Democratic Party together. In an effort to placate Henry Jackson, he was persuaded to send a proposal to the Soviet Union in 1977 that undermined the Vladivostok-SALT II agreement. Cyrus Vance, secretary of state, delivered the proposal to the Soviet Union. It was grossly inequitable, calling for deep cuts in the Soviet ICBM forces (70 percent of its strategic nuclear weapons are land-based ICBMs) but not in strategic bombers and submarine missiles, where the United States had a clear advantage. It also called for a ban on Soviet Backfire bombers. Previously considered medium-range (and later excluded from the SALT II agreement), the Backfire was reclassified as a long-range strategic bomber. America now claimed that the Backfire could reach the United States from the Soviet Union, although it had only enough fuel to fly one way at military speed. The new proposal also allowed the United States to continue developing cruise missiles. Both of these new conditions contradicted the Vadivostok proposals. William Hyland, one of Kissinger's staff, said that he knew the Soviets would never accept such an unfair proposal. Brezhnev, disturbed by this overtly unilateral proposal, rejected it.

President Carter was deeply committed to eliminating nuclear weapons. During his term in office, he frequently called for détente and a reduction of nuclear weapons, combined with a ban on direct or indirect military intervention in the world, a freeze on further modernization of weapons, and a comprehensive test-ban treaty.

Indeed, in his inaugural address, he called for elimination of all nuclear weapons.

Unfortunately, during his presidency, the Soviets made détente and Carter's commitments difficult. They airlifted Cuban troops to Angola and Ethiopia (these Cuban troops support and protect Gulf Oil facilities in Angola); supported intervention in South Yemen; supported the invasion of Cambodia by Vietnam; and, finally, invaded Afghanistan. Of course, the Committee on the Present Danger capitalized on these actions.

In fact, these events should have spurred America to negotiate even harder with the Soviet Union. Throughout this time, Brezhnev was promoting a freeze on further modernization and a complete test-ban treaty. Indeed, in July 1980, the Soviets agreed in principle to voluntary on-site inspection during negotiations on the treaty.

But the U.S. hawks were not at all in favor of the freeze or a complete test-ban treaty and wished to continue building the MX, Trident II missiles, cruise missiles, Pershing II missiles, and the strategic B-1 and stealth bombers. They believed in the exotic fantasy put forth by Team B—that the Soviets were planning to fight and win a nuclear war and that our only hope was to regain American nuclear "superiority." (Throughout the SALT II negotiations, however, and even now, both superpowers agree that there is at present strategic parity.)

Throughout the Carter Administration, the Committee on the Present Danger, and another like-minded lobbying group, the American Security Council, propagandized their new doctrine: (1) a huge buildup of Soviet military power; (2) the Soviet drive for world conquest; and (3) the Soviet doctrine of fighting and winning a nuclear war.

The American Security Council boasted a national membership of 230,000 and formed a group called the Coalition for Peace Through Strength, to which 42 percent of the elected members of the House and Senate belonged. The council produced several films that were frightening depictions of Soviet military strength and were full of lies and half truths. (*The Price of Peace and Freedom* was shown on 200 local TV stations and was viewed by 50 million Americans.) It alleged, among other things, that the Soviets never abide by their treaties. In fact, there have been 16 treaties on nuclear weapons negotiated between the Soviet Union and the United States. Despite alleged infringements on both sides, there have been no proven substantial violations by either party. The American Security Council was and is funded by millions of dollars—from private individuals, military-industrial corporations, and others. The films it has produced influenced millions of Americans to change their mind about détente late in the 1970s. Many well-intentioned people now said: "You can't trust the Russians" and "The Russians are ahead." Even intelligent and moderately well-informed journalists and TV and radio interviewers were convinced by this brilliant propaganda exercise.

President Carter, unfortunately, lost his way on nuclear weapons as he accepted advice from Henry Jackson and from his national security adviser, Zbigniew Brzezinski. Carter also was obviously influenced by the pressure exerted by the Committee on the Present Danger. Cyrus Vance and Paul Warnke eventually left the administration in disgust. The hawks worked hand in hand with Brzezinski, who in turn worked closely with Richard Burt, a *New York Times* reporter and well-known Washington hawk. A past assistant director of the International Institute for Strategic Studies in London, Burt frequently wrote stories that were fed to him straight from the Pentagon, with little or no critical journalistic comment. Once I called him after he produced a verbatim report on a meeting of the Committee on the Present Danger. I told him the data in his article were biased and untrue, and he replied, "Madam, when you have a similar meeting, we will report that." So Physicians for Social Responsibility organized a conference in New York on the medical consequences of nuclear war, using Cyrus Vance as a moderator. Vance had just resigned as secretary of state and spoke movingly about his concerns of nuclear war. Neither Mr. Burt nor *The New York Times* covered this unique event. Mr. Burt now is assistant secretary of state for President Reagan. During the five days preceding the Reagan election, *The New York Times* published five full-page articles by Burt about the antiquated, rusting, useless U.S. military force.

In 1979, President Carter and Chairman Brezhnev signed the SALT II treaty in Vienna. But during the subsequent SALT hearings before the Senate Foreign Relations Committee, Senator Frank Church "discovered" the Soviet troop brigade in Cuba. The CIA later admitted that these troops had been in place since 1962, but the atmosphere in the Senate became so charged with emotion that Church had sounded the death knell of SALT II. Soon thereafter, following the tortuous year of the Iranian hostage crisis, the USSR invaded Afghanistan, and the American public, almost in relief, transferred its wrath from Iran to the reliable and time-trusted enemy, the Soviet Union. SALT II was over. It was never ratified by the United States Senate. The hawks had won.

The European Factor

Preceding the brief life of SALT II, other events were occurring. Between 1969 and 1972, Willy Brandt, in West Germany, developed a policy of *Ostpolitik*: A nonaggression pact was initiated and signed between West Germany and the Soviet Union; West Germany recognized East Germany as a separate state; West Germany established diplomatic relations with Poland and Czechoslovakia; and a four-power agreement was signed in Berlin. This reduced East-West tension enormously, and the West German fear of a Soviet invasion virtually disappeared.

Senator Mike Mansfield, sensing the atmosphere of reduced tension, advised that the number of U.S. troops be reduced in West Germany. But his suggestion badly frightened the Soviets, who foresaw the void filled by German soldiers. Haunted by the memories of twenty million World War II dead, they initiated talks on mutual and balanced force reductions, insisting that together with Soviet and U.S. troop reductions, the number of German troops must also be reduced; but for various technical reasons the negotiations have never borne fruit.

Instead, the U.S. forces were mysteriously strengthened. (By 1982, the U.S. contribution to NATO had increased to $122.3 billion per year.) To justify the buildup of troops and money, America issued warnings of a Soviet blitzkrieg—although at no time during the Cold War had the USSR ever indicated that it would risk nuclear holocaust by invading West Germany.

During these years, American scientists had developed the neutron bomb, a modified hydrogen bomb that killed people with intense radiation while producing a smaller blast effect than an ordinary hydrogen bomb. The radiation was intended to penetrate and stop Soviet tanks, which were expected to be used in a blitzkrieg on West Germany. Helmut Schmidt was persuaded by the United States to accept the bomb, much to his discomfort, and revulsion was exhibited by an outraged European public. The neutron bomb is considered by the U.S. and NATO military officials as a usable first step if conventional battle lines fail. It therefore must be considered a possible trigger for nuclear war.

Schmidt was also troubled in 1977 by some of his advisers, and by some American strategic weapons experts in Bonn at the time, who told him that he could no longer rely on American support for German security. One of these Americans was Fred Iklé, the present undersecretary of defense for policy.

So in October 1977, Schmidt countered these U.S. threats and innuendos by delivering a speech at the International Institute for Strategic Studies in London, where in the context of the modernization and replacement by the USSR of its twenty-one-year-old intermediate-range SS-4 and SS-5 missiles by SS-20 missiles, he suggested that the West rectify the nuclear balance in Europe.

The NATO high command met this request in mid-1978, recommending NATO deployment of intermediate-range missiles in Europe that could strike at the Soviet Union. Many Germans felt that this move could threaten détente, which had enabled millions of East and West Germans to visit and call each other more frequently than in the previous decade and had allowed West German exports to Eastern Bloc countries to triple.

In September 1979, Kissinger gave a speech in Brussels, advising that Europe could no longer rely on the U.S. strategic umbrella because the United States would not risk destruction of its civilization to protect Western Europe. America had to develop the capability to fight small-theater nuclear wars, implying that a U.S.-Soviet nuclear war could be fought on European-Soviet ground, excluding American territorial involvement. This scared the hell out of the Europeans. Kissinger left out two obvious facts: Such missiles would be U.S.-controlled, and the USSR obviously would retaliate against the United States if they were used.

Schmidt then recommended that other NATO nations—Italy,

Holland, Belgium, and Great Britain—accept these new American missiles. The missiles chosen—air- and sea-launched cruise missiles—were very controversial during the SALT II negotiations and so were put under temporary control in a protocol to SALT II, which was to last until December 31, 1981.

On October 6, 1979, Chairman Brezhnev spoke in East Berlin. He announced that the Soviet Union would dismantle an unspecified number of its medium-range missiles in Europe and remove 1,000 tanks and one Soviet division from East Germany if NATO agreed to forgo its decision to deploy new missiles in Europe and entered into immediate negotiations with the USSR. Brzezinski immediately dismissed the proposal as propaganda, although Brezhnev indeed carried through with his promise and removed both troops and tanks. A few months later, Brezhnev also offered to freeze all further deployment of SS-20s in return for negotiations. This offer also was rejected.

On December 12, 1979, a two-track decision was made to deploy a total of 464 ground-launched cruise missiles and 108 Pershing II missiles. Both are first-strike weapons and part of the new war-fighting strategy; the ground-launched cruise missiles signal the end of arms control agreements, and the Pershing IIs signal the beginning of launch-on-warning systems. The cruise missiles were to be distributed in the countries previously listed, but the 108 Pershing II missiles would be placed only in West Germany. The deployment of the missiles was made contingent on ongoing arms-control talks. In 1980, the Americans also adhered to their promise to remove from Europe 1,000 of the 7,000 U.S. tactical nuclear weapons already deployed.

The NATO decision sparked a fear in Europe that had been latent for the first thirty-five years of the nuclear age. Europeans began to realize that the United States probably was ready to fight its nuclear war in their arena. This fear was compounded by well-publicized pronouncements by Reagan Administration officials that America could fight and win a nuclear war. The president himself announced that a limited nuclear war might be fought in Europe without pressing the button. It was obvious to the European public that there were no moderates in this new government, only-hard-line hawks who hated the Soviets. The U.S. defense budget also signaled planned spending of $1.5 trillion over the next five years to build up a nuclear arsenal designed to fight and "win" a nuclear war.

The European public erupted with anger and indignation in 1981 and 1982. Huge marches were organized in most capital cities, and governments strained under the political pressures exerted by their people.

President Carter left office as he had entered: warning about the threat of nuclear war. In his inaugural address, he had said he wished to eliminate nuclear weapons from the face of the earth, and in his farewell speech, he said that a nuclear war would last a long afternoon with the equivalent of a World War II every second. He was a good man but misguided and misled, and not strong enough to avoid being outmaneuvered by the hawks—a handful of hostile people who had gained enormous power in a political vacuum created by the lack of knowledge and by widespread apathy of the vast American electorate.

Germs of
Conflict:
The Third World

President Reagan keeps talking about worldwide Soviet expansionism. Yet, of the 164 nations in the world, the Soviet Union has significant influence in only 19. Back in 1958, a total of 31 percent of the world's population and 9 percent of the world's gross national product—outside the Soviet Union—were under its influence. But by 1979, the figures had dwindled to 6 percent of the world's population and 5 percent of the gross national product. Since the 1960s, it has lost influence in key countries such as China, Egypt, India, Indonesia, and Iraq. Since World War II, the only time the USSR has used large numbers of Soviet troops outside its own territory (excluding the Warsaw Pact nations) has been in Afghanistan.

Frequently the American press has misrepresented events in foreign countries. Incorrect or adulterated reporting has had a serious effect upon American public opinion, which in turn has often distorted American foreign policy. It is vital that Americans understand their own recent history.

Recent U.S. Interventions in Latin America*

Terrible events have occurred in Central and South America in the name of the Monroe Doctrine. Since the 1917 Russian Revolution, movements for self-determination in Latin America

---

*Material for the following section has been obtained from Noam Chomsky, Edward S. Herman, James Bamford, and George H. Crowell.

usually have been labeled "Communist"; any U.S. intervention is justified in the name of anticommunism. To maintain its economic power, the United States trains client military personnel at numerous bases and training schools and sends mobile units and advisers to serve on an in-country basis. This training has placed great weight on ideological conditioning. U.S. military training also has helped to build a network of personal relationships between the United States and Latin American military cadres. Military aid, from the wealthier power and from joint maneuvers and logistical training, have strengthened the bond. Over a hundred thousand Latin American military personnel have been trained by the United States; since 1946, over forty-five thousand Latin American officers have trained at the U. S. Army School of the Americas alone, a school often called a "training center for future dictators" and sometimes identified in Latin America by its historic function as the "school of coups."

The CIA is an integral part of the U.S. military establishment. It operates in secret, so a large portion of its activities are unknown to the public. The total number of cases of CIA involvement in active subversion of established governments (and attempts at political murder) run into the thousands. In Brazil in 1964,

> the CIA was able to bribe its journalists, subsidize its politicians, conspire with military factions, infiltrate and subvert the labor movement, and engage in extensive propaganda campaigns—in short, it could virtually disregard the sovereignty of this large and theoretically independent country. The catch, of course, is that Brazil was not an independent country—U.S. penetration was already enormous by the 1960s. . . . The Brazilian military and much of its economy were already "denationalized" with strong ties and dependency relations to the United States; and U.S. business had a substantial presence in Brazil. . . . It was hard to separate U.S. business and CIA activities in Brazil before 1964.

CIA intervention in Brazil occurred with "weapons on a huge scale, together with bribery, black propaganda, and practically open conspiracy with military officers, and massive institutional subversion." This was a prime factor in the military coup in Brazil in 1964.

The U.S. National Security Agency is another power used by the United States for intelligence-gathering around the world. It employs from fifty thousand to sixty thousand military and civilian personnel and deploys an enormous array of electronic gadgetry to monitor communications all over the globe, gathering information on any activity it considers subversive.

Argentina

In March 1976, Argentina was taken over by military rulers. Since then, twenty thousand Argentine citizens have disappeared after arrests by security forces. The government imprisoned hundreds without charges and restricted hundreds more by making house arrests and otherwise limiting their movements. Human conditions continued to worsen. The media were censored. Thousands of clandestine cemeteries have been found; since 1976, more than a thousand victims have been buried in some of them. And yet President Reagan certified Argentina for military aid in December 1983, reversing Carter's ban of 1977. There are stories of ordinary middle-class people being removed from their families in the middle of the night, taken out in helicopters, and dropped into the sea. Grieving mothers tried vainly to pressure the government for the whereabouts of their loved ones. Physicians from Argentina came to American hospitals to work and were still so intimidated that they could hardly talk about what happened at home without fearing for their lives. In December 1983, the people of Argentina elected a new government led by Raul Alfonsin—the first civilian president in Argentina in seven years. He is prosecuting, interrogating, and jailing former military leaders for their crimes.

Chile

In 1970, a physician named Salvador Allende was elected president in Chile by democratic vote. During his campaign he had promised to nationalize the economy and to end the exploitation of Chile by foreign capital. The country had been under repressive regimes in the past, but now Allende would help his people with education, health care, and food for all. The United States and the CIA, along with IT&T and PepsiCo, saw his efforts as a threat to their vital interests. These agencies, together with President Nixon, Henry Kissinger, Richard Helms, and chairman of the Joint Chiefs of Staff General Brown, engineered a coup that stirred discontent among the Chilean people and the labor unions. A vast press campaign was coordinated via CIA connections in Europe and Latin America. It linked Allende to the Soviet Union and concluded that he posed a direct threat to "democracy and freedom" in the Western Hemisphere. The CIA began a series of covert propaganda actions and support for terrorist activities, which lasted from 1970 to 1973. Designed to stir discontent and fear among the Chilean people, they led to a coup d'état in September 1973. The Chilean military overthrew Allende and then assassinated him. The international banks were coordinated to reduce their credit facilities to Chile from $300 million to $17 million. Direct American investment fell from $1 billion in 1969 to less than $100 million in 1972. Swiss banks played a key role in this economic strangulation. Since then, Chile has been ruled by a repressive military dictator, General Augusto Pinochet, supported by the government of the United States. Tens of thousands of Chilean people have been tortured and killed; the torture techniques are taught by the CIA at the International Police Academy in Panama. Chile's wealth remains in the hands of a few. One million people—about 10 percent of the population—have fled. The junta has been supported by the Chase Manhattan Bank, the Bank of America, First National City Bank, Irving Trust, and Bankers Trust. Other American corporations in Chile include Dow Chemical, IT&T, General Motors, General Electric, Textron, and General Tire & Rubber Company.

Cuba

In 1959, Fidel Castro overthrew Cuban dictator Fulgencio Batista. Batista, with recognized ties to organized crime, had ruled that country for twenty-five years and had supported the economic monopoly of the American corporations. At the time, most Cubans were illiterate and malnourished. Diseases such as hookworm, malaria, and tuberculosis were endemic. Since the revolution, almost all Cuban people have become literate. Most endemic disease has been eradicated, and health care is uniformly good.

Indeed, during the Carter Administration, the U.S. surgeon general traveled to Cuba to observe its efficient health-care system.

Because many Americans lost large capital investments in Cuba, the U.S. government petulantly refused to establish relations with Cuba after the revolution. It imposed a total embargo on trade, forcing Cuba to turn to other countries for economic support. Literally pushed into the hands of the Soviet Union, Cuba subsequently has had to endure enormous hardships in trade and economic well-being. Because no ship traveling to Cuba can dock in an American port, many European countries find trade with Cuba economically inefficient. The United States has tried on many occasions to destroy the Castro regime; its most famous attempt was the ill-conceived Bay of Pigs invasion, orchestrated by the CIA and Cuban exiles from Florida. The Cubans have performed miracles with their people in the past twenty-five years, but their rigid political system has been exacerbated by a mandatory relationship with the Soviet Union. It is interesting to speculate how Americans would have reacted if a foreign power had tried to unseat its new government soon after its own revolution.

El Salvador

Ever since the Spanish conquered this region in 1524, a powerful minority has dispossessed the vulnerable majority of native Indians from their lands and resources and has exploited their labor. The original Spanish conquest was violent; the various forms of oppression imposed since have been consistently enforced by violence. The colonial conquerors in El Salvador and Guatemala have exacted tribute, imposed forced labor, resorted to debt peonage, enslaved native peoples, bought African slaves, and exercised brutal retaliation against any who resisted. Political independence from Spain in 1821 brought no relief to the oppressed. On the contrary, it gave a freer hand to the landholding elite of El Salvador and Guatemala.

In 1881, under U.S. and European pressure, the government of El Salvador abolished all communal forms of land tenure, paving the way for the wholesale expulsion of peasants and consolidating vast tracts of land to coffee magnates. Coffee became the major export crop in El Salvador. By the turn of the century, it dominated the economy and has remained the primary export ever since. The wealthy elite owned the coffee crops. When the world coffee market collapsed in 1931, thousands of peasants rebelled against a system that had methodically denied them all sources of livelihood. In the 1930s, Salvadoran security forces working for the rich killed some 30,000 peasants.

At present, privileges of the wealthy in El Salvador are maintained. The population is 4.8 million; 2 percent, dominated by 14 families, own 60 percent of the most fertile land and produce coffee, cotton, sugar, and beets for export; 90 percent of the people own 22 percent of the land. In 1971, a total of 6 families held as much land as 80 percent of the rural population. The number of rural families possessing no land at all increased from 30,000 in 1961 to 167,000 in 1975. This desperate pervasive poverty is evident in ramshackle housing and spindly-legged, malnourished children. Infant mortality is 60 percent. The average caloric intake is 40 percent below the recommended minimum and is the lowest in Latin America. Ninety percent of the people earn less than $100 per year.

Refugees number 800,000—20 percent of that country's population. In El Salvador, doctors, nurses, and health-care workers, as well as patients in operating rooms, were shot down in cold blood by soldiers. The Salvadoran Army entered the National University (which includes the nation's only medical school), where they killed students; occupied buildings; and ransacked and destroyed equipment, libraries, and records. From 30 to 40 percent of the nation's physicians have left the country. The military controls the availability of blood. El Salvador is the only nation in Central America in which food aid is distributed by the government, and the country is ruled under emergency decrees that permit the detention of people not suspected of any crime, and the use of confessions extracted under torture.

There are virtually no prisoners of war, and, contrary to the Geneva Conventions of 1949, most prisoners have been executed. All legal and judicial safeguards that guarantee rights and due process have been suspended by the military. Approximately 40,000 civilians have been murdered in El Salvador since 1979.

Health care is treated as a subversive activity by the El Salvador government. Well-documented evidence indicates that the overwhelming majority of violent deaths have been perpetrated by the military government and right-wing paramilitary death squads; and clandestine guerrilla movements have inevitably arisen because the government does not permit nonviolent political opposition. The present U.S. administration insists that the fundamental problem in Central America is the threat of Soviet or Cuban domination in the area. In fact, the problems are poverty and the helplessness of millions of human beings. Many people in Latin America have joined the struggle for independence. Most of them are Christians; a few are Communists. They are seeking justice and self-determination.

Today the United States has approximately $100 million invested in El Salvador. Some of the main corporations there are Texas Instruments, Chevron, Phelps Dodge, Kimberly-Clark, Texaco, and Crown Zellerbach. Since World War II, the United States (through its Military Assistance Program [MAP], its International Military Education and Training program [IMET], and its Office of the Public Safety [OPS]) has provided extensive training to Salvadoran military and police officers in the many forms of counterinsurgency. It has also offered a thorough indoctrination in anticommunism. Since October 1979, the United States has supplied more than $100 million in lethal military equipment to bolster the threatened military government—more than six times the military aid provided to El Salvador during the previous twenty-nine years. In 1981, a so-called free election was held. But the left did not participate—to do so would have been suicidal. A right-wing government was elected. The country's most feared killer, Roberto D'Aubuisson, was one leader who emerged from the rigged election. Amnesty International has declared that El Salvador practices gross violations of human rights. Yet every six months the Reagan Administration declares that human rights continue to improve in El Salvador and sends there more military equipment, openly acknowledged to be used by the death squads.

Guatemala

In 1944, a nonviolent revolution led by students and supported by the urban middle classes overthrew the despotic Guatemalan President Jorge Ubico. For the first time in four centuries, major social reforms were instituted. They reversed the oppression of the poor, ended forced labor, encouraged union organization and social security measures, and redistributed land from the great wealthy plantations to rural peasants.

But most of the country—500,000 acres of the most fertile land—was owned by a Boston-based company, United Fruit. This company had penetrated Central America in the late nineteenth century and came to own, directly or indirectly, Guatemala's only Atlantic port, as well as the major railroads in Costa Rica and in Honduras and nearly 900 miles of railroads in Guatemala and El Salvador. It established an immense network of plantations in Honduras, Costa Rica, Nicaragua, Panama, Jamaica, and the Dominican Republic.

The plantations contributed directly to the U.S. market and made little or no contributions to local economies. United Fruit enjoyed a variety of tax exemptions and profit remittances. The company wreaked social and political havoc in these countries. They paid minimal wages, and almost all the workers' money was spent in company-owned workshops. This company and others throughout Central America were closely allied with archconservative landlords and the military.

In 1954, newly elected President Jacobo Arbenz took measures to expropriate 387,000 acres of land owned by United Fruit. The land was not under cultivation at the time, and he offered the company compensation commensurate with its declared tax value. But United Fruit had consistently undervalued its property to reduce an already insignificant tax liability. At the same time, peasant laborers intended to form a union to help improve wages and working conditions. Secretary of State John Foster Dulles, whose law firm had prepared the United Fruit Company contracts with Guatemala in the 1930s, began a campaign to smear the reform government as part of an international Communist conspiracy. His brother Allen Dulles was director of the CIA. United Fruit Company launched a massive public-relations campaign in the United States, accusing the Arbenz government of being Communist. Some of the listed supporters in this effort were Claude Pepper, Mike Mansfield, Henry Cabot Lodge, President Eisenhower, John and Allen Dulles, Arthur Hays Sulzberger of *The New York Times*, and journalists from the *Miami Herald*, *Christian Science Monitor*, *San Francisco Chronicle*, UPI, *Time*, and *Newsweek*. The CIA planted Soviet arms in adjacent Nicaragua, with the support of that country's dictator, Anatasio Somoza, making it seem that the USSR was involved. They also organized and financed a military coup from neighboring Honduras, which overthrew Arbenz and replaced him with a U.S.-trained Guatemalan army officer, Carlos Castillo Armas. Some months later, United Fruit Company gradually disappeared. Under the rule of Castille Armas, trade unions and political parties were abolished. Eight hundred *campesinos* (peasants) were killed in the first two months; 9,000 political arrests were made in the first year.

In 1966, guerrilla resistance arose again, only to be put down by the puppet government with the aid of U.S. intervention, which provided police training, weapons, military advisers, and $6 million in aid to the Guatemalan armed forces. The violence was excessive. A 1980 State Department report concluded, "To eliminate a few hundred guerrillas, the government killed perhaps 10,000 Guatemalan peasants." The Guatemalan government has since ruled with such terror that President Jimmy Carter suspended military assistance because of their inadequate attention to human rights. At present, Guatemala has a population of 7.7 million, of whom 65 percent are rural; 2.1 percent of the landowners hold 72.2 percent of the land, on which they grow crops almost exclusively for export.

Some 80,000 civilians have been murdered in Guatemala since 1954. Recently a report in *The New York Times* described hideous murders by government soldiers using rusty machetes. They hacked and killed children, pregnant women, and babies. They picked up children by the feet and smashed their heads against walls, or tied ropes around their necks and strangled them. Babies were thrown in the air and bayoneted. On March 23, 1982, the president, General Romeo Lucas Garcia, was replaced by General José Efrain Rios Montt. A born-again Christian, Montt was reported to have been systematically killing peasants in rural areas, using the Army. He is quoted as having said, "We have no scorched-earth policy. We have a policy of scorched Communists." Recently, Rabbi Arthur Hertzberg, vice president of the World Jewish Congress, described Guatemala as a "charnel house." President Reagan has said that he thinks Rios Montt's government was "getting a bum rap." It has since been overthrown by General Oscar Mejia.

The United States instituted this form of despotic government in 1954 and supports Mejia, supplying him with helicopters and other military equipment in the name of anticommunism. From 50,000 to 80,000 peasants fled that country in 1982 alone.

Nicaragua

America firmly supported the rule of the Somozas in Nicaragua for more than forty years. Anastasio Somoza Debayle once told Luis Echeverria, then president of Mexico, "You should envy me. I have no problems. All I have to do is what Washington wants me to do." The United States has exploited and controlled Nicaragua since the 1850s, when an American investment group led by Cornelius Vanderbilt instituted a transit system there. The United States was once also interested in establishing a canal across that country and in protecting mining and banking interests there; U.S. Marines landed in Nicaragua in 1909 for that reason. They withdrew in 1910 after establishing a government satisfactory to the United States, but invaded in 1912 to quell a rebellion. A treaty was forced on Nicaragua, giving the United States exclusive rights to any canal across the country. New York banking interests gained control of the Bank of Nicaragua and the nation's railroads. They exploited the coffee export trade; they manipulated currency at the expense of the poor. A U.S. Marine detachment of at least one hundred men occupied Nicaragua until 1925. They returned in 1926 and remained until 1933, departing only after setting up the National Guard under the control of Somoza's father, who eliminated a people's movement by murdering its leader, Augusto Sandino. The United States consistently supported the Somozas despite their failure to protect democratic freedoms, hold elections, or free the economy from the dynasty's stranglehold. In 1979, the people of Nicaragua—businessmen, Church leaders, and students, both middle-class and left-wing—rose up against this dictator, who controlled virtually all the country's wealth and corporations. With great sacrifice of civilian lives at the hands of Somoza's National Guard, the revolution prevailed. A nationalistic government, with the general support of most of the people, assumed power. They called themselves Sandinistas, after their dead hero. By 1981, the country had achieved self-sufficiency in food production. Health and medical care were available to the rural poor, illiteracy had been reduced from 50 percent to 12 percent, and land was being distributed to formerly landless peasants. There was a high degree of democratic participation at the local level, and representatives were elected to a national governing council. Churches, concerned for the poor, supported this revolution. But soon after the revolution, the country found itself deeply in debt. Somoza, in exile, had removed hundreds of millions of dollars from Nicaragua to banks in Florida. President Carter, intending to support the new government with several hundred million dollars, refused to send a final $15 million because the U.S. government said Nicaragua was aiding a rebellion in El Salvador. The Reagan Administration continued the cutoff, although it admitted that Nicaragua had stopped aiding the Salvadoran insurgents. Since then, the United States has advanced a variety of explanations for a policy of unremitting hostility toward the Sandinista government. It is, in fact, based on Nicaragua's left-wing politics and behavior. Is it left-wing to want to feed and educate the majority of one's people? Nicaragua has established economic relationships with France, Sweden, Finland, and Brazil. Because it got no support from the United States, it was forced to ask the Soviet Union for financial support.

Now the CIA is arming and training Somozan supporters in Honduras and in Costa Rica. It has more than 150 agents based in Honduras, and dozens more in neighboring countries. A recent American visitor to Honduras confirms that the country is teeming with American troops. The CIA is conducting the largest covert operation mounted in nearly a decade, attempting indirectly to overthrow the Nicaraguan government. It has supplied money and military equipment to paramilitary groups fighting under the banner of the Nicaraguan Democratic front, a coalition of Nicaraguan exile groups intent on toppling the Sandinistas. And it has enlisted the aid of Argentina and Israel to support these Nicaraguans trained in Honduras. (In 1983, the United States had armed the military in Honduras to the tune of $62 million.) The CIA has conducted a series of huge military training exercises involving thousands of U.S. ground, air, and naval forces. In January 1984, an unpublished report of the House Armed Services Committee stated that the United States has taken advantage of exercise Big Pine II to create "a substantial semipermanent military capability" in Honduras, with construction of airstrips, housing, radar facilities, ocean piers, roads, and an eleven-mile-long tank trap. Honduras has been a remarkable area of stability in Central America for many years—a true democracy that had an election as recently as 1980, when it elected its first civilian president in a decade. But U.S. military support is almost certain to destabilize this small country. The Nicaraguan Democratic Front makes frequent forays into Nicaragua. At present, an estimated twelve thousand to fifteen thousand counterrevolutionaries are supported and organized by the United States, operating inside the country and conducting guerrilla warfare. What are the ethics of the United States when it covertly intervenes to destroy a government attained by a majority revolution of its people? Colombia, Mexico, Panama, and Venezuela have offered to help mediate the problems in Nicaragua, and all have been rejected by the United States, as has a six-point peace plan proposed by the Sandinista government, and an offer by Fidel Castro for a bilateral removal of all foreign troops from the country.

In an address before the General Assembly of the United Nations on October 8, 1981, Daniel Ortega Saavedra of Nicaragua referred to the history of U.S. aggression:

> The emergence of the Monroe Doctrine, America for the Americans, was to represent the aggressive will of Yankee expansionism on the continent, and from 1840 onwards our people were no longer to benefit from the influence of those ideals of democracy and freedom, but rather to suffer interference, threats, the imposition of treaties contrary to the sovereignty of our countries . . . blackmail with the presence of the United States fleet in our territorial waters, military interventions, the landing of Marines and the imposition of corrupt governments and one-sided economic treaties. More than 784 acts hostile to the right our countries to sovereignty have occurred on our continent since that time, and more than 100 of them since 1960.
>
> Why were our countries insulted, invaded, and humiliated on more than 200 occasions from 1840 to 1917? Under what pretext, since at the time there was not a single socialist state in the world and the Czar ruled over all the Russians? Treaties and loans were imposed on us; we were invaded; we were given the status of protectorates under the same thesis of

national security, which was first called the Monroe Doctrine. . . .

How can we explain the numerous acts of aggression and interference and the landings that occurred between 1917 and 1954 in Latin America, when there was still no Cuban revolution and Cuba could not be accused of interference . . . ?

The United States did not take over Cuba and Puerto Rico in 1898 . . . to save Caribbean territories from the influence of the Soviet Union since the latter was not yet in existence.

The United States did not land Marines in Vera Cruz, Haiti, and Nicaragua, nor did it from 1903 onward arm the most formidable naval force ever seen in Caribbean waters to resolve the East-West conflict to its own benefit. It was simply defending the interests of its territorial expansionism, the interests of its financiers and its bankers, of those business tycoons who were beginning to beset Latin America.

This history is well chronicled. Soviet-Cuban Communist expansionism is only an excuse for the preordained economic expansionism of the United States of America. It is obvious that the military assists such expansionism. The threat of the Nicaraguan revolution is a threat to U.S. economic interests.

The fate of human beings in many of these countries is not unlike the atrocities that occurred in Hitler's Germany. Yet their governments still are eligible for support by the United States because they are "anti-Communist." So was Hitler.

American Intervention in the Eastern Hemisphere

Iran

In 1953, President Eisenhower, urged by his secretary of state, John Foster Dulles, gave the signal to launch a CIA coup in Iran. The coup overthrew a much-loved premier, Mohammed Mossadegh, because he had nationalized the British oil companies. The CIA reinstated the shah on the Peacock Throne after returning him from exile. Iran never accepted the autocratic shah with his hated secret policy (SAVAK) and resented America for removing its beloved premier. Eventually, in 1979, the shah was overthrown and fifty-two American hostages were taken. The bitterness engendered by such action could well have thrust the United States and the USSR into a superpower confrontation. The patriotic fervor created among many Americans during those months of the hostage crisis was frightening; indeed, I saw a young messenger walking through the halls of the Children's Hospital at Harvard, wearing a T-shirt that read "Nuke Iran." Yet most Americans did not fully understand the reasons for Iran's resentment.

Vietnam and Cambodia

In a ten-year undeclared war, America sent half a million soldiers into Vietnam and bombarded the country with three times the tonnage of bombs dropped on Germany and Japan in World War II. There were approximately two million casualties. Agent Orange was used as a defoliant over hundreds of thousands of acres of Vietnamese territory, making a virtual desert of some of the most lush tropical forests in the world. Napalm was used on thousands of innocent men, women, and children.

In 1969, Henry Kissinger and Richard Nixon authorized the secret bombing of Cambodia. B-52s bombed "boxes"—areas of land half a mile wide by three miles long—to root out nonexistent North Vietnamese bases. The secret war in Cambodia continued for just under four years. At one stage, the number of B-52 sorties was as high as 81 per day (in Vietnam, the maximum had been 60 per day). The total tonnage of bombs dropped was 539,129, almost half of them in the last six months of the war. Thousands of square miles of densely populated fertile areas in Cambodia were blackened, and hundreds of thousands of people were killed. Much of the ancient irrigation system was destroyed, and a lot of the rice-growing areas fell into ruin.

The United States also allowed Prince Sihanouk to be deposed. Thus was assured the destruction of a beautiful, peaceful country held together by a delicate coalition of forces guided and directed by the intensely nationalistic Sihanouk.

The United States supported the government of Lon Nol, a weak and ineffectual ruler. He was opposed by the Chinese-backed

Pol Pot, who armed and trained hordes of young adolescent soldiers—the Khmer Rouge—in the name of communism. After the secret bombing of Cambodia, Pol Pot and his young soldiers murdered at least one million Cambodians. They committed the most frightful atrocities against their people, nailing old woman against houses and then burning the houses, slaughtering children, and murdering anyone who seemed to have an education. Almost three million people died during those years of the war; a whole civilization was almost destroyed. Relief came only after Vietnam—an ancient enemy—invaded the country and displaced the Pol Pot regime. To this day, Pol Pot is supported by China and by the United States. America at first recognized Pol Pot as Cambodia's official representative in the United Nations, and later recognized a coalition of forces, of which Pol Pot continues to be a main component. And Vietnam, lacking American financial support after the war, has had to rely totally on the Soviet Union.

America also supplies moral, political, and economic support to South Africa's oppressive regime of apartheid, which separates husband from wife and forces people to live in subhuman conditions just because they are not white.

Soviet Interventions

Afghanistan

Since the nineteenth century, the Afghan monarchy had maintained order in a society riddled with deep ethnic, tribal, and religious diversity. The rulers had also maintained a policy of international nonalignment; in return, the Soviet Union had left the Afghans alone. In 1973, Prime Minister Mohammad Daud staged a coup and overthrew his cousin, King Zahir Shah. Daud's regime was corrupt and cruel. He was courted by the shah of Iran, who wished to extend his influence throughout the Persian Gulf. Daud accepted the shah's hated SAVAK—secret police—to help him "root out Communist influence" from the Afghan civilian and military service.

The Communists consisted of two rival groups, which until that time had posed no threat to the country's stability. One faction had originally supported Daud, but he eventually lost Communist support. The Soviet Union was unhappy that the shah, with American influence, was invited to participate in Afghan affairs, and was further distressed by his vehement opposition to the Communists. The Soviet Union and the Communist Party of India worked to unite the opposing factions. Daud moved closer to the Washington-Tehran axis, which really alarmed the Soviet Union, its southern border in danger of becoming destabilized.

In a clumsy attempt to overthrow the Communists, Daud inadvertently instigated a coup in April 1978, bringing a Marxist-Leninist government to power. The USSR, the CIA, and SAVAK were all taken by surprise. But the Soviets were obliged to support the new government. New leader Hafizullah Amin consistently ignored Soviet advice, and he moved too fast to force an impoverished and illiterate agrarian society into the twentieth century. Amin also began to develop close associations with the United States through Ambassador Adolph Dubs.

The Soviet Union tried to get rid of Amin in September 1979, but the wrong man was killed. Amin now assumed complete control. Eventually, in December 1979, the USSR had Amin and his family killed, replacing him with Babrak Karmal and invading Afghanistan with eighty-five thousand troops in order to bring "stability" to the southern Soviet border. In so doing, it aroused the wrath of the world. This was the first time the USSR had moved its troops beyond its borders (and those of the Warsaw Pact nations) since 1945.

The Soviets continue to be plagued by rivalry between the two Communist groups. There is evidence that one of the factions is cooperating with the Afghan rebels fighting the invading army. Senator Birch Bayh was chairman of the committee that approved CIA aid to the rebels through Pakistan.

Obviously, the Soviet Union did not invade Afghanistan because it needed oil from the Persian Gulf; it is the largest producer of oil in the world today. It invaded when its stable, nonaligned neighbor was destabilized by the 1978 coup and by the disturbing influence of the shah and the CIA. It was confronted by a Communist but pro-American country on its southern border, just as America had been confronted with a pro-Soviet regime in Cuba some twenty years earlier, to which it had responded with the Bay of Pigs invasion. Apparently both the Soviet military command and

Soviet Intelligence argued against military intervention. The Kremlin overruled the military and KGB advice and took defensive action in response to an unacceptable challenge to strategic Soviet interests in an area of vital concern. Soon after the invasion, an all-party committee of the British House of Commons concluded:

> The Soviet Union did not go into Afghanistan earlier because the Afghan regime prior to 1978 had been stable, even though not Marxist. Once the Communist regime had been established, the USSR had the double incentive of ideological commitment to the maintenance of Communist gains, in line with the Brezhnev doctrine, plus the desire to restore stability on its borders.

At this time, no one knows how many people have been killed, although some estimates suggest more than 100,000 fatalities. There may be 3 million refugees in Pakistan, according to the Pakistani government, although some people feel this estimate is too high. There are 115,000 Soviet troops in Afghanistan. The Soviet Union is having a difficult time maintaining order among these troops. Many of them are unhappy with their role there. They are also dying of endemic hepatitis and apparently are freely using drugs. Evidence suggests that the Soviet Union has been using mycotoxins (yellow rain) on the Afghan people. However, these data have come only from the U.S. State Department and have not yet been verified by the United Nations or any other independent agency.

Unfortunately, the Soviet Union invaded Afghanistan just as U.S. anxieties ran high, generated by the hostage situation in Iran. The anger, indignation, and frustration of the American people toward Iran was projected immediately onto the Soviet Union and its illegal invasion of Afghanistan.

Poland

In 1980, a new union movement called Solidarity developed in Poland. Workers rushed to join—ten million of the eleven million in the labor force. The government eventually capitulated to their demands—the right to form independent unions, the right to strike, reduced censorship, and access to state-controlled television and radio for the unions and the Church. They were developing freedom of speech and had an enormous consensus throughout the country, under the leadership of Lech Walesa.

But Poland was deeply in debt, the result of Prime Minister Edward Gierek's cavalier economic attitude during the previous ten years. Food became scarce. Even soap was difficult to obtain (new mothers were discharged from the hospital prematurely for fear their babies might become infected, because supplies of soap were inadequate). As a result, the movement got out of control, and Walesa was not able to moderate some of the more militant people within the unions. Finally the militants called for a national referendum on the future of the Communist government in Poland and re-examination of Poland's military alliance with the Soviet Union. The whole world wondered what the Soviet Union would do with this challenge coming from one of its Warsaw Pact countries. But the USSR knew that if it invaded Poland, all hell would break loose. In the nuclear age, this is not politically indicated, so the Polish government itself outlawed Solidarity. By the end of 1982, it had been almost destroyed. During this uprising by the union, there was some bloodshed—and the death of the spirit of liberation. I identify with the Polish people because my maiden name is Broinowski.

The Soviet Union violated the Helsinki Declaration of 1975, in which the East and West coupled recognition of the existing frontiers of the Warsaw Pact nations with the agreement that all signatories adhere to basic concepts of human rights. It seems clear that the USSR never can feel secure when it has to disenfranchise its Warsaw Pact allies by destroying their yearnings for self-government and human rights.

Events in Poland have been tragic, and events in Hungary, Czechoslovakia, and other Warsaw Pact countries have caused consternation in the West as well as internal bitterness. It also is true that the war in Afghanistan is an immoral war and that Soviet intervention there is illegal. By the same criteria, the massacres, genocidal activities, and repression practiced by governments in Central and South America and supported by the United States of America are illegal and immoral. Most Third World countries, and other Western countries resent both the USSR and America for their economic and military interventions. It is time that the superpowers, as they posture for bilateral nuclear disarmament, agree to sign a treaty in which they promise not to intervene in other countries. The United States would not be able to suppress or subvert people in other countries. The Soviet Union would have to stop "supporting" or, conversely, "repressing" national revolutions around the world.

Only if this happens will the world be safe from annihilation. It is time for Third World and Western countries to rise up and demand that the superpowers start behaving themselves. To this end, former Canadian Prime Minister Pierre Trudeau initiated an international cooperative effort to produce real and constructive arms control. Obviously, the nuclear forces on both sides serve to support and bolster the conventional forces used by the superpowers to subvert and monopolize small countries for their own ends.

We have looked at American misperceptions of the USSR. It is also important for America to understand how the Soviet leaders view the world. The Soviet Union is the only Communist country flanked by hostile Communist nations—China and the Warsaw Pact countries. If the USSR were to invade Western Europe, the Warsaw Pact allies would hardly move rapidly to support its offensive efforts and would, in fact, probably fight against it. There are five large nuclear nations in the world. Four of them have their weapons targeted on Soviet cities. Each could destroy the USSR. Imagine U.S. fears if Canada were China, Mexico were NATO— including the British and French nuclear forces—and the Soviet Union were about to deploy Pershing IIs and cruise missiles in Mexico. The Soviet leaders have every cause to be realistically frightened and perhaps a little paranoid. (I was interested to discover during my visit to the Soviet Union that they are more afraid of China than they are of America.) Perhaps if there were less belligerence, the Soviet Union might feel freer to moderate its tough posture within Poland. But while present conditions prevail, if one Warsaw Pact country falls to free expression, the others will obviously follow. If moves could be made to reassure the Soviet Union that it is safe from Western or Chinese aggression, perhaps it might moderate its stand in Poland. It has done this to some extent in Hungary.

One reason the South Korean commercial airliner was destroyed was Soviet paranoia, induced by a new U.S. military posture in the North Pacific. This article from *The Nation* describes the dynamics of this policy:

WHERE FLIGHT 7 FLEW

TENSIONS IN THE NORTH PACIFIC

WALDEN BELLO AND PETER HAYES

"This region, I believe, is most probably where we shall witness confrontation with the Soviet Union," Adm. Robert Long, then chief of the U.S. Pacific Command, told a Japanese reporter a few months ago. In the aftermath of the September 1 downing of a South Korean commercial airliner by a Soviet fighter, Long's words have taken on an unintended immediacy.

Northeast Asia, where the tragic incident occurred, is one of the world's most militarized areas. Soviet and U.S. forces there are in a state of tense confrontation. The South Korean plane flew close to the Soviet naval base at Petropavlovsk, on the Kamchatka Peninsula, home port for the Northwest Pacific nuclear-missile submarine fleet. It was shot down over Sakhalin Island, site of several important Soviet communications and aircraft facilities, after allegedly being mistaken for an American RC-135 spy plane.

In recent years both the Soviet Union and the United States have engaged in major military buildups in the area. The Russians have deployed about one-third of their 250 SS-20 theater nuclear missiles and the same proportion of their new long-range Backfire bombers. According to Adm. Nata-oishi Sakonjo of Japan, an expert on defense policy in the region, Soviet missiles and aircraft are deployed primarily for use in the event of a ground war with the People's Republic of China. Reagan Administration propaganda to the contrary notwithstanding, their purpose appears to be largely defensive.

Perhaps the most accurate assessment of the balance of forces in Northeast Asia was provided by former Defense Secretary Harold Brown, who wrote in his recently published *Thinking About National Security* that the U.S.-Japan-China alliance "must truly be a nightmare to the Soviets and the modest cooperative steps [taken by the three nations from]

1975-80 have . . . tilted the politico-military balance against the Soviets to a degree that significantly exceeds the advantages accruing to them from their substantial build-up in the region during the late 1960's and 1970's."

Indeed, over the past three years, the Reagan administration's arms escalation has been the prime cause of instability in the region. The thrust of the Pentagon's strategy is to pit the Navy, the only U.S. service that enjoys clear-cut superiority over its Soviet counterpart, against the Soviet fleet in an area where the Russians are geographically highly vulnerable.

The United States now periodically deploys several aircraft carrier task forces in the area; before this Administration, only a single carrier task force was assigned to it. U.S. battle groups hold regular exercises in the Northwest Pacific just off the Sea of Okhotsk and in the Sea of Japan. The Seventh Fleet, which patrols the western Pacific and the Indian Ocean, is stronger than it has been in years, having been augmented by the battleship New Jersey (temporarily on gunboat diplomacy duty off Central America), which has been refitted with cruise missiles, and by America's newest nuclear-powered carrier, the 90,000-ton Carl Vinson. The ships of the U.S. Pacific Command, which includes those of the Third Fleet in the eastern Pacific, now make up almost half the Navy's forces.

The Navy's moves cannot be divorced from its longstanding obsession with outstripping the "upstart" Soviet fleet under Adm. Sergei Gorshkov. During the years immediately after the Vietnam War, the Navy's expansion plans were frustrated by a popular mood of antimilitarism, budgetary constraints and skepticism on the part of civilian authorities. But when Ronald Reagan, a longtime favorite of the service, became President, the Navy's views became policy.

The harmony between the Navy brass and the Administration has produced the "Lehman Doctrine," named after Secretary of the Navy John Lehman, a former consultant to Boeing and a member of the Navy Reserve, who has called for the "achievement of outright maritime supremacy." In order to attain that goal, the Navy will expand to a 600-ship fleet, including fifteen aircraft carriers and four recommissioned World War II battleships armed with cruise missiles. To make the Soviet Union an "isolated island," as Lehman put it, the Navy's primary mission has been shifted from a defensive one of protecting vital sea lanes to an offensive one of "force projection" against the Soviet fleet and Soviet coastal targets [see James A. Nathan, "Return of the Great White Fleet," *The Nation*, March 5].

By increasing its presence in the home waters of the Soviet Pacific fleet, the Navy hopes to dissuade the Russian naval command from sending substantial task forces out of port, enabling the U.S. fleet to exercise unchallenged control over the Pacific and Indian Oceans.

The strategy of confrontation is, of course, backed up by contingency plans for dealing with any "incidents" that occur in the area. Such incidents are an ever-present possibility in the Northwest Pacific, where the two opposing fleets boldly venture into each other's training maneuvers.

Under U.S. naval doctrine, it is preferable to outmaneuver and overwhelm the enemy in one location than to fight it all over the high seas. Such a strategy gives the United States the edge in the Pacific: the Soviet fleet's main area of operation is the almost landlocked Sea of Japan, where its maneuverability is limited. The five narrow straits that lead to the open Pacific can be easily mined, blockaded or bombed. U.S. battle groups, by contrast, have the immense advantage of operating in the open seas, supported by land-based aircraft launched from Japan and South Korea. As the Joint Chiefs of Staff point out in their last "defense posture" statement, a major U.S. "advantage is the ability of American forces—including those in Japan and Korea—to bottle up the Soviets' Pacific fleet at Vladivostok."

What Harold Brown calls the Russians' strategic "nightmare" would become reality in a battle in the Sea of Japan or the Sea of Okhotsk. Two U.S. carrier battle groups assigned to the Seventh Fleet would be arrayed against only one small Soviet carrier, which is designed for antisubmarine warfare, in the Northwest Pacific, forcing the Russians to rely on cruise-missile firing ships, submarines and land-based aircraft.

The Seventh Fleet and the Air Force and Marine air units based in Japan and South Korea have about 440 aircraft available for use in offensive operations against the Russians.

When the U.S.-equipped air forces of Japan and South Korea are included, the balance of power tips against the Russians. Even though they enjoy numerical superiority, their planes are inferior to those of the United States. The Bear heavy bomber, boasts one American admiral, "would not get within 1,000 miles" of a U.S. battle group. It is unlikely that the long-range Backfire bombers would be able to penetrate the screen of U.S. interceptors and fighter-bombers. And the Russians have nothing to match the *enfant terrible* of the U.S. offensive force: the ultramodern F-16, which is capable of carrying nuclear weapons. A squadron of F-16s is now based in South Korea, and another will soon be deployed in Misawa, in northern Japan.

In short, the Soviet Pacific fleet would get little help from air power, which is the decisive factor in modern naval conflicts. The two other tactical arms of the Soviet fleet—its missile-firing surface ships and its submarines—would have to break through the mined or blockaded straits leading out of the Sea of Japan, and the noisy Soviet submarines would have to contend with U.S. antisubmarine forces, which a former Navy Secretary has described as "awesome."

To support its independent capabilities, the United States is strengthening its military alliances with Japan, South Korea and China:

§ The United States and Japan have planned joint twenty-four-hour patrols in three of the straits leading out of the Sea of Japan, and Japan has promised to join the United States in mining or blockading those "choke points" in the event of war.

§ To place North Korea, a Soviet ally, on the defensive, the United States has upgraded South Korea's defense status to the equivalent of the European theater's—that is, from a "significant interest area" to a "vital interest area"—and has indicated its intention to deploy neutron bombs on the Korean peninsula. The Pentagon has advocated linking the United States to Japan and South Korea in a "triangular alliance," which would permit military operations that are not possible under present bilateral pacts—for example, the mining of the strategically important Tsushima Strait.

§ The United States is integrating China into its war

plans. In addition to urging a "continuing program of military-to-military contacts and prudent assistance in defensive weaponry," Defense Secretary Caspar Weinberger's "Defense Guidance" for 1985–89 calls for U.S. "logistical support" for "Chinese military maneuvers to tie down the Soviets' Pacific Fleet, tactical air squadrons, and its approximately 50 army divisions on the Sino-Soviet border" in the event of war.

Those initiatives have brought tensions in the area to flash point. The Navy brass's desire to put Admiral Gorshkov in his place and the Reagan Administration's ill-disguised belief in the feasibility of a "limited war" could prove to be an explosive combination.

The destabilizing effect of the limited-war doctrine that guides contingency planning at the Pentagon should not be discounted. As then-Assistant Secretary of Defense for International Security Affairs Francis West put it last year in Congressional hearings on "seapower projection":

> A strategy of global flexibility does not necessarily mean simultaneous, intense conflict worldwide. Quite the opposite. It means assessing the opponent's strength on the entire global chessboard, assessing the capabilities of theater criticalities, and assigning moves and counter-moves designed to terminate the conflict speedily and with minimum escalation, while protecting the interests of the United States and its allies.

West based that strategy on the assumption that the Soviet Union "is a mature global superpower in the 1980s." The problem, of course, is that the Russians have stated time and again that a limited war—either conventional or nuclear—with the United States is not possible. It would quickly escalate to global war. Moreover, the lessons of the 1905 Battle of Tsushima, when the Czar's Baltic fleet went down before the guns of the imperial Japenese Navy in the strait, which leads into the Sea of Japan, are deeply ingrained in the minds of Soviet commanders.

It is important to place the shooting down of the South Korean passenger plane in the context of the rapid escalation of the arms race, largely promoted by the United States, in the

Northeast Asia-Northwest Pacific region. Perhaps that tragic affair will serve to draw public attention to the buildup and provoke second thoughts in the Pentagon and the Navy among the adherents of pre-emptive strikes and limited war.

International Conventional Arms Trade

Concomitant with the constant wars and insurrections between and within Third World countries is the growing arms trade. Many Third World countries, too poor to afford food, medical care, or education for their people, are buying enormous quantities of sophisticated weapons. The USSR and America are the leading "salesmen," selling arms to friend and foe alike. (France is the third major conventional-arms seller, followed by the United Kingdom, West Germany, and Italy.) During the period from 1974 to 1981, the United States made Third World arms sales that exceeded those of the USSR by about $9.1 billion. But in nominal terms, the Soviet Union and the United States are very close in Third World arms sales.

Over a recent four-year period, the Soviets outnumbered the United States in sheer numbers of weapons delivered. The major European suppliers have also become serious competitors for arms markets in every region of the Third World, particularly in Latin America. Of course, numbers may not compensate for quality or levels of sophistication in the weapons actually delivered to a particular region. Well-trained personnel using top-quality equipment may ultimately prove more important in a nation's ability to wage successful conventional war than its inventory of conventional weapons.

Since Ronald Reagan entered the White House in 1981, international arms sales by the United States have increased enormously. In 1982 alone, orders totaled over $23 billion. Total sales during the four-year Carter Administration were only a few billion dollars less than the total transfers made by the United States for the twenty years from 1950 to 1970. And President Reagan is responsible for a 30 percent increase in fiscal 1982 over fiscal 1981.

In America, arms bazaars are held several times a year. Here the latest weapons—missiles, tanks, guns, planes—are displayed, often adorned with bikini-clad girls. Sheiks and arms buyers from all over the world attend, while weapons salesmen and Pentagon military officers pour inviting words into their ears.

President Reagan has also proposed dropping restrictions on arms sales to Argentina, Guatemala, Pakistan, Ecuador, Chile, and Brazil. (President Carter barred military sales to these countries because of their poor record in human rights.) In 1981, a total of $25 million in "aid packages" was sent with congressional approval to the El Salvador military. Reagan proposed another $25 million for fiscal 1982. Added to the $10 million in military aid from the Carter Administration, this amounts to $60 million in fiscal 1981 and 1982—four times the value of all U.S. arms sales to El Salvador from 1950 to 1980. For 1983, Reagan proposed $110 million.

The major motivation behind this enormous growth in arms sales is profit. Probably a similar motivation exists for the Soviet Union—although it operates from a nonprofit system, it has a balance-of-payments problem. Approximately half (fifty-two) of all national governments in developing countries are now under military domination. Forty-nine of these fifty-two governments practice citizen repression under law, and 40 show a consistent pattern of extreme repression, including torture. The United States provides military support to twenty-seven of these countries; both superpowers, as well as other nations, export weapons to repressive regimes.

The discrimination between conventional and nuclear weapons is less and less distinct. The sea-skimming radar-guided French Exocet missile, which sank a British destroyer in the Falklands, is one example. Technologically sophisticated weapons are indiscriminate in the violence they cause. Fragmentation bombs are made of plastic, which cannot be identified in a human body by X ray (nor, incidentally, can the cluster bombs that were sent to Israel by the United States). During the 1960s, the number of military deaths worldwide equaled the number of civilian deaths in war. But in the past 10 years, 3 civilians have died in war for each soldier. As Ruth Leger Sivard says, "It is no longer the men who fight, but rather those for whom they are fighting who become the main victims of war." Sixty-five major wars have been fought since 1960. They have involved the territory of 49 countries, which represent two thirds of the world's population and 40 percent of its land area. In these 25 years, more than 10.7 million people have been killed. Many of these countries will soon be able to fight with nuclear weapons; by

Top 25 FMS Contractors, FY 1980
(in thousands of dollars)

	1980	1979 (Rank)
1. **General Dynamics Corp.**	$ 992,958	$ 517,998 (2)
2. **Northrop Corp.**	859,401	472,282 (3)
3. **United Technologies Corp.**	749,047	249,048 (5)
4. **McDonnell Douglas Corp.**	471,238	638,853 (1)
5. **Raytheon Co.**	435,468	132,113 (8)
6. **Sam Whan Corp.**	266,306	*
7. **FMC Corp.**	232,933	65,267 (20)
8. **Hani Development Co. Ltd.** and **Al Mabani Joint Venture**	217,558	*
9. **Harsco Corp.**	205,393	70,508 (19)
10. **Chrysler Corp.**	197,089	*
11. **General Electric Co.**	175,597	101,442 (13)
12. **Mi Ryung Construction Co. Ltd.**	171,340	*
13. **Lockheed Corp.**	148,536	141,812 (7)
14. **General Agencies** and **Sam Whan Joint Venture**	144,306	*
15. **Westinghouse Electric Corp.**	140,101	85,266 (15)
16. **Boeing Co.**	131,542	*
17. **Saudi Maintenance Co. Ltd.**	128,834	*
18. **General Motors Corp.**	109,071	50,692 (25)
19. **Teledyne Inc.**	108,541	53,237 (23)
20. **Hughes Aircraft Co.**	95,533	86,423 (14)
21. **Textron, Inc.**	81,960	109,158 (10)
22. **American Telephone and Telegraph Co.**	78,773	61,832 (21)
23. **Sperry Corp.**	72,705	75,138 (16)
24. **Rockwell International Corp.**	59,327	*
25. **Hyundai Construction Co. Ltd.**	58,338	290,486 (4)
Total, Top 25 Companies	**$6,331,895**	**$3,984,775**
Total FMS Awards	**$8,157,571**	**$5,329,876**

*Not among top 25 FMS contractors during FY 1979.
Source: "Foreign Military Sales, Top 25 Companies and Their Subsidiaries Ranked According to Net Value of Military Prime Contract Awards," for Fiscal Years 1979 and 1980. Chrysler contracts for FY 1979 are from the DoD Public Affairs division.

1981, 54 nations owned research or nuclear power reactors, which are essentially bomb factories. They produce plutonium as a by-product of nuclear fission, and plutonium is the fuel for nuclear weapons.

Etiology: Missile Envy and Other Psychopathology

To promote the cause of "strength" in the nuclear age by arguing for more bombs is a classic example of prenuclear thinking. Before 1945, it was true that the more conventional weapons the country possessed, the safer it was. Since 1945, any attempt by one of the two superpowers to engineer a superiority in numbers of nuclear weapons has been met with a catch-up game by the other. By participating in the crazy logic of nuclear-war-fighting scenarios, America is engineering her own suicide. Before nuclear weapons, the United States was virtually invulnerable to the threat of military invasion, with two huge oceans to the east and west and two friendly countries to the north and south. Before nuclear weapons, there was never any real attempt even to develop antiaircraft defenses in the United States. It still is true that no country can hope to invade the United States. But, by following America's lead, the Soviet Union now could obliterate this great country within several hours.

The truth is that America has placed its destiny in the hands of a few frightened Soviet politicians, who are being continuously provoked by the threat of ever more destabilizing weapons and delivery systems, as well as plans to fight and win a protracted nuclear war. When I was in the USSR in 1979, our delegation met with high-ranking Soviet officials, including the two diplomats who negotiated SALT II. They were very worried about the threat of nuclear war and terribly concerned about the planned deployment of the ground-launched cruise missiles and Pershing IIs in Europe.

They talked constantly about World War II and their twenty million dead, and they seemed more frightened of China than of the United States—probably because of their long history of previous invasions by Mongols and Tartars over hundreds of years. They have virtually no important allies in the world, and I think they are acutely aware that if they invaded Western Europe, most of the Warsaw Pact countries would fight against them. The Soviet Union is ringed by countries that harbor American military bases, missiles, nuclear weapons, listening posts, and intelligence systems.

As a physician, I have admitted clinically paranoid and frightened patients into acute medical wards. From long experience, I abstained from sticking needles into them or hurting them because they might have been provoked to harm themselves or me. Instead, I tried to understand what was really happening in their troubled minds. Such an approach required a lot of courage on my part, as well as immense patience and love, but usually it paid off. The patients would open up and share their troubled thoughts, so I could engage them in a constructive, therapeutic dialogue.

In the same vein, I would humbly suggest that it is medically contraindicated to frighten the Soviet leaders. If America continues to provoke their anxieties and fears, they could, in their paranoia, initiate nuclear war.

It is also imperative that Americans learn about the history and culture of other countries, including that of the Soviet Union. The behavior of nation-states is very much conditioned by their past experiences, in the same way that individual human beings are products of their genetic makeup (genotype) and the way their emotional environments have shaped their behavior, particularly during childhood. The people in the Soviet Union and their leaders behave in rigid, uncompromising ways, as they and their ancestors have done over hundreds of years. They have a proud cultural history of great art, music, and literature. But until the 1917 Revolution, they were a nation of millions of starving serfs, a wealthy middle class, and an extremely rich nobility. Unfortunately, the grand ideals upon which that revolution was based, centered primarily on care for others and the society, collapsed in ruins as Stalin took over the leadership in 1929.

After years of internal bloodshed and massacres, Stalin's reign of intimidation was replaced by a series of rigid, unimaginative leaders, who declined to move far from the authoritarian rules of Stalin—although without the bloodshed. Over the past thirty years or so the USSR has moderated its behavior toward its citizens. Where once dissidents were killed automatically, they now survive, proclaim their views, and are even permitted to hold interviews with the eager Western press. Jewish emigration fluctuates in a way often related to international pressures and events. There is no unemployment problem in the Soviet Union; all have access to free medical care and free education, and the price of food has remained low for twenty years. All citizens are automatically given several weeks' annual vacation, and the standard of living is incomparably higher than in prerevolutionary days.

Many scholars of the present-day Soviet Union are convinced that its leaders are sincere in their attempts to negotiate the control and reduction of nuclear weapons. These scholars are also convinced that if the Soviet leaders felt less intimidated and threatened by the hostile actions and words of the U.S. government, they would feel free to allow increased moderation in their Warsaw Pact countries, to permit more emigration of Jews, and possibly to relax some of the rigid internal restrictions in the USSR.

The Tribal Mentality

Why do nations feel obliged to act with such hostility and self-righteousness toward each other? Perhaps the mobilization of people in nation-states had its origin in the dynamics of the tribe. Millions of years ago, people needed to live together in order to survive, forming tightly knit bands that were defensive and aggressive toward any other threatening group. It certainly is possible that this tribal mentality was stamped into our genes as a product of evolution—a Darwinian "survival of the fittest" necessity. But such a mentality is anachronistic in the age of genocide. Nationalism is just a sophisticated term for tribalism. The same feelings are provoked when "The Star-Bangled Banner" is played—pride, unity, comradeship, self-righteousness, and a certain sense that we would fight for the principles enunciated in that song. National anthems in most countries in the world evoke similar feelings of tribalism. It is high time for people to realize that nationalism now means possible extinction of one's own country as well as of the human race. We must all try to direct these parochial instincts toward a sense of altruism, pride, compassion, and love for the family of man.

As I work with millions of people, teaching them the medical effects of nuclear war, I find that their instinct for survival overcomes their primitive nationalistic urges. The survival instinct is the strongest physiological drive we possess, more powerful than those for eating or reproduction. People faced with imminent prospects of extinction suddenly become transformed when they realize that in order to save themselves and those they love, they must help others who are totally alien to them. These feelings are possessed by everyone. We were not put on earth to make ourselves happy. The path to true happiness lies in helping others.

In my more regressive moods, I often have thought that if Martians invaded earth, all nations would unite in a self-righteous comradeship to do battle with the aliens. Will the alien threat that unites us all today—the omnipresent threat of instant annihilation at any time—have the power to save us?

There is a theory that man is an evolutionary aberrant not designed to survive in the long run. In fact, man is a wondrous beast. The human brain developed and evolved in a very short evolutionary time-span. As soon as he stood on his hind limbs and developed an opposing thumb, which enabled him to hold tools and weapons, he became a threat to other living creatures, including his own species. Certainly, the rapidly developing intellect couched in the huge neocortex of the brain allowed him to kill dangerous animals and members of threatening tribes.

Most, if not all, of our emotions still originate in the primitive midbrain, at the base of the brain. The large cortical lobes are used to rationalize and justify what our midbrain is telling us to do. No person on earth is totally rational. All human behavior is motivated to some degree by primitive emotional responses and reactions. We have been conditioned to fear, hate, feel jealous, or to respond in other ways to certain stimuli. Many of our emotions have their origins in childhood. For instance, I might meet a woman who, because of the shape of her ears, the tone of her voice, or her powerful personality, reminds me of my dear mother. Without consciously making a connection, my reaction to this stranger would be colored by a far more complex relationship. These powerful feelings have absolutely nothing to do with the woman herself; she simply triggered feelings that I carry around with me all the time. We all have feelings like this, liking some people immensely and disliking others. It is not difficult to understand these reactions if one takes the time and effort to understand the most important early influences within one's own childhood.

We also tend to project our feelings of inadequacy, fear, or hatred onto other people. Ronald Reagan told me during a meeting in the White House that the Soviets are evil, godless Communists. When I asked him if he had ever met one, he said no. That is an example of Mr. Reagan projecting his fear and hatred onto the Soviets. This nasty side of people is called our dark side. We all have a dark side. We never like to admit that we are haters or that we are jealous or that we are really a mass of fear and insecurities. It is far easier to dislike other people and blame them for our feelings. How many times have we heard others say, as we say ourselves, "She makes me feel awful" or "He makes me feel frightened"? Nobody can make us feel anything. Each of us is responsible for his or her own feelings. Other people can trigger these feelings, but we allow ourselves to feel them. They are nobody else's fault.

In a tribal sense, people seem to derive deep feelings of well-being by projecting their fears and hatred in a unified fashion onto a common enemy. This dark side can become evil personified. Hitler was an absolute master at mobilizing the dark side of the German people. He was so brilliant at this technique that the Germans unified in their hatred and killed tens of millions of people. This projection of the dark side becomes mass paranoia and mass psychosis.

Americans are taught to dislike and in many instances even hate the Soviets. There is a compulsory course taught in the Florida high schools called Americanism vs. Communism (nicknamed AVC by the schoolchildren); in Texas, children are taught the evils of communism; other states conduct similar educational campaigns. This sort of childhood conditioning serves to justify the projection of the dark side. Nations behave in this way very much as individuals do.

If we are to survive as a species, we must stop this paranoid projection, both personally and collectively. The place to start is with family and friends. Pick the person whom you dislike most, seek him out, and talk to him. Discover what he really thinks of you and tell him honestly what you think of him and why (if you understand your own conditioning). Make friends with him. Nothing is more disarming than vulnerability. That is what we must do with the Soviets. It is really not too difficult; it certainly takes some courage, but it is eminently rewarding and very satisfying.

Another emotional dynamic that needs to be examined is love. In our society, we are taught that we need love and people should give it to us. In a marriage, unhappiness often results when one partner does not feel loved or understood by the other. We need these emotional reinforcements. The only way to true happiness is to give love and have no need. In my marriage, I have found that if I blame my husband for my unhappy state, I don't get his love. But if I abandon my selfish needs and I give him what he needs, making no demands—just loving him—the tables turn. The total renunciation of my expectations leads to conflict resolution. The only way a relationship can work is for each partner to capitulate on his own desires and to reach out to the other—in other words, to negotiate from a position of so-called weakness and not one of strength. It *always* works. To make oneself vulnerable in any conflict situation is a sign of real courage and strength. When two wolves are involved in a death struggle, the losing wolf typically recognizes his failures and bares the jugular vein in his neck to this attacking opponent. The other wolf then capitulates and walks off.

On this planet, the superpowers are married to each other. They must either live and work together, respecting their differences, or they will die together. The marriage vow is appropriate for a future life-preserving relationship between the United States and the Soviet Union: For better, for worse, for richer, for poorer, in sickness and in health, forsaking all others, till death do us part, according to God's holy name, I pledge thee my troth. Each superpower must learn that the true path to conflict resolution is to forget selfish needs and wants and pragmatically to make the first move. Typically, throughout most U.S.-USSR arms-control negotiations, the Americans have made the first move and have taken the initiatives in certain areas. Usually the Soviets follow. They are rigid and slow, but they follow. A good example of capitulation and unilateralism was Jack Kennedy's initiative in his American University speech, when he unilaterally stopped testing nuclear weapons. From this initial move, other unilateral moves followed on both sides. This is conflict resolution at its most potent.

Men and Women

Men and women are psychologically and physiologically different. Each has a most important role to play in the world, but unfortunately, women play second fiddle on most occasions. Although American women won the vote sixty-five years ago, they have done virtually nothing with it. There are virtually no women in high office. For various reasons—feelings of inadequacy, lack of knowledge, lack of energy contingent upon childbirth and child-rearing—women have stayed in the background while men have made virtually all significant and major decisions. Now the world is ready to blow up. Women are worried, but men still make most of the decisions.

A man named Mark Gerzon recently wrote a book called *A Choice of Heroes* in which he examines the state of the world. He determines that it is in a serious dilemma and that certainly in the United States decisions are made by a small minority—white Anglo-Saxon males, middle-aged and older. Because these people have created such enormous problems, Mr. Gerzon asserts that we need to examine their psychological pathology. Typically, these men never show emotion, never admit mistakes, and are very dependent upon others of the same sex for peer group approval. They are always sure of themselves; they are always right; and above all, they are always tough and strong. He suggests that in the nuclear age, these men need to redefine strength and courage for themselves, to become men who have the courage to show weaknesses and fallibilities, to admit mistakes, to show emotion, even to cry when appropriate. It takes extraordinary strength and inner courage for man to be able to do this. A weak, unattractive man never shows any emotion or even admits to having emotions, never is fallible, never admits to making a mistake, hides behind his defense mechanisms, and builds missiles. One could call this dynamic a case of acute missile envy. Such men, who in fact hold the reins of power in Washington, in the Iron Triangle, and throughout the land.and the world, are anachronistic in the nuclear age.

A typical woman is very much in touch with her feelings. She cries when necessary and has a strong and reliable intuition. She is not afraid to admit she has made a mistake and generally is interested in life-oriented human dynamics. She innately understands the basic principles of conflict resolution. Most of these women know how to get to a man's deepest emotions. Most men, when in love or infatuated with a woman, will open up and reveal their true feelings, which they would ordinarily not have the courage to do, particularly when dealing with male colleagues and friends.

Women are nurturers. Their bodies are built anatomically and physiologically to nurture life. Not all women can have babies, and some do not even desire them, but many have a will to give birth. Mothers or not, most women care deeply about the preservation of life. Women are also capable of capitulation and can move into conflict resolution if they make a conscious decision. It is almost always the woman who makes the initial move to seek marriage or partner guidance counseling if there are problems in a relationship.

One of the reasons women are so allied to the life process is their hormonal constitution. After I went through pregnancy and the birthing process, I was emotionally and physically engrossed in my children. I was very frightened lest one of them have a congenital deformity. I was totally delighted by these perfect little human beings. After the births, if one of the babies cried in another part of the house, I was still so attached to them that my breasts prickled with milk. I have never been so fulfilled in my whole life and felt that giving birth was the most creative and loving thing I ever did. I would have happily done so every year until menopause. In fact, for the first time in my life, I knew I would give up my own life to save another human being—my baby. To a certain extent, these feelings are induced by the female hormones estrogen and progesterone, which are secreted in large quantities by the placenta, and probably by the hormone that induces and controls lactation. Indeed, women's psyches are influenced by hormonal levels— varying sometimes in different stages of the menstrual cycle and often influenced by the changes evoked by the contraceptive pill, which can involve depression, loss of libido, and general malaise.

Men, on the other hand, are men because of their hormonal output of androgen. If a male fetus does not have the capacity to respond to male hormones secreted by his testicles, he will develop anatomically into a female. But if a male has normally functioning androgens, he develops big muscles, a deep voice, secondary sexual characteristics, and body hair. He is typically more psychologically aggressive than women. Some people contend that this is the result of conditioning. I am sure that some aggressive behavior in men is conditioned, but some must also be hormonally controlled. I have observed clinically that when a man develops cirrhosis of the liver and loses the ability to metabolize and break down the small quantities of female hormones secreted by his adrenal glands, he becomes both physically and psychologically feminized. He loses his body hair, his testicles atrophy, his skin becomes soft, and he becomes more sensitive psychologically. And if a woman is given male hormones over a prolonged period of time, for a medical condition, she will develop big muscles, her body hair will increase, her voice will deepen, and she will become more aggressive psychologically.

Some recent work has shown that little boys under the age of six are more aggressive than girls of the same age. Teachers in Educators for Social Responsibility observed that primary school boys become excited when playing video games and, having lost, walk away feeling energetic and aggressively disappointed. Girls will play for a while, but they don't become nearly as emotionally involved as the boys, and walk away after several games because they are bored.

Some men have recently described to me the fascination that killing holds for them. One man, now a deeply religious person, described to me some of his childhood activities. He used to catch a frog, hold it in the palm of his hand belly up, and pierce its belly with a very sharp stick. He would then hold it over a fire, turning it slowly on the stick as it roasted. He said he had feelings of ecstasy as he watched the frog squirm and burn to death. A French film producer, who used to be a correspondent, interviewed Nazi torturers. Initially, the cruelty and killing made him physically sick, but as he got used to it, he described an almost orgasmic fascination with killing—almost a feeling of omnipotence.

What is it about their most primitive feelings that makes these men enjoy killing? Women know almost from birth that they can experience the ultimate act of creativity, but boys and men lack this potential capacity. Do they replace it with a fascination with control over life and death and a feeling of creative omnipotence? Perhaps the men reading this book will look into their souls and examine the validity of these questions.

Another dynamic operating in the arms race is that of overt sexuality. As I watch adolescent boys and young men in their twenties driving their girlfriends around in souped-up hot rods, it is obvious that they are demonstrating their virility. I suppose at that age, with life and the whole world ahead of them, these young boys and men are bursting with energy and their newly discovered sexuality. But I wonder how many of them really ever grow up.

I am reminded of a frequent experience one meets in general practice. Often a young couple, aged seventeen and twenty, come in, with the girl pregnant. As soon as the girl delivers and becomes a mother, she turns into a woman overnight, emotionally mature and extremely responsible for this new life. Almost always, the boy remains an emotional child and often runs away from his responsibilities by leaving his wife and baby. As I observed many couples, it seemed to me that often these men never mature. They continue to flirt with death, playing with dangerous toys—motorbikes, racing cars, weapons, and war.

The hideous weapons of mass genocide may be symptoms of several male emotions, reflecting inadequate sexuality, a need continually to prove virility, and a primitive fascination with killing. I recently watched a filmed launching of an MX missile. It rose slowly from the ground, surrounded by smoke and flames, and elongated into the air. It was a very sexual sight indeed; more so when armed with the ten warheads it will explode with the most almighty orgasm. The names used by the military are laden with psychosexual overtones: missile erector, thrust-to-weight ratio, soft laydown, deep penetration, hard line, and soft line. A McDonnell Douglas advertisement for a new weapons system proudly proclaims that it can "shoot down whatever's up, and blow up whatever's down." Sexual inadequacy in a powerful leader is illustrated by the following example: Hitler once invited a young woman to his room. He stuck out his arm in a Nazi salute and in a booming voice said,

> I can hold my arm like that for two solid hours. I never feel tired. . . . My arm is like granite—rigid and unbending, but, Göring can't stand it. He has to drop his arm after half an hour of this salute. He's flabby, but I am hard.

The American missiles are smaller than the Soviet missiles, a fact that is used to good advantage by the generals to persuade Congress of the need for more money. Boeing constructed a model of the different sizes of missiles, painting the American ones blue and the Soviet ones red. The generals take this model to House and Senate hearings to say: "But Senator, how do you feel when America has these small blue missiles and Russia has these great big red missiles?" They always get what they ask for.

General Patton described war as "the cataclysmic ecstasy of violence." The chairman of the Committee on Public Information during World War I said, "Universal military training means more than national safety and defense. It means national health, national virility. . . . There is not a weakness in American life that it would not strengthen." A Spanish saying goes, "When a nation shows a civilized horror of war, it receives directly the punishment for its mistakes. God changes its sex, despoils it of its common mark of virility, changes it into a feminine nation, and sends conquerors to ravage it of its honor." A quote from Ireland: "Bloodshed is a cleansing and sanctifying rite, and the nation that regards it as a final horror has lost its manhood."

The psychologist Carl Jung described two basic psychological principles that govern human behavior: the anima, or feminine principle, and its masculine corollary, the animus. Both principles, present to some degree in all human beings, have a positive and a negative aspect. The positive anima is the nurturing, caring, loving principle, which women embody and that also is present powerfully in some men. The negative anima is the petulant, bitchy characteristic, best epitomized when a man and a woman have a fight and the man becomes very petulant, refusing to talk for several days. The positive animus is the principle that motivates people to become active in relationships or in the world, to take the initiative, and to become confident, positive, and powerful. Many men embody this principle, but most women have a very undeveloped positive animus, except if they feel their children are threatened. The negative animus is a competitive, egocentric, evil, powerful principle, which often can lead to killing, either in a psychological or a physical sense. Many men also are filled and motivated by the principle of negative animus, which, indeed, has the world in its

Missile envy

grip. When a woman attacks a man verbally and emotionally, her negative animus is operating.

Individuals face a formidable challenge in the nuclear age because of the survival imperative. They must learn to understand the basic principles that underlie and motivate their behavior and to determine how they can enhance the growth of the positive anima and animus and diminish the negative aspects. One person who, perhaps more than anyone else, embodied these positive principles was Jesus. He was soft and loving, caring and nurturing, but He also had a powerful drive to correct evil and help people do the right things, and sometimes He could be positively aggressive if the need arose. He expressed righteous indignation and moral outrage when He observed people abusing others, and He uttered some very profound psychological truths. He was probably the most brilliant, well-balanced psychiatrist who ever lived.

Women have a very important role to play in the world today. They must rapidly develop their own power so that they can move out into local, national, and international affairs, using their positive animus to save the children of the country and of the world. Through the women's liberation movement, they have learned that they are as intelligent as men and can be as powerful or more powerful, as the occasion arises. They also have developed a confidence in themselves that is delightful to see. The age of woman has arrived. If we don't stand up and rapidly become elected to the highest offices in the country, changing America's national policies from those of death to those of life, we will all be exterminated. I don't mean that in doing this women should abrogate their positive feminine principle of nurturing, loving, and caring. I mean they should tenaciously preserve these values but also learn to find and use their incredible power. The positive feminine principle must become the guiding moral principle in world politics.

Women also need to teach men how to get into contact with their emotions. I am married to a very beautiful man, who in the past ten years has learned to recognize and talk about his emotions. But still he is a man. Sometimes I still am surprised when I ask him how he felt about a person or a situation and he gives me a chronology of events. I have to say to him again and several times more, "But I am not interested in how it happened. How did you feel?" I think it is difficult for men consciously to recognize their feelings and emotions, let alone to talk about them. I think it somehow makes them feel demeaned and probably very vulnerable to have to admit that they feel rejected or hurt.

The women's liberation movement has encouraged men to become more nurturing and gentle. By staying at home and minding the children, they have become more empathetic with women and the lives women have lived in the past. These men often find they become closer to their offspring and develop tremendous satisfaction when they are involved in the nurturing process. This, of course, usually enhances the relationship between the two parents.

Most of the men who lead American society are married, and most of them have children and grandchildren. When I speak to a hall full of uninformed people about the medical effects of nuclear war, it is invariably the women who rise up in their seats and who develop a power that they previously lacked. I am sure that I am tapping into the instinct that a woman has to protect her children. The positive animus takes over. But, so often at the end of a lecture, men will come up to me and point out that I did not give the correct number for the cruise missiles, or correct some other statistic. The women usually will jump down their throats and scream, "That's the sort of thinking that's going to kill us!" The men look very shocked and retreat, hurt. They have obviously not let the appalling material I have just presented enter their psyches and have studiously avoided the logical emotional response by clinging to their rational exposition of numbers and tunnel-vision perspective and statistics.

On the whole, men are fascinated with numbers and how things work. They are comfortable operating from a rational perspective, ignoring the real emotions that motivate their every action and feeling. It is time for the positive feminine principle in women and the nurturing, caring side of men to take over and assume the lead.

Men often accuse me of being too emotional. It is absolutely appropriate to be emotional as one contemplates the fiery end of the earth.

Politicians

Most politicians practice prenuclear thinking—they have not taken into their souls the hideous consequences of nuclear war and translated these effects into their own lives. They continually vote for more and more missiles, bombs, ships, planes, satellites, and radars without giving the logical conclusions of their actions a second thought. They have been conditioned to think that more military installations in their districts will create more jobs, and that is better for their re-election prospects.

I took the Physicians for Social Responsibility film *The Last Epidemic* down to Washington to show it to Congress. This is an excellent short film with statements by admirals, ex-CIA officials, and scientists who have been involved in the arms race, and it graphically describes the medical consequences of nuclear war. The room was packed with people, but they were mostly aides and staff people. I asked where the senators and representatives were, and their staff told me that they were too busy to attend—too busy, perhaps, being courted, wined and dined, and cajoled by the defense contractors and the Pentagon.

Many of these people practice psychic numbing, a term aptly coined by the psychiatrist Robert Lifton. They have rarely contemplated—morally, ethically, or emotionally—the logical consequences of their daily actions as they vote to prepare the earth for a global holocaust. The few politicians who have seen this film or have been present during a lecture on the medical consequences of nuclear war have almost always had their psychic numbing shattered. It is easy for a physician to establish the doctor-patient relationship with any audience and to personalize in a professional way the frightful consequences of nuclear war. We do this every day with our seriously ill patients, as they must be made aware of the enormous consequences of their diagnosis. After a realistic appraisal of their diseases, they will then be prepared to undergo the often very unpleasant side effects of therapy.

People who have been shocked into reality about their disease characteristically enter the five stages of grief. The first stage is shock and disbelief, which will last for days or weeks. The whole situation seems unreal and will, it is hoped, go away. The next stage is one of deep depression, so profound that they can lose their appetite and their libido. They lose weight, wake early in the morning, and have no energy to live a normal life. This stage may last for months and is followed by or combined with the stage of anger—railing against God for their illness. The next stage may be bargaining with God—if they do the right thing, maybe God will let them live. The final stage of grief is adjustment and acceptance of death or reality. If the patient has been allowed time to pass through the other stages of grief, he will then finally be able to die at peace with himself and his Maker.

Many people, faced with the imminent prospects of nuclear war, will enter this same grief process. It is extremely painful psychologically—most people avoid these feelings if they possibly can. But only if people let themselves experience the true gravity of the nuclear period will they be motivated to alleviate the situation. The angry phase is the most constructive period. When a person is angry, his adrenal glands, which are located just above the kidneys, pump out the hormone adrenaline, which raises the blood-sugar level, pushes up the blood pressure, and turns on the neurons. Angry people become motivated to decide what they must do to survive. Acceptance also is a useful phase. When people have stopped battling with reality, they have more energy to devote to constructive solutions.

I showed *The Last Epidemic* to the staff at *The Washington Post*. Ben Bradlee gathered his people into a large room, and, before the film began, defense correspondents and others were arguing about various military strategies and saying, "What about the Russians?" I said I would not answer them until they had watched the film. When the lights went on, there was stunned silence in the room. Several of the journalists were in tears, and Ben Bradlee said, "I guess I'm numb." I said, "No you're not. You've entered the first stage of grief." I went on to explain the psychological response that people have to such material. They were fascinated. Later, Walter Pincus, the Pentagon correspondent, came up to me and said, "That was the best presentation I ever heard." He explained that he listened to presentations every day about weapons and strategies, professionally produced by the military corporations, but that he had never heard the issue discussed in these terms before. A new facet to the problem had been presented. Emotions are seldom discussed by the people in the media or in the Iron Triangle.

It is imperative that our representatives be exposed to the emotional consequences of their actions. Politicians practice old modes of thinking. They believe that the more bombs America has, the safer it will be. They don't seem to recognize that more bombs increase the risk and probability of nuclear war simply because, as more people handle the bombs and delivery systems, statistically the chances for risk and error increase.

The total number of nuclear warheads also is a very important factor to consider. As the arsenal increases, the global ecological system becomes more and more threatened. In fact, more nuclear weapons increase the insecurity of American and the earth.

Sexuality and National Security Politics

Power, seductive and corrupting, has become the ultimate goal of politicians. In his book *The Price of Power,* Seymour Hersh describes how decisions were made by Nixon and Kissinger in an arbitrary fashion, often to protect their own power and prestige. The decisions were based not on morality or ethics but on their egocentric self-interests.

For instance, they were warned by some officials during the war in Biafra that without American intervention, one million people could be dead within a month. Because Henry Kissinger was having some difficulty with personal relationships in the State Department, nothing was done, and hundreds of thousands of people died of starvation in Africa.

The president of the United States has ultimate power and can start a war if he so desires. There are no immediate checks and balances to prevent these decisions from being made.

In his book, Hersh discusses the Soviet menace and reports that it was considered "soft" not to be tough on the Soviets. These sexual dynamics still prevail in the Reagan Administration and in the House and Senate.

Lyndon Johnson desperately wanted to be seen as a man, according to the author David Halberstam. "He wanted the respect of men who were tough, real men, and they would turn out to be hawks." Johnson had two categories: men and boys. The men were "activists-doers who conquered business empires, who acted instead of talked." Boys were "the talkers and the writers and the intellectuals, who sat around thinking and criticizing and doubting instead of doing." Halberstam called Johnson "more than a little insecure." He was acting out his sexual insecurities in the world and in so doing was the catalyst to the deaths of hundreds of thousands of people. Had he had the wisdom and courage to examine his childhood and to discover the origin of his insecurities, he could well have become a more whole man, perceived by many as a leader. He would have become a true hero instead of having to leave in disrepute and humiliation. Johnson lacked a well-developed positive anima, and his negative animus obviously was trying to compensate for his insecurity. His dark side was projected upon the world.

In *A Choice of Heroes*, Gerzon describes the sexual dynamics in the Johnson Administration:

> One high-level State Department aide who witnessed many planning sessions recalled how Johnson's decision-makers reenacted this predictable masculine drama. "I watched the Doves trying to phrase their arguments so as not to look soft," said James C. Thomson, who now directs the Neiman Foundation at Harvard. "But, the Doves were intimidated by the brass and the hardliners. Particularly those who had not served in the Armed Forces, such as Humphrey, were vulnerable to the uniform. They never rebut the techno-military 'We've got to be tough' language that the Generals and the Hawks used."

In these tribal power games, the bottom line always is the zero-sum mentality—I win if you lose, and vice versa. There is no middle line or compromise if the masculine ethic is to be preserved. This is the football-game mentality. Boys are taught in school to be intensely aggressive in sports, and the word "kill" frequently is used to drum up the necessary energy to win. If men *have* to prove their masculinity to each other, the safest way to do it is through sports. The ancient tradition of the Olympic games is a healthy, wholesome way for countries to act out their tribal impulses and for men (and, indeed, women) to prove themselves in competition. I have often thought that the solution to the aggressive needs of the men who control the superpowers would be an annual wrestling match between the Kremlin and the Pentagon. These men could lock each other in intense body-to-body physical combat. If necessary, matches could be arranged monthly to alleviate built-up aggressions.

It always is the old men who send the young men off to die in their wars. Countries traditionally maintain departments of state or departments of foreign affairs full of diplomats who negotiate when difficulties arise between countries. But if the negotiations break down, the countries start to kill each other's people. How primitive! Never do people who make the decision to kill get killed—it is the boys who usually don't even know what the dispute is about, let alone understand the intricacies of international politics. This dynamic has been occurring for thousands of years. Now it must stop, because any conventional superpower war will most certainly escalate the nuclear war.

How many leaders of the world have ever witnessed the explosion of a hydrogen bomb—felt the heat hundreds of miles away, like a furnace door opening next to their faces, watched the flash through their closed eyes and hands and seen the bones of their hands light up, watched an adjacent battleship rise up in the water like a splinter and disappear? How many of these old men emotionally understand the magnitude of destruction in these small suns? I would venture to say none.

How many leaders of the world have ever watched the miracle of birth? How many leaders of the world have helped a child to die and supported the parents in their grief before and forever after? Each life is as precious as any other, and the magnitude of suffering involved in a single death is vast.

General Public: Psychic Numbing

Although most people were relieved when World War II ended after Hiroshima and Nagasaki, they were shocked nonetheless by these dreadful new bombs. General fears about nuclear war increased during the era of Dulles brinksmanship in the Eisenhower Administration and recrudesced when America and the USSR began testing bombs in the atmosphere. Linus Pauling and other scientists and physicians predicted that the high levels of radioactive fallout concentrating in the milk and in children's teeth could increase the incidence of cancer and leukemia in these children many years later. The days of nuclear fallout were followed by the Cuban missile crisis, where nuclear war might have been only hours away. People in America were so frightened that they started to build fallout shelters, and some were so provoked by anxieties that they bought guns to protect themselves from their neighbors. This generalized fear helped to bring about the Limited Test-Ban Treaty; America and the Soviet Union could continue their nuclear testing, but only underground, in order to eliminate atmospheric fallout.

Out of sight is out of mind, and people's fears of a nuclear war rapidly disappeared. The superpowers quietly and efficiently continued to test and to increase their arsenals without any public interference or adverse world opinion.

The world's people lapsed into a state of psychic numbing and pushed the fear of nuclear annihilation into their collective subconscious. Occasionally, if an air-raid siren sounded, some would be reminded of the days of air-raid drills in school—scrambling under desks, hiding in the corridors, or covering their heads with pieces of paper to protect themselves against a nuclear bomb.

The old nuclear anxieties began to rear their heads again when SALT II failed to be ratified by the U.S. Senate, when the MX was authorized by President Carter, and when Reagan came riding into power on a platform of winnable nuclear war. The Reagan Administration continued to make wildly provocative statements about firing nuclear warning shots across the bow of the Soviet Union and having a limited nuclear war in Europe without pressing the strategic button. Physicians for Social Responsibility began to hold symposia across the country on the medical consequences of nuclear war. These captured the imagination of the media, and once again nuclear war became a prime topic of conversation in many American households as well as in Europe and the Soviet Union. Many thousands of people, alerted to the horrific medical effects, were thrown into the grieving process and emerged as activists. Millions voted for a nuclear freeze in the 1982 elections (it passed in eight out of nine states), while 79 percent of people in a March 1983 Harris poll supported a nuclear freeze.

Yet most of these people had not really been through the grieving process. Although they had become sensitized in a superficial way to the medical dangers of nuclear war, they really had little concept of the magnitude of the arms race in their own country, let alone in Europe or the world at large.

People avoid facing nuclear reality by several mechanisms:

They practice displacement activity. This dynamic is best illustrated by animal experiments. If you put rats in a cage and threaten them with a lethal situation, they tend to ignore it and run away to another part of the cage, engaging in activities that are totally irrelevant to their life-threatening situation. Most people do this every day. They worry about their work and their families and ignore the overwhelming danger that hangs over them like a Sword of Damocles every minute of their lives.

They practice manic denial. Some people deny nuclear reality with a vengeance. They indulge in hot tubs, Jacuzzis, fancy cars, gourmet foods, fur coats, and fashionable clothes. In pre-World War II Germany, there was an atmosphere of manic hedonism very like the egocentric, pleasure-seeking activities of present-day America and Europe.

Some people are truly ignorant about the imminence of nuclear war. I met a young man, age twenty-one, at a party recently. He was intelligent, but he asked me if the bomb dropped on Hiroshima was nuclear, and he had absolutely no knowledge of the nuclear arms race.

Other people justify the possession of nuclear weapons by saying, *"What about the Russians?"* Some psychiatrists feel that people's fear of nuclear war is projected onto the Soviets. By transforming them into inanimate objects, we can talk about killing hundreds of millions of people and have no feeling about it. In so doing, we have lost our humanity. This extension of the tribal dynamic is overlaid by the profound fear of nuclear war, which is an obvious threat to both tribes.

Another example of denial is exhibited by millions of fundamentalist Christians, led by Jerry Falwell and others. They believe that the world will be consumed by fire, as in nuclear war, and that one third of men with the mark of God on their foreheads will go straight up to heaven. They call this event *the rapture,* and many of them are actually praying for it to happen.

Everyone is scared of his or her own death, and very few people ever face this reality until a lethal diagnosis has been made. Even then, some people refuse to accept the fact that they are dying. But to face the death of life on earth is so much more painful than even one's own death. I think I have reached the stage where I could die at peace and accept that reality. I could even accept the death of my children because I know they have to die sometime. What I absolutely cannot accept is the death of life on the planet. We may be the only life in the whole universe. When I was a little girl, I used to derive a great sense of emotional security in the knowledge that the world would go on if I were to die.

All these mechanisms are used to avoid the very unpleasant feelings of grief and responsibility. People who are forced to accept reality are forced to accept responsibility for their world. This involves changing the priorities in their lives: The exigencies of daily living would become secondary to their need to find solutions to their dangerous dilemma. Why make sure the children clean their teeth, eat nutritious food, or are exposed to a good education when they could be vaporized within the next ten years?

By ignoring the true reality of the imminence of nuclear war, we are practicing passive suicide. Our society is in the grip of a pervasive mental illness that will lead to its death. Certainly, it takes courage and guts to face the dreadful facts and to accept responsibility to save the world. But this course of action is very satisfying and the only way for parents to ensure a future for their children. Preventing nuclear war is the ultimate parenting issue; nothing else matters.

We all behave very much like the Jews in Hitler's Germany after Hitler wrote *Mein Kampf*. They ignored his calculated plans and said, "It will never happen to us, because we're Germans." Even when they were being carted off in the cattle cars, many of them still denied the reality of their situation.

Repressing fear takes more mental energy than accepting the feelings of loss and grief that are associated with reality. People often tell me that they feel much more energetic once they have allowed themselves to go through the stages of grief. They become joyous people with a sense of mission, and they find that they are able to achieve extraordinary results in society toward ending the nuclear arms race, both at a local and a national level.

It is absolutely inappropriate for anyone to feel psychologically comfortable in this day and age. The physician and writer Lewis Thomas recently gave a speech in which he said that ever since he acknowledged the imminence of nuclear war, he can't listen to beautiful music without feeling an overwhelming sense of grief for the world—a world without Paris and other wonderful cities, a world where the children have no sense of a future. What an absolute tragedy!

Children

Our children are in a terrible dilemma. A survey that focused on their feelings about nuclear war was conducted by Drs. John Mack and William Beardslee between 1978 and 1981. Sponsored by the American Task Force on the Psycho-Social Impact of Nuclear Disasters for the American Psychiatric Association, the survey was conducted among one thousand high school and grammar school students in Boston. Asked what they thought about nuclear age, the majority of these children said that they had no future. Similar surveys conducted by the *Houston Post* and by the *Boston Globe* produced the same findings.

New Zealand children surveyed in 1976 were found to be very optimistic about their future, but a 1982 study unearthed a feeling of pessimism very like that of American children. Doctors in Europe report that their children seem to be similarly afflicted.

I have worked with children for years as a pediatrician. My patients, all afflicted with a lethal genetic disease called cystic fibrosis, die any time from birth to age thirty. Children are unable to deny harsh realities. They seem to lack the mechanism to repress unpleasant thoughts and so are extremely vulnerable to fears about nuclear war. The reality of the nuclear threat is apparent to them every day as they watch television and read the newspapers. They merely have to listen to President Reagan make a speech in which he renames the MX missile "the Peacekeeper" to realize that they are living in an insane world. Children also seem to have an intuitive "sixth sense" about the truth, which adults usually lack. Some of my young patients have said to me, "I'm going to die tonight" when it was not clinically obvious that they were, and they did. Children are so honest and straightforward that their comments are often disarming to adults, who prefer to dismiss their profound truths as childish thinking and therefore not to be taken seriously. Jesus recognized their simple veracity when he said, "Out of the mouths of babes and sucklings thou has perfected praise."

Some of the comments that children make about the arms race are so close to the bone that it makes one cringe.

Piper Herman, age twelve, at Swampscott Junior High School in Massachusetts, said, her voice trembling,

> I just get so scared thinking that tomorrow I might not wake up, and that would just be the end. Because anyone can just push the button. We are studying Russian culture in school; they really are similar. We don't really know that much about what our government is doing, and the people in Russia know even less about what their government is doing.

Karen Zacarias, age twelve, from Swampscott, said,

> You know, I feel sorry for the Russians. We both have nuclear bombs, but we are the only country in the whole wide world who has actually dropped one and killed all those people. We're scared of Russia, but they must be super-scared of us.

Catherine Rich, age twelve, from Swampscott:

> I had nightmares of the bombs slowly floating towards me. I could feel my blood spurting all over the place. But, now it is better knowing it will all be over so fast. I feel scared, but relieved at the same time. It's like having cancer and at least being told you have it.

Susan Sweeney, age seventeen:

> As for a career, it seems like it is a waste to go to college and to build up a career and then get blown up someday. And, children—I would love to have kids, but I don't want to have them if they have nothing to live for. . . . Everyone's building up these nuclear weapons just to have one more than the other guy. Everyone's power-hungry. It will get to the point where one guy will say: "You may have more bombs than I, but I am going to get you first."

Stacey Sweeney, age fourteen: "I think all the leaders in the nation should fight it out in the boxing ring and leave us all out of it. It is really scary."

Susan Sweeney:

What scares me is that President Reagan wants to build up the military. He is trying to say that this way we'll be more secure, but what he is saying is making me more scared. . . . At least with Carter, the Russians could relax a little. Do we want Brezhnev all jittery?

Bob Genduso, age fourteen, said, "I don't think one country would ever have the guts to use them. Even if we are the only one that has ever done it, I think the leaders have more sense."

Stacey Sweeney:

But if leaders have so much sense, why have we had so many wars? And didn't they say that World War I would end all wars? Nobody even remembers why that one started, do they?

Susan Sweeney: "That's what's so scary. I just don't like being kept in the dark. It seems like the whole future of the world is in the hands of about ten people."

Stacey Sweeney:

I have nightmares, not about a nuclear war, but about not being here afterwards. Nothing is in the dream, really like fog. Try to picture nothing. The world is not the way it is meant to be.

Maybe a million years ago, someone could have done something, but now that all these countries have all these defenses built up ready to fight, it is really too late to do anything. We should be thinking, "They're people, just like we are." We should be working together, not against each other.

My own daughter, who is eighteen years old, said to me out of the blue the other day, "Mommy, I don't think I'll ever have any babies." And she loves babies.

We have brought these children into a world where they have no sense of a future. How could we do this to the people we love most in our lives and for whom we want the very best?

Some psychiatrists think that our children are dropping out, becoming part of the "me now" generation, and indulging almost universally in drugs and alcohol largely because of their total pessimism about the future.

They feel emotionally and almost physically abandoned by their parents. Many adults work hard to make sure their children receive good educations, are well-clothed, and are "psychologically secure." Yet these parents indulge in the societal dynamics of pervasive psychic numbing, furthering their careers while totally ignoring the fact that their children could be annihilated any day. Some children feel almost desperate in their abandonment. One eighteen-year-old girl approached my husband after he gave a lecture in Florida and said that she and her friends are frantic.

One little boy wrote to President Reagan and said, "President Reagan, you've lived your life. I haven't finished playing yet."

Rachel Bunker, from Framingham High School in Massachusetts, wrote a letter to the Boston Globe, saying,

> In the event of nuclear war, the youth of the world has the most to lose. Having no legal power in decisions needed to halt the arms race, we cry out for the right to live our lives in peace without the fear of nuclear annihilation.

These children receive extremely mixed messages from adults. They watch thousands of hours of television annually, observing blood-chilling violence that is rarely tempered by human emotion. They have been trained to accept that a violent society is normal. Some children act out the violence in schools, on the streets, and in their homes. There is a coldheartedness about some of these children that is most distressing. Many of them come from broken homes; in some areas of the country, such as Palo Alto, a large percentage of school students come from single-parent families. These children have rarely witnessed self-discipline in their parents and have observed less adult discipline in society. So their role models do not predispose them to accept responsibility and self-discipline as adults. They will inevitably grow up psychologically damaged, inheriting a world laced with nuclear weapons and ticking like a time bomb ready to explode any day.

When children reach late adolescence, they begin to develop psychological defense mechanisms that inure them to the scary subject of nuclear war. It is ironic that primary and secondary school children are acutely conscious of the threat of nuclear war, where young adults are almost sublimely unaware of the dangers. Often when I speak at colleges, I find it very difficult to arouse the audience in sufficient measure. Girls clad in designer jeans often get up halfway through the lecture on the medical effects of nuclear war and prance out with smirks on their faces. I appeal to them, pointing out that they are inheriting the world and that they have their whole future to look forward to, but they seem strangely unimpressed and uninvolved. Many of my children's friends, attending college, say the apathy is frightening. Their peers seem interested only in graduating and getting good jobs where they will make a lot of money. This attitude has perplexed me for several years, but I think I understand it now. These young people were born after the Limited Test-Ban Treaty went into effect in 1962. They grew up during the Vietnam War and Watergate, when nuclear war was never mentioned, and right through the benign 1970s. When Reagan was elected and talk of nuclear war began again, they had passed the age of susceptibility; they had developed a secure, stable vision of the future, and their egos had been formed and were refractory concerning the issue. Many older Americans remember the bomb scares and fallout in their youth and are very susceptible to having these old wounds reopened, if they will allow themselves the pain.

It amazes me that most secondary schools in America still avoid the subject of nuclear war—the single most important issue in students' lives. Teachers often feel embarrassed to teach the subject because they have no clear-cut answers. Yet Educators for Social Responsibility have found that children experience a tremendous sense of relief when adults show concern about their feelings and fears. We must work with them to try to find positive ways to stop and reverse the arms race. Students have actually formed national organizations, working together to get nuclear war curricula in their schools. They organize petitions and letter-writing drives to the press and the Congress, and they go to Washington to lobby.

Physicians, educators, and family counselors have found that the only way for parents to give their children some sense of emotional security in the nuclear age is to take responsibility for their children's future, to change the priorities of their own lives, and to start working to get rid of the bomb. During the adolescent rebellion phase, children whose parents are totally uninvolved in this issue take the weight of the world on their shoulders and bitterly resent the apathy and disinterest displayed by their parents for their future lives. Children whose parents are deeply involved in trying to stop nuclear war rebel against their parents' interest in such a "stupid subject." Our three children have behaved like this, and in a way it has given them the freedom to lead relatively carefree adolescent lives in the nuclear age.

Parents often ask me at meetings if they should discuss nuclear war with their children or what they should do when their child asks if he or she will grow up. My answer always is, "Become more involved in the issue and your child will relax and say, 'Mommy and Daddy are working to fix the situation.'"

As we think about our children, we must remember that they are being exposed continually to the pressures to buy war toys, many of which simulate nuclear war scenarios. As with the video games, they are conditioning our children to accept the prospects of nuclear war.

Scientists

Like all doctors, I have been trained to keep my emotions and biases from entering into decisions when treating patients. We can be empathetic but not sympathetic; otherwise, we may not be able to bring ourselves to make the necessary clinical decisions that will benefit patients.

When I graduated from medical school in 1961, I thought I knew all there was to be known about medicine. My arrogance and ignorance were gradually tempered by the vicissitudes of life, and I have since become a much better doctor. By learning to understand myself and my unconscious conditioning, fears, angers, and insecurities, I was better able to understand my patients' needs.

Most scientists and doctors are male. The ethic to which they subscribe studiously avoids the role of emotion in the thought process. It is appropriate that pure science be approached unemotionally, but scientists are in trouble. With unbounded zeal, they have pursued the secrets of the universe like little boys let loose in a toy store. They have rarely set foot outside their ivory towers to explain to the general public how these scientific truths can and will be applied to affect the world in which we will live. Most laymen remain frighteningly ignorant about the near-fatal state of our planet; yet the scientists rush ever forward with more technological breakthroughs while remaining invisible to public scrutiny.

In the years after World War II, a few honorable scientists realized the magnitude of the dilemma created by atomic bombs. Since then, these people have worked to try to end the nuclear arms race and to alert the public to its dangers. Unfortunately, they are a tiny minority. The wealth and power of the corporations and political system back the majority of avid scientists who are wedded to the discovery of ever more frightful ways to wreak havoc on the earth.

As Sir Solly Zuckerman has said,

Scientists are the alchemists of our times. They are the originators of the dreadful secrets whereby man can release the energy of stars on earth. Why are they so blocked and unconscious about their past and why are they still doing it? Why do they see no need to accept responsibility for their actions and to teach the people what they have done to the world?

I suspect that these people know that what they do is wrong, but the problems they try to solve are extremely interesting intellectually. I asked Joe Weitzenbaum, professor of computer science at MIT, why these men work on systems of genocide, and he said, "Do you know why? It's incredible fun." They are faced with an insoluble problem, like how to MIRV a missile, and they solve it. The intellectual prestige and the approbation from their colleagues must be rewarding. Grants flow in from the Pentagon and corporations. The scientist is set. His ego is gratified, and he does well financially, which is good for his family. As long as he can avoid thinking about the end result of his work, he can be emotionally comfortable.

Many scientists who leave military work say that all other jobs are comparatively boring. But there is more to life than intellectual excitement. When people face death at the end of their lives, the most important and significant part of their journey has been their relationship with other people, particularly their families. How can these people die with clear consciences when they realize on their deathbeds that they had played a role in preparing for the deaths of millions of their brothers and sisters, including those they love most?

Robert Lifton has coined the word "nuclearism" to describe the process of fascination and near-worship that some scientists, military people, politicians, and others have with the nuclear bomb. These people worship at the feet of the bombs and deify them, rationalizing that because of their potential for damage, they must be blessed with some innate goodness.

Many people are frightened of their own deaths. Some deal with this fear by actually playing with death in order to give them some power over it. This dynamic is called counterphobic mechanism. It may, indeed, be operating in many of these scientists. Certainly, one of the reasons I entered medicine was my own fear of death and my unconscious need to understand the process of the pathological mechanisms that lead to death.

In 1981, I was invited to speak at Sandia Labs in New Mexico, which are engaged in turning the devices designed at other nuclear labs into military weapons. Over five thousand scientists and ordnance engineers work at these labs, as well as at Los Alamos Lab, some miles away in the hills of New Mexico. The scientists at Sandia met in a large corrugated iron shed, where they gather periodically for lectures. They crowded into this makeshift hall, and there was standing room only. I was quite nervous because I knew I was facing a potentially hostile audience. I have a very careful clinical lecture about the medical and ecological effects of nuclear war, and at the end of this description I begged the scientists to leave their jobs, admitting to them that I knew such a decision would be very difficult.

I took questions, and the first man who stood up said, "You were quoted in the Boston Globe as saying that anyone who works for the nuclear industry is either dumb, stupid, or highly compromised." I could feel a rush of feeling in the hall that "at last we've got her." I was very careful and admitted that I had made such a statement and that I was wrong to have said that—in other words, I capitulated totally to my questioner. Deflated, he sat down. Most of the successive questions were hostile, but I was very polite and considerate and the meeting went very well. At the end, the scientists lined up to talk to me, and several of them said, "That was a very good lecture. They needed to hear this," pointing to their colleagues. No one took personal responsibility. They projected their dilemma onto their colleagues.

It is time for those scientists who are involved in the hideous military arms race to face their own consciences. They must take the initiative to remedy the situation they have created. As physicians have described the medical effects of nuclear war and the stages of grief consequent to this knowledge, many people who had repressed feelings of grief, fear, and guilt about their previous involvement in the arms race seem to have been given permission to speak of these fears for the first time. It is becoming acceptable to be against nuclear war; five years ago it was considered unpatriotic to mention the adverse properties of nuclear weapons.

Thanks to the endeavors of our scientists, we now have the technology to solve most problems facing the human race—overpopulation, hunger, energy depletion, polluted air and water, and the myriad medical ailments facing man. If these same scientists decided that they would work for the benefit of humanity and not for its death, they would earn eternal gratitude from the family of man. Such a challenge probably is the most wonderful and creative project any humane scientist could fulfill. I beg my colleagues to leave the business of death and to exercise their talents to preserve life.

The Military

Many men in the Pentagon do not like nuclear weapons. They know that, with them, wars can no longer be fought. Some have left, taking their considerable expertise with them to educate the general public about nuclear weapons and nuclear war from a military perspective. Others remain in the services, deeply disturbed about the ever-increasing nuclear stockpile.

The majority of men running the services remain committed to nuclear weapons. They plan and strategize about various ways to fight nuclear war RAND style, and they have enlarged their list of targets in the Soviet Union to forty thousand. They have innumerable plans for any international contingency that may arise, and the integrated plan for these strategies is the highly classified secret SIOP, or Single Integrated Operational Plan.

These people compensate for the fact that they really know they can't fight proper wars any longer by displacing their frustration. They indulge in the drive to build and experiment with increasingly complicated technology and weapons systems, which, of course, are enormously expensive.

So the military forces grow stronger and bigger, not just in the superpowers, but also in Europe and in smaller nations all over the world. Men have not learned to behave any differently. The whole ethic of masculinity is tied up with being tough and courageous, *macho* and fearless, and they cling to this behavior by building more weapons with almost frantic desperation.

The military trains its recruits to reject emotion in a cruel and violent way, so it can turn them into professional killers. Drill instructors use the terms "maggot," "faggot," "snuffy," "pussy," or "woman" to knock their men into shape. This talk is demeaning both to women and to the men's own feminine side. They are trying to destroy the feminine principle. The drill instructors often are physically cruel with their recruits; in the past, some young men have even been killed in training.

The result of this training is described in *A Choice of Heroes*. Men in battle develop a tremendous sense of comradeship under the adversity of battle, as they suffer and die next to each other. Only then do these men feel free to cry and show their fear. They even hug and kiss each other to demonstrate their love once they have proven their masculinity. What a tragedy of errors!

Men also love to dress up in uniforms and costumes. They have done this for years. I suppose it could be similar to the female drive to look colorful and attractive. For centuries, men have either strutted around in high heels, lipstick, and wigs or worn gorgeous robes and cloaks, as in the Elizabethan period, or resorted to extravagant uniforms bedecked with feathers, medals, ribbons, and shiny boots. The uniforms bestow conformity, and conformity is another sign of insecurity. The uniforms reinforce the peer group pressure to conform to the masculine military ethic.

When my brother, Richard, was a little boy, all he ever drew were big pictures of planes dropping bombs on ships and shooting each other, full of blood and violence. He used to walk around for hours holding an airplane, making loud engine noises, and driving us all crazy. Other men recollect with chagrin their similar childhood memories. I never gave my sons guns; nevertheless, the youngest made his own guns out of sticks and bits of wood and played violent games. Some people say that little boys should be allowed to act out their violent fantasies so when they grow up they don't need to behave like that anymore. But many men remain intoxicated by violence and potential violence. They watch with fascination the killing power apparent in the speed of military planes; racing cars; and the slow, awesome might of Trident submarines. All their lives they have been seduced by the John Wayne image—the touch, *macho* hero who shows no emotions while he kills people and who always is right. They have been conditioned to believe that such men are to be emulated.

Men acting on these impulses in the First and Second World wars were so eager to prove their virility that they faked their ages and signed up by the hundreds of thousands. But recruits are cruelly disillusioned with the romantic notion of toughness, even though at the time some of them derive a strange pleasure from killing. Many soldiers come home from war psychotic and depressed from their harrowing experiences. All people crack under sufficient stress: The intense fear of death and the hideous thought of killing—not just other men but also women and children—often are too much for normal men to handle without a severe emotional reaction. They have failed to understand that the image of John Wayne represents an emotional cripple, and they learn a painful lesson about reality and the human brain. War never creates the wonderful experiences that men expect. The fantasy is rather like the unreal, old-fashioned love stories where lovemaking never induced pregnancy.

Although society did not welcome returning Vietnam soldiers with open arms, it continues to idolize veterans of past wars. This glorification of war by a male-dominated society is a tacit sanction of institutionalized killing. We say we are a Judeo-Christian society, yet we condone mass murder.

It is said that all wars are fought according to the rules of the last war. American society still is fascinated with prenuclear heroes like John Wayne. Ronald Reagan is to some a prenuclear hero—strangely anachronistic and almost willfully ignorant as he struts on the nuclear stage. But he taps into people's tribal archetypal need for masculine heroes who will protect them. Current American thinking about strength and toughness and superiority is analagous to prenuclear thinking. With this tough masculine ethic comes a subliminal fear of war and of being killed. But modern man has conquered even this personal fear of proximal death, of bullets ripping through flesh, and of burned, charred bodies. He has built weapons that can be dropped from on high so the bodies cannot be seen. He relies on buttons that can be pressed from thousands of miles away. He ignores the fact that another button, also pressed, will spill blood all over America. He feels a primitive need to kill, but also to hide from the actual killing and to block out reality.

I was present at a meeting on Capitol Hill in Washington when nuclear war was discussed. The generals and officials were calm and rational throughout the presentations while numbers and strategies were discussed. Several hours later, I stood up and laid out the clinical details of nuclear war in stark detail. General Daniel Graham, a member of the Committee on the Present Danger, exploded like a champagne bottle being uncorked. He was fine as long as nuclear war was not discussed from a medical or emotional perspective, but as I explained the clinical details, his dark side erupted and was directed at me and toward the Soviets.

Another time I was invited to speak on a Chicago television program. I thought I would be alone, but at the last minute a retired brigadier general turned up to participate in the discussion. For ten minutes he talked in a calm, polite way about nuclear war and the possibility of the world being blown up. He also used some factually incorrect information. As the arc lights were turned off at the end, he turned to me and aggressively said, "You should go to Russia." I thought for several seconds, decided to let him see the true fear in my soul, and said to him, "I fucking want my kids to grow up." Well, he could talk with absolutely no emotion about nuclear war and the deaths of hundreds of millions of human beings, but when a lady said "fuck" to him, he was undone. He went wild and almost physically attacked me. The producer came running out to separate us; there was nearly a brawl on the floor of the TV studio. The exchange made me realize that a lot of these military characters have an extraordinary amount of anger. It probably is this anger and hostility, generally kept under control, that motivate them in their military careers. I decided then that it was very important to try to uncover these emotions, to stop being polite and skating around on the surface of the issue.

On another occasion, I visited SAC headquarters in Omaha (I was surprised to find that their motto is "Peace Is Our Profession"). The SAC commander-in-chief, General Bennie L. Davis, discovered that I was about to visit, and he wanted to see me. I was looking forward very much to seeing the control center and the B-52s but wasn't allowed to get near any of that stuff. Instead, I was given two briefings: One compared the American and Soviet arsenals and pointed out how far behind the United States was on practically all weapons and equipment; the other involved the Air Force's interpretation of the nuclear freeze. I felt as if I were back in the Soviet Union, being presented with a whole load of propaganda—simple lies and half truths. It was humiliating and demeaning for an intelligent person to sit through such obviously fabricated material. As I asked increasingly penetrating and difficult questions, more and more officers covered with medals quietly slipped through the doorway and sat on chairs lining the wall. I felt as if I were being surrounded. I later asked the Methodist minister who had come with me why all the other men had to come in, and he said there was safety in numbers. What an eerie experience!

I was whisked out and taken up to see the general. His room was large, and on several tables there were tall models of missiles. He was a tall, thin, older man who immediately started plying me with veiled, hostile questions. I was very sweet but gave him as good as I got and answered his questions with a lot of facts and data. Although the meeting was supposed to last only fifteen minutes, he seemed not to want to let me go. I think he supposed I would be easy to convince, but I was not. Finally he asked me rather aggressively if I had children, and I told him about my three beautiful children. I asked him if he had grandchildren. He said, "Yes," and I said, "How many?" and he said, "Two," and I said, "How old?" and he said something like "Two and six months." Suddenly the atmosphere in the room changed. I saw by his eyes that I had gotten to his soul. We ended up with a polite shake of the hands. Apparently, everyone outside his room had been very worried, wondering what on earth was keeping the general as he talked to this woman. The atmosphere was very tense.

Later I read that he had testified on the Hill and reassured people that American strategy was not now one of mutual assured destruction, but that the policy now was counterforce and war fighting—in other words, winnable nuclear war. I wish I had known that before I had seen him; I would have moved in even more strongly.

The Industrial Complex

Every Sunday, the business sections of *The New York Times* and the *Boston Globe* are full of advertisements for engineers and scientists and computer specialists to work on C^3I and ABM systems, guidance and delivery systems, satellites, and the like. It would appear at a cursory glance that much of the U.S. economy is geared to sophisticated killing techniques.

The corporations operate with a dynamic all their own. Their one motivation is profit, and they will do anything—literally anything—to make money. If the managing director or chair of the board of a company does not satisfy the profit motive, he (usually he) is fired. There is absolutely no moral integrity to this whole business, and no one person is in charge. Corporate enterprise is extremely well oiled, finely tuned, and very energetic, and it holds the future of America and the world in a strangling, viselike grip. The staff in large firms have been trained to honor and respect their employers, and there is tremendous peer group loyalty engendered by the management. Along with this dynamic goes conformity. No one steps out of line, no one is game enough to speak the truth or voice concern or doubt. Anyone who did would almost certainly lose his job.

I have been on the speaking circuit for many years, but apart from some Rotary Club luncheons, I have never been asked to speak to any corporations. Corporations, usually a rich source for speaker requests, obviously don't want to expose themselves to my medical message, or they would have to face the psychological and moral consequences of their behavior. They prefer to remain deliberately unconscious.

On a few occasions when my colleagues or I have had the

opportunity to confront these people, they always justify their life's work by blaming the Soviets. Projecting the dark side has been the rationale of the arms race right from the early days of SAC and the RAND Corporation.

The real motive of the military corporations is greed: to make money in any way possible. The military avenue has proved to be extremely successful for many firms. It has been refined to such an extent that government appropriations and money are almost self-generating, like spontaneous combustion. The logical conclusion of this very successful financial enterprise will, indeed, be combustion of the world.

In many ways, it seems to me that the deity of America has become money. The vital world interests, which the Pentagon vows to protect, really are only vital financial interests for trade, or strategic minerals, or raw materials. Six percent of the world's population uses 40 percent of the world's natural resources. In truth, America has only one vital interest to protect and that is its wonderful, ethical, moral principles. It is rapidly losing—indeed, it has very nearly lost—these guiding values of its soul, replacing them with a rapacious quest for more and more money.

Prognosis: How Long Will the Earth Survive?

In August 1979, President Jimmy Carter issued Presidential directives 58 and 59. Presidential Directive 58 called on the Defense Department and other agencies to study the capacity of the government, from the president on down, to withstand a nuclear strike. It included: (1) plans to move military and political leaders out of Washington; (2) hardened silos for personnel and equipment; and (3) creation of a network of command posts for military and civilian leaders in time of war. Presidential Directive 59, or PD-59, outlined a war-fighting strategy with a "flexible response" to limited nuclear war, maximizing the potential target structure in the USSR. The prime targets are to be Soviet military and industrial institutions and the country's political leadership. It (1) called for forty thousand targets in the USSR; (2) emphasized the need to target in a timely, redundant, and flexible fashion; and (3) outlined the weapons potentially needed. It described a prolonged nuclear war lasting for weeks or months and provided for a "secure strategic reserve"—that is, a missile force in reserve, not to be used in the early stages of conflict. This could deter Moscow from launching a major nuclear strike at a later date.

These directives still are classified as secret. They were issued (or leaked) to Richard Burt at *The New York Times* just before the Democratic National Convention in 1980, but they were not even referred to by the convention delegates, even though they represented formal acceptance of new concepts of targeting and nuclear war-fighting doctrines.

266

The lack of public response to these plans was almost more frightening than the plans themselves. The collective psychic numbing evident at the Democratic National Convention made it clear that America had not awakened to the ominous preparations for nuclear war. Never before had I seen plans of this sort made public. Until then, the deterrence formula of mutually assured destruction (MAD) had stood—massive reciprocal damage to both sides, enough to dissuade each from initiating a nuclear war.

It was obvious from the literature in 1979 that a vast planning network of scientists, industrialists, Pentagon officials, and politicians were involved in producing weapons to fight and win a nuclear war. The scientific developments had been under way for almost a decade, led by weapons laboratories sponsored by the government, by the University of California—Los Alamos in New Mexico and Lawrence-Livermore in California—and, in Albuquerque, by Sandia Laboratories, which is run by Western Electric. As the accuracy of the missiles and delivery systems increased, it became possible to pinpoint hard targets, or missile silos. This strategy is called counterforce nuclear war.

The strategic thinking behind fighting and winning a counterforce nuclear war, from the U.S. vantage point, goes like this:

1. The Soviet Union has emphasized ground-based strategic weapons, so that 70 percent (6,012 nuclear weapons in 1,398 missiles) of their bombs are land-based in silos. About 24 percent are in submarines that are noisy and easy to detect and track. (They have some 2,000 nuclear weapons in missile-carrying submarines, but only 15 percent, or 300 nuclear weapons, are at sea at any one time.) Only about 6 percent of their intercontinental weapons, or 440 nuclear bombs, are in bombers.

2. The United States has approximately 18 percent (2,127 bombs in 1,027 missiles) of its strategic nuclear weapons based on land; 50 percent (5,728 nuclear weapons) are in its noiseless, invulnerable submarines—60 percent or about 3,400 nuclear weapons are at sea at any one time—and approximately 32 percent, or over 3,500 bombs and missiles, are in large, intercontinental B-52 bombers.

Hence, the Soviet Union's strategic-weapons arsenal is much more vulnerable to U.S. first strikes, which can be used effectively only against ground-based missiles. The United States already has very accurate "silo-busting weapons" on 300 Minuteman missiles (3 Mark 12A hydrogen bombs per missile). It is on the verge of constructing the MX missile, a huge rocket with 10 independently targeted hydrogen bombs in the nose, each capable of landing on a different silo very accurately. Also, the Trident II or D-5 missile is scheduled for deployment in 1989. This missile is to be launched from the Trident submarine. Seven subs have been launched, with 13 or more planned. Each submarine carries 24 missiles, and each missile delivers 8 hydrogen bombs. (Each Trident submarine carries enough weapons to destroy most major cities in the Northern Hemisphere.) Each hydrogen bomb is exceedingly accurate and will be guided to its location from its sea launch by a satellite system called NAVSTAR.

The MX and Minuteman take 30 minutes to reach their targets after launching, and Trident II from 15 to 30 minutes, depending on the location of the submarine. Cruise missiles also are highly accurate, although quite slow, taking from one to three hours to reach their targets. However, they can be launched from B-52s, B-1 bombers, or stealth bombers just off the coasts of the USSR, so that planes can evade the anti-aircraft facilities of the USSR.

I stress accuracy because it is an extremely important factor in the destruction of missile silos. Yield (the size of the explosion) also is important, but you can destroy a missile silo far more effectively with a small, highly accurate hydrogen bomb than with an inaccurate larger hydrogen bomb.

The United States also is working actively on antisubmarine warfare. It is developing tracking stations using sonic waves to detect Soviet subs, which are relatively easy to find anyway because they are so noisy. The United States has about 90 sophisticated fast-attack submarines designed to destroy Soviet subs. It also is qualitatively more advanced in the area of antisatellite warfare. Eventually such technology may enable the United States to destroy Soviet information satellites in time to prevent the USSR from detecting the launch of first-strike U.S. missiles. If the Soviets could detect MX or Trident II launches, they might well launch their missiles immediately, and the American bombs would hit empty silos.

The scenario of a first-strike war goes like this: The first-strike missiles are launched with a calculated allocation of two hydrogen bombs to each Soviet missile silo. The first wave of 1,400 H-bombs will explode in the air just above the missile silos, and a second wave of 1,400 H-bombs will arrive seconds later and explode on the ground on top of the missile silos. The jolting and dislocation resulting from this massive attack will be so severe that although every missile will not necessarily be destroyed, it will have received a severe shakeup and will be incapable of being launched.

At the same time, the air bases in the Soviet Union containing the strategic bombers will have been destroyed along with the Soviet Command, Control, and Communications (C^3) facilities, many of which are located in major cities, and also the major military installations. The Soviet satellites will be destroyed just before the attack begins, and the submarines will also be destroyed as the first strike takes place.

This is termed a "winnable limited nuclear war," and the doctrine for this sort of war is more clearly enunciated in a Pentagon five-year defense concept signed by Defense Secretary Caspar Weinberger and leaked to Richard Halloran of *The New York Times* in the summer of 1982. The document is called Defense Planning Guidance. Complementary doctrines, called National Security Decision memoranda, mandate that the Defense Department will provide a program for implementing President Reagan's nuclear war policy. This is the first policy statement of a U.S. administration to proclaim that U.S. strategic forces must be able to prevail in a protracted nuclear war. ("Prevail" means having more nuclear weapons at the end of the war than the enemy does.) Such a war will also feature intensive electronic warfare and possibly chemical and biological weapons. The Defense Planning Guidance also calls for antisubmarine warfare, economic warfare with the Soviet Union, guerrilla warfare in Eastern Europe, and forced intervention in Southeast Asia and the Persian Gulf if necessary, without invitation by U.S. allies. The plan requires the assumed destruction of "nuclear and conventional military forces and industry critical to military power."

To implement this plan, the Reagan Administration wants to build 17,000 hydrogen bombs, including 8,000 sea-, ground-, and air-launched cruise missiles, Pershing II missiles, MX and Trident II missiles, and neutron bombs. The United States already has 11,500 strategic hydrogen bombs; the Soviet Union, 8,500. Robert McNamara, secretary of defense in the 1960s, determined that 400 equivalent megatons would kill up to one third of the Soviet people and destroy two thirds of their industry. This number was declared, at that time, to be an adequate "deterrent."

The Soviet Union is just now deploying in submarines long-range, highly accurate cruise missiles, although it cannot yet threaten us with the quick Pershing II missiles that it can launch from a country adjacent to the U.S. border. It does not have an incredibly accurate land-based missile like the MX or a sophisticated, accurate, sea-launched missile like the Trident II. But almost certainly it will develop these if the arms race is not stopped. The late Soviet Premier Yuri Andropov said that the USSR would match the United States, weapons system to weapons system, as it has always done in the past.

Scientists who have participated in the design of these weapons at the Los Alamos Lab say that if there is a first-strike counterforce nuclear war between the superpowers in the next ten to twenty years, a huge quantity of radioactive fallout will be created by the thousands of ground-burst hydrogen bombs. Cubic miles of rock and dirt will be atomized, rendered radioactive, and injected into the stratosphere and troposphere in the mushroom cloud. If most of the other nuclear weapons are used as well, an *On the Beach* syndrome could be created. That means lethal fallout for every human being on earth within weeks. Nuclear winter would quickly follow. This medical scenario dictated by first-strike nuclear war is being actively planned by President Reagan and Caspar Weinberger as well as by the Pentagon.

The psychological problem related to first-strike nuclear war is very frightening. If the Soviet leaders feel that their weapons are threatened at any instant by a surprise attack, they will respond in the same way that they will respond to use of the Pershing II missiles in Europe: with a launch-on-warning policy. But the Soviet detection and computer network is far less sophisticated than that of the United States, and the United States currently is blocking sales of sophisticated technology to the Soviet Union. Problems have been associated with even the relatively sophisticated U.S. computer fail-safe system over the past few years. In the early 1960s, false alerts were triggered by a flock of geese that the early-warning system interpreted as a fleet of Soviet missiles, by a rising moon, and by a shower of meteorites. In November 1979, someone plugged a war-games tape into the fail-safe computer, and the machine mistakenly decided that the USSR really had launched a nuclear attack. The whole Western world was put on nuclear alert for six minutes; three U.S. squadrons of planes armed with nuclear weapons were ready to take off; at the seventh minute the president was to be officially notified, but they could not find him. When the mistake was realized, we were thirteen minutes from potential annihilation. People reassured us that such a mistake always would be detected, but thirteen minutes really is too close for comfort. The *Manchester Guardian* and the Canadian papers carried head-lines reporting the mistake; *The New York Times* had a tiny article near the obituaries. That was in 1979. The reaction now would probably be more vocal because the media and public have become more sensitized in recent years to the dangers of nuclear war. A six-minute lead time with the Pershing II, or a thirty-minute lead time with the paranoid situation of "use 'em or lose 'em" in a threatened first-strike attack could well induce an accidental nuclear war.

Two men called the National Command Authority (NCA) have been delegated the responsibility for deciding when to launch a nuclear war and whether it is to be a pre-emptive first-strike nuclear war, a launch-on-warning nuclear war, or a retaliatory attack. These two men are the president of the United States, Ronald Reagan; and the secretary of defense, Caspar Weinberger; or their duly designated alternates.

On December 6, 1982, at 4:00 P.M., I met with President Reagan and his daughter Patti Davis for seventy-five minutes. Reagan entered the downstairs library of the White House in a somewhat diffident fashion and proceeded to reassure me when I told him I was nervous being in the presence of the American president. We sat around a long table. He sat at its head, and I next to him, with Patti at the other end.

I opened the conversation by saying that he probably didn't know who I was, but he interrupted and said that he knew I was an Australian and that I had read *On the Beach* by Nevil Shute when I was young, and that's how I became involved in the issue of nuclear weapons. I then told him that I had been frightened by the incessant buildup in nuclear arms since I was fourteen, and that I began studying medicine in 1956 when I was seventeen and learned about the effects of radiation on cellular mechanisms and genes. At that time, high levels of radioactive fallout were being recorded in the Northern Hemisphere, with strontium-90 and other radioactive elements concentrating in the milk and the deciduous teeth of young children. I told him that I feared to bring my first baby into this nuclear world in 1963 but that I had had three babies because I was selfish and loved children. I also told him that I'm deeply religious and consider what I do to be a spiritual mission.

He replied that he, too, doesn't want nuclear war but that our ways of preventing it differ; he believes in building more bombs. He moved immediately into tactics and strategy and seemed not to be interested in discussing the medical, scientific, or ecological consequences of nuclear war. He said that the Soviet Union is stronger than America; that it wants to take over the world, with communism dominating; and that it already has a base ninety miles off the American coast. He added that the domino theory had proven correct in Southeast Asia. I said that America similarly sees capitalism as the only answer for the world and that the superpowers are mirror images of each other. He said the Soviets were evil, godless Communists. I asked him if he thought they were all evil, but he declined to answer. I asked him if he had ever met a Russian, and he said, "No, but we hear from their émigrés."

I noted that America has the Soviet Union ringed by bases in Italy, Greece, Turkey, Britain, France, and other countries, and that many of these bases are equipped with nuclear weapons and missiles. He denied this fact. He then talked about the Soviet SS-20 missiles. When I pointed out that the nuclear balance between NATO and the Warsaw Pact is approximately equal because of the forward-based systems in Britain and Germany as well as the missiles in American submarines allocated to NATO, he declined to accept these facts. He replied that the Soviets have submarines, too. I then talked about the Pershing II missile's capability to reach Moscow from its launching point in West Germany in six to ten minutes, which could induce the USSR to adopt a computer-directed launch-on-warning policy. He noted in reply that the SS-20s could also reach Europe in six minutes. He seemed not to appreciate the strategic significance of the Pershing II missiles threatening part of the Soviet Command, Control, and Communications (C^3) centers in Moscow—the Pentagon Five-Year Defense Guidance indicates that they could be used for decapitation of Soviet C^3 centers.

I then talked about Paul Warnke, and he said that Warnke stood for unilateral disarmament. I asked him if he would see George Kennan, noted former U.S. ambassador to Moscow. He did not say yes or no but replied, "I know who he is."

At one point, Patti interrupted the conversation and said, "Dad, I know that what Dr. Caldicott is saying is correct, because I have a 1982 Pentagon document to prove it." He looked at her and said, "It's a forgery."

I discussed the fact that the Soviet Union is flanked by Communist countries hostile to the USSR. Of the five nuclear-armed nations in the world, each of three—Britain, France, and China—could destroy the Soviet Union as an entity. He denied this, particularly in reference to China because, he said, they lack an adequate delivery system. I replied that the loss of Moscow and Leningrad alone would be a virtual destruction of the USSR. He did not accept this.

He then said, "Talking of saving millions of people, the Russians have a great civil defense system." I asked him where he got these data from; he didn't seem to know. I asked if they came from T. K. Jones; he didn't seem to know who Jones was. The president said that the Soviet Union has been decentralizing and hardening its industry, and burying it. I replied that for evacuation and civil defense, they have a lousy highway system, which I had seen, and that none of their civil defense systems would do any good. I quoted the 1979 CIA report that was highly skeptical of Soviet civil defense.

I told him about the recent Soviet television program during which three American and three Soviet physicians appeared uncensored on USSR national television for one hour, describing to two hundred million Soviet people the medical consequences of nuclear war. I said that one of the American doctors told the Soviets that their civil defense system was useless. The president said that he knew who *they* are. He also said that two hundred million Soviets could not have watched that program because they don't all have television sets. I replied that I had not known this fact but that I would check it. (I have since checked with the U.S.

physicians who were on the program and have learned that the program was shown twice nationally in a three-day period and that between one hundred million and two hundred million people saw it.)

We talked about the money spent on defense, and the president said that the USSR has outspent America over the past years. I then told him about the two reports prepared by the CIA on Soviet defense spending—the "Team A Report" and the "Team B Report"—and pointed out that he was quoting from the "Team B Report," which subsequently had been proven inaccurate. He didn't seem to know the difference between the two reports until I mentioned that the "Team B Report" was prepared under the guidance of George Bush when he was CIA director. He then said that George's report was the right one.

The president said that a freeze would lock the Soviets into a position of superiority. When I noted that the United States leads in numbers of nuclear weapons, he replied that the Soviets are ahead in megatonnage and missiles. I explained that missiles were only the delivery vehicles and that the important thing to assess was the number of bombs.

He said that the USSR has violated the ABM treaty. I said they had deployed only one ABM system around Moscow, which they are allowed by the treaty.

He said the Soviets could track U.S. submarines from space by watching the deep wake of the subs. (These are unsubstantiated data, as I found when I later questioned Admiral Noel Gaylor, former commander-in-chief of U.S. forces in the Pacific.)

I said that America was ahead in killer submarines. He stated that the Soviet Union was ahead. In fact, the Warsaw Pact has 126 and NATO 110 nuclear-powered attack subs, but the NATO subs are substantially superior. He said that the USSR has defied détente and had been building up a huge arms inventory with nuclear weapons, many tanks, and troops. I showed him the data in the manual published by the Center for Defense Information (CDI), run by Rear Admiral Gene LaRocque, U.S. Navy (Ret.). They indicate that although the Warsaw Pact has 63,000 tanks, NATO deploys over 50 types of antitank weapons and has a total of almost 500,000 in Europe. The same data repeat that NATO leads the Warsaw Pact in the total number of ground forces in Europe. He said these data were wrong. He also said that the former high-ranking military officials who run the CDI were not credible. I stated that America had also defied détente by MIRVing its missiles and that this technology was not outlawed by the SALT I Treaty because at that time only America could MIRV. However, the Soviet Union started MIRVing in 1975. I showed him a CDI graph indicating that America leads the Soviet Union in numbers of strategic weapons, both now and during the 1970s. He did not believe the graph.

He said that we have not built a new missile in fifteen years and that the USSR is on its fifth generation of new missiles. (Because America has been continually upgrading and modernizing its missiles, it has not needed to build entirely new ones.)

He told me that the Soviets are far advanced in sea power and have built many submarines in the past ten years. He also cited the new, huge USSR submarine class called the Typhoon. I told him that American submarines were noiseless and impossible to track, in contrast to the Soviet subs, which were less capable, very noisy, and easy to track. I pointed out that America carried five thousand strategic weapons on her submarine fleet while Russia had only two thousand. He seemed uninterested.

He replied that the land-based strategic systems were more important than submarine-based weapons because they can be launched to arrive at their targets in thirty minutes. His remark was intended to defend his START proposal, which asks the USSR to cut back its land-based systems from five thousand to twenty-five hundred nuclear warheads, while it allows America to increase from approximately twenty-one hundred to twenty-five hundred land-based warheads. I replied that submarine-launched ballistic missiles also can reach their targets in thirty minutes or less, but he said the subs are difficult to contact. (The only reason for instant contact with submarines would be for a pre-emptive first-strike attack; otherwise, the submarine-launched strategic weapons are to be used for a retaliatory strike.)

He said that the Soviet Union could get to the western coast of Europe in ten days and that America will continue to maintain a first-use policy of nuclear weapons to deter such an event. He added that we would never use them, to which I replied, "unless we are losing."

He said the Soviet Navy has blockaded and is practicing war games at all the strategically important points on the seas and that this is why America is getting Japan to rearm so it can defend its territories a thousand miles out from the islands. I said that the American Navy is far more powerful than the Soviet Navy, but he refused to accept my statement. I also said that a fight between the USSR and America at sea could start a nuclear war. He didn't reply.

I then cited the unilateral moves toward the Soviet Union that President Kennedy made in a speech at American University in June 1963. I talked about Nixon going to China even before diplomatic relations were established and about Sadat's heroic visit to Jerusalem, and I asked, or rather begged, him to go to see Andropov. He replied that just after he had been shot, he had made a move toward Brezhnev by writing a letter to the Soviet leader. The reply came months later; he said it was hard-line and implied that it was no use reaching out to the Soviets.

He stressed that America must be strong, and that after World War II, when the United States was the only country with nuclear weapons, it helped its former "enemies" in their postwar recovery and showed restraint. To this I replied that General MacArthur had wanted to use nuclear weapons on China but that President Truman stopped him. But Reagan said the only thing the Soviets understand is strength and that their missiles were far better than America's missiles. I told him that almost all the Soviet missiles were liquid-fueled, but he seemed not to understand what that means. (This is antiquated technology; such missiles require hours for launching. Almost all U.S. strategic missiles are solid-fueled and can be launched almost immediately.)

I assured him that every time I'm interviewed by *Tass* or *Izvestia* I give the Soviet reporter's card to the FBI, but he wasn't interested. He seemed continually to have his own agenda and didn't appear to listen much or to consider seriously my statements or replies.

He then pulled out some papers from a small desk pad on which he had written in longhand. He quoted some material saying that the freeze campaign was orchestrated by Russia and that we were KGB dupes. I looked at him and said, "That's from the *Reader's Digest*." He shook his head and said, "No, it's not; it's from my intelligence files." If I am not badly mistaken, it was copied straight from the John Barron article in the October 1982 issue of *Reader's*

Digest. He said that Communist and left-wing groups organized the huge June 12, 1982, rally in New York City, alluding to Americans for Democratic Action and others. He implied that we were being manipulated, and I said that he must think we were very unintelligent to allow ourselves to be so manipulated. I told him that I am one of the leaders of the movement and that I have never met a Communist in it, to which he replied that I might not know I was being manipulated.

I told him that I speak as a citizen of the world, and the whole world is frightened about nuclear war. I then read to him a statement from an eight-year-old girl named Rachel Conn:

I know the big countries of the world think they have to have nuclear weapons to be strong, and that they think they have to have more nuclear weapons than the other countries or else they wouldn't be strong. I think it would be better to be less strong than to blow up the world.

He did not respond to this statement, but instead pulled from his pocket a map of Oregon showing the concentric rings of destruction from a nuclear explosion and another map of America showing the location of nuclear weapons facilities. He said these were handed out to primary school students in Oregon and that children should not be frightened in this way. I said maybe not like *that,* but this is the reality of the world in which they live, and children pick up the information anyway from television, as Rachel did. I told him that as a pediatrician, I treat dying children, and that they often have a sixth sense and know when they are going to die.

At no time during the discussion was there acrimony. I leaped in at many points during the conversation to correct his statements, but he was not at all receptive to my remarks. In fact, often he seemed not to hear me. I'm sure that the sense of despair I felt at the end of the meeting was apparent in my demeanor. I don't think he sensed my concern as he said good-bye and left the room. The interview was especially troubling in light of Reagan's consistent opposition to every arms control treaty in the nuclear age.

The secretary of defense makes up the other arm of the NCA. Caspar Weinberger knew little about nuclear weapons or arms control before he became secretary of defense. Robert Scheer, *Los Angeles Times* reporter, interviewed Weinberger and George Shultz at Bechtel during the 1980 campaign; both of them said Scheer could ask about anything but foreign policy or defense, because they knew nothing about these topics. Weinberger, an attorney from California who was previously secretary of health, education, and welfare, and director of the office of the military budget, was known for severe cutting of social programs to save money. Unfortunately, he has done the reverse with the defense budget. He and his president plan to spend $1.8 trillion over the next five years, which will amount to about $2.5 trillion when cost overruns in production and other incidentals are included. Actually, the Defense Department is a misnomer. It is really the Department of Offense—a War Department. There is no defense against nuclear weapons. If the Soviet Union launches one hundred missiles at one hundred U.S. cities, one hundred missiles will land.

In the early days of Reagan's presidency, the *London Guardian* reported that "cartoons of atomic explosions, airplanes and warships were used to help President Reagan grasp the options for U.S. military spending. Visual aids were taken to the White House by Caspar Weinberger, Secretary of Defense."

The authoritative *Armed Forces Journal* tells how Pentagon staff were ordered to revamp the usual tables and graphs on budget proposals. One chart showed "different size mushroom clouds," the smallest representing the strategic forces under President Jimmy Carter, and two bigger ones, the alternatives being discussed by the Reagan Administration. Programs for the tactical air forces were depicted for the president by "different sizes and shapes of airplanes, a cartoon rendition of a fighter bomber—one the same size, but loaded with bombs under its wings, and a third with its nose missing."

Devising the cartoons proved arduous, and Pentagon "action staff" had to work overtime. An informant told the *Journal:* "There were so many revisions, it was difficult to keep track." The visuals, which were more than three feet wide, were vetted by Frank Carlucci, the deputy secretary of defense, before being shown to Reagan. This information was reported in the *London Guardian* in October 1981.

Here are some excerpts from speeches Reagan made in October

1981, when talking about limited nuclear war in Europe, as reported in the *International Herald Tribune* of October 21, 1981:

> When asked if he thought an exchange in nuclear weapons between the United States and the Soviet Union would be limited or if escalation was inevitable [Reagan replied]: "I honestly don't know. I think again, until some-place—all over the world this is being, research going on, to try and find a defensive weapon. There never has been a weapon that someone hasn't come up with a defense, but it could—and the only defense is, well, you shoot yours and we'll shoot ours, and if you still had that kind of stalemate, I could see where you could have the exchange of tactical weapons against troops in the field without bringing either one of the major powers to pushing the button."
>
> "The intermediate range—and this is to call your attention to where SALT was so much at fault—is that we have our allies there who don't have an ocean between them, so it doesn't take intercontinental ballistic missiles; it just takes ballistic missiles of the SS-20 type."

I was visiting Europe when he twice commented during news conferences that it would be possible to fight a nuclear war in Europe without pressing a button. The comment badly frightened the Europeans, who were convinced that America was planning to fight its nuclear war with the Soviet Union in Europe without involving the continental United States. This, of course, is a misconception. Most senior military men say that once a nuclear war started in Europe, a global nuclear holocaust would be triggered between the superpowers within hours or days. Dr. Desmond Ball, an Australian strategist writing for the International Institute for Strategic Studies in London, estimates that fatalities in a tactical nuclear war in Europe would range from two million to twenty million if there were some restraints on the use of nuclear arms, and up to two hundred million without restraints. He said that strategic analysts take the view that it is possible to conduct a limited and quite protracted nuclear exchange in such a way that escalation can be controlled and that a war would end before nuclear exchanges reach an all-out level. However, extensive review of the C^3I

network of the United States shows that from fifty to one hundred Soviet warheads could destroy most of the communications centers, the satellite ground terminals, the early-warning radar facilities, and the very-low-frequency communications stations. And some ten to twenty high-altitude nuclear detonations could disrupt high-frequency communications. Because of the vulnerability of the C^3I system, nuclear war could neither be limited nor controlled. The United States probably has a similar targeting strategy for the Soviet Union. (As noted previously, both C^3I systems are very vulnerable to disruptions.)

In our society, anybody who contemplates the murder of a single individual is considered either mentally unstable or a potential criminal. But people within this administration are making statements about nuclear war that contemplate the death of hundreds of millions of human beings. Consider the following statements:

President Reagan, on the chances of survival in a nuclear war: "It would be a survival of some of your people and some of your facilities, but you could start again."

George Bush, vice president of the United States: "If you believe there is no such thing as a nuclear winner, the argument [that nuclear superiority is meaningless] makes sense. I don't believe that."

Frank Carlucci, former deputy secretary of defense: "We need more than counterforce. I think the Soviets are developing a nuclear-war-fighting capability, and we are going to have to do the same."

Paul Nitze, former arms control negotiator: "The Kremlin leaders want to achieve military victory in a nuclear war, while assuring the survival, endurance, and core of their party."

Richard Pipes, former top presidential adviser on Soviet affairs: "The [nuclear] contest between the superpowers is increasingly turning into a qualitative race whose outcome can yield meaningful superiority." Pipes also said in 1981: "Soviet leaders would have to choose between peacefully changing their Communist system or going to war." He also advised Americans during the same period that they had better start preparing themselves psychologically for nuclear war.

Eugene V. Rostow, arms control chief for the first two years of the Reagan Administration: "We are living in a prewar and not a postwar world."

Richard N. Perle, assistant secretary of defense: "I worry less about what would happen in a nuclear exchange than about the effect the nuclear balance has on our willingness to take risks in local situations." Perle has stated publicly several times that he does not believe in arms control between the United States and the USSR, yet he is one of the main architects of the START and INF proposals, and the new round of Geneva negotiations. He said that "cosmetic agreements" on arms control are "in the long run fatal for the democracies of the West. Democracies will not sacrifice to protect their security in the absence of a sense of danger. And every time we create the impression we and the Soviets are cooperating and moderating the competition, we diminish that sense of apprehension." In other words, agreement with the Soviet Union is impossible, and under such circumstances the self-fulfilling prophecy will prevail: We cannot avoid war if we are preparing to fight it.

Charles Kupperman, an employee of the Arms Control and Disarmament Agency: "It is possible for any society to survive a nuclear war." Also: "Nuclear war is a destructive thing, but still in large part a physics problem."

Deputy Under Secretary of Defense James P. Wade, Jr., said before the House Appropriations Committee, "We don't want to fight a nuclear war, a conventional one either, but we must be prepared to do so if such a battle is to be deterred, as we must also be prepared to carry the battle to our adversary's homeland. We must not fear war."

Colin Gray, an Englishman and top arms control adviser to the Reagan Administration, wrote in *Foreign Policy* magazine in 1980:

> The United States should plan to defeat the Soviet Union and do so at a cost that would not prohibit U.S. recovery. Washington should identify war aims that, in the last resort, would contemplate the destruction of Soviet political authority and the emergence of a post-war world order, compatible with Western values.

President Reagan, during the 1982 European trip, said to the British Parliament that with a military buildup combined with diplomatic, economic, and propaganda campaigns, the Marxist-Leninist system might collapse into "the ash heap of history."

Laurence Beilenson, a former Hollywood attorney, is a close friend of President Reagan and claims that when he was counsel for the Screen Actors Guild in the 1930s, he was responsible for turning Reagan against the Communists. I quote from his book *Survival and Peace in the Nuclear Age* (published in 1980):

> For our survival and peace in the nuclear age, what should we do? Realize that whatever we do, nuclear war is likely sooner or later. Prepare the best shelter (civil defense) for our population that money and brains can buy. Go all out to develop an active defense. Know that treaties are a trap and avoid them except in the case of temporary settlement treaties and alliance treaties, and understand that they, too, will be broken. Comprehend that diplomacy is only a patching tool; use it for that purpose, though sparingly, but do not harbor the illusion that diplomacy can do more than patch. Forget SALT. Build up our nuclear deterrent to strive for superiority. In short, employ armed might as our tool of choice for survival and peace.
>
> Nuclear war, however, is not inevitable. We should devote our utmost endeavor to prevent it by avoidance, as well as deterrence.

President Reagan was so impressed with Mr. Beilenson's book that he quoted it in a speech to the War College in 1981.

In October 1983, President Reagan

> . . . told a group of congressmen that he had not realized until recently that most of the Soviet Union's nuclear defenses were concentrated in its system of heavy land-based missiles. Mr. Reagan reportedly added that he realized now that his proposals for the Soviets to dismantle their heaviest missiles, without similar concessions by the United States, were interpreted by many as one-sided. Several listeners said afterward that while they appreciated Mr. Reagan's new negotiating flexibility, they were flabbergasted at his comment and wondered whether Mr. Reagan was being sufficiently briefed on critical issues.

Again in October 1983, Mr. Reagan told Thomas Dine, the executive director of the American-Israeli Public Affairs Committee, in a telephone conversation,

> You know, I turn back to your ancient prophets in the Old Testament and the signs for telling Armageddon, and I find myself wondering if, if we're the generation that is going to see that come about. I don't know if you've noted any of those prophecies lately, but, believe me, they certainly describe the times we're going through.

T. K. Jones, deputy under secretary of defense: "The dirt is the thing that protects you from blasts and radiation. If there are enough shovels to go around, everybody's going to make it. It's the dirt that does it."

Desmond Ball, a leading authority on strategic policy, and research associate at the International Institute for Strategic Studies, said, when asked about Reagan's shift toward a nuclear-war-fighting policy:

> It is coming closer to reality, but more than likely it won't become a reality because you can't do it. What is dangerous is that these characters will think that they can do it . . . that they have the capabilities for controlling a nuclear war . . . and they don't. They are deluding themselves. They are deluding themselves in strategic terms because the United States has now put itself in a position where in places, most specifically in Europe, but also in other places, where if push comes to shove they will rely on the ability to deter the Russians by threatening to have a limited nuclear attack.

Dr. Herbert York, formerly of the Manhattan Project and former director of California's Lawrence-Livermore Laboratory, and director of defense research and engineering under President Kennedy:

> What's going on right now is that the crazier analysts have risen to higher positions than is normally the case. They are able to carry their ideas further and higher because the people at the top are simply less well-informed than is normally the

case. Neither the current President nor his immediate backers in the White House nor the current Secretary of Defense have any experience with these things, so when the ideologues come in with their fancy stories and with their selected intelligence data, the President and the Secretary of Defense believe the last glib person who talked to them.

The Reagan Administration has encouraged a steady expansion of military influence in decisions on national security. And to aggravate the problem, pending legislation before Congress would shift the legal status of the chairman of the Joint Chiefs of Staff from adviser to commander. He and his successors would then theoretically have authority to issue orders in their own names.

Inadvertent Nuclear War and Weapons Accidents

I often lie awake at night thinking about accidental nuclear war. I cannot understand logically how we are still here and how it has not yet happened. I feel lucky to wake up in the morning and celebrate another day. Like a dying patient, life becomes infinitely more precious as I notice the blue sky after a magnificent blizzard, or drown in the perfume of a gardenia blossom, or look into the eyes of a newborn baby and behold the innocence and deep, archetypal wisdom gazing out at the world with total trust. It is in this context that I now describe some of the ways in which our world can be destroyed by accident.

Computers

I have described the frequent false alerts caused by an inadequate computer network. In the 18-month period from January 1979 to June 1980, there were 3,703 alarms. Most were routinely assessed and dismissed, but 152 of them were serious enough to have represented a potential attack.

All but 3 of the 152 alarms were caused by misleading or ambiguous information received from infrared sensors aboard U.S. satellites or from early-warning radar. The false alarms were received by North American Air Defense Command (NORAD) headquarters in Colorado. Five of these were serious enough for

U.S. bomber and intercontinental missile crews to be placed on alert. Of the other three alerts, one was caused by a war-games tape fed into a computer in November 1979, and the other two, in June 1980, by a defective silicon chip in the computer system. There was also an unspecified number of false alarms caused by random failure in computer and communications equipment. Before the June 1980 accidents, specific records of such events were not kept. NORAD spokesman said such events may happen two or three times a year.

The computer equipment that gives warning of nuclear attack on the United States is acquired in much the same way as the equipment used to process armed services payroll and military leave records. According to Senators Gary Hart and Barry Goldwater, the procedures for procurement of automatic-data-processing equipment by the government are "highly regulated, complex, and fragmented." As a result, delays and technical obsolescence are practically guaranteed. This information came from the Goldwater-Hart Report to the Senate Armed Services Committee in November 1980. John Bradley, a former senior test and evaluation engineer, was fired by the Department of Defense in 1979 after he revealed the system's faults. He went over the heads of the Defense Department and complained to the National Security Council that

. . . the Goldwater-Hart Report is a baby-step forward. What we need is a giant-step. The fact is, the computer hardware in this system was obsolete when it was installed, and it is now 10 years old. As for the software, it lacks the ability to take these false alarms, assess them, and come to a positive conclusion within microseconds, instead of having to do it by means of telephone conferences, which eat up vital minutes. It is well within the state of the art for computers to perform this function.

He said there are ten false alerts for every one revealed to the press. He also said the system was slow, cumbersome, and inaccurate. It fails, on an average, once every thirty-five minutes.

In 1979, the General Accounting Office (GAO)—the investigating body of Congress—assessed the Worldwide Military Command and Control System (WMCCS) developed during the 1960s. It consisted of 158 different computer systems operating at 81 separate locations. The GAO concluded that the old system was in bad shape, could not be improved by piecemeal modernization, and needed replacement. President Reagan has recently decided to spend $18 billion to modernize the C^3I system as part of a program to expand and improve the entire U.S. strategic nuclear capability over the next 10 years.

Two false alerts occurred in the computer system on June 3 and June 6, 1980. During the first incident, about one hundred B-52s armed with nuclear weapons were prepared for takeoff, together with FB-111 airplanes. The crews were ordered to start their engines, and battle-control aircraft were prepared for flight, one of which took off in Hawaii. Silo-based missiles were brought closer to the firing stage as the crews were put on a higher state of alert. This all happened after a duty officer at the Strategic Air Command received computer data indicating that Soviet intercontinental and submarine ballistic missiles were on their way toward the United States. Officials revealed that in each instance, President Carter's Airborne Command Post, a modified 747 airplane crammed with communications equipment and based at Andrews Air Force Base, was also prepared for takeoff. In these two accidents, satellite and radar early-warning information was fed into a special NOVA computer built by Data General Corporation at Cheyenne Mountain. Although, in fact, no attack was under way, the computer sent spurious messages to the Strategic Air Command reporting that large numbers of land- and sea-based missiles had been launched. The messages were received in Omaha, and lights immediately began to flash on an electronic map of the Strategic Air Command. Shortly after the alerts began, the officers in Omaha were said to have held a brief "conference" by telephone with officers at Cheyenne Mountain and at the Pentagon Command Center. A Pentagon aide said it took from two to three minutes to determine that the computer had malfunctioned and to see that the alerts were turned off. Subsequently it was determined that these false alerts were provoked by an electronic component about the size of a dime and worth forty-six cents. Although the mistake was discovered within three minutes, it took twenty minutes for the strategic forces to resume normal operations.

Assistant Secretary of Defense Thomas Ross declined to discuss the wider implications of the false alarms: Specifically, he refused to comment on the suggestion that an alert could set off a series of escalating responses in the United States and the Soviet Union, which could precipitate a nuclear confrontation. "I am going to duck that question," he said. Mr. Ross also declined to disclose whether the United States knew if the Soviet Union had experienced similar mishaps that caused concern in this country. Assistant Secretary of Defense Gerald Dineen said, "I hope that they have as secure a system as we do, that they have the safeguards we do." At this time there are no available data about French, British, or Chinese false alerts.

After these near-disasters, the military concern seemed to be that the computer system was too slow to respond to an attack from the Soviet Union and that American weapons would have been destroyed before they could have been fired. The press voiced little consternation about the fact that, had America launched its nuclear weapons by mistake, the computer error could have provoked a massive Soviet retaliatory nuclear strike on the United States.

Early-warning systems capable of detecting Soviet nuclear attacks seconds after they are launched include ground-based radar near the Arctic Circle, infrared satellites that detect missile exhaust, and new radars in Massachusetts and California (Pave Paws) that detect Soviet submarine-launched rockets. The information collected by these systems is continually fed into computers at the Air Defense Command at Cheyenne Mountain and to the Strategic Air Command in Omaha, the National Military Command Center in the Pentagon, and the Alternate Military Command Center (an underground bunker at Fort Ritchie, Maryland). Upon receiving signs that an attack is under way, preparations are immediately made for launching U.S. nuclear forces, while officials monitor any new information and decide whether or not to inform the president and other senior officials. But it takes Soviet land-based missiles only thirty minutes to reach the United States and submarine-launched rockets from ten to fifteen minutes.

Recently, adolescent boys have learned how to break into secret computer systems, including the computer system of Los Alamos Lab. They do this for fun and for the intellectual challenge. The idea for the plot in the film *WarGames* probably was derived from such sport. These young men call themselves hackers. Some evidence suggests that the computers controlling the nuclear weapons systems may not be immune to such intrusions. An article by Bernard Bereanu, a mathematician, describes the "inherent random behaviour of complex software of Early Warning Systems" and predicts that with the drastic reductions in warning time that will accompany new missile systems, it is only a matter of time before accidental nuclear war occurs.

Electromagnetic Pulse (EMP)

A single Soviet warhead detonated 250 miles above Nebraska could blanket the entire nation with electromagnetic pulse energy, with peak fields of 50,000 volts per meter—strong enough to shut down all power and communications throughout the country. Although this pulse would have little effect on human beings, it would paralyze the United States and throw its armed forces into total confusion.

EMP was first discovered in 1962 when an atomic test, conducted 800 miles southwest of Hawaii and 248 miles above the earth disrupted many of the electrical and communications systems on the islands. The true significance of this effect was not realized until the 1970s, when military engineers discovered that solid-state integrated circuits are a billion times more likely to be destroyed by EMP than primitive vacuum tubes. It is extremely difficult to shield communications systems from such an enormous pulse. Apparently Soviet manuals and magazine articles are full of references to EMP. I quote: "To achieve surprise in a modern war, high-altitude nuclear explosions can be carried out—to destroy their system of control and communications and to suppress the antimissile and antiradar defense radar system. . . ."

Communications satellites carry more than 70 percent of all long-distance military messages. For some time, the military believed that satellites would be immune to all but a nearby nuclear blast. But in the early 1970s, physicists discovered that the radiation from a nuclear blast in space travels vast distances and knocks electrons out of a satellite's skin and innards, causing an EMP-type surge. The pulse is clearly different from the terrestrial EMP but is even stronger (about 1 million volts per meter), driven directly into the satellite's electronic heart. A relatively small explosion of two megatons just outside the upper atmosphere at an altitude of from 50 to 75 miles would damage an unprotected satellite in geosynchronous orbit 22,300 miles above the earth. The kill range could easily be extended by increasing the size of the bomb.

Actually, an expectation of 50,000 volts per meter on earth might be too conservative. The Pentagon and some French physicists envision a pulse of about 100,000 volts per meter. If they are correct, the nominal protection the Pentagon has tried to build into communications networks, missiles, radar, and radios would almost certainly be useless. An EMP attack by either country on the other would trip circuit breakers throughout the power grids, silence telephone lines, lobotomize computer memories, and throw the armed forces into disarray. Civilian and military planes alike, their solid-state controls and radios knocked out, would attempt, perhaps unsuccessfully, to make emergency landings. Most of the military would be without electricity. Emergency backup power would support Cheyenne Mountain in the Colorado Rockies, the nerve center of the North American Air Defense Command, but the supersecret satellites that warn exactly where to expect a rain of Soviet warheads could be knocked out. The Defense Command's other eyes—the U.S. early-warning radar— would be blinded, as predicted in the Soviet manual. Communications with the outside world would be cut off, leaving the nerve center unable to respond. At strategic-bomber bases, B-52 flight crews could find that the planes would not start because the electronic ignition systems would be dead. Even if the president could take off in his airborne command post (hardened against EMP), it is possible that the radio range would be sharply reduced and the satellites used to relay the president's messages would be out of action.

Theodore B. Taylor, one of the inventors of the miniaturized hydrogen bomb, says there are roughly fifty exotic effects from a nuclear blast, including many types of EMP, gamma radiation, X rays, and electron effects from bomb debris. However, because of classification, he is unable to elaborate on these effects in any great detail.

William Broad, writing in *Science,* says, "Someone standing in an open field would feel no shock, not even a tingling, during an EMP attack. EMP passes harmlessly through human flesh, glass, wood, and plastic, knocking out machines, rather than people." However, someone in contact with or close to a metal object might be shocked or burned. The bigger or longer the object and the better the human connection, the greater the jolt. It would be hazardous to touch a toaster because it plugs into the national power grid, or to iron a shirt, adjust a television, wear headphones hooked up to a home stereo, talk on the telephone, ride a train on miles of metal rails, lean against a chain-link fence, or take a bath (unless the pipes were plastic).

The Department of Defense, in an apparent afterthought, tells of the human threat on the very last page of the EMP manual: "The energy collected in a long wire might cause electrocution or burns," it warns. "Such conditions are not generally expected." Expected or not, such a jolt to a fraction of the U.S. population could represent death or injury to hundreds of thousands of people.

Broken Arrows (Accidents with Nuclear Weapons)

A nuclear weapon dropped and exploded accidentally by one superpower near the territory of the other could trigger a nuclear war, just as Soviet uncertainty about the Korean jetliner caused that plane to be destroyed. Accidents with nuclear weapons probably are much more frequent than even the unclassified data reveal. Obviously, as the number of nuclear weapons increases, the probability of an accident increases. America has some thirty thousand nuclear weapons; the Soviet Union, twenty thousand. About four new hydrogen bombs are made or recycled every day in the United States and probably a similar number in the Soviet Union. And Britain, France, and China have nuclear arsenals. According to a Department of Defense unclassified document, there were thirty-two accidents involving U.S. nuclear weapons between 1950 and 1980. It is interesting to note that after the report of a nuclear accident in the spring of 1968, there is not another report until September 1980, when the Titan missile in Damascus, Arkansas, exploded. Obviously, there were accidents between 1968 and 1980, but this information still is classified. During the 1950s, there were nineteen crashes of planes involving nuclear weapons. None of these exploded, but many of them distributed radioactive materials around the site of the crash. During the 1960s, there were twelve more in the unclassified literature. The most serious were as follows:

1. On January 24, 1961, a B-52 on airborne alert developed structural failure of the right wing over Goldsboro, North Carolina.

Two weapons separated from the aircraft during the breakup of the plane at an altitude ranging from two thousand to ten thousand feet. The bombs were both twenty-four-megaton bombs, which is equivalent to twenty-four million tons of TNT. The total energy of TNT released during World War II was three million tons. One bomb crashed, and five of its six safety catches were triggered. Had that bomb exploded, it would have destroyed much of North Carolina.

2. On March 14, 1961, the second serious accident involved a B-52 failure near Yuba City, California. All the crew bailed out at ten thousand feet, except for the commander, who stayed with the aircraft to four thousand feet, steering it away from populated areas. Two nuclear weapons on board were torn from the aircraft on ground impact. Luckily, the high explosives did not detonate.

3. On January 13, 1964, a B-52 crashed during severe turbulence near Cumberland, Maryland, in isolated mountains. The plane contained two hydrogen bombs.

4. On December 8, 1964, at Bunker Hill Air Force Base, Indiana, another plane crashed into a B-58 on an icy runway. The B-58 slid off the runway, and its left main landing gear struck a concrete electrical manhole box, igniting the aircraft. Portions of the five nuclear weapons on board burned. The report states that contamination by radioactive material was limited to the immediate area of the crash and was subsequently removed.

5. On January 17, 1966, over Palomares, Spain, a B-52 and a KC-135 collided during a routine high-altitude air-refueling operation. Both aircraft crashed. The B-52 carried four nuclear weapons; one was recovered on the ground and another from the sea on April 7, after extensive search and recovery efforts. High-explosive materials from two of the weapons exploded on impact with the ground, releasing large quantities of plutonium. Approximately 1,400 tons of plutonium-contaminated soil and vegetation over 640 acres were scraped up and imported to the United States in 4,827 steel drums, to be dumped straight into the ground at the Savannah River waste-storage facility in South Carolina, where the average rainfall is four inches per month. Plutonium is one of the most carcinogenic, toxic substances known to man.

6. On January 21, 1968, over Thule, Greenland, a B-52 returning from Plattsburgh Air Force Base in New York crashed and burned some seven miles southwest of the runway while approach-

ing the base to land. The bomber carried four nuclear weapons, all of which were destroyed by fire. Radioactive contamination occurred in the area of the crash, which was on the sea ice, and 237,000 cubic feet of plutonium-contaminated ice, snow, and water, with crash debris, were removed to an approved storage site in the United States during a four-month operation.

7. The last declassified accident occurred in September 1980 at Damascus, Arkansas, when an Air Force repairman dropped a heavy wrench socket, which rolled off the work platform and fell toward the bottom of a silo. The silo contained a Titan II missile with a nine-megaton warhead. The socket bounced and struck the missile, causing a leak from the pressurized fuel tank. About eight and a half hours after the initial puncture, fuel vapors within the silo ignited and exploded the liquid fuel. One man was killed; twenty other people were injured. The nine-megaton hydrogen bomb was catapulted hundreds of yards away and was found lying in a field next to a grazing cow. Had this weapon exploded, its effect would have been approximately 720 times greater than that of the Hiroshima bomb.

Four days before the Titan missile accident in Arkansas, a B-52 armed with nuclear weapons caught fire while on a runway at Grand Forks Air Force Base in North Dakota. State emergency officials learned of the accident by intercepting an Air Force message about a "broken arrow" on the plane. The Pentagon refuses to confirm or deny the accident.

The Stockholm International Peace Research Institute estimates there were 125 U.S. nuclear-weapons accidents, major and minor, between 1945 and 1976, or about one every two and a half months. All the admitted accidents so far have been in the Air Force, but recently the Navy acknowledged the existence of classified documents, dated from March 1973 to March 1978, entitled "Summary of Navy Nuclear Weapons Accidents and Incidents." The documents are hundreds of pages long.

On January 14, 1969, while ammunition was being loaded onto aircraft aboard the U.S.S. Enterprise, a bomb accidentally detonated, causing a series of explosions and fires on deck. The carrier, located seventy-five miles south of Pearl Harbor, was believed to have had nuclear weapons on board.

Obviously, more accidents have taken place. It would seem imperative that this information be declassified so that the people of the world can calculate the number of times they have been on the brink of disaster. The bombs are our bombs, made with our money, and the Pentagon is our department, and the military are our servants.

Location of Nuclear Weapons in the United States

A recent *New York Times* article refers to a book entitled *Nuclear Battlefields*, written by William M. Arkin and Richard W. Fieldhouse and published by the Institute for Policy Studies in Washington. According to the book's authors, nuclear arms are deployed or stored in 28 states. South Carolina has the largest nuclear arsenal, with a total of 1,962 warheads (the state serves as a base for submarines armed with ballistic missiles); and New York comes in second, with 1,900 warheads stored at various locations throughout the state, including the Seneca Army Depot, Griffiss Air Force Base, and Plattsburg Air Force Base. The other leading states in numbers of weapons stored are North Dakota, California, Texas, and Michigan.

The information in *Nuclear Battlefields* refutes the popular notion that arms are stored primarily at air bases and missile silos in the Midwest. Its conclusions are frightening indeed: that a total number of 14,599 warheads are stored or deployed in 670 locations throughout the United States.

Official government policy on the subject of nuclear arms storage is silence: The Pentagon will neither confirm nor deny the exact location of nuclear weapons anywhere in the United States. Presumably their stance is intended to protect the general public from undue alarm. Certainly it is not for the sake of national security. Evidence strongly suggests that the Soviets already know where most of our nuclear weapons are stored.

Terrorist Attacks

The Pentagon Five-Year Defense Guidance Plan reflects concern about foreign terrorists trying to steal nuclear weapons:

The existing program and efforts to improve the security of nuclear weapon sites overseas must be sharply accelerated.

New methods are being devised to protect nuclear weapons storage facilities in the U.S., Europe and South Korea. Some weapons are small enough to be carried; others must be moved by truck.

Colonel Linton of the Defense Nuclear Agency said information had been received that terrorists in Europe might have been planning to break into sites where nuclear artillery shells and other tactical weapons were stored.

There were seventy nuclear-related threats in the United States during the 1970s. The most serious was in 1974, when Boston was threatened with a nuclear explosion, which proved to be a false alarm. A special team of engineers and scientists based in Las Vegas and called the Nuclear Emergency Search Team (NEST), was then assembled to respond to terrorist blackmail and threats. Of course, it would be almost impossible to find a small nuclear weapon in a large city, because the very small amount of radiation emitted by the plutonium or uranium trigger of the bomb would be practically impossible to detect. If such a clandestinely placed bomb exploded, it could conceivable initiate a nuclear war. The host government, not prewarned of such an event, might misinterpret the source of the attack during the confusion.

Lateral Proliferation of Nuclear Weapons

In 1983, only five countries in the world owned nuclear weapons—the United States, the USSR, Great Britain, China, and France. Yet at the time, a total of forty-eight countries could have manufactured nuclear weapons because they were operating either nuclear-power reactors or nuclear-research reactors. A nuclear reactor is a bomb factory; it generates plutonium, which is the trigger for nuclear weapons. Thus a global thermonuclear holocaust could well be triggered by a conflict between two small nations.

An example: England is a nuclear nation; Argentina is close to the manufacture of its first nuclear weapon. During the Falklands dispute, America reluctantly sided with Britain, and the USSR with Argentina. Had the war gone badly for either side, it could have escalated into a superpower confrontation, particularly if nuclear weapons had been used by either Britain or Argentina. In August 1983, the Reagan Administration approved the sale of 143 tons of heavy water to Argentina, even though Argentina has not signed the nonproliferation treaty. Such a move may hasten its bomb program.

Israel, according to the CIA, has many nuclear devices; South Africa, perhaps with the help and cooperation of Israel, almost certainly tested a nuclear weapon in September 1979; Colonel Khaddafi of Libya is financing Pakistan's bomb project; South Korea and Taiwan are on the verge of nuclear weapons capability. These "hot spots" in the world obviously will be nuclear trigger points in the future.

As the Third World becomes progressively more deprived of the basic staples of life and America continues to grow richer (6 percent of the world's population consuming 42 percent of the world's natural resources), the new nuclear nations of the world will doubtless focus their frustration upon the rich. The anger in many Third World countries toward both the United States and the USSR is overt. In the near future, a small nuclear nation could well threaten to destroy New York or Moscow.

Military Personnel

Military personnel who handle nuclear weapons are part of the Personnel Reliability Program (PRP). More than 100,000 individuals belong; they must show evidence of emotional stability and good social adjustment and have no history of alcohol or drug abuse. Physicians routinely assist in the screening process and periodically monitor those selected. On page 323 of the 1979 report "Hearings Before a Sub-Committee of the Committee on Appropriations of the House of Representatives," these data were reported: In 1975, a total of 5,128 people were removed from access to nuclear weapons because of violations of the PRP; in 1976, a total of 4,966; and in 1977, a total of 4,973, an annual rate exceeding 4 percent. Reasons given for removal in 1977 included alcohol and drug abuse—the primary drug abused was marijuana, but more than 250 people were removed for abuse of drugs such as heroin and LSD. In the same year, 1,289 were removed for "significant physical, mental, or character trait or aberrant behavior, substantiated by competent medical authorities," which might "prejudice reliable performance of the duties of a particular critical or controlled position." In addition, 828 were disqualified for negligence, 350 for court-martial or civil convictions of a serious nature, and 885 for evidence of "a contemptuous attitude toward the law."

When I was in Phoenix several years ago, I spoke with women who dated the men who work in the Titan missile silos. These women said that their dates frequently took drugs, including LSD, while on duty. Titan missiles contain one hydrogen bomb each, equivalent to nine million tons of TNT. They can be launched only when each of two men inserts a key simultaneously into the control board. Each man is armed with a pistol; one is to shoot the other if he shows signs of abnormal behavior.

Obviously, the C^3I system is so complex that human errors will be frequent. The equipment is as fallible as those who designed and constructed it. We all make mistakes when we feel well, but mistakes occur with increasing frequency when we have a mild virus infection, such as influenza or a cold, or when we suffer even minor emotional duress.

Danger also lurks among seemingly normal military personnel. A retired admiral recently told me that there is no system so fail-safe that an intelligent person could not bypass it to initiate a nuclear war if he were really determined. A physician colleague told me that when he was an officer on nuclear submarines, each man was given a special and secret part of the code for launching nuclear missiles. The system invariably broke down when one man would say to the other, "I'm going to the head [bathroom]; my code is so-and-so. Please cover for me." Nuclear weapons can be launched from submarines without their receiving commands from the president or other high officials.

Leaders

Over the past four centuries, seventy-five chiefs of state have led their countries for a total of several centuries while suffering from severe mental disturbances. In this century, at least six English prime ministers and a large number of cabinet ministers were sick while in office. In the United States, Franklin Roosevelt and Woodrow Wilson had advanced atheroma (hardening) of the arteries of the brain during their last months in office; and Eisenhower had a heart attack, a major operation, and a mild stroke when president. The first U.S. secretary of defense, James Forrestal, was frankly delusional when relieved of office. He thought that the sockets of beach umbrellas were wired to record everything he said, and at one point he thought that some planes overhead were Soviet bombers.

The characteristic signs of hardening of the cerebral arteries are loss of energy and adaptive capacity, inability to concentrate, lapses of memory, periods of confusion, emotional instability, and irritability. A modern leader frequently is faced with making decisions under extreme emotional stress while suffering from sleep deprivation. If he is already handicapped with the symptoms just described, obviously he will be unable to function adequately. Even healthy people experience severe mental aberrations from prolonged sleep deprivation, for mild to moderate sleep loss leads to the inability to sustain intellectual efforts.

It is interesting that top leaders in the world do not have to submit regularly to routine medical and psychiatric examinations. Airline pilots, who are responsible for, at the most, several hundred lives, are examined every six months. World leaders could now kill hundreds of millions of human beings. I think in the nuclear age it is medically indicated that leaders of nations with nuclear weapons be similarly assessed.

Therapy

During the process of writing this book, two very obvious conclusions have dawned on me:

1. America must really be planning to strike first in the nuclear war because the counterforce weapons were designed with such extraordinary accuracy simply to hit silos full of missiles. If America waited until the Soviet Union initiated the nuclear war, all of these new, tremendously expensive, and sophisticated weapons would be rendered useless because they would hit only empty silos.

2. Because of the extraordinary vulnerability of the C³I system, the American arsenal is designed only for first use—not even for a second strike. Most of the system would be utterly devastated if the Soviets were to strike first. The president and his deputies would be dead. The communications systems to launch the rockets would be destroyed, and the secondary command system would also be destroyed.

What an extraordinary situation! Even Lewis Carroll could not have invented a more fantastic tale.

The only way to prevent nuclear war is to use the democratic system. Many people have lost faith in politics and consider it to be dirty and somewhat beneath them. Yet the American political system, as well as those of most of the democracies in the Western world, are wonderful organizations. If used effectively in the next several years, they can determine the future of the life process on this planet.

On the whole, politicians are quite ignorant about the predicted medical and ecological consequences of nuclear war, as well as of the intricacies and implications of all the different weapons systems for which they continually spend money. It is urgent that these politicians be educated to understand that we are on the verge of destroying ourselves.

In the past, doctors and medical scientists have educated politicians about the causes of smallpox, malaria, and many other contagious diseases. As a result of this education, elected representatives appropriated money to establish vaccination programs on an international scale to eradicate smallpox. Mass-immunization programs have prevented our children from dying of tetanus, whooping cough, diphtheria, polio, and measles. With scientific and medical advice, the politicans have cleaned up the sewage systems and sterilized the water supplies. Consequently, the average life expectancy of the population has increased from the forties to the seventies.

A large percentage of the American annual budget is appropriated for the practice of preventive medicine. But we now face the single most important medical catastrophe in history, the final epidemic of the human race. We must once again demand that our politicians are appropriately educated and become involved in saving our lives.

Thomas Jefferson said, "An informed democracy will behave in a responsible fashion." It is the responsibility of every American to educate himself or herself about the vast ramifications of the nuclear and conventional arms race, about the military-industrial complex, about past American intervention in other countries, and about present U.S. foreign policy. All this is vital because any superpower confrontation could end in nuclear holocaust.

Understanding this subject is more important than any other reading you have to do. It should become the number one priority in your life. Such activity might preserve the life of your family.

The next step for you as an informed citizen is to become involved in the education of your friends, relatives, and business and professional acquaintances, and to reach out to others in your local communities to ensure that they, too, understand the gravity of the issue. Learn to use the media constructively. I find if I supplement my local newspaper with daily readings of *The New York Times* I am kept extremely well informed. If you disagree with anything you read in the press, write a letter to the editor. Call the manager of your local TV station or Dan Rather or other national anchorpeople if they are not covering an important story in an adequate way. Organize public meetings in your churches, city halls, and movie theaters; promote discussion and controversy everywhere you go, so you will encourage people to start thinking about and debating the subject.

Unless we elect a House, Senate, and administration that support and will work for bilateral nuclear disarmament, the world is doomed. We must elect a majority who support these principles, and after the election we must keep Congress on a straight and narrow track, riding them like racehorses, using spurs and whips if necessary.

You must investigate the platform of members of and candidates for the Senate and House in your state and local districts. Elicit their attitudes toward all aspects of the arms race and foreign policy, and their attitudes toward the Soviet Union. Attend their local meetings as they run for election and ask them intelligent, penetrating questions about the issues that worry you most. Don't be satisfied with tangential replies. Make sure they answer you in an intelligent fashion. If you disagree with their positions, make it known. Write letters to the newspapers; call talk-back radio and TV shows; get on radio and TV yourself. Educate the editorial boards of your local newspaper and TV and radio stations. Take along a delegation of physicians from your local Physicians for Social Responsibility chapter. Show *The Last Epidemic* and shatter their psychic numbing. If you educate your local media, the job is half done.

Nuclear war must become the number one issue of every election. What does the economy matter if the world is on the brink of instant annihilation? Prevention of nuclear war must become as sacred as mother's milk or apple pie or Social Security—an issue upon which all politicians vote correctly to stay elected, and that includes the president.

If you adequately educate your community, you will find the politicians scrambling to become better educated themselves. The debate will be lively and stimulating. All incumbents must be answerable for their past voting records. Because the issues are so clear-cut, the best person will surely be elected. This may all sound difficult, but it is very rewarding work. What issue deserves more time and effort?

Let me give you a wonderful example of a success story. Representative Nick Mavroules, Democrat of Massachusetts, was a hawk and had voted fairly consistently for nuclear weapons. In the winter of 1980, I was invited on a cold night to go to Rockport, Massachusetts, to speak in a small village church about nuclear war. The church was packed and the audience responded enthusiastically. A local woman, Betty Tuttle, who had been looking forward to a peaceful retirement, became very involved and concerned and started a chapter of WAND (Women's Action for Nuclear Disarmament—an organization I had founded several years before). She and other women worked like man doing all the things I have just suggested, and Mavroules swung around and started advocating an end to the nuclear arms race and a freeze. Thomas Trimarco, the man running against Mavroules, was a hawk, but was beaten by several thousand votes after a long, hard race and intensive debate by the electorate. Mavroules later acknowledged that WAND had been a major factor in his victory, and now he is a leading House opponent of the MX and a proponent of the freeze.

The same community process must occur in the Senate races and in the presidential race. Only the people of this nation have the power to alter the political agenda. I have often heard people say that you can't fight City Hall. Nonsense! No matter how much money the corporations pour into the coffers of the politicians via political action committees or individual contributions, it is the people who ultimately have the power to elect or defeat politicians. Here lies the profound strength of the American political system and all other democracies. Don't forget that most elections are won or lost by a few thousand votes.

In 1980, only 26 percent of the American public voted for President Reagan. I come from a country where voting is compulsory. If you don't vote, you get fined. So people are obliged to understand who and what they are voting for. I find it extremely worrisome that most Americans don't take the time to vote, let alone to become informed about the issues of their nation. At this moment, people are struggling and dying around the world to create their own democracies. Yet many Americans who have been given the privilege choose to ignore the enormous responsibility implicit in living in a democracy. Freedom means privilege, and privilege means knowledge and responsibility.

At this point in history, the United States has been invested with the responsibility for saving the world. No other country has this opportunity. History has bequeathed the fate of the future of life on earth to the American democracy. Will she react in time or not?

The work begins now. Training the elected politicians will be somewhat like training children. We will have to watch them like hawks. Every vote must be noted. The electorate will need to know the legislative calendar so they can call or write to their politicians telling them how to vote. All weapons systems must be *verboten*; the nuclear freeze must be immediate and mandatory.

People must learn to understand how money for weapons is appropriated, which committees on the Hill do what. (All weapons and military systems are determined by two main committees in each legislative body—the Armed Services committees and the Appropriations committees.) People must learn which legislators serve on these committees, who chairs them, and what their electoral districts are. The agendas of these and other relevant committees must become public knowledge and be printed in the newspapers and discussed on the TV news so that people can lobby frequently at the appropriate times to influence the outcome of important votes. People must visit their legislators in large numbers, either in their home districts or on special trips to Washington to ensure that their congresspeople and senators are continually representing the future of their children. The plans for nuclear war are developed in an ethical and scientific vacuum. Medical and ecological data are never considered. The Pentagon and politicians are actively planning for America's suicide. They must be made answerable immediately for this extraordinary irresponsibility.

There will, of course, be stiff competition from the corporations, banks, insurance companies, and Pentagon lobbyists. However, nothing threatens a politician more than a challenge to his or her political survival; hence, the people ultimately hold the power. People will feel proud and will develop confidence in themselves and their country as they demonstrate the positive influence that can be brought to bear on their own government.

All of this may sound unduly optimistic, but it is easy to do and will create a new sense of joy and well-being among the American people. They will have healed their ailing democracy.

If one case of rabies were diagnosed in the city of New York, it would hit the national headlines. The few deaths from cyanide incorporated in Extra-Strength Tylenol became the subject of intense FBI investigations. It is terribly difficult to make people understand that the threat of nuclear war is just as imminent (and much more probable) as was taking a capsule laced with cyanide at the height of the scare. The media exposure on this overriding issue has been minimal. There is a story on the history of and preparation for nuclear war far bigger than Watergate ever was—the arbitrary decisions, the fraud and corruption, the psychic numbing, the enormous and ubiquitous power and influence of the military-industrial complex, the complicity of the politicians. Yet the majority of the press and TV people who interview me have only a limited, superficial knowledge of this subject, and some are almost totally ignorant of it.

I find this situation truly appalling. *The New York Times* produces a supplement on homes and furnishings once a week. Why don't they begin to give similar coverage to the vast subject of nuclear war and its preparation? The same could be said for most of the newspapers and TV stations in the country. The *Boston Globe* and *Los Angeles Times* have recently produced excellent supplements on the arms race, but they are virtually alone. *The New York Times* has thirty sportswriters and only a couple of defense and military affairs correspondents.

The TV networks are only gradually learning that nuclear war is a subject to be covered. CBS produced an excellent series called *The Defense of America,* but although good, it only superficially covered this enormous subject. ABC has made a most provocative and excellent drama about the aftermath of nuclear war called *The Day After* (and an excellent movie, *WarGames,* depicting the vicissitudes of the NORAD computer systems, has been well received by the public).

Television is an excellent medium and the single most important influence in the country. Yet it is difficult to persuade the

TV networks to broadcast ads depicting the medical dangers of nuclear war, because they cite the equal-time rule, whereby people having the opposing view will demand a hearing.

Several years ago, I visited the director of advertising at ABC to investigate the possibility of doing some ads using physicians depicting nuclear war as the ultimate medical issue. The ABC attorney came in halfway through the meeting and said in a loud and abrupt way, "What's your bottom line?" I said, "What do you mean?" and he repeated the question. I fumbled around for an answer and finally said, "Nuclear disarmament," and he jumped on me and said, "That's controversial." When I asked him what he meant, he said that Alexander Haig, then secretary of state, could demand equal time because he believes the only way to prevent nuclear war is to build more bombs. In other words, the adversary to my position would be the government of the United States, which is supposed to be elected to protect the health and well-being of the citizens.

Because the planet is terminally ill, there is a grave urgency about our work. In the past, traditional arms control negotiators sometimes have stopped single weapons systems, but on the whole they have just sanctified and justified continuation of the arms race on both sides. They and their colleagues in the Pentagon and the corporations also have developed an obscure mystical language for the arms race to confuse the public. Because of patient demands, physicians recently have learned to demystify the language of medicine so that patients become adequately informed about their illnesses. Similarly, it is time to demystify the arms race. There are no professional "arms controllers." If there were, surely we would have had real arms reductions by this time.

It also is time to change our way of thinking about arms control. I prefer not to use this phrase at all. Let's talk about rapid bilateral nuclear disarmament and abolition of nuclear weapons. It must be rapid because even if we achieve a freeze we still have fifty thousand nuclear weapons; even if we move down to five thousand within five years, that still is ample to kill most people in the world. (Carl Sagan's data imply that a hundred megatons could destroy the earth.) Physicians treating a terminally ill patient never compromise. They work on that patient twenty-four hours a day for weeks or months, and occasionally the patient survives. A similar degree of dedication must be shown by the world leaders and their people if we are to save the earth.

After the Pentagon prepared its Five-Year Defense Guidance Plan for protracted winnable nuclear war, I prepared a five-year plan for rapid nuclear disarmament. It has three phases (the last two are adopted from a proposal made by George Kennan):

- a bilateral verifiable freeze on production, deployment, and testing of any more nuclear weapons or delivery systems, to be achieved by the superpowers within one year
- 50 percent across-the-board cuts in all nuclear weapons and delivery systems; each superpower can select which bombs it chooses to discard—to be completed within two years
- two-thirds cuts in the remainder of nuclear weapons and delivery systems bilaterally—to be completed in two years

At the end of five years, the United States would have five thousand bombs and the Soviet Union three thousand. This still is not enough of a reduction, but I would hope that the momentum and goodwill generated would be sufficient by the end of that time to proceed rapidly to zero.

Some people say I am naïve to suggest this time frame and such a severe degree of disarmament. I believe it is naïve to suggest that the world will continue unscathed by nuclear holocaust. We must implement such a plan immediately. It is important to define an objective goal. People tend to procrastinate unless they have a defined time limit, and there is no time to waste. Only if the superpowers begin to exert nuclear self-discipline will they be in a position to exert pressure on other nuclear nations and to lobby to prevent further proliferation of nuclear weapons.

Roger Fisher, a lawyer at Harvard, has suggested a scheme that may help prevent nuclear war. He advises that the codes the president needs to start a nuclear war be buried in the pericardium of the heart of one of the men who normally carries the "football" (the case containing the nuclear war codes) behind the president. Should the president decide to start a nuclear war, he would have to slice open the man's chest to retrieve the codes. Apparently some military people were horrified at this suggestion and said, aghast, "But that would mean killing a man if the president wanted to start a nuclear war."

Conversion from a War Economy to a Peace Economy

After World War II, America took the initiative and quickly converted its economy to peacetime uses. It also behaved in a mature, statesmanlike way on the international scene when it instituted the Marshall Plan, which helped revivify the disastrous economic situations of the European Allies. It also instigated programs that have allowed Japan to develop one of the most successful peacetime economies in the world.

The American corporations that are involved in the arms race are run by very intelligent people who will quickly perceive that the people of America will not allow the wartime economic system to continue to flourish. They will put their heads together and will be motivated to design equipment that will be used to the benefit of people both in the United States and internationally.

The world urgently needs adequate production and equitable distribution of food. It needs vast production of medicines and vaccines, and redistribution of medical expertise and medical supplies to the millions of suffering people in the Third World. Adequate distribution of birth-control techniques is required to prevent an increase in global population growth from 4.5 billion now to 6 billion in 2000. Reforestation of many areas of the world is a mandatory priority, since trees currently are used to provide fuel for the poor countries, and trees recycle carbon dioxide to produce oxygen. The riches of the sea must be equitably distributed among all nations on earth and must not be mined only by those few Western nations that currently possess the technology and expertise to do so. All the world's natural resources must be shared and used for the benefit of the family of man and not hoarded and wasted on production of weapons. Millions of the world's people must be delivered from their situation of illiteracy and poverty—a vicious cycle that perpetuates endemic overpopulation and hunger.

The air and the water of America and large ports of the world are fast becoming irretrievably polluted with carcinogenic and mutagenic poisons produced by industry to make profits. There are 4.5 million known toxic chemicals, and 375,000 new ones are produced annually. Most have never been adequately tested for carcinogenicity, and most are released to the environment, often illegally. Many of these chemicals are by-products of industries that produce plastic throwaway materials we don't need.

America needs to tighten its belt. My husband and I visited Cuba in November 1979. Before the revolution, malaria, hookworm, tuberculosis, and gastrointestinal diseases were endemic there. Cuba now has one of the best medical schemes in the world—so good that Dr. Julius Richmond, President Carter's surgeon general, visited Cuba to develop ideas for America's healthcare system. Prerevolution illiteracy was about 40 percent; now it is almost negligible. The education programs are excellent. Nevertheless, life is still spare. There is no choice of clothes in the shops—one type of shoe, one type of trousers—and a limited variety of foods. The government has helped its people enormously, and the people are grateful.

We returned to Christmas in America with the stores just dripping with luxury and affluence. We knew then that if America redefined its priorities, it could help feed many of the world's people. Americans do not have a God-given right to be the wealthiest people in the world to the detriment of millions of others. These poor countries are now developing their own nuclear weapons, and they are justifiably angry. Who will they drop them on?

Men are very smart—so smart that they have learned to destroy themselves. They could with a little effort and ingenuity develop a global economic system (excluding the production and sales of weapons) that would benefit the Western corporations, as well as all the countries on earth. For several years, the Third World has been pleading for such a move, but the selfish Western nations have refused to cooperate or to contemplate ways to alleviate the plight of the poor. Yet it is obvious that the global situation is all interconnected and relevant to prevention of nuclear war.

All such a scheme would take is creative initiative with the right motivation. If people see that in the end, they, too, will benefit as wealth is equitably shared around the world, thus making the world a safer place, they will become enthusiastic about such an endeavor. This is not pie-in-the-sky talk; it is pragmatic and ultimately reasonable and rational. It will take place only if the people in the wealthy Western democracies educate themselves about the plight of mankind and decide for their own well-being that they and their politicians will create the solutions. The powerful politicians who met in Williamsburg in 1983 to discuss the global economic crisis behaved like emasculated pawns. They made soothing noises but did absolutely nothing to change the situation.

Conversion of a corporation from war to peace can be achieved not just by a decision of the corporate heads but also by initiative from the workers. In England, the Lucas Aerospace Industry used to make parts for missiles. After many years, the workers became concerned about the global implications of their work. They called in some consultants and asked, "With our technical skills, what can we make that would benefit mankind?" So the consultants designed electric cars, dialysis machines, and mass-transit systems. The workers then took these plans to the management and said, "We are not going to make missiles anymore. We are going to make this equipment." Management was surprised but was influenced.

Other workers and high technologists are beginning to leave the military industry because of profound moral concern. They have formed an organization called High Technologists for Social Responsibility. These people help each other find jobs doing peaceful work. At the moment, however, such jobs are not easy to find. We need to create the political climate that will channel government money into peaceful industry and abolish appropriations for weapons production. It's easy. We, the people, ultimately control our government through the vote! We own the White House; we own the Pentagon and the Congress. They are our bombs; we paid for them.

Some scientists and their colleagues also are becoming alarmed about the implications of their occupations. I gave a speech at the American Association for the Advancement of Science meeting early in 1982, and a man named Bill Perry, who was the director of public relations for Lawrence-Livermore Lab, heard me talk. He was taken aback by the information I presented, even though he worked right in the middle of a weapons organization. He spent the next week at the meeting checking around with other scientists to determine if I was a credible spokesperson. Most assured him that I was. He then said to himself, "If only half of what she says is valid, we are in terrible trouble." He contemplated his dilemma for several months and then decided to leave the lab and work for the passage of the nuclear weapons freeze in California. Rarely have I seen such an elated man. He addressed a large meeting in San Francisco's Grace Cathedral, where he recounted the history of his conversion, and he said, "I feel like a clean man." More people need to open up their souls to the truth and develop the courage to do what Bill Perry did.

George Kennan has articulated the dilemma eloquently:

We have gone piling weapon upon weapon, missile upon missile, new levels of destructiveness upon old ones. We have done this helplessly, almost involuntarily, like the victims of some sort of hypnotism, like men in a dream, like lemmings heading for the sea, like the children of Hamelin marching blinding behind their Pied Piper, and the result is that today we have achieved, we and the Russians together, in the number of these devices, in their means of delivery, and above all in their destructiveness, levels of redundancy of such grotesque dimensions as to defy rational understanding. . . .

I find the view of the Soviet Union that prevails today in our governmental and journalistic establishments so extreme, so subjective, so far removed from what any sober scrutiny of external reality would reveal, that it is not only ineffective, but dangerous as a guide to political action. This endless series of distortions and oversimplifications; this systematic dehumanization of the leadership of another great country; this routine exaggeration of Moscow's military capabilities and of the supposed inequity of its intentions; this daily misrepresentation of the nature and the attitudes of another great people—and a long-suffering people at that, sorely tried by the vicissitudes of this past century . . . this reckless application of the double standard to the judgment of Soviet conduct and our own; this failure to recognize the commonality of many of their problems and ours as we both move inexorably into the modern technological age . . . these, believe me, are not the marks of the maturity and realism one expects of the diplomacy of a great power.

We must reach out to the Soviets, who are people like ourselves. We must demystify the Soviet culture, as they must learn to understand ours. Cultural exchanges and scientific exchanges must increase, and trade between the superpowers must become the utmost priority. The USSR for years has been begging to become a major trading partner of the United States. Let's do it. Let's move toward them as Richard Nixon once did with that long-hated enemy, Red China. Overnight, China became an ally and a major trading partner. If we did the same thing with the Soviet Union, weapons involving our two countries would become anachronistic. It is simple, obvious, and easy. We must drop our ancient need for a tribal enemy and grow up and become responsible nations.

It is true that we have the secret of atomic energy locked in our brains forever. But this does not mean we can't alter our behavior. Once we practiced slavery, cannibalism, and dueling. As we became more civilized, we learned that these forms of behavior were antithetical to society, so we stopped. We can just as easily stop making nuclear weapons, and we also can stop fighting and killing each other. We must move beyond war, because any small conventional war in the nuclear age could trigger a nuclear war. It was difficult initially to design and construct the weapons, but it would be very easy to dismantle them. It just needs a decision. Disposal of the plutonium will be neither easy nor safe; permanent disposal may, indeed, be impossible.

Einstein said we must change the way we think. The answer lies, in fact, in the brilliant psychological teachings of Jesus. If we follow His admonitions and practice what He preached, it will be easy to make friends with the Soviet Union.

Ye have heard that it was said by them of old time, Thou shalt not kill; and whosoever shall kill shall be in danger of the judgment; but I say unto you, that everyone who is angry with his brother without a cause shall be in danger of the judgment.

Therefore if you bring thy gift to the altar, and there rememberest that thy brother hath ought against thee, leave there thy gift before the altar, and go thy way; first be reconciled to thy brother, and then come and offer thy gift.

Blessed are the peacemakers; for they shall be called the children of God.

In other words, the anger is the instinct behind the kill. We must stop projecting our anger and dark side out onto others.

> Why beholdest thou the mote that is in thy brother's eye, but considerest not the beam that is in thine own eye? Or how wilt thou say to thy brother, Let me pull out the mote out of thine eye; and, behold, a beam is in thine own eye? Thou hypocrite, first cast out the beam out of thine own eye; and then shalt thou see clearly to cast out the mote out of thy brother's eye.

This admonition is very relevant for the people of America. They must learn to understand their own past and present history before they can possibly start criticizing that of the Soviet Union.

> Ye have heard that it hath been said, Thou shalt love thy neighbor and hate thine enemy. But I say unto you, Love your enemies, bless them that curse you, do good to them that hate you, and pray for them that despitefully use you. For if ye love them which love you, what thank have ye? for sinners also love those that love them. And if ye do good to them which do good to you, what thank have ye? for sinners also do even the same.
>
> Ye shall be children of the Most High: For he is kind toward the unthankful and to the evil. He maketh his sun to rise on the evil and on the good, and sendeth rain on the just and on the unjust. Be ye therefore merciful as your Father also is merciful.
>
> Blessed are the merciful: for they shall obtain mercy.

These admonitions obviously are directed in modern times toward the Americans to love the Soviets. In other words, we have to learn to love our enemies.

The American Catholic bishops have written a pastoral letter on nuclear weapons and nuclear war, using the teachings of Jesus as a moral foundation. Other churches and Jewish organizations have made similar statements about the total immorality of the preparation for and probability of nuclear war.

Many people are moving toward this ultimate solution. Newsman Walter Cronkite recently told me that for years he has been in favor of unilateral nuclear disarmament. He thinks that America should totally disarm within ten years and some of the money saved should be used to create satellites and communications systems to educate the people of the world about how to live in peace. The money could also be used for food programs and to help the industrial conversion process from weapons to peace. He said that he favors passive resistance—that if tens of thousands of people just sat down in front of Soviet tanks, what could they do? He said we should make the arms negotiators sit at the table, and stop the clock and lock the door until they achieve appropriate arms reductions.

It is time for people to rise to their full moral and spiritual height, to take the world on their shoulders like Atlas, forgetting all other priorities in their lives, and to say, "*I* will save the earth." Each person can be as powerful as the most powerful person who ever lived. I have achieved a lot in a foreign country. I am an Australian and a woman, but neither of these factors has been an impediment. Think how much Americans could achieve by using and working through the democracy they have inherited from their forebears. All it takes is willpower and determination.

This quest is a spiritual adventure. It is time for mankind to achieve spiritual fulfillment. Each person has much to offer. However, it is imperative that the ego be controlled. Ego needs are enormous and can be extremely destructive when working with others. I have learned in this work that if my ego becomes dominant and I engage in negative thoughts, things always go wrong. If I meditate or pray and decide simply to do what is right—not because it *feels* right but because it *is* right—and I drop my own egocentric needs, things always fall into place in the most amazing way. Such action is enormously rewarding. As we work with others, we must remember only one thing, and that is our final common goal: elimination of nuclear weapons. We don't need our egos fulfilled; we need only to fulfill our destiny on the planet in the twentieth century: to save the world. We must learn to reinforce and support one another. True happiness lies in helping one another. We are all sons and daughters of God, and under the universal horror of the nuclear Sword of Damocles, we will be united to work together in mutual respect and peace.

No other generation has inherited this enormous responsibility. We have been given the privilege of saving all past and all future generations, all animals, all plants. Think of the enormous variety of delicate butterflies; think of the gorgeous birds of the earth, of the endless designs of fish in the sea; think of the beautiful and exotic flowers with their gorgeous and seductive perfumes; think of the proud lions and tigers and of the wondrous prehistoric elephants and hippopotamuses; think of what we are about to destroy.

Rapid nuclear disarmament is the ultimate issue of preventive medicine.

It is the ultimate parenting issue.

It is the ultimate Republican and the ultimate Democratic issue.

It is the ultimate patriotic issue.

Above all, it is the ultimate religious issue.

We are the curators of life on earth; we hold it in the palms of our hands. Can we evolve spiritually and emotionally in time to control the overwhelming evil that our advanced and rational intellect has created? We will know the answer to this question in our lifetime. This generation will die having discovered the answer.

Notes

INTRODUCTION

Nevil Shute, *On the Beach* (New York: William Morrow and Company, 1957).

Robert Jay Lifton, *Death in Life* (New York: Basic Books, 1983).

David Barash and Judith Eve Lipton, *Stop Nuclear War* (New York: Grove Press, 1982).

Richard Halloran, "Pentagon Draws Up First Strategy for Fighting a Long Nuclear War," *New York Times*, May 30, 1982.

THE TERMINAL EVENT

World Health Organization, *Effects of Nuclear War on Health and Health Services* (Geneva, 1983).

Kevin N. Lewis, "The Prompt and Delayed Effects of Nuclear War," *Scientific American*, Vol. 241, No. 1, July, 1979.

Jonathan Schell, *The Fate of the Earth* (New York: Avon, 1982).

Desmond Ball, *Can Nuclear War Be Controlled?* Adelphi Papers, No. 196 (London: International Institute of Strategic Studies, 1981).

Ambio: A Journal of the Human Environment, Royal Swedish Academy of Sciences, Permagon Press, Vol. 11, No. 2–3, 1982.

Frank H. Ervin, John B. Glazier, Saul Aronow, David Nathan, Robert Coleman, Nicholas Avery, Steven Shohet, and Calvin Leeman, "Human and Ecological Effects in Massachusetts of an Assumed Thermonuclear Attack on the United States," *New England Journal of Medicine*, Vol. 266, No. 22, May 31, 1962.

Victor W. Sidel, H. Jack Geiger, and Bernard Lown, "The Physician's Role in the Postattack Period," *New England Journal of Medicine*, Vol. 266, No. 22, May 31, 1962.

314

Report of the Secretary-General, United Nations, *Nuclear Weapons* (Brookline, Mass.: Autumn Press, 1980).

John Hersey, *Hiroshima* (New York: Knopf, 1946).

Japan Broadcasting Corp., ed., *Unforgettable Fire* (New York: Pantheon, 1981).

John Constable, "Burn Casualties," in *The Final Epidemic,* edited by Ruth Adams and Susan Cullen (Chicago: Educational Foundation for Nuclear Science, 1981).

Schell, *The Fate of the Earth.*

Ambio, Vol. 11, No. 2–3.

Judith Miller, "U.S. Delays Buying Morphine to Avoid War-Ready Image," *New York Times,* February 14, 1983.

Steven A. Fetter and Kosta Tsipis, "Catastrophic Releases of Radioactivity," *Scientific American,* Vol. 244, No. 4, April, 1981.

Henry Way Kendall, Physicians for Social Responsibility Symposium on the Medical Consequences of Nuclear Weapons and Nuclear War, Harvard Medical School, February, 1980.

Federation of American Scientists, "Effects of Nuclear War," *Public Interest Report,* Vol. 34, No. 2, February, 1981.

Ervin et al., "Human and Ecological Effects"; Sidel et al., "The Physician's Role."

Herbert L. Abrams, "Infection and Communicable Diseases," in *The Final Epidemic,* edited by Ruth Adams and Susan Cullen (Chicago: Educational Foundation for Nuclear Science, 1981).

The Defense of America, CBS series, 1981.

Jennifer Leaning, "Civil Defense in the Nuclear Age" (Cambridge, Mass.: Physicians for Social Responsibility, 1982).

Robert Scheer, *With Enough Shovels* (New York: Random House, 1982).

K. S. Gant and C. V. Chester, "Minimizing Excess Radiogenic Cancer Deaths After a Nuclear Attack," *Health Physics,* vol. 41, No. 3, September, 1981.

Assembly of Mathematical and Physican Sciences, National Research Council, *Long-Term Worldwide Effects of Multiple Nuclear Weapons Detonations* (Washington, D.C.: National Academy Press, 1975).

Ibid.

Schell, *The Fate of the Earth.*

Barrie Pittock, "Atmospheric Effects Reappraised," *Australian Physicist,* Vol. 19:189, 1982.

Schell, *The Fate of the Earth*.

R. P. Turco, O. B. Toon, T. P. Ackerman, J. B. Pollack, and Carl Sagan, "Nuclear Winter: Global Consequences of Multiple Nuclear Explosions," *Science*, December 23, 1983.

Paul Ehrlich, John Harte, Mark A. Harwell, Peter H. Ravan, Carl Sagan, George M. Woodwell, Joseph Berry, Edward S. Ayensu, Anne H. Ehrlich, Thomas Eisner, Stephen J. Gould, Herbert D. Grover, Rafael Herrera, Robert M. May, Ernst Mayr, Christopher McKay, Harold A. Mooney, Norman Myers, David Pimentel, and John M. Teal, "Long-Term Biological Consequences of Nuclear War," *Science*, December 23, 1983.

THE IRON TRIANGLE

Benjamin Taylor, "Pentagon Seeks $239 Billion to Continue Build-Up," *Boston Globe*, February 1, 1983.

Rone Tempest, "U.S. Defense Establishment Wields a Pervasive Power," *Los Angeles Times*, July 10, 1983.

Ibid.

Howard H. Hiatt, "Sounding Board: The Physician and National Security," *New England Journal of Medicine*, Vol. 307, No. 18, October 28, 1982.

Gordon Adams, "America Held Hostage," *Nuclear Times*, April, 1983.

Tempest, "U.S. Defense Establishment Wields a Pervasive Power."

Clyde Haberman, "Japan Holds '84 Rise in Arms Spending to 6.9%," *New York Times*, July 13, 1983.

David Treadwell, "Arms Costs Figure Heavily in Economy," *Los Angeles Times*, July 10, 1983.

Ibid.

Fred Kaplan, *The Wizards of Armageddon* (New York: Simon and Schuster, 1983).

Fred Kaplan, "Herman Kahn: Nuclear Strategist Who Took 'Rational View,'" *Boston Globe*, July 10, 1983.

Orr Kelly and K. M. Chrysler, "While Protestors March, Bomb Business Flourishes," *U.S. News and World Report*.

Ibid.

Ibid.

Herbert York, *Race to Oblivion* (New York: Simon and Schuster, Clarion Book, 1970).

"Frightened for the Future of Humanity," *New York Times*, April 24, 1983.

Robert Scheer, "Teller's Obsession Becomes Reality in 'Star Wars' Plan," *Los Angeles Times,* July 10, 1983.

Ibid.

Solly Zuckerman, *Nuclear Illusion and Reality* (New York: Viking Press, 1982).

William J. Broad, "Expanding the Underground A-War," *Science,* Vol. 218, October 22, 1982.

"U.S. Atom Arms Tests at a Post-1970 Record," *New York Times,* October 24, 1982.

Samuel H. Day, "The Nicest People Make the Bomb," *Progressive,* October, 1978.

Scheer, "Teller's Obsession Becomes Reality in 'Star Wars' Plan."

Ibid.

Wayne Biddle, "Publish and Perish Catch in Defense Research," *New York Times,* June 26, 1983.

John Powers, "Pentagon Is Back at School . . . Quietly," *Boston Globe,* September 6, 1981.

Ibid.

Steve Burkholder, "The Pentagon in the Ivory Tower," *Progressive,* June, 1981.

Ibid.

Helen M. Caldicott, *Nuclear Madness* (Brookline, Mass.: Autumn Press, 1979; reprint, with Epilogue, New York: Bantam, 1981).

Gordon Adams, *The Politics of Defense Contracting: The Iron Triangle* (New Brunswick, N.J.: Transaction Books, 1981).

Bob Adams, "Muffled Drums," *St. Louis Post Dispatch,* April 17, 1983.

Tempest, "U.S. Defense Establishment Wields a Pervasive Power."

Michael W. Johnson, "Keeping Up in Weapons," *Boston Globe,* May 9, 1982.

Stephen Daly, "Arms Industry's Hot Stocks," *New York Times,* September 9, 1983.

Adams, "Muffled Drums."

Ibid.

John Hanrahan, "Fat City," *Common Cause,* May-June, 1983.

Bob Adams, "Defense 'Revolving Door' Could Lead to Conflict Critics Say," *St. Louis Post Dispatch,* April 19, 1983.

Ibid.

Kenneth B. Noble, "Thayer Quits as Defense Deputy over Expected Charges by S.E.C.," *New York Times,* January 5, 1984.

"Boeing Severance to 3 in Pentagon Under Inquiry," *New York Times*, March 16, 1983.

Adams, "Defense 'Revolving Door' Could Lead to Conflict Critics Say."

"A Revolving Door for Defense Jobs," *Los Angeles Times*, July 10, 1983.

Bob Adams, "Congressmen Who Can Get Helped," *St. Louis Post Dispatch*, April 18, 1983.

Adams, *The Politics of Defense Contracting: The Iron Triangle.*
Ibid.
Ibid.
Ibid.
Ibid.

Bob Adams, "Camaraderie Parlayed into Defense Orders," *St. Louis Post Dispatch*, April 22, 1983.

Adams, *The Politics of Defense Contracting: The Iron Triangle.*

David Wood, "B-1 Symbolizes Power of Military-Industrial Complex," *Los Angeles Times*, July 10, 1983.

Adams, *The Politics of Defense Contracting: The Iron Triangle.*

Tempest, "U.S. Defense Establishment Wields a Pervasive Power."

David Wood, "Spending Eludes Civilian Control," *Los Angeles Times*, July 10, 1983.

Richard Halloran, "Why the Military Has Four Tactical Air Forces: A Case Study," *New York Times*, June 12, 1983.

Tempest, "U.S. Defense Establishment Wields a Pervasive Power."

Wood, "B-1 Symbolizes Power of Military-Industrial Complex."

Gordon Adams, "The B-1 Bomber: An Analysis of Its Strategic Utility, Cost, Constituency and Economic Impact," *Report* (New York Council on Economic Priorities, 1976).

Charles Mohr, "Lockheed's Grip on Washington," *New York Times*, October 17, 1982.

David Shribman, "The MX's Economic Impact," *New York Times*, December 7, 1982.

Robert Scheer, "California Wedded to Military Economy, But Bliss Is Shaky," *Los Angeles Times*, July 10, 1983.

Rone Tempest, "'Beltway Bandits' Ring Washington," *Los Angeles Times*, July 10, 1983.

Hanrahan, "Fat City."

Jonathan Alter and Mary Lord, "Cutting Waste at the Pentagon," *Newsweek*, July 11, 1983.

Tempest, "U.S. Defense Establishment Wields a Pervasive Power."

Wood, "Spending Eludes Civilian Control."

"Federal Inmates in Connecticut Making U.S. Missile Parts," *Boston Globe,* May 9, 1983.

Rone Tempest, "Kremlin System Looks Familiar," *Los Angeles Times,* July 10, 1983.

Franklyn D. Holzman, "A Gap? Another?" *New York Times,* March 9, 1983.

Fred Kaplan, "Soviet Arms Budget Stirs Debate in U.S.," *Boston Globe,* February 16, 1983.

PATHOGENESIS: THE PATHOLOGICAL DYNAMICS OF THE ARMS RACE

Kaplan, *The Wizards of Armageddon.*

Ibid.

Ibid.

Jim Calogero, "Conference at MIT Stresses Disarmament," *Boston Globe,* December 5, 1982.

"Standing at the Brink," *Mother Jones,* September-October, 1982.

Daniel Ellsberg, "Call to Meeting," Preface to *Protest and Survive,* edited by E. P. Thompson and Dan Smith (New York: Monthly Review Press, 1982).

Desmond Ball, "International Security, U.S. Strategic Forces: How Would They Be Used?" *Harvard and MIT,* Vol. 7, No. 3, Winter 1982–83, pp. 31–60.

Gregg Herken, *The Winning Weapon: The Atomic Bomb in the Cold War* (New York: Knopf, 1982), pp. 256–74.

Verbal communication with Daniel Ellsberg, December 1983.

Center for Defense Information, "U.S.-Soviet Military Facts," *Defense Monitor,* Vol. 11, No. 6, 1982.

Barash and Lipton, *Stop Nuclear War.*

Ibid.

Ibid.

Ibid.

Ibid.

Ibid.

Report of the Secretary-General, *Nuclear Weapons.*

Robert Aldridge, *The Counterforce Syndrome* (Washington, D.C.: Institute for Policy Studies, 1978).

Steven Roberts, "Administration Opens a Drive in Congress for MX," *New York Times,* April 21, 1983.

R. Jeffrey Smith, "Soviets Lag in Key Weapons Technology," *Science*, Vol. 219, March 18, 1983.

Aldridge, *The Counterforce Syndrome.*

Report of the Secretary-General, *Nuclear Weapons.*

Barash and Lipton, *Stop Nuclear War.*

Stansfield Turner, "The 'Folly' of the MX Missile," *New York Times Magazine*, March 13, 1983.

Herbert Scoville, Jr., *MX: Prescription for Disaster* (Cambridge, Mass.: MIT Press, 1981).

Hedrick Smith, "Politically Unprepared: The Administration Now Seeks to Buy More Time," *New York Times*, December 12, 1982.

Leslie Gelb, "New Deployment Needed, Maybe a New Strategy, Too," *New York Times*, December 12, 1982.

David C. Wright, "Missiles Too Accurate for Our Own Good," *New York Times*, October 8, 1982.

Dale Bumpers, "The MX? No," *New York Times*, October 22, 1982.

"Unguided Missile," *New York Times*, December, 1982.

Charles Mohr, "Pentagon Studies 'Midgetman' Basing," *New York Times*, May 16, 1982.

Charles Mohr, "Fleet of Smaller Missiles to Bolster MX Debated," *New York Times*, March 23, 1983.

"PACs of MX missile Contractors Doubling Campaign Contributions," *Washington Post*, October 14, 1982.

Aldridge, *The Counterforce Syndrome.*

Report of the Secretary-General, *Nuclear Weapons.*

Barash and Lipton, *Stop Nuclear War.*

STOP Project, "Doomsday in the North Country," *Project ELF*, Summer, 1982.

Barash and Lipton, *Stop Nuclear War.*

Aldridge, *The Counterforce Syndrome.*

Report of the Secretary-General, *Nuclear Weapons.*

Leslie Gelb, "The Cruise Missile," *New York Times*, September 2, 1982.

Center for Defense Information, "The Cruise Missile Era: Opening Pandora's Box," *Defense Monitor*, Vol. 12, 1983.

Charles Mohr, "Cruise Missile Passes Tests, But Its Critics Score, Too," *New York Times*, July 17, 1983.

Charles Mohr, "Pershings Put Moscow on 6-Minute Warning," *New York Times*, February 27, 1983.

Dusko Doder, "Pershing II and Soviet Concern," *Boston Globe*, January 25, 1983.

William Beecher, "Nuclear Jitters in Moscow," *Boston Globe*, November 13, 1981.

Bernard Gwertzman, "Reagan Intensifies Drive to Promote Policies in Europe," *New York Times*, January 20, 1983.

"Britons and U.S. Ad Agency Discuss a Campaign on Arms," *New York Times*, January 31, 1983.

Wood, "B-1 Symbolizes Power of Military-Industrial Complex."

Gordon Adams, "The B-1 Bomber: An Analysis of Its Strategic Utility, Cost, Constituency and Economic Impact."

Wood, "B-1 Symbolizes Power of Military-Industrial Complex."

Countervailing Strategy Demands Revision of Strategic Force Acquisition Plans, Report to the Congress by the Comptroller General of the United States (Gaithersburg, Md., August 5, 1981).

Christopher Paine, "Reagatomics, Or How to Prevail," *Nation*, April 9, 1983.

William Arkin, "More Weapons Nobody Wants," *Bulletin of the Atomic Scientists*, October, 1982.

Michael Klare, "The Conventional Weapons Fallacy," *Nation*, April 9, 1983.

Christopher Paine, "On the Beach: The Rapid Deployment Force and the Nuclear Arms Race," *Merip Reports*, No. 111, January, 1983.

Martha Wenger, "AirLand Battle Doctrine," *Merip Reports*, No. 111, January, 1983.

Michael Klare, "An Army in Search of a War," *Progressive*, February, 1981.

Ball, *Can Nuclear War be Controlled?*

Robert Levey, "Support Grows for U.S. School of Peace," *Boston Globe*, August 4, 1982.

PHYSICAL EXAMINATION

Some of the data cited subsequently in this chapter were updated according to information provided by the Center for Defense Information and are current as of April 1985.

Leslie H. Gelb, "Korean Jet: Points Still to Be Settled," *New York Times*, September 26, 1983.

John F. Burns, "Jet Incident Improves Picture of Russian Military," *New York Times*, September 18, 1983.

David Shribman, "U.S. Experts Say Soviet Didn't See Jet Was Civilian," New York Times, October 7, 1983.

"The New Peace Candidate," Boston Globe, January 17, 1984.

Richard Halloran, "Spread of Nuclear Arms Is Seen by 2,000," New York Times, November 15, 1982.

Scheer, "Teller's Obsession Became Reality in 'Star Wars' Plan."

William J. Broad, "Rewriting the History of the H-Bomb," Science, Vol. 218, No. 4574, November 19, 1982.

Center for Defense Information, "U.S.-Soviet Military Facts."

R. Jeffrey Smith, "Soviets Lag in Key Weapons Technology."

Center for Defense Information, "U.S.-Soviet Military Facts."

Report of the Secretary-General, Nuclear Weapons.

Center for Defense Information, "U.S.-Soviet Military Facts."

Ibid.

Barash and Lipton, Stop Nuclear War.

William M. Arkin, "Nuclear Security: The Enemy May Be Us," Bulletin of the Atomic Scientists, November 1983.

Center for Defense Information, "U.S.-Soviet Military Facts."

Jerome B. Wiesner and Emma Rothschild, "Expand the Arms Talks," New York Times, November 11, 1983.

Report of the Secretary-General, Nuclear Weapons.

Barash and Lipton, Stop Nuclear War.

Center for Defense Information, "U.S.-Soviet Military Facts."

Ibid.

Randall Forsberg, "Confining the Military to Defense as a Route to Disarmament," World Policy Journal, Vol. 1, No. 2, Winter 1984.

Ibid.

Ibid.

Ibid.

Roy Gutman, "The Nay-Sayer of Arms Control," Long Island Newsday, February 18, 1983.

Forsberg, "Confining the Military to Defense as a Route to Disarmament."

Ibid.

Ibid.

Personal communication with Steven Goose, Fellow, Center for Defense Information, Washington, D.C., 1983.

Walden Bello and Peter Hayes, "Tensions in the North Pacific," The Nation, October 1, 1983.

Richard Halloran, "Uncle Sam Pays a High Price for Being in 359 Places at Once," *New York Times*, July 24, 1983.

Ibid.

Clergy and Laity Concerned, "U.S. Bases in the Philippines," *U.S. Bases in the Philippines: Springboards for Intervention, Instruments of Nuclear War;* originally published in *Southeast Asia Chronicle*, special issue on the Philippine Bases, No. 89, May, 1982.

Ibid.

Ibid.

John O. Iatrides, "To Meet Greek Needs," *New York Times*, March 2, 1983.

Philip Taubman, "Role in Panama of U.S. Military Causing Strains," *New York Times*, May 24, 1983.

Desmond Ball, *A Suitable Piece of Real Estate* (Sydney, Australia: Hale and Iremonger, 1980).

Darlene Keju and Giff Johnson, "Kwajalein: Home on the Range," *Pacific Magazine*, November-December, 1982.

Palau, Self-Determination vs. U.S. Military Plans, Publication of Micronesia Support Committee, Honolulu, May, 1983.

Steven R. Weisman, "The Influence of William Clark," *New York Times Magazine*, August 14, 1983.

Jeff Gerth, "Problems Promoting Democracy," *New York Times*, February, 1983.

Forsberg, "Confining the Military to Defense as a Route to Disarmament."

Ibid.

Ibid.

John Noble Wilford, "Mapping in the Spage Age," *New York Times Magazine*, June 5, 1983.

"The Super-Charger—Featuring Three New Games," Star Path Corporation, 1982, P.O. Box 209, Santa Clara, Calif.

Flora Lewis, "Lemmings in Space," *New York Times*, January 6, 1984.

Jim Nesbitt, "'Defender' Ron Scores Zillions With Students," *Orlando Sentinel*, March 9, 1983.

David Hoffman, "Offensive Capability of Shuttle Confirmed by Officials at NASA," *Washington Times*, March 11, 1983.

"Shuttle Needed for Space-Based BMD System," *Aerospace Daily,*

Ziff Davis Publishing Company, Washington, D.C., Vol. 121, No. 6, June, 1983.

Thomas Karas, *The New High Ground* (New York: Simon and Schuster, 1983).

Ball, *A Suitable Piece of Real Estate.*

Lou Cannon, "President Goes to the Movies, Skips New Hampshire for NOW," *Washington Post*, June 13, 1983.

In Our Defense, film produced by Bill Jersey, Foundation for the Arts of Peace, San Francisco, 1983.

Ball, *Can Nuclear War Be Controlled?*

Knut Royce, "In Case of N-War, It's Government Officials First," *Seattle Post Intelligence*, May 10, 1983.

Knut Royce, "Destabilization Results When Over-Confidence Pushes Button," *Seattle Post Intelligence*, May 11, 1983.

Ball, *Can Nuclear War Be Controlled?*

Ibid.

Ibid.

Ibid.

Ibid.

Ball, *A Suitable Piece of Real Estate.*

David Burnham, "The Silent Power of the NSA," *New York Times Magazine*, March 27, 1983.

Ball, *A Suitable Piece of Real Estate.*

Robert Lindsey, *The Falcon and the Snowman* (London: Penguin, 1979).

Home on the Range, an Australian documentary film, produced by Gil Scrine, 1982.

Ball, *A Suitable Piece of Real Estate.*

Irving Wallace, David Wallechinsky, and Amy Wallace, "The Forgotten War," *Parade Magazine*, June 12, 1983.

Ball, *A Suitable Piece of Real Estate.*

Ibid.

Ibid.

Ibid.

Ibid.

CASE HISTORY

William Appleman Williams, *America Confronts a Revolutionary World, 1776 to 1976* (New York: William Morrow and Company, 1976).

Thomas Boylston Adams, "The End of Colonialism," *Boston Globe,* March 13, 1983.

Louis M. Hacker, *The Shaping of the American Tradition* (New York: Columbia University Press, 1947).

Williams, *America Confronts a Revolutionary World.*

George F. Kennan, "America's Unstable Soviet Policy," *Atlantic Monthly,* November, 1982.

Henry Steele Commager, "Outmoded Assumptions," *Atlantic Monthly,* March, 1982.

Ibid.

Ibid.

Kennan, "America's Unstable Soviet Policy."

George F. Kennan, *The Nuclear Delusion* (New York: Pantheon Books, 1982).

Bernard Feld, "Einstein and the Politics of Nuclear Weapons," *Bulletin of the Atomic Scientists,* Vol. 35, March, 1979.

Kennan, *The Nuclear Delusion.*

Barash and Lipton, *Stop Nuclear War.*

Scheer, *With Enough Shovels.*

Kennan, "America's Unstable Foreign Policy."

David Halberstam, *The Powers That Be* (New York: Alfred A. Knopf, 1979).

Peter Goodchild, *J. Robert Oppenheimer: Shatterer of Worlds* (London: British Broadcasting Corporation, 1980; and Boston: Houghton Mifflin Company, 1981).

Kennan, *The Nuclear Delusion.*

Barash and Lipton, *Stop Nuclear War.*

Kennan, *The Nuclear Delusion.*

Jerome D. Frank, *Sanity and Survival in the Nuclear Age* (New York: Random House, 1967, 1982).

Alan Wolfe, *The Rise and Fall of the "Soviet Threat"* (Washington, D.C.: Institute for Policy Studies, 1979).

Forsberg, "Confining the Military to Defense as a Route to Disarmament."

Barash and Lipton, *Stop Nuclear War.*

Ibid.

Forsberg, "Confining the Military to Defense as a Route to Disarmament."

Barash and Lipton, *Stop Nuclear War.*

Zuckerman, *Nuclear Illusion and Reality.*

James Fallows, *National Defense* (New York: Random House, 1981).

Center for Defense Information, *Defense Monitor,* Vol. 11, No. 6, 1982.

M. R. Montgomery, "The Press and Adolf Hitler," *Boston Globe Magazine,* January 30, 1983.

Halberstam, *The Powers That Be.*

Noam Chomsky and Edward S. Herman, *Political Economy of Human Rights: The Washington Connection and Third-World Fascism* (Montreal: Black Rose Books, 1979; and Boston: South End Press, 1979).

Ibid.

Ibid.

Ibid.

James Bamford, *The Puzzle Palace—A Report on America's Most Secret Agency* (Boston: Houghton Mifflin Company, 1982).

Stephen Schlesinger and Stephen Kinzer, *Bitter Fruit* (New York: Doubleday and Company, 1982).

George H. Crowell, "Central America and the Arms Race" (Paper presented to the Socialism and Economic Justice Subgroups of the Social Ethics Working Group, American Academy of Religion, New York, December 21, 1982).

Stephen Kinzer, "Human Rights Aide Defends U.S. Policy," *New York Times,* January 20, 1983.

James A. Nathan and James K. Oliver, "Conserving Containment," *U.S. Foreign Policy and World Order,* 2nd ed. (Boston: Little Brown, 1981).

James Garrison, *The Russian Threat* (London: Gateway, 1983).

Gabriel Garcia Marquez, "The Solitude of Latin America," *New York Times,* February 6, 1983.

Juan Mendez, "Reagan's Argentines," *New York Times,* December 22, 1982.

Crowell, "Central America and the Arms Race."

George Crile, "Toppling Managua's Regime," *New York Times,* December 3, 1982.

Walter La Feber, "Making Revolution Opposing Revolution," *New York Times,* July 3, 1983.

Alan Riding, "Violence Rules Central America Despite Pacts and Plans for Peace," *New York Times,* January 23, 1983.

"Central American Politics at a Glance," *New York Times*, December 5, 1982.

"Health and Human Rights in El Salvador, A Report of the Second Public Health Commission to El Salvador" (Boston and New York: Committee for Health Rights in El Salvador, 1983).

Garrison, *The Russian Threat.*

Crowell, "Central America and the Arms Race."

William Shawcross, *Sideshow* (New York: Simon and Schuster, 1979).

Seymour M. Hersh, *The Price of Power* (New York: Summit Books, 1983).

Garrison, *The Russian Threat.*

Ibid.

Walden Bello and Peter Hayes, "Tensions in the North Pacific," *The Nation*, October 1, 1983.

Richard Grimmett, *Trends in Conventional Arms Transfers to the Third World by Major Suppliers, 1974 to 1981* (Washington, D.C.: Congressional Research Service, Library of Congress, 1982).

William Hartung, "Weapons for the World," *Council on Economic Priorities Newsletter*, December-January, 1981–2.

Ruth Leger Sivard, *World Military and Social Expenditures* (Leesburg, Va.: World Priorities, 1982).

Hersh, *The Price of Power.*

GERMS OF CONFLICT: THE THIRD WORLD

Cox, *Russian Roulette.*

Ibid.

Ibid.

Ibid.

Scheer, *With Enough Shovels.*

Ibid.

Cox, *Russian Roulette.*

Ibid.

Scheer, *With Enough Shovels.*

ETIOLOGY: MISSILE ENVY AND OTHER PSYCHOPATHOLOGY

Mark Gerzon, *A Choice of Heroes* (Boston: Houghton Mifflin Company, 1982).

Eleanor E. Maccoby and Carol Nagy Jacklin, "Sex Differences in Aggression: A Rejoinder and Reprise," *Child Development*, Vol. 51, No. 4, December, 1980.

Hersh, *The Price of Power*.

David Halberstam, *The Best and the Brightest* (New York: Random House, 1972).

William Beardslee and John E. Mack, "The Impact of Nuclear Developments on Children and Adolescents," *Psychosocial Aspects of Nuclear Developments*, American Psychiatric Association, Task Force Report 20, 1981.

Barbara MacIntosh, "The Nuclear Nightmare," *Houston Post*, December 13–15, 1981.

Olive Evans, "Handling Children's Nuclear-War Fears," *New York Times*, May 27, 1982.

David Arnold, "The Young and Nuclear War—How Exactly Do They Feel?" *Boston Globe*, October 29, 1981.

Peter Pringle and William Arkin, *S.I.O.P.* (London: Sphere Books, 1983; and New York: W. W. Norton, 1983).

Gerzon, *A Choice of Heroes*.

G. William Domhoff, *The Bohemian Grove* (New York: Harper-Torch Books, 1974).

Richard Pollak, "Covering the Unthinkable," *Nation*, May 1, 1982.

John E. Mack, "But What About the Russians?" *Harvard Magazine*, March-April, 1982.

PROGNOSIS: HOW LONG WILL THE EARTH SURVIVE?

Richard Burt, "Carter Said to Back a Plan for Limiting Any Nuclear War," *New York Times*, August 10, 1980.

Center for Defense Information, "Force Level Calculator" (Washington, D.C., 1983).

Center for Defense Information, *Defense Monitor*, Vol. 11, No. 6, 1982.

Aldridge, *The Counterforce Syndrome*.

Halloran, "Pentagon Draws Up First Strategy for Fighting a Long Nuclear War."

Verbal communication with J. Carson Mark, Former Head, Theoretical Division, Los Alamos Scientific Laboratory.

John Bierman, "Nuclear Warning System Rapped," *Boston Globe*, November 10, 1980.

Ball, *Can Nuclear War Be Controlled?*

In Our Defense, film produced by Bill Jersey.

Center for Defense Information, "Cost Defense Guidance Plan," *Defense Monitor*, Vol. 12, No. 2, 1983.

Scheer, *With Enough Shovels.*

Gutman, "The Nay-Sayer of Arms Control."

Text of President Reagan's Address to Parliament on Promoting Democracy, *New York Times*, June 9, 1982.

Laurence Beilenson, *Survival and Peace in the Nuclear Age* (Chicago: Regnery/Gateway, 1980).

Scheer, *With Enough Shovels.*

Steven R. Weisman, "Clark's Move to Interior Makes External Waves," *New York Times*, October 16, 1983.

A.P., *Chicago Sun-Times*, October 29, 1983.

Richard Halloran, "Military Influence Is Seen Expanding," *New York Times*, November 2, 1983.

Arthur Macy Cox, *Russian Roulette* (New York: Times Books, 1982).

Bierman, "Nuclear Warning System Rapped."

David Blundy and John Bierman, "The Computer That Keeps Declaring War," *Times* (London), June 22, 1980.

Cox, *Russian Roulette.*

Jim Bencivenga, "C-Cubed! New U.S. Entrant in Military Technology Race," *Christian Science Monitor*, October 16, 1981.

"Two False Alerts Traced to 46¢ Item," *New York Times*, June 18, 1980.

"Missile Warning Computer Errs Yet Again on Attack by Soviets," *Boston Globe*, June 6, 1980.

"New False Warning of Attack Is Given," *New York Times*, June 9, 1980.

Richard Halloran, "Computer Error Falsely Indicates a Soviet Attack," *New York Times*, June 6, 1980.

Richard Burt, "False Nuclear Alarms Spur Urgent Effort to Find Flaws," *New York Times*, June 30, 1980.

"That Nuclear Alarm Wasn't False," Editorial, *New York Times*, June 30, 1980.

Ball, *Can Nuclear War Be Controlled?*

Christopher Hanson, "Doubts Cast on Security of Military Computers," *Boston Globe*, July 4, 1983.

Bernard Bereanu, "Self-Activation of World Nuclear Weapons Systems," *Journal of Peace Research*, Vol. 20, No. 1, 1983.

William J. Broad, "The Chaos Factor," *Science*, January/February, 1983.

"How Many Bomb Mishaps?" *Christian Science Monitor*, December 26, 1980.

"Summaries of Accidents Involving Nuclear U.S. Weapons, 1950 to 1980," from Department of Defense data, n.d.

Steven Talbot and Jonathan Dann, "Broken Arrows, Broken Sleep," *Los Angeles Times*, March 18, 1981.

Richard Halloran, "U.S. Heightening Defenses Against Nuclear Terrorists," *New York Times*, October 24, 1982.

"If Nuclear Terrorists Ever Threaten, Team Will Respond," *Los Angeles Times*, October 24, 1982.

Sivard, *World Military and Social Expenditures*.

Milton Benjamin, "A U.S. Shift on N-Sale Policy," *Boston Globe*, August 18, 1983.

Edward Markey, *Nuclear Peril* (Cambridge, Mass.: Ballinger, 1982).

Samuel H. Day, Jr., "The Afrikaner Bomb," *Progressive*, September, 1982.

James E. Muller, "An Accidental Nuclear War," *Newsweek*, March 1, 1982.

Verbal communication with Admiral Gene LaRocque, Center for Defense Information, Washington, D.C.

Frank, *Sanity and Survival in the Nuclear Age*.

Ibid.

Index